Jesus and Christian Origins

Jesus and Christian Origins

A Commentary
on Modern Viewpoints

HUGH ANDERSON

NEW YORK   OXFORD UNIVERSITY PRESS   1964

232
An 23

Dedicated to My Wife

Preface

In the first phase of the demythologizing debate, inspired by Rudolf Bultmann, attention was focused chiefly on the problem of myth in general and the mythological statements of the New Testament in particular. While this first interest has never really flagged, the center of the stage has latterly been occupied by the question of faith and history, the question of the Christ-kerygma and the historical Jesus. Especially in the last decade, and under the impetus of the now widely known "new quest" of the historical Jesus, there has been a complete reversal of the position of the nineteenth century, for which the Christ of dogma presented the worst stumbling block and the Jesus of history hardly constituted any problem at all. Jesus of Nazareth has in fact become *our* biggest problem. That this is so is no cause for dismay. The unrest of the Church, the Church's theologians, and Biblical critics before the supreme mystery of the central figure of our historic religion may be taken as a sign of health.

In an almost unimaginably short space of time the discussion about the relevance and significance of the historical Jesus for Christian faith and theology has gathered momentum so rapidly that it has already given rise to a very extensive and often highly technical literature, most of it emanating from German sources. We are therefore profoundly indebted to the handful of Anglo-American scholars who have acted as transmitters of recent German research and have thus helped us to stay abreast. It is not easy, however, to share the optimism of a few of them that we have already arrived at a new day of community of understanding between German and Anglo-American theology and New Testament criticism. In this regard, the wish may only be father to the thought. Or alternatively, it may be, and probably is, true that a somewhat select group on this side, by reason of their own broad scholarly background as well as the good fortune we enjoy today of scholarly interchange, have become sensible of a growing unity. But the vast majority of us still find it hard to listen to, much harder to sympathize with, the opinions of the other man concerning the investigation of the New Testament and of Christian origins, particularly when these opinions are forged in a tradition and intellectual climate that are quite different from our own. There is, moreover, the added vexation that much of the controversy of the last decade or two has been couched in a language that is, to say the least, obscure, and not readily understood by the people. Bearing this in mind, and out of the conviction that, in a world which is fighting for its future and wrestling with the question of the peaceful coexistence of nations and individuals, provincialism in the science of New Testament criticism and theology is at all costs to be avoided, what I have sought in these pages is mainly a clarification of the salient issues that have of late been raised with respect to the historical Jesus and the beginnings of Christianity.

There is no way to understand what has been taking place in the field of New Testament study on the wider international front save by tracing the "critical" and "theological" lines that led up to and eventually beyond the stance held by Bultmann. In the earliest section of this book I have attempted to do just that, even though it means once again going over ground (not uncritically, as I hope) that has been covered in other works. I have not tried to enter into the many philosophical repercussions of the recent debate: I am not qualified to do so. I have been content to set the discussion almost entirely within the framework of New Testament studies. And if, indeed, even here I have touched on but a few of the great historic problems of Christian origins, I can only plead the boundless scope of the subject and the limits of my own competence.

Inasmuch as we shall be constantly engaged at the critical level with the problem of the historical Jesus, it ought perhaps to be said here that Jesus of Nazareth is not primarily a problem at all. I remember with thanksgiving how the late Professor A. J. Gossip never wearied of telling those of us who were his students (and how we needed the advice amid our preoccupation with the refinements of the critical and theological disciplines!) that Jesus is not first and only an academic question to be solved, but a life lived out, a dream of God come true, God's Amen to men.

I wish to pay tribute to Professor G. H. C. Macgregor of the University of Glasgow (his death occurred some months after this preface was first written). I shall always be grateful for his inspiration as teacher and his continual encouragement and help through the years as a friend.

My present colleagues, Professor Frederick Herzog (Systematic Theology) and Professor John Strugnell (Old Testament), have given freely and gladly of their time to discuss with me, in a most helpful way, a number of important questions. They have also brought to my attention some periodical literature that might otherwise have escaped my notice. Their assistance, perhaps most of all where we have most disagreed, is deeply appreciated.

My typist, Mrs. Alfreda Kaplan, of Durham, North Carolina, has gone far beyond the duties of a copyist and has at many points been a very valuable mentor. I am much indebted to my friend, the Reverend Colin Campbell of Williamwood Church, Glasgow, Scotland, for his generous help with proofreading. I am pleased also to record my thanks to the librarian and staff of the Divinity School Library of Duke University for their unfailing kindness and courtesy.

H. A.

Duke University
North Carolina
January 1963

Acknowledgments

Acknowledgment is hereby made to the following publishers for permission to quote:

CAMBRIDGE UNIVERSITY PRESS, London, for the quotations on page 73 from W. D. Davies and D. Daube, eds., *The Background of the New Testament and Its Eschatology,* and on page 275 from W. L. Knox, *St. Paul and the Church of the Gentiles.*

T. & T. CLARK, PUBLISHERS, Edinburgh, for the quotation on page 23 from Karl Barth, *Church Dogmatics,* Vol. IV, Part 2, translated by G. W. Bromiley.

HARPER & ROW, PUBLISHERS, INC., New York, for the quotation on page 178 from W. Klassen and G. Snyder, eds., *Current Issues in New Testament Interpretation.*

HODDER AND STOUGHTON, LTD., London, for the quotation on page 151 from Günther Bornkamm, *Jesus of Nazareth,* translated by Irene and Fraser McLuskey with J. M. Robinson.

Interpretation for material in Chapter 4 from Hugh Anderson, "Existentialist Hermeneutics," *Interpretation,* XVI (April 1962).

JOHN KNOX PRESS, Richmond, for the quotation on page 11 from Karl Barth, *The Humanity of God,* translated by J. N. Thomas and T. Weiser.

DIVISION OF CHRISTIAN EDUCATION, NATIONAL COUNCIL OF CHURCHES, for the Scripture quotations, which are from the *Revised Standard Version of the Bible,* copyright 1946 and 1952 by the Division of Christian Education, National Council of Churches.

OLIVER & BOYD, LTD., Edinburgh, for the quotation on page 6 from Paul Althaus, *The So-called Kerygma and the Historical Jesus,* translated by D. Cairns.

SCM PRESS, LTD., London, for the quotation on page 305 from Eduard Schweizer, *Lordship and Discipleship* (published in the United States by Alec R. Allenson, Inc., Naperville, Ill.), and for the quotation on page 4 from Walter Eichrodt, *Theology of the Old Testament,* Vol. I, Old Testament Library, translated by J. A. Baker.

THE SOCIETY FOR PROMOTING CHRISTIAN KNOWLEDGE (S.P.C.K.), London, for the quotation on page 78 from C. W. Dugmore, ed., *The Interpretation of the Bible.*

THE WESTMINSTER PRESS, Philadelphia, for the quotation on page 4 from Walter Eichrodt, *Theology of the Old Testament,* Vol. I, Old Testament Library, translated by J. A. Baker. Copyright © 1961, SCM Press, Ltd.

Contents

Introduction   3

I The Shift Away From the Historical Jesus   16

The Primary Problem of Christian Origins   16
Schweitzer's The Quest of the Historical Jesus   18
Barth's Denigration of Historicism   22
Bultmann's Attitude Toward History   24
The Historisch *and the* Geschichtlich   26
Bultmann and Form-Criticism   29
Bultmann and the Christ-Kerygma   34

II The Resilience of the Historical Approach   56

E. Stauffer: Reversion to Historical Scientism   57
Historical Criticism in American Biblical Scholarship   61
*Representative Historical-Critical Positions in Recent British
Biblical Scholarship*   76
*The Question of Historical Criticism and Its Relation
to Theology or Faith*   95

III Toward a Solution of the Jesus of History—
Christ of Faith Problem   104

Event-Interpretation   105
Call and Congregational Response   114
The Raw Materials of Christology in the Person and Message of Jesus   118
Christ the Mid-Point of the Line of "Sacred History"   134

IV Features of the "New Quest"   149

Manson's Teaching and Bornkamm's Jesus   150
Contrasting Views of the Character of the Gospel Tradition   152
Fatherhood and Sonship   155
The Problem of Messiahship   160
The Eschatological Sayings of Jesus   165
The Framework of the Gospels   168
Critique of the "New Quest"   169

V The Resurrection of Jesus Christ   185

The Centrality of the Resurrection   185
Attempts at Historical Reconstruction   189
The Empty Tomb Tradition   192
Galilee and Jerusalem   195
The Question of What Happened in the Resurrection   199
Bultmann's Understanding of the Resurrection   205
I Corinthians 15:3–8   211
Mark's Easter Witness   218
Matthew's Easter Witness   222
Luke's Easter Witness   226
John's Easter Witness   233
Salient Easter Motifs   237

VI Earthly Suffering and Heavenly Glory   241

The "Secret" of the Messiah   243
The "Meek King"   247
The One Anointed with the Spirit   253
The Humiliated-Exalted One   262
Confessions of the Exalted Jesus Christ   267
The Lord's Supper   291
The Church, the Body of Christ   297

Conclusion   307

Notes   319
Selected Bibliography   355
Index of Scripture References   361
Index of Authors   366

Jesus and Christian Origins

Introduction

The attention of our age is gripped mainly by the exciting new conquests that have been made in the natural sciences and technology. Yet we should not overlook the fact that this has also been an age of rapid change and great ferment of ideas and opinions in the cultural sciences, and not least in theology and Biblical studies.

No doubt the kaleidoscopic pattern of modern views and theories in theology and Biblical studies reflects some of the salient characteristics of our era. The dissolution of old loyalties, the sweeping away of old landmarks, and the restlessness and despair occasioned by the tragedies of two World Wars have made their mark on the theologian and Biblical scholar no less than on the artist, composer, and writer. In the story of man there have been relatively peaceful eras when history itself constituted no very serious difficulty, when men seemed to be living in the glow of history's high noontide, as in the golden age of Greece, in the Renaissance, in late-Victorian England with its superoptimism about the future. Our own time is different. History is today, as Rudolf Bultmann has observed, our most serious problem. The cultural sciences have lately been engrossed with the question of history and the meaning of history.

The prevalent concern with history has profoundly affected modern trends in Biblical theology, in the fields both of Old and New Testament. In recent Old Testament study the old, yet always new, problem of "faith and history" has been very prominent. The ongoing discussion concerning the relationship between the facts of Israel's history and the theological expressions of Israel's faith enshrined in her historical tradition has lately been brought into sharp focus by G. von Rad's *Theology of the Old Testament,* completed in 1960.[1] Taking as his point of departure the proposition that the Old Testament is a "history book," von Rad has conceived Old Testament theology basically in terms of *Heilsgeschichte* or "salvation-history." In this view what is presented to us in Israel's historical tradition is a history created and shaped by God's Word, and what is offered to us in the Old Testament is a selection of theologically significant confessions of Israel's faith in the God who acted mightily toward her. Von Rad's critics have been quick to detect in his position a violent rift between the recounting of Old Testament *Heilsgeschichte* and the historical-critical version of Israel's history built up by Old Testament researches through the years. It is thus contended by the critics, especially in relation to the historical emergence of the phenomenon of Yahweh religion, that the real facts of Israel's history have been replaced by an accidental collocation of religious ideas, arising here and there in various existential situations, that genuine historical happenings and historic meanings are therefore severed. The opposition to von Rad's *Heilsgeschichte* portrayal of Old Testament history is well summed up by W. Eichrodt.

There must be an absolute refusal to surrender a real historical foundation to the faith of Israel, or to interpret the conflicts between the statements of the OT version of history and that discovered by critical scholarship in a merely negative way as proof of the unimportance of the historical reference of religious statements. . . . The link between the testimony of faith and the facts of history is not therefore a topic to be excluded from the scope of OT theology, but calls for continuous and careful attention, if the claim of Israel's faith to be founded on facts of history is to be anything more than a mental device for overcoming the problem of history, and lacking, in the last resort, any kind of binding authority.[2]

The flourishing debate about "faith and history" among contemporary Old Testament theologians runs parallel to the movement in New Testament studies, inspired by Bultmann, in which the problem of the connection between the New Testament message and historical fact has come to the center of scholarly interest. How is the Church's faith in and proclamation of the exalted Christ linked up with the historical person of Jesus of Nazareth and his message? Our present anguish over the so-called Jesus of history–Christ of faith problem was scarcely felt by the nineteenth-century historians.[3] So long as scholars were governed by a thoroughly positivistic approach to history, the question of the relation of the New Testament kerygma to historical reality could scarcely emerge as a pivotal concern. They were preoccupied instead with securing a place within the framework of human history for the man, Jesus of Nazareth. Their aim was to reconstruct the biographical data of his life by penetrating what they conceived to be the dogmatic crust with which the true and original gospel had been overlaid. The resultant picture drawn by the *Leben-Jesu-Forschung* was that of a scaled-down, human Jesus, in the bare facts of whose history faith was straightforwardly located. The outcome to the conviction that when we had the bare facts about Jesus we had everything that mattered for faith was a theology drained of the *Mysterium Christi*.

Around the turn of the century, however, signposts were erected that were to give a new direction to New Testament studies. M. Kähler classified the Gospels not as biographies of Jesus but as Easter confessions of the Church's faith in Jesus Christ.[4] W. Wrede, regarding the "Messianic secret" in Mark's record as a purely dogmatic device, gravely impugned the hitherto well-accepted historical reliability of the Marcan outline of Jesus' life.[5] A. Schweitzer undertook his massive critique of the nineteenth-century works on the life of Jesus and concluded by drawing his own thoroughgoing, eschatological portrait of Jesus.[6] Over against the Ritschlian view of the kingdom of God in the message of Jesus as a hoped-for, this-worldly goal, realizable by human plan and program, J. Weiss demonstrated the apocalyptic-eschatological nature of the New Testament documents, and showed that in them the kingdom of God is affirmed as always and only God's gracious gift to man.[7] W. Dilthey, moving away from objective historiography and emphasizing the need for the interpreter of an ancient text to be passionately involved in the subject of which the text speaks, helped pave the way for the modern German historiographical stance.

Only after a lapse of some twenty years did the full force of the new views that were then being forged begin to make itself felt, with Karl Barth's relegation of the work of historical criticism to a subsidiary place and his advocacy of the supreme importance of "theological exegesis." Barth's strictures against *Historicismus* were only less severe than those of Bultmann, who, after the prominence enjoyed by Barth's dialectical theology in the 1930's, became undoubtedly the central figure in the European theological debate until now. The classic role assumed by Bultmann in the present century has been that of arch-enemy of the nineteenth-century type of quest of the historical Jesus.

With Bultmann, Form-criticism of the Gospels led to the conviction of the impossibility of the old quest of the historical Jesus, and the existentialist view of history led to the conviction of its theological illegitimacy.[8] Bultmann has in fact fundamentally stood for a synthesis of advanced critical New Testament research and the major cultural trend in German thought furnished by the existentialistic analysis of Heidegger's *Sein und Zeit*. It is probably distrust and suspicion of the latter that have made many Anglo-American Biblical critics reluctant to participate directly in interrogation of Bultmann's findings in the former. I imagine that many English-speaking New Testament scholars entertain toward Bultmann's appeal to Heidegger something of the same feeling Paul Althaus expresses toward F. Gogarten's somewhat rigid distinction between objective history and existential history:

> Why such far-fetched explanations, why all this philosophical carping at "objective historicity" and the so-called subject-object mode of thinking? . . . What has interest in the reliability of the narratives, in the fact that the history of Jesus really happened, got to do with metaphysical thinking, with a subject-object mode of thinking? It seems to me that this great display of historical-philosophical and epistemological considerations obscures the simplicity of the question which is here in dispute.[9]

However, despite the objections of some of Bultmann's opponents, it would be no better than a caricature to think of him as forsaking the New Testament for philosophy. The first foundation of Bultmann's structure is indeed his critical work on the New Testament and on the beginnings of Christianity. As Form-critic, he has understood the Gospel tradition as the creation of the primitive Christian community's faith in the exalted Christ, and therefore as "kerygmatic" and not a source for the history of Jesus. As himself a product of the History of Religions School, and as Bousset's successor at the University of Giessen, he has been greatly influenced by Bousset, such as in the view that, in the formation of the earliest Christian religion, the syncretistic influences of the Hellenistic mystery cults of the dying and rising savior gods, Attis, Osiris, and Dionysos, played a decisive part. In his *Theology of the New Testament,* Bultmann follows the lead of Heitmüller and Bousset in assuming that such Hellenistic churches as those of Antioch, Tarsus, and Damascus formed a link between the first Palestinian church and Paul, and that Paul was therefore able to draw upon the Hellenistic kerygma of these churches.[10] The weight of emphasis with Bultmann falls accordingly not only upon the primacy of the Pauline kerygma in the New Testament message, but upon the kerygma's indebtedness to the Hellenistic world, and in particular upon what Bultmann regards as the pre-Christian Gnostic redeemer myth. As interpreter of the Fourth Gospel, Bultmann has gone even further in this direction. For whereas Paul has still combined Gnostic redemption ideas with the Jewish apocalyptic element, the Fourth Gospel, minus the editorial recensions by which, in Bultmann's judgment, it was adapted to suit orthodox circles in the early Church, presents redemption entirely in Gnostic terms not as a visible event in history, but as a present process (John 3:19; 5:24 f.; 11:25 f.: 12:31). The redeemer is present not so much in history as in the word of preaching or the message from above.[11]

In all of this, despite his early work on Jesus [12] with its attempt to understand the meaning of Jesus' person only through the words of his teaching, Bultmann has hardly laid any stress at all upon the historical person of Jesus of Nazareth, but has instead brought the kerygma of the Christ into high relief. He has thus been the kerygmatic theologian *par excellence.* Now the second foundation of Bultmann's structure is that he has called for the demythologizing of the kerygma and has invoked the aid of Heidegger's existentialistic analysis as a means of clarifying the existential possibilities enshrined in the kerygma.

In the Bultmannian structure of the New Testament proclamation the coexistence of the unique divine act in Jesus Christ and its demythologization by means of the analysis of human possibilities, resulted in Bultmann's being attacked from two sides, by critics on the "left" and critics on the "right." The views of Bultmann's critics on both sides have already been presented with admirable clarity by John Macquarrie in his study *The Scope of Demythologizing.*

Just as earlier Graf Paul Yorck and W. Dilthey had held that the Christian "understanding of existence" could be attained without any necessary reference to Jesus Christ at all, so latterly such critics of the

"left" as Karl Jaspers and Fritz Buri have contended, against Bultmann, that the logic of demythologizing demands the abandonment
of the kerygma with its proclamation of a decisive historic event of the
past, and the understanding of Christianity simply as a philosophy
of existence.

Among orthodox critics on the other side, Helmut Thielicke, for
instance, has asserted that Bultmann has reduced the Christian message to subjectivism, and so has lost the objective historicity of Jesus
as an event *extra nos*.[13] Karl Barth has also struck at the very roots
of Bultmann's hermeneutics by rejecting the idea of an existentialist
pre-philosophy as the final norm of New Testament exegesis. For
Barth there is no hope of understanding what the New Testament has
to say through any element that does not come from the illumination
of the Holy Spirit. Consequently, we betray the sovereignty of the
Word and denature it when we relegate the prior event of Jesus Christ
to that which is only secondary, the understanding of our human condition. It is in the context of this altercation with Bultmann on the
subject of hermeneutics that Barth attacks him for severing the
kerygma from the event it proclaims and so for giving the Christ-event
only a peripheral place within it.[14]

Macquarrie, for his part, does not try to effect a synthesis between
the extremes of the critics, but seeks rather to show that the two facets
of Bultmann's position, proclamation of a decisive historic divine act
and the analysis of human possibilities, can properly be held together
and constitute a genuine paradox. Whether he has made his case is an
open question that could be decided only by following through his
arguments in detail. At all events, it would now appear to be beyond
dispute that Bultmann always tried at least to differentiate the kerygma
from the Gnostic type of redeemer myth by holding that it bears witness to a unique historic occurrence, the occurrence of Jesus Christ,
which in the recent past of the primitive Church inaugurated the
eschatological event of redemption. Yet at the same time so one-sided
was his emphasis on the Christ-kerygma and so strict his veto on the
retrospective question about the historical Jesus that his own pupils,
not surprisingly, became fearful of the danger inherent in his position
of dissolving the kerygma into a timeless Christ-myth or Christ-idea.

Out of this situation arose the post-Bultmannian discussion of the
possibility of a "new quest" of the historical Jesus, opened up by
E. Käsemann's Marburg paper of 1954.[15] The story of the discussion

has already been told with erudition by James M. Robinson.[16] The subsequent debate of recent years has given rise very rapidly to an extensive literature, including the appearance of a large volume of essays published in East Germany in 1960 under the title, *Der historische Jesus und der kerygmatische Christus*.[17] To sift out, collect, and evaluate the many views that have been put forward would be a mammoth task. I can only hope in the following pages to touch on the most strategic points.

I have the impression that Anglo-American scholarship has in the main conjured up a picture of the "new quest" as an entirely unitary movement. Certainly the dynamic for all the "new seekers" has been the wish to go beyond Bultmann in renewing the question of the significance of the historical Jesus for Christian theology. But there has all along been a variety of nuances in the different approaches made to the problem.

At the first Käsemann concentrated simply on the need for us to hold on to the unity between the message of Jesus of Nazareth and the Church's proclamation of the Christ. The question raised by him was this: assuming the point of view of Form-criticism that the Gospels are community confessions of the risen Christ, can we get back into the pre-Crucifixion life of Jesus and investigate the relation between the words of Jesus and the Church's post-Easter message of the Christ? He suggested that we should try to establish criteria for deciding those features in the tradition which properly belong to the historical figure of Jesus, and went on to propose that the elements most likely to be authentic are those which cannot be traced to Judaism and have least of all been "kerygmatized" by the primitive Christian community.

Latterly, in his influential programmatic essay on the "new quest," J. M. Robinson has gone further in attempting to define its *modus operandi*. The point of departure for Robinson is the inability of the older objective historical methodology to grasp the inward existential reality of Jesus' life. He therefore takes up the new weapon of modern historiography, handed on by W. Dilthey and more recently by R. G. Collingwood, as a means of access to the innermost being or selfhood of the historical Jesus. We are asked by Robinson to distinguish between "what can be known of Jesus of Nazareth by means of the scientific methods of the historian" and "Jesus of Nazareth as he actually was," that is, in the hidden depth of his person, in his aim and intention. The purpose of the "new quest" must therefore be "to test the validity of the kerygma's understanding of existence with *Jesus'* existence." [18] In pursuit of this aim, its procedure must be to unite existential openness with historical-critical analysis. Again, G. Born-kamm's *Jesus of Nazareth,* which will be discussed at some length in Chapter IV, appears, on the face of it, to be a plea that the only stand-point from which we can enter into the history of Jesus is that of Easter, since only from such a standpoint can we perceive the indis-soluble interpenetration of history and kerygma in the Gospel witness to Jesus.

There have, however, been signs of a certain disparity of outlook among the post-Bultmannian group. Käsemann himself, for instance, perhaps as a result of Bultmann's protests or of what others, such as Fuchs, were making of the "new quest," has become increasingly lukewarm on the subject. Similarly H. Conzelmann has recently held that there is no necessary connection between faith and the historical Jesus. On the other hand E. Fuchs and G. Ebeling have veered back to a positive attitude toward the nineteenth-century quest and, in particular, toward the notion of the Jesus of history as the "ground of faith."

From the first, Fuchs has defended the idea that Jesus' message falls within the framework of his conduct, that he is the bringer of God's Word not only in his words, as advocated by Bornkamm and Robinson, but in his person and his deed. So Fuchs has reflected upon Jesus' acts, his living in love for others, his faith, and his absolute decision for God even unto the death of the Cross. The event of Jesus, which is given expression and interpreted in the words of Jesus, is given expression also in the apostolic kerygma—Jesus has remained decisive. The post-Easter faith of the Church is a recapitu-lation of Jesus' own faith. The kerygma's summons to decision echoes Jesus' own summons to decision. Fuchs can say in fact that Jesus' own certainty of God *is faith,* and if we let ourselves be led by the texts of the New Testament we are confronted with the faith of those who themselves have entered in upon the faith of Jesus. Fuchs thus lays considerable stress on the communal nature of faith, whereby the "speech-event" (*Sprachereignis*) that is Jesus Christ is not a private word of God addressed to the individual man, but a word that in-volves him in, and comes through, the community of faith.[19]

In close affinity with Fuchs's approach is that of G. Ebeling.

Ebeling delineates the structure of faith as existential attitude. But within the structure of the faith act that takes place among men Ebeling includes the faith of Jesus himself. Going back to the historical Jesus, he describes him as the witness to faith, whose work is consummated in the Easter faith response of his disciples so that he has now become for them the "ground of faith." [20]

There has thus reappeared with Fuchs and Ebeling the same understanding of Jesus as the "ground of faith" as characterized the work of the Ritschlian theologian, Wilhelm Herrmann. Out of this has lately arisen talk of the emergence on the horizon of the Bultmannian movement of a "neo-liberal" strain.[21] Whether this trend can gather sufficient momentum to establish itself, despite opposition, as the dominant one in German theology in the later years of this century, only the future will tell.

For the moment many will no doubt take comfort and encouragement from the fact that two of Bultmann's disciples have shown their willingness to seek illumination on the question of the historical Jesus from the reappropriation of former views and insights, albeit in terms of our present situation. There may be a needed corrective here to the present climate of thought in many of our theological seminaries. The false exaggeration of Bultmann's "modernism" by some of his interpreters has led some among the present generation of theological students to despise old interpretations and concepts, and to believe that with our appearance all wisdom and all knowledge have for the first time come to light. *Vixere fortes ante Agamemnona!* Karl Barth, who has reacted more vigorously than most against the theology of the nineteenth century, has none the less said wisely:

> The 19th century is *not* to be dismissed, nor is its theology. I could not follow the rule *De mortuis nihil nisi bene* (speak nothing but good of the dead) simply because the theologians of that time are not dead. "In Him they all have life," in the greatness and within the limitations in which they once lived. *Et lux perpetua lucet eis* (and the eternal light shines upon them). And thus they live, excitingly enough, also for us. They will not cease to speak to us. And we cannot cease to listen to them.[22]

With regard to the reception accorded the "new quest," so far as one can discern, there has been relatively little critical concern over it in Great Britain or America, probably because it has there been somewhat unquestioningly accepted as no more than a welcome revival of the old quest. On the continent of Europe, Bultmann has quite impenitently resisted the "new quest," and has classified the work of his pupils as reversion in one way or another to positivistic historical-psychological interpretation. In his pronouncement of July 1959 at the Heidelberg Academy of Sciences, he once again tolled the bell of the *Dass*—in talking of the event of Jesus Christ we can never go beyond the "thatness" of the Cross, present now as God's Word in the Church's proclamation.[23] *That* the Cross has happened he will not deny. *How* and *why* it happened he will not ask. Barth, from his own position, also has remained skeptical of any kind of "historical" affirmations about Jesus that are still dependent upon historical-critical research: he has expressed his suspicion of the "new quest" of the historical Jesus proposed by Bultmann's disciples, "the authoritative New Testament men, who to my amazement have armed themselves with swords and staves, and once again undertaken the search for the 'historical Jesus'—a search in which I now as before prefer not to participate." [24] Again from a younger theologian of the Barthian school, Heinrich Ott, has come a vigorous objection to the "new quest." Ott revises Kähler's affirmation that the historical Jesus conceals from us the living Christ to the statement that the positivistic acceptance of a worldly actuality conceals from us the genuine depth of "history" (*Geschichte*). Events relating to Jesus understood as brute facts are only a secondary abstraction. What is primary is the "image" (*Bild*) or "appearance" (*Erscheinung*) of Jesus Christ. The "appearance" of Jesus Christ, that is to say, the actual historical Jesus, and not the so-called historical Jesus of the *Leben-Jesu-Forschung,* belongs fundamentally to the same ontological order as the Biblical Christ-image. Accordingly the distinction between the historical Jesus and the Christ of the kerygma cannot be sustained and entry into the factual history of Jesus is quite impossible.[25]

The foregoing survey may have served to show how fluid and many-sided is the ongoing debate about the significance of the historical Jesus for Christian theology—of one thing only we may be sure, that the debate is not finished. On the whole problem of the Jesus of history, Dr. W. C. van Unnik has recently suggested that we must distinguish between two different sets of questions, the "historic" and the "dogmatic," as he has called them. In the former what is at stake is the question of how in the New Testament the first Christians came to look upon the man, Jesus of Nazareth, as the final revelation of

God for the present as well as for the past. In the latter the question is how this message of Jesus the Christ touches us in our world, and how it can best be preached, interpreted, and responded to in the present generation. The two sets of questions, as van Unnik has recognized, are of course constantly intertwined with each other. We cannot, to be sure, abstract ourselves from the needs and demands of our own historically conditioned situation or hermetically seal off the "historic" questions today from all that has happened since the failure of the *Leben-Jesu-Forschung* through the rise of Form-criticism, of dialectical theology, and of existentialist theology. But, with this *caveat,* the distinction made by van Unnik seems to me to be a useful one.[26]

The claims of modernity and the demand for interpretation of the message of Jesus Christ in terms of our present situation notwithstanding, a certain priority, if not autonomy, has still to be assigned to the "historic" questions that we have to ask in confrontation with the New Testament. We should never forget that alongside Bultmann's contribution as existentialist theologian stands his work as noted historical researcher in Christian origins. There has been a tendency, however, among recent theological interpreters of Bultmann, to accept somewhat uncritically the radical results and conclusions of his researches in the beginnings of Christianity.

The tendency to overlook the "historic" problems of the New Testament and Christian origins is exemplified in Schubert Ogden's theological essay, *Christ Without Myth.* In endeavoring to meet the "dogmatic" needs of the moment, he allows himself to make what appear to me to be sweeping generalizations about the intention of the New Testament as a whole. "The only final condition for sharing in authentic life that the New Testament lays down," he writes, "is a condition that can be formulated in complete abstraction from the event Jesus of Nazareth and all that it specifically imports." [27]

Is this really what the whole New Testament is saying? Has the modern theologian succeeded in discovering the one true message of the New Testament unmistakably and finally? It would be comforting to think that all old doubts and questions concerning the New Testament and early Christianity had at last been settled. But instead, in the very act of listening for the gospel from the New Testament as a guide to our present theological understanding, we are not only confronted with a plurality of confessions of Jesus Christ, but also find

ourselves in a situation of great uncertainty with regard to the historical complexities of primitive Christianity, not least what Easter has
meant to the men of the New Testament, and the ambiguous role of
Paul, the character of his kerygma, and the influences that played
upon him.

Behind the question of how the message of Jesus Christ is to be
understood and interpreted now lie intricate and unresolved problems
of Christian origins, whose significance for the contemporary "Jesus
of history"–"Christ of faith" debate can hardly be overemphasized.
Possessed though we may be today by a tremulous sense of urgency
about communicating the message of Jesus Christ to a world that
appears to be dying of its own worldliness, we still may not despise
or neglect study of the so-called "smaller historic" details, e.g. the
"historic" question of the meaning of Easter for the New Testament,
the Gnostic issue in its bearing on Christian origins, the influence of
the Hellenistic mystery cults on Paul, and the formulation of the
Pauline kerygma. The "historical Jesus problem" is an extremely
complex issue, impinging on the fields of New Testament background
and introduction, theology and doctrine, and methods of historical
research.

Since, in our discussion of modern viewpoints on the "Jesus of history"–"Christ of faith" question, we are concerned chiefly with the
"historic" issues of how primitive Christianity, as represented by the
New Testament, came to believe in and to preach Jesus as the Christ
of God, we have seen fit to use the title *Jesus and Christian Origins*.
Chapter I deals mainly with Bultmann's approach to the New Testament and the formative influences behind it. In English-speaking
scholarly circles there has undoubtedly been a good deal of antipathy
to Bultmann's position. Anglo-American Biblical critics have perhaps
too often tried to dismiss recent movements in German theology and
criticism, with all their varied nuances, simply by disparaging reference, in an uncritical and undifferentiated way, to "neo-orthodoxy."
But in this day of the cold war and of ever-increasing international
tensions, when the Churches are being constrained to think and talk
and act in terms of ecumenicity, we are surely under obligation also to
try to transcend the boundaries of scholarly provincialism and to
attain a genuine openness toward opinions from outside that may
never have occurred to us or may perplex us. Equally so, it is incumbent on those who, on our side of the fence, are attracted by the new

German hermeneutical and historiographical stances, not to assume an attitude of haughtiness toward the scientific historical research that has remained most typical of their own scholarly traditions and has frequently stood as a safeguard against the recrudescence of crudely mythological views or anarchic speculations and superstitions. We have to take account of the conditioning factors that lie behind the basic methodological and hermeneutical differences between Anglo-American and German Biblical scholarship. Accordingly, in Chapter II we seek to evaluate certain normative historical-critical points of view, that have certainly retained their vitality despite the Bultmann trend.

Chapter III explores some efforts on the part of individual scholars to probe beyond the normal historical-critical understanding toward a more satisfying solution to the "history-faith" problem. I have thought it preferable to let the reader have the discussion of Chapters II and III in front of him before taking up the subject of the "new quest" in Chapter IV. For although the "new quest" has sprung out of the Bultmann fold and might fittingly have been included at the close of the first chapter on Bultmann, it lives also in the historical-critical camp to the extent that it is ready to rely on the methods of historical criticism as a means of penetrating the history of Jesus.

Chapter V is devoted to the pivotal question of the meaning of the Easter event for the New Testament. Chapter VI seeks to explicate the "humiliation-exaltation" theme that appears to permeate the various confessions of Jesus the Christ in the New Testament documents, and this is followed by a brief concluding statement.

I

The Shift Away From the Historical Jesus

The Primary Problem of Christian Origins

The problems of Christian origins are very numerous and complex. M. Goguel once remarked that even an incomplete bibliography of modern works on the beginnings of Christianity would more than fill a volume of over five hundred pages. In the Preface to the English edition of his monumental *Dogmengeschichte,* von Harnack observed that the most difficult part of the history of dogma is the beginning, because in it are the seeds of all later developments, and also because it is hard to know what material to select as the most important from the history of primitive Christianity. Every form of inquiry into the rise of Christianity, environmental-historical and theological as well as dogmatic, is confronted with the dilemma of where to start and what to choose.

It is said of the famous Scottish divines, Marcus Dods and Alexander Whyte, that when they used to go for their Saturday afternoon walks together, they always in their conversation struck straight across country to Jesus Christ himself. When we take up the subject of the beginnings of Christianity, he is the great converging point, to which we have to strike straight across the great expanses. Learned scholars of the Church, dogmatician, theologian, and Biblical critic, have done just that with a kind of unwavering instinct. "It certainly is the first duty of the historian," wrote von Harnack, "to signalise the overpowering impression made by the Person of Jesus on the disciples,

16

which is the basis of all further developments." [1] A. Schweitzer contended that the central concern of the historical study of primitive Christianity must be to discern and describe how the teaching of Jesus developed through Paulinism into early Greek theology and so led to the history of dogma.[2] While M. Goguel, devoutly interested as he was in the sociological laws operative in the rise and growth of the Christian religion, maintained that "the real problem is not only to discover how Christian theology and dogma were formed, but also, what is specially important, to discover how the Church developed its constitution," he none the less began his inquiry on the birth of Christianity with a full discussion of the source-question of the nature and meaning of the Church's Easter faith in Jesus as the risen and glorified One.[3]

Von Harnack, Schweitzer, and Goguel—to take only these three examples of scholars of diverse interests and outlooks—pointed, each in his own way, to the necessity of trying to bridge the gap between Jesus and his Church as the foremost task of the investigator of Christian origins. This inescapable and pre-eminent question of the connection between Jesus of Nazareth and the earliest Church has become one of the liveliest and most widely debated issues of recent years. It was in the face of this problem and in confrontation with Bultmann's massive concentration upon the kerygma of the Christ that E. Käsemann declared in 1954 that "we cannot deny the identity of the exalted Lord with the incarnate Lord without falling into docetism, and depriving ourselves of the possibility of distinguishing the Easter faith of the Church from a myth." [4] The problem is implicit already in the designation "Jesus Christ," even though we are hardly aware of it when we take these words upon our lips confessionally. "Jesus" is the name of a particular and definite historical person: "She will bear a son and you will call his name Jesus" (Matt. 1:21). "Christ" on the other hand is a titular dignity conferred by the Church upon this "Jesus" and denoting for him an exalted status and a unique relationship to God.

The historic problem of how this merger between apparent incommensurates, the name "Jesus" and the title "Christ," could have taken place was described some time ago by Sir Edwyn Hoskyns and Noel Davey as "the riddle" lurking behind every fragment of the New Testament. "The riddle is a theological riddle, which is insoluble apart from the solution of an historical problem. What was the relation be-

tween Jesus of Nazareth and the primitive Church? That is the riddle." [5] That is the axial question of Christian origins, to which Käsemann drew attention once again in 1954. Contemporary interest has
lain in attempting to discover and work out the unity between Jesus
of Nazareth and the Christ of the Church's kerygma. But when we
go behind this present phase, as we have to do in order to see it in
perspective, we find a quite different story.

The nineteenth-century Liberal quest was intent on driving a wedge
between the historical Jesus and the Christ of the kerygma. In making the cleavage, the Liberal historians fastened onto the human
Jesus, the portrayal of whose history was the abiding theme of their
researches, as the great object of their faith. The impression we now
get in retrospect is that, having differentiated between the man Jesus
and the Christ, and having envisaged the need to choose between
Jesus *or* the Christ, they voted wholeheartedly for Jesus. In our own
century the vote has swung. There has been something of a landslide
away from the historical Jesus to the Christ of the Church's kerygma,
the Christ of the Church's faith, as the center of theological interest.[6]

We have now to consider some of the more important factors which
have helped to produce this quite distinctive change of temper.

Schweitzer's The Quest of the Historical Jesus

In his powerful book, Schweitzer records the many attempts made
between 1778 and 1901 to distill out of the Gospels the essence of
what Jesus really did and taught. The basic presupposition of the
Leben-Jesu-Forschung was that the primitive Church, and so the
Evangelists themselves, had misunderstood Jesus, and that now at
length, through the instrumentality of scientific historical reconstruction, a needed corrective could be supplied. Whereas Reimarus, the
somewhat enigmatic eighteen-century genius, had pointed to the significance of the eschatological elements in the Gospels, the Liberal
Protestant scholars, of whom von Harnack was a leading representative, persistently maintained that access to the historical reality of
Jesus of Nazareth could only be gained by penetrating and hacking
away the underbrush of eschatology. So they made a concerted drive
to push past the eschatological and apocalyptic ideas of the Gospels
as simply accommodations to an ancient local and temporal *milieu,* in

order to arrive at the historic features of Jesus' life and teaching which could be seen to be of timeless value.

The Liberal Lives of Jesus, which arose out of these fundamental premises, Schweitzer castigated as unjustifiable modernization, tailored to suit the requirements, as the case may be, of the modern idealist, rationalist, socialist, or romanticist. The very existence of such a startling variety of pictures of Jesus could perhaps be taken as a sign that not a single one of them was accurate.

There is nothing more negative than the result of the critical study of the life of Jesus. The Jesus of Nazareth who came forward publicly as the Messiah, who preached the ethic of the Kingdom of God, who founded the Kingdom of Heaven upon earth, and died to give His work its final consecration, never had any existence. He is a figure designed by rationalisation, endowed with life by liberalism, and clothed by modern theology in an historical garb.[7]

It is important to notice that the arrows of Schweitzer's criticism were directed not at historical study as such, but at the jejune results achieved by its practitioners in the case of Jesus of Nazareth. The most cherished convictions of the historical scholars, particularly of the latter part of the nineteenth century, were left unscathed by Schweitzer —their understanding of history as an assemblage of facts of the past, their unshakable confidence, inspired by the recent striking advances made by the natural sciences, in the ability of the truly objective historical inquirer to extract the real facts from such old documents as came under his scrutiny. The substance of Schweitzer's complaint against the composers of the Liberal Lives was indeed that they were not *objective* enough, but were altogether too much conditioned by the subjective desire to clothe Jesus in the garb of a Victorian gentleman, and so gave us a lay figure, too respectable to offend us, too unmysterious to claim our reverence, too diminutive in stature to account for the rise of the Church of Christ.

Accordingly Schweitzer proceeded without hesitation to his own delineation of Jesus, which he could regard as objective because he sought to push Jesus back into his own time and thought-world, so remote and alien from our own. Unlike the Form-critics of a later date, Schweitzer repudiated Wrede's attack on the historicity of the Marcan record on the ground of Mark's employment of the "dogmatic" device of the "Messianic secret." Against Wrede, Schweitzer

maintained that the "secret" in Mark has to do not with Jesus' Messiahship, but with the wider and all-embracing mystery of Jesus'
eschatological preaching of the Kingdom of God. In the eschatological
world-view of Jesus, Schweitzer found the true "dogmatic" element of
the Gospels, and relentlessly pressed his case that this "dogmatic"
element constituted precisely the actual historical element. The in-
choateness and disorder of the Gospel records has therefore been
occasioned not by mere accidents in the transmission of the tradition,
but by the explosive power of the inward decisions of Jesus, whereby
the course of his history was determined.[8] Impelled inexorably by his
overwhelming belief in the imminent end of the world and in his own
Messianic Parousia in the very near future, he lived and at last was
crushed by death in his prodigious but unsuccessful effort to bring all
ordinary history to a close.[9]

Schweitzer's Jesus, living and dying to end history and bring in
a future that never came, thoroughgoing apocalyptist, deluded visionary, is characterized by nothing more than by *Schwärmerei*. No doubt
Schweitzer brought us closer than did the Liberal critics of the von
Harnack tradition to the *Mysterium Christi* which pervades the Gospels. But, bent on letting us see Jesus as he really was in his own day
and place, Schweitzer put him far away from us, disclosing for us not
a man of flesh and blood, "tempted in all things even as we are," but
the history of a Faith that was disappointed, of a staggering Idea that
failed. Having rooted the whole history of Jesus in the failure of his
expectation that he would very soon usher in the kingdom of God,
Schweitzer, who had been zealous to keep in closer touch with the
historical facts than such as Wrede, was paradoxically left with only
one last recourse—to discredit the significance of historical knowledge
of Jesus and summon us to his Spirit, which is still at work in the
world as the Spirit of him who can come to us now only as *"One unknown."* [10] So it is that, with Schweitzer, the mangled body of Jesus,
hanging on the onward rolling wheel of the world, has become little
more than an everlasting symbol of the pathos of human existence and
of the possibility, divinely given to man, of transcending the conflicts
and sufferings of his history.[11]

Schweitzer's notion of the history of Jesus as, in its inward depth,
the living out of a tragic yet lordly error about the coming of the
kingdom of God, and of the inner history of Christianity as grounded
throughout on the non-occurrence of the Parousia, became particularly

influential for the Bern school of Martin Werner and latterly of his pupil, Fritz Buri, at Basel.[12] For this school it seemed no longer possible to speak in terms of faith in the historical Jesus Christ, seeing that his history was determined entirely by a mistaken apocalyptic world view. Nor on the other side was the Christology of the early Church anything more than a replacement for the apocalyptic end of the world which was eagerly anticipated but never arrived. Buri therefore came to look upon the Christological or soteriological formulations of the primitive Church as a secondary mythological interpretation that had no bearing on the real Christ. With faith in the historical Jesus Christ gone, and with the Church's Christology dismissed as a mythological fabrication, all that remains to us, according to Buri, is the "idea of Christ" as a perennial symbol of human existence as grace.[13] In the demythologizing controversy, Buri subsequently radicalized this point of view by pleading with Bultmann for the abandonment of the kerygma of Jesus Christ as a mythological residue and for the understanding of Christianity as a philosophy of existence.[14]

Neither theology nor historical study can be satisfied with the notion of the Bern School that the early Church sought compensation for the awaited cosmic cataclysm that never came by fancifully devising a dogmatic Christology. The Church's Christology was no mere substitute for the delay of the Parousia, but was inspired rather, to put it in the simplest terms, by a past to which it looked back and a present in which it rejoiced—the past in which the historical Jesus of Nazareth had brought God's grace near to men and had confronted them with the demand for love and faithfulness and truth simply because they were God's will then as they are now, and the present in which, through Easter, this grace and this demand were still near and still real.

Let us be clear then about the effects of Schweitzer's classic work. After about two centuries of unwearied scholarly endeavors to establish the facts about the historical Jesus, Schweitzer declared a moratorium on the old quest by dramatizing in his own portrait of Jesus as a fanatical futurist the very thing which the Liberals had minimized or eradicated, the eschatological element in Jesus' life and ministry. By his tremendous stress on the non-advent of the Parousia, for the inauguration of which and for nothing else Jesus died in vain, Schweitzer helped to pave the way for recent versions of the primitive Church's Christology which left no place therein for faith in the historical Jesus as the decisive revelation of God for the past as well as for the present. Whereas the Liberals, in their search for the truly human lineaments of Jesus, lost the Christ-character or the kerygma-character of his history, Schweitzer, himself no less resolved on scientific objectivity, all but submerged the historical Jesus in the dogmatic "concept of the Christ." If, as Günther Bornkamm states it, Schweitzer thus "delivered the funeral oration" of the Liberal quest, he was commemorating the death not of its time-honored method of critical study but of its results. It was from other quarters that Schweitzer's insights into the palpable limitations of the old quest were transmuted into a general critique of objective historical-critical methodology.

Barth's Denigration of Historicism

At the same time as the leaders of the Form-criticism school were arraigning the Liberal attempts to reconstruct a life of Jesus, a new voice was raised with prophetic zeal when, in the Preface to the second edition of his commentary on the Epistle to the Romans in 1921, Karl Barth protested against the historical scholars' readiness to attribute sovereign rights to scientific historical inquiry.[15] Barth's rigorous affirmation that the historical-critical method must not be regarded as the be-all and end-all in dealing with the Biblical witness fell, as Karl Adam, the Tübingen Catholic theologian, has put it, "like a bombshell on the playground of the theologians." Barth maintained that the increasing resources available to historical research from archaeology, philology, psychology, textual criticism, furnished no more than the means of a prelude or preamble to the one indispensable task of the Biblical interpreter, which is to expose "the Word in the words," to describe and define the *religious* content of the Biblical documents. So Barth proposed the replacement of "historical exegesis" by "theological exegesis" as the one means of bringing us face to face with the theme of the New Testament writings, namely the Christ-event, in its meaning for us.

Despite his eloquent plea that the function of the contemporary New Testament interpreter is to break down the walls of partition between, shall we say, Paul, and his own time, so that Paul himself speaks and the men of our day listen, Barth has certainly never given the slightest hint that the Christ-event, as attested by the New Testament, is to be refined into a timeless theological principle or religious concept, or that "historical" knowledge of that event can be dispensed with. But for Barth "historical" knowledge has its precise boundaries —it cannot go behind the texts of the New Testament itself, but must ever begin and end with them.

It will not be "the historical facts" which we have to find (or think we have already found) somewhere behind the texts, and which we then claim as objective reality. A conscientious affirmation and investigation of the true "historical element," i.e., the New Testament texts themselves and as such, is sufficiently difficult and important and rewarding to pose new tasks for each successive generation. It is in this that the necessary introduction consists. As against this, the investigation, and even the affirmation with varying degrees of assurance, of facts which lie in a vacuum outside the texts, can only mean the leading away into a Babylonian captivity in which there is no attestation of this event [the Christ-event], and can have nothing to do with the knowledge of this event.[16]

This insistence of Barth's that all discussion of Jesus Christ must be limited only to the New Testament witness explains his recent aversion to the attempt of Bultmann's disciples to revive interest in the possibility of historical reconstruction of the words and acts of Jesus.[17] While the early Barth's frequent references to the Christ-event as *Urgeschichte,* "primal history," ran the risk of substituting all that was implied by the prefix for the history itself, his continual refusal in the later parts of the *Dogmatics* to go beyond the New Testament texts has certainly not prevented him from stating the significance, within the presentation of the New Testament witnesses, of the past of Jesus of Nazareth as a man among men. According to Barth, the texts were really looking at this man and attesting his life. While from the standpoint of the texts, that is from the standpoint of Easter, we can see how the early Christian community thought of him as the one who still is what he was, nevertheless the past of the "Royal Man," Jesus of Nazareth, has remained utterly decisive for its faith and theology. The traditions of the Gospels are a monument to the memory of this man, who moved about among other men and yet was marked off from them "in His inescapability, in His critical function, in His unforgettable lordliness, in His irrevocability which bursts and transcends all the limits of His life and its time." [18]

In his reaction against objective historical research into the life of Jesus, Barth has obviously therefore not intended to minimize the sig-

nificance of the "historical Jesus" for Christian theology. Rather was
he concerned to demonstrate the inability of historical science, along
with all other human categories, to grasp the reality of this man, Jesus,
concerning whose person we must simply receive the witness of the
texts of the New Testament itself, without trying to go beyond them
or to add anything to them by our own highly developed scientific
skills and techniques. Barth's profound interest in upholding the importance of the man Jesus for Christian faith and theology has
afforded small consolation to those imbued with the spirit of scientific
historical scholarship. Rather, by Barth's refusal to go behind the
texts, by his exclusive preoccupation with theological interpretation,
with the specifically *religious* content of the New Testament documents, they have been roused to cry "reactionary, ultra-conservative,
fundamentalist." The Barthian demotion of "historical exegesis" and
exaltation of "theological exegesis" was bound to raise vehement protests from those enchanted with the long romance of historical critical
study and discovery of the time and world of Jesus and the primitive
Church, and particularly from those quarters in which an unremitting
struggle had been waged against narrow Biblicism and arid dog-
matism.

The Barthian revolt against objective historical method early found
an intuitive sympathizer in R. Bultmann, who was among the first
defenders of the school of Barth. Sharing Barth's antipathy to the
nineteenth-century *Leben-Jesu-Forschung,* but certainly not all of his
views, Bultmann has subsequently taken his own independent way,
until in him the revolt against the old quest of the historical Jesus has
reached its climax.

Bultmann's Attitude Toward History

It is necessary to begin by stating that, contrary to some Anglo-Saxon
opinions particularly, Bultmann has not run away from history, but
has been preoccupied with it and with the question of the claims of
Christianity as a historical religion. For one thing his researches in the
field of Christian origins have been a large part of his life's work. For
another he has affirmed that history is indeed our biggest problem
today. He cannot be understood as an arch-skeptic about history. Because of his later pronouncements on the kerygma, his interest in

Jesus of Nazareth in *Jesus and the Word* is perhaps too readily forgotten. His presentation of Jesus of Nazareth as rabbi, prophet, herald of the coming reign of God, and wonder-worker appears to leave room for the objective reality of events associated with Jesus. The opening gambit of Bultmann's *Theology of the New Testament,* in which he declares that Jesus is only one among other presuppositions for New Testament theology, and which has gained a certain notoriety, is not to be construed as a declaration of skepticism, but rather as an indication of his apathy, as Christian theologian, to the concrete historical element. Anticipating our later discussion of Bultmann's view of the Resurrection of Jesus Christ, we can also say that no more in this case does his interpretation constitute a blank denial of objective factuality. What is involved is not Bultmann's refusal to believe that there are certain events that cannot be established, but his unwillingness to allow us to assume the truth of some possible occurrences, in as much as they cannot be established.[19]

The heart of Bultmann's attitude toward history is not any skepticism of his, but rather his indifference to concrete historical facts or happenings in their pastness. This indifference is not new or unique with Bultmann. It has come to him as part of his inheritance. The Preacher of old once declared, out of his wisdom and maturity of experience, that "there is nothing new under the sun." So far as the history of theological thought is concerned, this is largely true. It certainly is true of Bultmann. Bultmann himself, of course, whether rightly or wrongly, has regarded his program of demythologization or existentialist interpretation as a repristination of Luther's *sola fide,* seeing it as a necessary means of overcoming that desire to cling to objective worldly events of the past which represents a fall into "works righteousness," into the domain of the Law, and so a refusal to accept faith's radical insecurity. But we are not here so much thinking of that part of Bultmann's heritage, crucial though it is. Nor indeed are we thinking of the Kantian distinction between the objective world of sense perception and the thing-in-itself, to which some have traced Bultmann's indifference to the concrete historical element in past events.[20]

What we have in mind is the more immediately constitutive background of Bultmann's outlook upon history, namely that revolution in historiographical standpoints which took place around the end of last century and in the earlier part of the present century. The anti-Liberal reaction was not an isolated phenomenon, confined to theological circles. The nineteenth century's whole notion of history as an exact science, comparable to the natural sciences, its unprecedented homage to objective, external facts, and its confidence in recovering them, were put in question during these years. Pre-eminent among critics of the older positivistic historiography were such commanding figures as Wilhelm Dilthey and Max Weber, who stressed more and more the importance of *subjectivity,* the need for the subjective self-engagement of the historian in the meaning and decisions of great individual forms of human being of the past, in the process of historical knowledge. This movement was not restricted to Germany, but later received prominence in England through the work of R. G. Collingwood, in whose view "history is for self-understanding," and in France through that of Raymond Aron.[21] Against the wide canvas of this fundamental reorientation in historiography is to be viewed Bultmann's attitude of indifference to the concrete historical element in events of the past. For Bultmann, greatly indebted as he is especially to Dilthey, the primary principle of hermeneutics is the principle of life-relationship to the subject (*Sache*) of which the ancient text speaks. With his subject the interpreter must become passionately involved. He must leave the self open to the possibility of radical decision as he confronts the meaning or intention latent in his subject. Applying this principle to the subject of which the New Testament texts speak, or shall we say the Christian "object," Jesus Christ, Bultmann is chiefly concerned not to repudiate its concrete historicity but to give pride of place to the question of meaning, allowing it to enter into the specification of the historic reality.

The Historisch *and the* Geschichtlich

The distinction between the *historisch* and the *geschichtlich* appeared already in the title of Martin Kähler's epochal book, *Der sogenannte historische Jesus und der geschichtliche, biblische Christus,* first published in 1892, and still basic on the present question and debate about the historical Jesus. Faced with the optimistic inquiries of the nineteenth-century scholars into the Gospels as sources for biographical data in the "Life of Jesus," and at the same time with the staggering variety of the portraits presented, Kähler sought to emancipate Christian faith from dependence on the scholars and the palpable uncertainties of criticism, and castigated what he called the "papal pretensions" of the historians. To his mind the historians were shutting out the ordinary man, and arrogating to themselves a monopoly of knowledge of Jesus, by declaring in effect that he was accessible only to those possessed of the necessary historical and critical resources. "How can Jesus Christ be the proper object of the faith of all Christians, if what and who He really was can be established only by a complicated investigation. . . . How can this uncertain deposit left by the corrosive acids of criticism, i.e. the historical Jesus, be the object of faith of all Christians?" [22] All we have in the New Testament is the disciples' confession of faith in the risen Jesus Christ. The risen Saviour is not "the historical Jesus *behind* the Gospels." Rather is he the Christ of the apostolic preaching, the Christ of the whole New Testament. The real Christ is the preached Christ, and the preached Christ is the Christ of faith. The Gospels themselves are Easter documents through and through. If we would know the real, *historic* (*geschichtlich*) Christ, we can only begin with the kerygma. It is via the kerygma that we come into touch with the *historic* in the sense of *what really happened* (*das Geschehene*). There is, therefore, neither the need nor the possibility of trying to return to bare facts in the life of Jesus lying behind the Gospels. Such facts belong to the realm of the *historisch,* and as mere occurrences could be the concern of the historian only as detached observer and reporter of the past.

There was, however, another angle to Kähler's approach. He did not intend to cast a cloud of doubt upon the events to which the Gospels bear witness. Consequently, in a manner reminiscent of pragmatism, he felt the necessity of harking back to the character "image" (*Bild*) of the historical Jesus. He faced the question of whether the picture of Jesus in the Gospels may not simply be a pious fiction, and concluded that the Gospel portrait of Jesus authenticates itself inescapably to historical reason. "All the biblical descriptions produce the irresistible impression of the completest reality. One might venture to predict how Jesus would have acted in this situation or in that—indeed, even what He would have said. Therefore we can have converse with this Jesus, and need for this purpose nothing more than the biblical representation. The picture of Him, so full of life, so singularly beyond the power of invention, is not the idealizing creation of the human mind; there His own being has left its imperishable impression." [23]

We might expect from this latter phase of Kähler's exposition that

he assigned considerable importance to the historical person of
Jesus.[24] But, on the contrary, Kähler associated historicity not so
much with the actuality of past events as with impact upon posterity
(as in *Geschichte*). Consequently, with all his stress on the preached
Christ as the only true Christ, he left the way open to fasten onto the
Christ of the kerygma as a symbol of the faith, to the neglect of the
historical Jesus and his significance for theology.[25]

Wilhelm Herrmann, Kähler's opponent at the turn of the century,
went behind the kerygma and extended the scope of the *geschichtlich*
to include not merely the kerygma of the Christ, but the "inner life"
of Jesus of Nazareth as the absolutely convincing ground of faith. In
Herrmann's conception, the "inner life" of Jesus, in the grandeur of
its moral influence upon history, could not be established for us or
given to us by historical criticism, the results of whose reconstructions
of the past as causal sequence of events (*Historie*) are always merely
more or less probable and have to be constantly modified. Accordingly, the absolute truth of the portrait of Jesus which the Christian
believer carries within him can only be compared and contrasted with
the relative truth obtained by historical research. Herrmann certainly
spoke like Kähler of the realism with which the New Testament picture of Jesus impresses itself upon us. But he disagreed with Kähler's
verdict that historical reason or historical judgment by itself can make
us sure of Jesus' historical reality. Bent on upholding the "unprovability" of faith, and sharing Lessing's view that it is impossible to
attach the conviction of faith to a purely historical decision, Herrmann
held that if we have a picture of Jesus at all, it comes to us only in and
through the Christian fellowship by the sheer moral power of Jesus
himself. "When we speak of the historical Christ we mean that personal life of Jesus which speaks to us from the New Testament, as the
disciples' testimony to their faith, but which, when we perceive it,
always comes home to us as a miraculous revelation." [26]

Bultmann subsequently gave a more radical turn to certain leading
insights both of his teacher, Herrmann, and of Kähler. Concerned
like Herrmann to preserve the "unprovability" of faith, he has gone
further and has rejected the notion of the historical Jesus as the
ground of faith for being a clinging still to this-worldly props for faith
and a quest for the objective verification of faith. He has thus con-
signed events relating to Jesus of Nazareth to the history of facts
(*Historie*), to which Christian theology must remain indifferent if it

is not to destroy the radical insecurity of genuine faith. So Bultmann was led to impose a veto upon the retrospective historical question, as it was asked by Kähler, about the character "image" of the historical Jesus. It was then left to him only to take up and develop Kähler's emphasis upon the Christ-kerygma. For Bultmann the Christ-kerygma is to be distinguished from the history of facts and is to be enclosed within the history of meaning (*Geschichte*), since the Christ-event takes on objective reality only when and where, through the Church's proclamation of its message, *it confronts me and effects a change in my understanding of myself*. The Christ-event is therefore *geschichtlich* or *escatologisch* as happening here and now *for me* in the Church's preaching. From this stress on the "for me" of the Christ-kerygma and the resultant disinterest in historicity as actuality of the past, it is but a short step both to Bultmann's proposition that there can be no talk about God's act in Christ which is not also at the same time talk about man, and to his appeal, for the purpose of existential interpretation of the gospel, to the categories of existence of Heidegger's existentialistic analysis, which has evoked so much discussion.[27]

We shall be going on from this brief account of some lines of connection between Bultmann and Herrmann and Kähler to consider Bultmann's work as historical critic of the New Testament. I think we can say even now that it is not necessary to suppose that Bultmann was forced to his existentialist attitude toward history by the negative conclusions of his historical researches in Christian origins. Operative in his environment all along were other conditioning factors, aside from his work as New Testament critic, that influenced him toward his existentialist view. It would be more correct to say that his scholarly study of the tradition of the Gospels and of the apostolic kerygma contributed simultaneously with these to the upbuilding of the existentialist interest in his thought in opposition to nineteenth-century historicism.

Bultmann and Form-Criticism

A little while before Karl Barth raised his voice in protest against historical exegesis, the rise of the Form-criticism movement in New Testament scholarship dealt a devastating blow at the old positivistic approach to the Gospels as annals or chronicles of the life of Jesus. Form-criticism did not appear suddenly out of nowhere around 1919. It had its own antecedents, only in light of which the new movement can be understood.

In the earliest years of the century, Hermann Gunkel, heir of the critical work of the Wellhausen school, became the pioneer of studies in Form-criticism in the Old Testament that were to be followed also by Hugo Gressmann and others later. The principle from which Gunkel started was that the writers of the Old Testament were not professionals, but compilers of the tradition. The tradition was the deposit of a great variety of literary types (*Gattungen*). Gunkel accordingly proposed that the primary task of Old Testament scholarship was to sift out each separate type and to study it in its unity, according to its form, content, style, and structure. Thereafter, each type had to be traced back to its *Sitz im Leben,* its life-situation in the daily environment and activity of the Hebrew people, at which stage the tradition was spoken, not written, and consisted of songs celebrating victory in war, funeral laments, sermons of the prophets, liturgies chanted in the practice of the cult, etc. Although the most elaborate results of Gunkel's brilliant analysis of Old Testament literary types according to their forms did not appear until the publication of his commentary on the Psalms in 1933, the wide-ranging possibilities of the Form-criticism of the Old Testament had already been demonstrated in his commentary on Genesis in 1901.[28]

The same principles enunciated by Gunkel were taken up and applied to the New Testament by a group of scholars since designated as the "Form-criticism school." [29]

The first principle of the new school was that the evangelical tradition of the New Testament did not begin with the written record of Mark, but had been transmitted orally at the preliterary stage in the so-called twilight period between the death and Resurrection of Jesus and the composition of Mark. Working back from the written Gospels, the Form-critics, led by M. Dibelius and R. Bultmann, engaged in an exhaustive examination of the oral traditions that circulated in the "twilight period," and of the laws governing their formation into written records, and so performed a notable service to New Testament scholarship.

One immediate consequence of the new concentration upon the stage of the oral tradition was the prominence given to the view that the tradition must have been transmitted initially in isolated fragments. The joining together of these separate fragments only took place later, either in the still preliterary stage of the transmission of the tradition, or more likely when it was committed to a written record. Thus K. L. Schmidt contended that the Gospel stories of Jesus were really so many disconnected units with no interrelationship to one another, like a string of pearls of which the string had been broken. The net result of this standpoint was a decline of interest in the problems that had occupied the older positivistic historical criticism, the question of the external framework of the life of Jesus and of considerations of context.

The second principle of Form-criticism was that, behind the oral tradition, lay the collective consciousness of the primitive Christian community. The whole evangelical tradition had been created or at least transformed by the earliest Church. Back of this principle stood Wrede's famous work on the "Messianic secret" in Mark. Wrede had maintained that the Marcan record of Jesus' ministry is dominated by the theological motif of the "Messianic secret." He called attention to those passages in Mark in which the demons recognize Jesus as Lord and make him known (e.g. Mark 1:23–25; 3:11–12), the healed demoniacs and sick people as well as the disciples are instructed not to divulge his Messiahship (e.g. Mark 3:12; 7:36), and Jesus himself teaches his disciples in an esoteric way about who he really is (e.g. Mark 4:10–13; 7:17–23; 8:30). In such passages is revealed Mark's doctrine that Jesus' Messiahship is to be a secret during his time on earth, known to none save the demons and the chosen disciples—only after the Resurrection will it be openly displayed. The problem with which Mark was faced then was that of explaining how, if on one side the demons and on the other the disciples were aware of the Messiahship of Jesus, it had not become more widely known during his lifetime. Mark's solution was that the knowledge of his "secret" was reserved only for the supernatural world, and that the disciples, because of their obtuseness, had never really comprehended what Jesus meant (e.g. Mark 4:13; 6:50–52). Wrede concluded therefore that Jesus was never in fact recognized as Messiah during his earthly ministry, but only after his Resurrection. It was Christian theology that interpreted his life messianically. So Mark's story, full as it is of inconsistencies, cannot be taken as history, but merely as the dogmatic invention of the theology of the early Church.[30]

Following the path of Wrede, Form-criticism showed by more per-

suasive arguments that in the Gospels no merely biographical groundwork is to be found for a life of Jesus, that the individual pericopes,
and the total framework of each Gospel, are to be understood as expressions of the community's faith, because all the traditions preserved by the community were felt to meet the indispensable needs
of the community's situation, in its cultic practice, its missionary concern, and its apologetic.

The description of the group of scholars who initiated the Form-
criticism movement as a "school" has tended to obscure the fact that
there was a fairly extensive range of opinion among them from the
first. For example, in his *Die Formgeschichte des Evangeliums,* published in 1919, M. Dibelius opened the new trail cautiously enough.
He found that the forms of the units of the tradition had been determined largely by the kind of people to whom they could be traced
back: preachers, teachers or missionaries. Yet while Dibelius clearly
saw that the tradition had undergone considerable change in the
preaching, teaching, and missionary interest of the primitive Church,
he did not deny the possibility of its historicity as going back in the
first instance to Jesus himself.

The more radical Bultmann, in whom, as we have seen, the existentialist interest was probably already present, and who was later to
become the champion of demythologizing, took the extreme step of
rejecting the idea that the Gospel traditionists had any kind of historical intention, and characterized the materials of the tradition about
Jesus as the legendary or mythological fabrications of the primitive
Christian community, which gave objective expression to its faith in
concrete stories regarding Jesus.

By contrast with Bultmann, M. Albertz exemplified a quite conservative approach to Form-criticism.[31] Reacting strongly against
Bultmann's negative conclusions concerning the historicity of the Gospel materials, Albertz endeavored to work back from the fixed literary
forms in the Gospels to the actual controversies which Jesus had with
his opponents. The conclusion he reached was that, despite the early
Church's adaptation of the traditions, their life-situation in the ministry of the historical Jesus is not irrecoverable—behind the tradition,
behind such stories about him as the Temptation account, stands
Jesus himself. This more temperate approach in Form-criticism has
borne good fruit. Impressed by the assistance the Form-critical
method can render in taking us past the Hellenistic overlay to the

older Palestinian tradition, J. Jeremias lately applied it to a detailed study of the parables of Jesus in an effort to penetrate behind the many accretions, grafted onto the parables by the early Church mainly for didactic purposes, and so to bring us into their life-situation in the ministry of Jesus.[32] The Post-Bultmannian circle of New Testament scholars may be said to have adopted the same positive Form-critical standpoint in view of their common acknowledgment that certain elements in the tradition must simply be taken as historical if we are not to succumb to a purely mythological Christology.

In the years after 1921, however, the method of analyzing units of the Gospel tradition according to their "forms" fell into relative desuetude in Germany, and made very little headway against the strong opposition of such British and American scholars as F. C. Burkitt, A. H. McNeile, and B. S. Easton. It was quickly noted that Albertz, the conservative, and Bultmann, the radical, while starting from the same base of operations, had reached completely divergent conclusions about the nature of the tradition. This lack of assured results, the obvious fact that a sizable proportion of the Gospel materials is characterized by its "formlessness," the uncertainty about how particular "forms" should be related to particular life-situations in the early Church, to say nothing of the fear inspired by Bultmann's negative conclusions about the historicity of the tradition, all contributed to the later prevailing distrust of the Form-critical method.[33] Yet Form-criticism did leave its own large legacy. Particularly in the hands of Bultmann it shifted the center of interest for much modern German scholarship from the historical Jesus to the Church and the Church's theology, and foreclosed the possibility of getting back, even if we so desired, to Jesus of Nazareth in his history. An echo of Bultmann's closing of the door against recovery from the Gospel tradition of the history of Jesus can be heard in the somewhat wistful and often quoted words of R. H. Lightfoot, more sympathetic than most English-speaking scholars to the Form-critical movement: "It seems then, that the form of the earthly no less than of the heavenly Christ is for the most part hidden from us. For all the inestimable value of the gospels, they yield us little more than the whisper of his voice; we trace in them but the outskirts of his ways." [34]

In Bultmann, the existentialist interest of which we have spoken, with the resultant indifference to the concrete objective element in past history, and Form-criticism, with its negative judgment on the historicity of the tradition, had combined to direct a powerful pincer attack upon the old quest of the historical Jesus. For Bultmann accordingly the Christ-kerygma became the axis of primitive Christianity, and all discussion of Jesus Christ must be limited to it alone.

Bultmann and the Christ-Kerygma

The "kerygma theology" of Bultmann is to be distinguished both from those "symbolic" interpretations of the historical Jesus which have their source in idealistic philosophy and from those theories in the history of criticism which have reduced the existence of Jesus entirely to a myth.

D. F. Strauss's first "Life of Jesus," published in 1835, was quickly followed by a storm of controversy among both orthodox and rationalists within the Christian fold. Convinced of the inability of the opposing tendencies within contemporary theology to account for the events of the Gospel history on either supernaturalistic or rationalistic lines, Strauss sought in characteristic Hegelian fashion to effect a synthesis by boldly proposing a new solution in the form of a consistent and comprehensive application of the mythological explanation to the Gospel narratives. His elaborate and microscopic investigation of the Gospel tradition led him to the conclusion that the historical material about Jesus had become so intermingled with myth that not nearly enough can be known about his person to constitute a foundation for the religious consciousness of men. Strauss therefore removed the emphasis from the historical person of Jesus to the *idea* of God-manhood embodied in him. It caused Strauss no concern at all that historical criticism could not in any way demonstrate that in Jesus the idea of God-manhood had reached its perfect external expression. The only significant thing for Strauss was that through Jesus Christ this idea of God-manhood could lay hold of the common consciousness as symbolizing the limit or goal of humanity's aspirations.

Quite different from all such "symbolic" representations is Bultmann's "kerygma theology." Again and again, Bultmann has reminded us that the eschatological saving-event, which is ever and anew brought near to men in the Church's kerygma, is definitely tied to the concrete historical destiny of a particular individual, Jesus of Nazareth. "The revelation consists in nothing else than the fact of

Jesus Christ."[35] So, for Bultmann, the salvation mediated by the kerygma resides not in an idea of God-manhood, of which Jesus is merely the bearer or symbol, as Hegelian philosophy might conceive it, but in the fact of Jesus' own person.

If Bultmann's view of the kerygma does not participate in any notion of a Christ-symbol or Christ-idea, even less so does it participate in the spasmodic denials of the historical existence of Jesus that have arisen since the work of Bruno Bauer around the middle of the last century. In the later stages of his stormy pilgrimage, tirading against the German theologians' cavalier dismissal of Strauss's mythological explanation of the Gospel portrait of Jesus, Bauer ended by asserting that there never was any historical Jesus, that the historical Christ and everything known and said about him belonged to the imagination of the primitive Christian community and had no connection with any man who belonged to the real world.[36] The furor raised by Bauer was stirred up once again in more recent times, not only in France but throughout Europe, by P.-L. Couchoud's rather eccentric monograph of 1924, refuting the historicity of Jesus. Couchoud's arguments were these: (1) Paul deduced the history of Jesus from a mythical drama of redemption; (2) the narrative of the Gospels comes directly from Old Testament prophecy, e.g. the Septuagint version of Psalm 22:17, "A crowd of dogs encircled me . . . they pierced my hands and feet"; (3) it is inconceivable that within the space of a generation the deification of a man could have taken place, especially on the territory of Judaism; (4) the Resurrection appearances were only the manifestation of an ideal Messiah, whose mythical history included a crucifixion episode.[37]

Since M. Goguel demolished Couchoud's case,[38] such thoroughgoing mythical theories of Christian origins have become museum pieces, aside from some spurious Communist propaganda. At all events Bultmann's "kerygma theology" is far removed not only from the view that Christianity is a mythical religion fabricated around a fictional figure, but also from the reduction of the historical Jesus to a symbol. Nevertheless, because Bultmann has made the Christ-kerygma of the apostolic Church the ground of theology, and because of his lack of interest in the content of the name Jesus and all that it implies behind the kerygma, there has always been latent in his position the grave danger of undervaluing the theological significance of the historical Jesus. There has in fact been recapitulated in Bultmann

the spirit of Kierkegaard's famous dictum that, even if we knew nothing whatever of the historical personality of Jesus, it would be enough
for faith if some disciple had bequeathed the word that God appeared
among us in the humble form of a servant, lived and taught in our
community, and died.[39] So far as his view of the kerygma is concerned, Bultmann has indeed narrowed this down still further, insist-
ing that when we ask how much of concrete history is embedded in the
kerygma, the only answer is the mere fact, the bare *Dass,* of the Cross
of Christ. Under these strict limits, the question arises as to whether
Bultmann has done anything like justice to the character assigned by
the New Testament to the kerygma, which undoubtedly makes constant allusions to the person of Jesus. The difficulty with Bultmann is
simply the lack of content of the actual name and figure of Jesus in
the Christ of the kerygma. The extent of Bultmann's evisceration of
the name, Jesus, can be gauged from the interchangeability of "Jesus"
and "the Christ" in the following quotation from his Heidelberg paper
of 1959.

It is often said, almost always in criticism, that according to my interpretation of the kerygma Jesus has risen in the kerygma. I accept this proposition. It is entirely correct, assuming that it is properly understood. It presupposes that the kerygma itself is an eschatological event, and it expresses
the fact that *Jesus* is really present in the kerygma, that it is *his* word which
involves the hearer in the kerygma. If that is the case, then all speculation
concerning the modes of the existence of the risen Jesus, all the narratives
of the empty tomb and all the Easter legends, whatever elements of historical fact they may contain, and as true as they may be in their symbolic
form, are of no consequence. To believe in the *Christ* present in the
kerygma is the meaning of the Easter faith.[40]

The exalted Christ who is present to the believer's faith in the
preaching of the gospel has here taken the place of the historical
Jesus, so that he no longer stands in our world and is no longer involved in our own historical humanity. The redeemer is deprived of
the "crown rights" accorded to him as the one exalted only because
he had previously ridden the ranks with men, accompanying them as
the one true brother and communicator of faith. While the heart of
Bultmann's theology is that, in the act of proclaiming and listening
to the gospel, Jesus of Nazareth becomes the Christ for us, we yet in
this moment of the only truly personal encounter, as Bultmann regards it, hear no Galilean voice and see no Galilean face. We are

alone before the presence of the transcendent Word in the terrible solitariness of isolation from the world and history and community. Shall we be saved in lonely confrontation with a Word from the Beyond that has not really penetrated the depths of our human estate, or freed from the trammels of the flesh by a Word that is not truly clothed with flesh?

Bultmann's de-historicized version of the kerygma, in which Jesus has become a hollow name, a ghostly figure abstracted from our world and our history, is to some extent an inevitable outcome of the idea of human nature with which existentialist theology operates. For Bultmann, appropriating Heidegger's categories, *Dasein,* human being, is choice, free personal decision. Every man, in the freedom of his being-in-the-world, is forever open to the danger of losing himself in the *Vorhanden,* in the impersonal and the neutral. Enticed to seek his security in worldly objects and worldly evidences, man becomes enslaved to the concrete, historical world around him. But man is pervaded with the universal mood of anxiety or dread, for he is secretly convinced that the security offered him by the world is merely illusory, that everything is crumbling away toward death, and that he is forfeiting his real life. The only way to find release from anxiety and to attain to authentic existence is, therefore, to abandon all ties with the world. In opposition to the philosophical notion that man can save himself by his own decision, Bultmann has tried to show that victory over the despair of *Dasein* can only come through an act of God in which is imparted the gracious gift of a new self-knowledge. But it is merely in the solitary instant of comprehending encounter with the kerygma, through which is mediated God's act of grace, that man is raised to the level of authentic existence. True human existence is thus comprised of broken and unrelated moments of encounter and decision, so that there is denied to it any temporal continuity and participation in the relativities of history. Such a view of human nature is one-sided. It takes no account of the fact that every man's present is compounded of his past and grows out of it, that existing is a continual movement from one web of human relationships to another, that man is always related to his world, his nation, his race, his church, his family. The acosmic overtone in existentialist theology's understanding of man makes it virtually impossible to give specific content to the figure of Jesus Christ as one involved in his world, the historical events of his time and place, or in a particular nexus of ordinary human relationships. The Christ of the kerygma must accordingly remain *unworldly* and non-historical.[41] Notwithstanding the truth we have already stated that for Bultmann the actual historical person of Christ is the origin, the point of departure, for Christianity, the human traces of that one who in the Biblical representation is Son of Adam and Son of Man, son of Mary and Joseph, and called by the name of Jesus, have been obliterated in the Bultmannian kerygma. The kerygma has become a kind of heavenly cryptogram, transmitted by the accredited messengers of the Church, and in it Jesus Christ is couched as an event revealed exclusively to faith.

On existentialist premises, there is another reason why the Christ of the kerygma can only appear as an unworldly and abstract figure. Since man cannot be saved by anything in the world, the Christ-kerygma, which as the sole vehicle of salvation has been given mythological expression in the New Testament, must simply be demythologized until no recognizable objective or worldly reality is left in it. It is of course the translation of the saving event, actualized in the proclamation of the kerygma, into the language of human possibility and human self-understanding that has called down upon Bultmann's head the theologian's complaint that he has reduced theology to anthropology by making the only possible divine event a phenomenon of the human consciousness.[42]

Bultmann's view of the kerygma is impregnated with the ideas he has held on Christian origins by reason of his well-established place in the *religionsgeschichtliche Schule.* "It is no accident," as Otto Eissfeldt remarked, "that the *religionsgeschichtliche Schule* was at the same time the school of *Gattungsforschung* and of *Formgeschichte,*" [43] The thesis developed by the History of Religions school concerning the "acute Hellenization of Christianity" and of the dependence of the primitive Christian proclamation and cultus on the Mystery religions of Hellenism in general and Gnosticism in particular has been so profoundly influential in the formulation of Bultmann's thought on the kerygma that it must be allowed to enter the picture. Once more the impetus toward comparative religious studies in the area of the New Testament, as of the Old, was provided by H. Gunkel's pioneering work at the beginning of this century. The phrase which soon became current thereafter was: "Christianity is a syncretistic phenomenon," a great blending of many tenets and practices drawn from the religious faiths of the ancient Near East.

Predominant in the unofficial, non-state Mystery religions of Hellenism, the cult of the Syrian Adonis, the Phrygian Attis, the Egyptian Osiris, and the Babylonian Tammuz, is the idea of the dying and rising again of the fertility deity. Their main function was to consummate the union of the initiate with the dying and rising god, so that thus his own salvation from death and rebirth, or deification, might be achieved. There is clearly a certain resemblance between this and Paul's concept of dying and rising with Christ. Moreover, Paul's terminology is similar to that of the Mysteries in his frequent employment of such words as *salvation, knowledge, wisdom,* and *mystery.* But since R. Reitzenstein accepted simply the fact that a straight line could be drawn from the Mysteries to the primitive Christian religion, there has been a persistent tendency not only in Germany but elsewhere, among such scholars, for instance, as Loisy and Kirsopp Lake, to magnify the likeness and minimize the salient differences between the Mystery cults and Christianity. Yet rebirth in communion with the vegetation deity is certainly not the same as resurrection with Christ, for in the former is presented a completely individualistic, timeless elevation from the lower to the higher realm of being, and in the latter a grafting into the body corporate of the historic community of the Church. Further, Paul's crucified and risen Lord and Saviour is rooted in a history that is as yet very close and real, so that the vocabulary he shares with the Mysteries is now filled with a quite specific and concrete historical content. Bultmann has, however, followed resolutely in the way of Reitzenstein. He has maintained, for example, that the interpretation of baptism offered by Paul in the sixth chapter of Romans originates from the Hellenistic Church—Paul understands the initiation rite handed down to him after the analogy of the initiation sacrament of the Mystery cults, the meaning of which is that the initiate shares in the fate of the cult-god, who has suffered death and awakened to life, like Attis or Osiris.[44]

We cannot here delay over the important question of whether there is any justification at all for the hypothesis, inherited by Bultmann from Heitmüller and Bousset, that Paul was dependent on the already Hellenized kerygma of such Hellenistic churches as Antioch and Tarsus, which stood between Jesus and the first Palestinian church on the one hand and himself on the other. We need only allude to what would seem, in the light of the very slim evidence at our disposal, to be a fair comment on the part of A. Schweitzer that it is impossible to prove the existence of a Hellenistic sacramental cult in a church like Antioch.[45] Heitmüller's appeal to Acts 6–8 and 11 as a good Hellenistic source is improbable since, as H. J. Schoeps has noted, it simply "expresses a tendency within the original Palestinian church." [46]

It is more in the forefront of our concern to comment on the effect that Bultmann's reading of Paul in terms of his being infused with the ideas and attitudes of the sacramental cults of Hellenism has had on his version of the kerygma. The History of Religions school spoke frequently about Paul's Christ-mysticism, and, by thereby implying the close proximity of what Christ meant for Paul to what the mythological figures of Attis and Osiris meant for their devotees, it tended to de-emphasize the truth that for Paul also Jesus "came in the flesh" (Romans 8:3) as an inescapable fact of recent history.[47] Out of its devotion to Hellenism, among other things, the school developed its own mystical theology and the concomitant thesis that religious language cannot be concerned with the world or history. It is but a short step from this to Bultmann's plea for the demythologizing of the kerygma and for the conception of it as the agent by which the individual man is given a new self-understanding through his confrontation with the Word of God in *lonely* encounter.

As a leading member of the History of Religions school, W. Bousset felt sure that syncretistic influences played an extremely important role in the formation of primitive Christianity. The religion of the earliest Church, developing along the lines of a *Kyrios* cult imported from Hellenistic circles by the first Christians, was in fact the direct product of the soteriological myths of the Mystery religions. Bousset contended in his influential work *Kyrios Christos* (1921) that Paul took over from the primitive Hellenistic communities their belief in Jesus as the great cult-hero, present with his Church and worshiped by it as *Kyrios,* a title widely used as a cultic name for the deity in the Mystery religions and for the Emperor in the official worship of Caesar, as Deissmann has shown from a variety of papyrus fragments.[48] The point of greatest interest for us here is that in answer to the question of how the attribution to Jesus of the high dignity of *Kyrios* could have arisen in the earliest Hellenistic churches, Bousset affirmed that it must have emerged "in the sphere of the unconscious, in the uncontrollable depths of the collective psyche of a community." [49] Through the creative imagination of the community, under the spell of the Hellenistic Mysteries, the gospel of Jesus has been replaced by a religion of salvation centering in a mystery cult of the Christ as *Kyrios*. Bultmann seems to have taken the next logical step in claiming that, instead of the historical person of Jesus, it is the mythical figure of the Son of God who has entered the primitive apostolic kerygma.

For the last forty years and more Bultmann and his pupils have laid very great stress on the points of contact and continuity between Gnosticism and the Christological formulations of the primitive Church. In so doing they have followed the broad conception of Gnosticism accepted especially by R. Reitzenstein. Reitzenstein widened the notion of Gnosticism, as applying particularly to those heretical schools which threatened the Church in the second century A.D. and had to be refuted by such orthodox Church Fathers as Irenaeus, to include a large variety of systems of thought and even ancient pre-Christian mythologies, a salient feature of which was the myth of the redeemed redeemer. Within Gnosticism, Reitzenstein embraced the amorphous, syncretistic religious ideas and ideals of Mandeism, Manicheism, and the Hermetic literature and assigned to them a maturation date before or around the beginning of the Christian era —despite the fact that only on the flimsiest grounds could we trace the Mandeans back beyond 400 A.D.,[50] that the founder of the sect of the Manichees did not appear until the third century A.D., and that the Corpus Hermeticum probably also belongs to the third century A.D. The comprehensiveness of Reitzenstein's "definition" of Gnosticism has given birth to confusion, for the term "Gnosticism" has since been made to pass for anything and everything in the world of declining antiquity. There is in fact no area of scholarly research that has been more hampered by lack of precise terminological definition than this. We do have a good deal of evidence for such well-developed Gnostic systems of thought in the second century A.D. as that of Valentinus, and our knowledge is being enhanced by continuing scrutiny of the Coptic Gnostic materials from Nag Hammadi. There is, therefore, wisdom in the suggestion put forward recently by some scholars that we should retain the term "Gnosticism" only for those heretical movements of the second century A.D. which were at first familiar to us from the polemical writings of the Fathers and latterly from newfound Gnostic sources.[51] In that case, no one would care to deny the existence in the first century A.D. (or even earlier), and certainly in the

New Testament itself, of phenomena that bear a close resemblance to the later Gnostic systems, phenomena for which R. M. Grant has employed the designation "proto-Gnostic." [52]

Men of incipient Gnostic or possibly Gnostic leanings had apparently found their way into the Pauline congregations. In accord with the typical Gnostic dualism of spirit and matter, that is well known to us from the systematized Gnostic forms of the second century, there were those in the Corinthian community who had spiritualized the Resurrection of Jesus Christ, and were almost certainly, in their eucharistic celebration, concentrating upon the spiritual, heavenly Christ (I Cor. 15). At Colossae certain "philosophers" were seemingly dissatisfied with the redemption offered in Christ and, under the sway of some astral cult, wished to incorporate in Christian worship veneration for the "elements of the world."

Again the language used by Paul is in places at least halfway toward the terminology of the later Gnostic systems. The antithesis between "spirit" and "flesh," between "faith" and "works," the idea of Christ as victor over the demonic world-powers who could not have brought the Lord to the Cross had they *known* who he was (I Cor. 2:8), of man's bondage to the "elemental principles" of the world (Gal. 4:3, 9), of the contrast between the "natural" man and the "spiritual" man (I Cor. 2:14 f.), could all have been drawn within the domain of later Gnosticism and given the special Gnostic twist. Perhaps most significant of all is Paul's thinking of himself as a "spiritual" man on whom has been bestowed the power to perceive the "deep things" of God (I Cor. 2:10), or as one in whose life the light of God has shone, bringing *knowledge* of "the glory of God in the face of Jesus Christ" (II Cor. 4:6). Most easily could this have been incorporated within the spiritual realm of *gnosis*.

Whether, in view of all this, we could justify Reitzenstein's verdict that Paul was "the first and the greatest of the Gnostics" is exceedingly doubtful, to say the least.[53] We must not overlook the other side of the picture: Paul's undoubted resistance to gnosticizing and spiritualizing interpretations. Whereas *gnosis* was often regarded as a magical alchemy that could rescue its possessor from this evil world of matter and endow him with the freedom of an ethereal spirit, a freedom that could too easily degenerate into libertinism, Paul derived from his Jewish heritage the notion that evil consisted in man's sinful rebellion against God, and he proclaimed the death of the historical

Jesus Christ as the means of man's deliverance to another kind of freedom, the freedom to live in righteous obedience to the will of God amid the ordinary stuff of the world and within the matrix of human relationships (Gal. 5:13–14); Paul's so-called Christ-mysticism, being "in Christ," in contrast with the usual Gnostic view of union with the redeemer god, was no absorption away from the world into lonely individual communion, but had searching ethical implications for life in community. Paul's emphasis on *agape* as supreme over all mysteries and all knowledge (I Cor. 13) was unparalleled among the Gnostics. Even if W. D. Davies is correct in the view that the essentially Rabbinic category of obedience is the clue to Paul's understanding of the death of Jesus, and that he consequently put less emphasis on its sacrificial aspect than on the perfect obedience of Jesus unto God, Paul to be sure did take over from the Palestinian tradition the interpretation of the Cross as an atoning sacrifice, stemming from the Jewish cultus and the juridical notions prevalent in Judaism (Rom. 3:25; 5:8 f.; etc.).[54] In this, coupled with his heavy concentration on the Eucharist as the means of institution of the New Covenant and the New Community (I Cor. 11:23–26), Paul is of course set directly over against Gnostic types of thinking.[55]

It is, nevertheless, impossible to deny that Paul must have imbibed many of the syncretistic religious ideas of the composite Hellenistic theology that permeated the intellectual atmosphere of his day and station and even infiltrated the popular mind. The History of Religions school made a notable contribution to scholarship by amassing a wealth of information illuminating this background against which Paul worked and lived. There were cross currents between the thought of Paul and the world of gnosticizing tendencies. However, it is clear that Paul did not accommodate himself to Gnostic trends of thought nearly so much as the "heretical" members of his congregations, who were allowing their understanding of the gospel to be distorted by syncretistic influences, and against whom Paul had to take his stand. It seems reasonable to suggest that the language and thought-forms of the contemporary *Weltanschauung* served Paul as an aid to the translation of the gospel in terms relevant to the situation of Hellenistic man in the Gentile world,[56] while at the same time he resisted any kind of modification of his absolutely Christocentric soteriology and never let the "for us" of the historic life and death of Jesus Christ become lost in the "with us" of the spiritual and exalted Christ. We witness that, in Paul's presentation of Jesus Christ in Galatians, the deliverer from blind Fate is not *knowledge* but Jesus alone, whose power exceeds both that of the Torah and of the demonic elements. What then shall we say of the situation after Paul? The Deutero-Pauline writings unquestionably exhibit a closer proximity to ideas of a Gnostic type, even if we cannot accept the judgment that the exposition of the Church in Ephesians as the "body of Christ" is of a highly Gnostic character.[57] More surely Gnostic motifs are found in Ephesians in the picture of the Saviour's journey through earth and heaven (Eph. 4:8–10), and in the notion of the dividing wall between the souls imprisoned in the underworld and the world of light (Eph. 2:14–18). Both Ephesians and Colossians appear to represent a more advanced stage toward *gnosis* than the great letters of Paul. Acts 17:18 gives us the key to what might have transpired in the Pauline congregations after the death of the apostle, for it is there recorded that when the Athenians heard him on the theme of Jesus and the Resurrection, they imagined he was speaking about the male god Jesus and the goddess Anastasis. So it is conceivable that members of the Pauline communities reinterpreted or misinterpreted Paul's original intentions by fastening onto the possibly Gnostic movement of his thought, expanding and developing it, and giving it a prominence it did not officially have with Paul himself. The Pastoral Epistles show us the other side of the coin, representing as they do, in their attachment to the Pauline Corpus, a bulwark and defense of the orthodox interpretation of Paul over against assimilations of his thought to "heretical" syncretistic ideas.[58]

We have gone far enough to demonstrate the uncertainty of Paul's role and position in relation to the gnosticizing tendencies that are embryonically present in his own proclamation of the gospel, and that had much more fully penetrated the Pauline churches. Bultmann for his part, however, has never been in any great doubt. To his mind Paul's interpretation and proclamation of Jesus Christ are steeped in the categories of the Gnostic redeemer myth. His view of the death and Resurrection of Jesus is the Gnostic conception of it as the cosmic saving-event, in which the "old" is done away and the "new creation" is inaugurated (II Cor. 5:17). Bultmann asks us to infer from Paul's statement that he knows Christ no longer "after the flesh" (II Cor. 5:16), that for Paul "Christ has lost his identity as an individual human person." [59] There could hardly be any more effective barring of the gates than this against a place for the historical person of Jesus in the kerygma. It is the mythicized Gnostic redeemer who has passed into the kerygma—the message is entirely "from above," and brings the presence of the spiritual world into this world.[60] Now we have to concede that the kerygma, employing the mythological terminology of the contemporary cultural environment, is interested chiefly in the elevation of Jesus to the rank of Cosmocrator, in the theological position of Jesus at the heart of the cosmic eschatological saving-event. But it is the elevation and theological position of *no other than Jesus*. Bultmann's reaction against the positivistic liberal delineations of Jesus, because they were concerned only with his human personality and took no account of the decisive eschatological action of God in him, may have been justified. But it is unreasonable, in view of the kerygma's repeated references to the historical Jesus, to swing to the other extreme and suggest that the New Testament has no interest whatever in his historical person and character. To base the judgment that Paul was quite unconcerned with the historical Jesus on his declaration to the Corinthians that he would henceforth know Christ no more "after the flesh" is surely quite unwarranted. This may well mean not that Paul was renouncing an earlier interest he had had in the human Jesus, but that, on his conversion to Christianity, he abandoned his previous notion of an earthly Messianic ruler, or, in the language of the contemporary debate, refused to seek his security in objectively proven external facts about the historical Jesus.[61]

It is necessary at this juncture to recall that Bultmann has of course always tried to differentiate Christianity from Gnosticism by his reiterated assertion that there is this much at least of historicity imbedded in the kerygma: the fact, the *Dass,* of the death of Jesus Christ as an event of the recent past. What are we to make of this claim that has figured so largely in the discussion about demythologizing? If the mere "thatness" of the Cross is all we can say about the historical person of Jesus, that and no more, then we may ask whether it is worthwhile or necessary to say even that. What can this bare, unapproachable, and cryptic fact, that may be mentioned but not asked about, proclaimed but not opened up or clarified, what can this tell us about our religion as a religion of historical revelation? If this and no more than this has entered into the kerygma, the kerygma is still merely an emergence in the non-disposable, the unworldly, and the unanswerable. Man remains by himself alone in his history, with no shadow of the God-man to accompany him. "Above him," as Gerhard Koch has put it, "there is the otherworldly God, behind him the force of humanity, before him the kerygma which calls to the stringent law of de-secularization." [62] If the sum total of concrete history behind the kerygma is nothing more than the inscrutable fact of the death of Christ, concealed in impenetrable mists, is it really a matter of any consequence to us at all that God chose to reveal himself in the historical Jesus Christ, in the Word made flesh? Are we not then given as a substitute for the paradox of the Incarnation, the paradox —if it be a paradox—of an unworldly kerygma that bears down upon the present world in the Church's preaching simply as a summons to decision to break with the world? In his wise book, *God Was in Christ,* which it were well for us, in the present atmosphere of New Testament interpretation, to read again, Donald Baillie reminded us of the risk we run of falling into sub-Christian and magical accounts of the salvation-event in Jesus Christ, "unless we remember that God saves us by revealing Himself to us, enlightening our minds with the knowledge of Himself, not in a 'Gnostic' sense, but by that method which was so intolerable and incredible to the Gnostics, the way of Incarnation in a real human life." [63]

Bultmann's treatment of the Fourth Gospel, which has been normative for his theology, illustrates further his submission to the "Gnostic thesis." R. Reitzenstein believed that he had found in the Iranian myth of the Primal Man, by which the soul is regarded as a divine being sent down from the world of light into the world of matter only to be released once more and called back again, a doctrine of fundamental significance for the origins of Christianity. Notwithstanding the tentativeness of much of Reitzenstein's brilliant research, Bultmann, with what is for him a surprisingly uncritical acquiescence, simply assumed that the existence of a pre-Christian Gnostic myth of the redeemed redeemer was a proven fact, and sought to demonstrate that it formed the basis of the Christology of the Fourth Gospel by adducing some rather fugitive parallels to scattered sentences in the Gospel from Mandean and Manichean sources, the Odes of Solomon, and such Gnostic texts as the apocryphal Acts of the Apostles. So, in Bultmann's presentation, the "Johannine Christ," while not altogether detached from history, has become clothed nevertheless in the garments of the Gnostic redeemer.[64] The Fourth Gospel, when it is stripped of the additions made to it by the ecclesiastical redactor in order to bring it into line with orthodoxy, can thus be classified as a Gnostic document.[65] It is not just a coincidence that in his theological interpretation of the Fourth Gospel, Bultmann has minimized the significance of the allusions to the Old Testament—it is in fact entirely in accordance with his view that the author of the Gospel in its pristine form consistently toned down the apocalyptic eschatological world-view in the interest of his account of the Christ as the revealed revealer in whose present the past and the future are absorbed.

Despite the appearance of undeniable gnosticizing tendencies in the Fourth Gospel, Bultmann's thoroughgoing Gnostic approach has, to be sure, not commended itself to many. For, although we cannot overlook the bearing of John's witness on the *presence* of the Christ with his Church, it is true also that he has never lost interest in the historical *past* of the earthly ministry of Jesus of Nazareth. "John is primarily concerned not with the Word as a philosophical principle but with the Word made flesh and manifested in human history in the whole life of Jesus Christ." [66] Indeed, John's concern reaches beyond the past of Jesus of Nazareth to the past of the witness of the Old Testament Scriptures to him in his incarnate life (John 12:41), and in this, too, is exhibited his unwillingness to detach the revelatory event from history.[67]

In general, the fallacy in Bultmann's attempt to trace not only the Johannine but also the Pauline doctrine of the Christ to a point of origin in pre-Christian or non-Christian Gnostic sources is the presupposition that the full-blown Gnostic systems of the second century A.D. had existed in mature, unchanging, and unchanged form for nearly two hundred years and had therefore throughout that period known none of the vicissitudes of growth and decay, rise and decline. Bultmann has never asked whether, for example, in Paul's time the Gnostic redeemer myth was in fact an established element of the surrounding thought-world on which Paul could have drawn, or whether gnosticizing interpretations of Paul may not themselves have been a step on the road to the later Gnostic structure. In the case of the Fourth Gospel, whose affinity with the sect of Qumran has been stressed by recent scholarship, we can say today that such traces of pre-Christian Jewish Gnosticism as have been found in the Qumran Scrolls—and they contain no indication whatever of a Gnostic-type redeemer myth—do no more than show that certain not very clearly defined *proto-Gnostic* trends within Judaism may have passed into early Christianity and constituted part of the environment of the Evangelist.[68]

To explain the apparent lack of interest of Paul or John in the historical life of Jesus as an integral part of their inheritance from Gnosticism, particularly from the Gnostic redeemer myth, is to be guilty of two errors. First, it means that we are participating in the dubious historical method of beginning with phenomena, in this instance first-century, *possibly* Gnostic phenomena, that are inaccessible and obscure because the documentary evidence is extremely slender, and then out of these trying to understand what lies before us in well-documented form in the New Testament writings. The sources for our knowledge of the syncretism of the Mystery religions, generally taken to belong to the Gnostic circle, are in fact quite fragmentary and difficult to comprehend. They consist, for the most part, of brief references and passing allusions in ancient authors, who were either themselves initiates of the Mysteries and so sworn to secrecy, or inveterate enemies with a "perfect hatred" of everything they were describing.[69] The Coptic-Gnostic texts, belonging obviously to the library of an ancient Gnostic community, discovered at Nag Hammadi in Upper Egypt around 1945, have enriched our previously existing store of knowledge of the "classical" Gnosticism of the second century A.D., but have so far shed very little light on the dark spots of the first century. Second, to try to interpret the New Testament out of something that can without reservation be called "Gnosticism" means subscribing to the improbable hypothesis that the fully-structured Gnostic system of the second century A.D. was already uniformly and unvaryingly present at any given instant in the previous nearly two hundred years.

This reduction of a long period of historical development, culminating in second-century Gnosticism, to a punctiliar "Gnostic moment of existence" that has dramatically influenced the New Testament proclamation, has reappeared in the Gnostic researches of Bultmann's disciples. In his monograph on Gnosticism in Corinth, W. Schmithals seems to assume that the developed Gnosticism of the second century originated in that form as a clearly defined pre-Christian movement, coming into Judaism from Babylon and now demonstrable from the literature of the sect of Qumran. The view of Schmithals that in its earliest days Christianity was permeated with Gnosticism owes much to Walter Bauer's unlikely suggestion that in Syria and Egypt Gnostic Christianity had prevailed for a long time before orthodox Christianity ever reached there.[70] The impression given by Schmithals is certainly that the struggle of the orthodox Church Fathers of the second century against the Gnosticism of their time was in every respect the same as Paul's struggle at least a century earlier. On every front the only great opponents against whom Paul had to contend were the same Gnostics referred to in II Corinthians 10–13, whom Schmithals, with no regard for chronology, is able to describe as if they were the second-century Gnostics who are well known to us.[71] In conflict with the Gnostics, Paul has hardly been able to resist the impact on his own thought and preaching of their ideas, their pessimistic attitude toward the world, their notion of salvation from the world through union with the mythical Gnostic redeemer.

In the first volume, published in 1934, of an as yet uncompleted trilogy on Gnosticism, Hans Jonas described the main themes of Gnosticism: the dualism of a transcendent God and an alienated world, the imprisonment of the human soul in the labyrinth of the world whose darkness is penetrated by a redeemer bringing light from the beyond, and the *gnosis* by which alone man is able to escape from the world and be saved. He then extended the range of the term "Gnosticism" to include almost every facet of syncretism in the entire Near East in the period of waning antiquity, and found "Gnosticism" in Philo, in Neo-Pythagoreanism, in Neo-Platonism, in pagan writings like the Hermetica, in Christian theologians like Clement of Alexandria and Origen and earlier, of course, in the New Testament itself, and lastly in the Mandean and Manichean movements.[72] But here is the significant thing: the avowed aim of Jonas is to search amid this welter of heterogeneous Gnostic materials and diverse syncretistic trends for what he calls the "autonomous essence" of Gnosticism, its unified understanding of man and the world, its dualistic-anticosmic spirit.[73] Jonas admits that his purpose is a philosophic one: over against the atomization of the subject of Gnosticism into many different motifs from separate traditions, as reflected in W. Bousset's work of 1907, *Hauptprobleme der Gnosis,* he wishes "to restore an intelligible unity to the baffling multiplicity of its expressions." [74] In the sequel it transpires that Jonas has viewed Gnosticism as a static entity, undifferentiated in content, stretching from the pre-Christian era into the early Christian centuries, possessing a unitary view of man and his world, and wielding of course a tremendous influence on the New Testament and the beginnings of Christianity. The unitary

Gnostic point of view thus becomes for Jonas the basic criterion from which highly differentiated and individual expressions of Gnostic ideas in the ancient world can all be explicated. Just what is this Gnostic point of view that stretched in its oneness and sameness over the first two centuries of our era and more, pervading the first century and the New Testament itself as much as the second, defying the march of time? It can hardly be overemphasized that our knowledge of it comes properly only from the second-century Gnostic systems, and not from the first century: it need hardly be emphasized that it bears a striking resemblance to modern existentialist theology. The transcendent God who participated in the pre-cosmic drama enacted in the heights of the supranatural world solicited the attention of the "classical" Gnostic less than his own self-knowledge did. His mythological speculations about the origin of the cosmos and of man only served to express and illumine his own self-understanding. The goal of his self-knowledge was freedom, freedom from the domain of the cosmos, from the tyranny of creation and every other tyranny, from the Old Testament law and all law. In the Valentinian *Gospel of Truth* we read: "He who knows is a being from above. If he is called, he hears, he replies, he turns to him who calls him. . . . He knows like a man who has been drunk and awakens from the drunkenness in which he was, returning to himself and restoring what belongs to him." [75] The emphasis we find here on restoration to authentic self-understanding has of course figured very prominently in Bultmann's existentialist interpretation of the New Testament.

This merging of the past in the present, this swallowing up of the historical process in a sovereign philosophy of existence that belongs both to the "now" of our time and the "then" of the first two Christian centuries, has not surprisingly aroused the suspicion that in the thoroughgoing "Gnostic thesis" of Christian origins, taken over somewhat uncritically by Bultmann and members of his group from Reitzenstein and the History of Religions school, we have a case of special pleading, of contemporary philosophical principles and presuppositions determining historical judgment. "No historian will seriously suppose," declares Johannes Munck, "that Gnosticism could be exempt from time and death, so that a suppositional continuation of a Gnostic movement could have a constancy which is not to be found in, for instance, the far better documented history of the church." [76]

Our rather lengthy discussion has been necessary if only to bring us to this point. Precisely here do we discern how in Bultmann the wedding of advanced historical research in Christian origins and existentialist theology has produced a somewhat Gnostic understanding of the kerygma as an unworldly message from above, through which the hidden Christ, the redeemer, is revealed to the hearer possessed of the existentialist pre-understanding (*Vorverständnis*) that enables him to respond. There is little doubt that in Bultmann's version of the Christ-kerygma lies at least the lurking danger of the same absorption of the historical Jesus in the heavenly Christ as there was in the Corinthian church, where accommodation to the notion of Jesus as the Heavenly Man was in peril of going too far among members of a strong gnosticizing tendency (I Cor. 15). The "new quest" of the historical Jesus undertaken by certain of Bultmann's pupils since 1954 can thus be seen to have arisen as an attempt to arrest the trend towards a Docetic Christology in Bultmann's position.

Aside from the "new quest," Reitzenstein's theory of the dependence of the primitive Church for its Christological formulations on a pre-Christian Gnostic redeemer myth has lately been rigorously contested. In a recent detailed study, Günter Wagner has again opened up the question of whether Paul's thoughts on Christian baptism in Romans 6:1–11 derived from the initiation rites of the Mystery cults, from the notion of regeneration through sacramental union with the dying and rising cultic savior god. In light of a comprehensive investigation of the history of modern criticism's various presentations of the "Mystery hypothesis," and of such scanty and late documentary evidence as exists for the ceremonies performed in the Mysteries, he is led to the conclusion that the notion of a mythical dying and rising god in the Hellenistic cults at a time before Paul is ill-founded. He has then revived the view that Paul's concept of baptism into the death of Christ and union with him in his Resurrection comes primarily not out of the Mystery religions but out of the Old Testament ideas of corporate personality and of the incorporation of the individual into the community of the people of God through his participation with the Exodus generation in God's act of deliverance from Egypt and the crossing of the Red Sea. So in Paul there is a historical realism that is quite foreign to the Mysteries, for his thought is grounded in the unique historic event of the Cross and Resurrection of Jesus Christ, which is now actually present to faith and comes through the Church's message not as a means of absorption in the divine but as a call to discipleship, to take the way of Jesus with all its consequences and to share the fate of Jesus.[77]

Once more, C. Colpe has recently maintained that while gnosticizing tendencies were certainly present at a pre-Christian stage, the Gnostic redeemer myth has almost certainly arisen out of Docetic interpretation of Christ.[78] We are thus remembering today with a fresh sense of urgency that there has in fact been longstanding opposition to R. Reitzenstein's constructions in relation to primitive Christianity. One recalls Edwyn Bevan's claim that there is no hint of the figure of the redeemer in any non-Christian Gnostic source.[79] One recalls also that F. C. Burkitt held that the Gnostic systems were Christian systems, that the prime factor in the rise of these systems was the eschatological one, the non-arrival of the Parousia.[80] Although we need not linger over the earlier or most recent critiques of the "Gnostic thesis," we should say that the question assuredly cannot now be settled merely by uncritical appeal to Reitzenstein. There is a warning here: the theologically minded, who have not unjustifiably been excited by the contemporary relevance of Bultmann's existentialist theology, may not, in so far as that theology has been linked up with a particular and evidently questionable reading of Christian origins, discount the importance of the historic questions of primitive Christianity or dismiss the validity and necessity of continuing historical research on the pretext that it is irrelevant to faith.

In this chapter we have discussed the forces operative in Bultmann's shift from the historical Jesus to the kerygma and have looked also at some aspects of his interpretation of the kerygma. His conviction, from a radical Form-criticism standpoint, that the tradition about Jesus was the product of the creative imagination of the primitive Christian community, his distinction between the *historisch* as mere objective occurrence of the past and the *geschichtlich* as event which comes to us as personal encounter, his existentialist view of man with its atemporal and asocietal overtones, were all driving relentlessly toward the foreclosure of the question concerning the historical Jesus. The searchlight must accordingly be thrown entirely on the Christ-kerygma. We have seen how Bultmann's understanding of the kerygma is conditioned not only by existentialist analysis but by a concomitant interpretation of the New Testament message that owes a great deal to his place in the History of Religions school and to his indebtedness to Reitzenstein's "Gnostic thesis."

Today, in the Anglo-Saxon world as elsewhere, in view of prevailing misunderstandings, we need to recognize what has been Bultmann's most passionate concern in focusing on the kerygma and advocating its demythologization. To call him a "modernist" and have done with it is certainly a travesty of his position. Rather has he been preoccupied in his historical researches with the problem of the character of the primitive Christian kerygma. It is in fact the age-old message of Jesus Christ that he fervently desires should address itself to contemporary man. Only, if it is to address itself to men now, as God's truly offensive call to surrender the world we so cherish, it has to be rid of the false scandal of the obsolete mythological world view, ideas, and language, in which it has been clothed in the New Testament, and translated into a language and conceptuality relevant to the human situation in the twentieth century. We have spoken about Bultmann's shift from the historical Jesus. We have to be clear what is meant. It is not that for Bultmann every trace of the name of Jesus is erased. Indeed, as we have previously suggested, his quarrel with the nineteenth-century quest of the historical Jesus has been that in its preoccupation with objective biographical facts about the human Jesus and in its "psychologizing" concern with his personality, it had nothing whatever to say about his destiny as the decisive, eschatological, saving action of God.[81] Bultmann's own most ardent wish has been to preach, in language suited to the needs of the day, the message of that Jesus Christ in and through whose historical fate the decisive, eschatological, saving act of God takes place. Nowhere does it become more clear than in Bultmann's presentation of Johannine theology, set forth with considerable evangelical intensity in his *Theology of the New Testament,* that the specific historical man Jesus, the pronouncer of the "I am," is the Son, the Revealer, who brings the truth of God and the glory of God into the world—albeit not visibly, but only to believers (John 14:17; 16:13 ff.).[82]

Yet here is the rub. If all we may know of Jesus Christ is that he is the "I am" of revelation, the discloser of God exclusively to faith, then what is left to us after all from his having lived in our world? We are left of course, according to Bultmann, with the kerygma of the Christ, in which is enclosed one tangible historical event, the bare fact of the death of Christ. What of this death in its nakedness and nothingness, this devouring of Jesus by the world and its evil powers, that could by a sheer act of God's grace give rise to the kerygma in which

Christ is preached? We ask instinctively: the death of *whom*? the death of what kind of person? But all such questions are forbidden us by Bultmann; they merely betoken our craving for worldly security and our refusal to accept the radical insecurity of faith's genuine "openness" toward the God who can only come to us out of the future and not from the past. The kerygma must remain in unanswerability. The message is from the transcendent realm, otherworldly. If it is not to be reduced to a worldly phenomenon, in the moment of encounter with it we can have no recourse to anything outside, no relation to the humanity of Jesus. All that appears to be given to us is the "mathematically punctual" event of preaching, from which the historical reality of Jesus is eliminated, and the equally punctual event of faith it elicits. Is there not here the grave peril of relapse into something very like a Gnostic enthusiasm for the present instant of fulfillment into which both past and future are merged—only now the heightened, pneumatic experience of the Gnostic is transposed into an existential-dialectical interpretation of the kerygma?

Some years ago Donald Baillie applied the new title of "Logotheism" to the theology of the early Barth because he felt that the austere Barthian theology of the Word, with its unconcern about the historical life of Jesus, was hardly a theology of the Word-made-Flesh.[83] On one side, in relation to his view of the kerygma, the title of "Logotheism" might most justly be applied today to Bultmann, to the extent that for him Jesus Christ is taken up and absorbed in the message of the absolutely transcendent God. On the other side, of course, I am not unaware that Bultmann's translation of the Biblical understanding of God, history, and the world into the understanding of man has called down on him the charge of anthropocentrism. Whereas Barth and Bultmann have both continued to disavow any and every attempt of historical criticism to reach the facts about Jesus behind the tradition, in the later reaches of the *Dogmatik,* certainly only and always from the standpoint of the New Testament witness, Barth has been able to speak in a very evocative way about the place and significance of the "Royal Man" in the Church's theology.[84] It is, however, when the reality of Jesus is declared theologically irrelevant and replaced by Bultmann with a dehistoricizing existentialist interpretation of the kerygma that the paradox of the Word-made-Flesh is most of all emptied of content.

It is no wonder that, while in the first phase of the demythologizing debate the main interest was in myth and the mythological elements in the New Testament, latterly the problem of kerygma and history, which had not been far from the heart of things all along, has occupied the center of the stage and is the dominant problem in what we have come to know as the new quest of the historical Jesus. How much of history has the New Testament raised into the kerygma? How can Jesus become known to us, and has he any significance for faith? Is Bultmann's narrow concentration on the close correlation of saving event and faith a true representation of Luther's *sola fide,* justification by faith alone? Is mythology commensurate with law, and kerygma with gospel?

These are the questions which are currently causing considerable travail of soul in the German theological controversy. When we turn to compare the situation in Britain and America, due allowance has to be made for the fact that in neither of these countries is discussion carried on so much under the weight of centuries-old ecclesiastical tradition or so much under the shadow of the commanding figure of Luther as in Germany. Yet the questions being asked in Germany today are of universal import. They transect national boundaries. They are vital to all who are concerned about the preaching of the message of Jesus Christ in the contemporary world. Why then, we ask, the reserve among most scholars in the English-speaking world in contrast to the German agonizing on the Christological problem? Why does Anglo-Saxon Biblical scholarship, in particular, appear to continue its work in its relatively undisturbed and independent way, with its old confidence in the historical method for the most part unshaken? We shall seek some answers in the next chapter.

II

The Resilience of the Historical Approach

From the period of the Enlightenment, and in its heyday in the nineteenth century, the scientific historical research on the life of Jesus that flourished under the aegis of liberal theology passed through different stages. Under the influence of rationalism, it occupied itself with the ethical precepts of Jesus on the love of the Father God and the unique value of the individual human soul, and with his own moral example. Later in its anti-intellectualist reaction against rationalism, it concerned itself with the religious personality, the soul, the God-consciousness of Jesus. There was latent in this "religious" interest in the person of Jesus the possibility of a new probing in depth of the Christological problem of the relation between Jesus and the apostolic proclamation of the Christ. But in its more radical form, as we see from the breach that was developed between the figures of Jesus and Paul at the end of the nineteenth century, the "back to Jesus" movement continued as always to be motivated by the desire for release from the dogmatic formulations of Paul and from the enigmatic and mysterious Christ-figure, presented in the doctrinal statements of the Church's Creeds. From around the turn of the century, the Jesus-research of liberal theology and criticism was subjected, as we have noticed, to a series of stunning blows, the full effects of which were only felt subsequently with the work of Barth and Bultmann. In this chapter we must try to understand why, in face of the rising tide in Europe of *Gemeindetheologie* and *existentialistische Exegese*, with the consequent decline of interest in the historical person of Jesus, in

56

Great Britain and America concern with historical reconstruction of the life of Jesus has survived quite sturdily. We must also endeavor at the close to make a frank assessment of the historical approach to Jesus. But first let us see how even in Germany the most rigorous kind of historicism has not altogether been blotted out.

E. Stauffer: Reversion to Historical Scientism

It need hardly be said that, despite the claim of "dialectical theology" that pursuit of the historical Jesus was a wild goose chase, Biblical scholarship even in Germany has never allowed Jesus to fade from the picture. One thinks of such a critic of Bultmann as Julius Schniewind and of his contention that our salvation is grounded in one who was involved in all the relativities of history and that the eyewitness reports received about Jesus in the tradition are an indispensable part of the apostolic preaching of the Christ. One thinks also of Joachim Jeremias as leading custodian of exacting historical, environmental, and philological research. But critics like Schniewind and Jeremias have not been entirely impervious to the spirit of "kerygma theology." Nor have they been unaffected by Form-criticism's demonstration of the difficulty of getting behind the tradition to the Jesus of history. It is different with F. Stauffer, who, despite his obvious sensitivity to the kerygma in his *New Testament Theology*, has retained a supreme confidence in the ability of objective historical criticism to recover the facts about Jesus from the Gospel records, when these are supplemented by external sources.

Stauffer is quite unconvinced by the theologians' claim that recovery of the facts about Jesus is a pipe dream. With real bravado he has embarked on a revival of scientific Jesus-research on the basis of an extensive investigation of the whole New Testament period.[1] The great quandary of the historian of Jesus is how with any certainty to separate the historical facts from the dogmatic bias in the Gospel records. The way out of the quandary proposed and put into effect by Stauffer is to muster from the surrounding world of the New Testament such extraneous documentary sources as bear direct or indirect testimony to the story of Jesus, and to use them as a means of checking and clarifying the Gospel narratives. Taking these sources as his aid, chronology as his guide, and the history of Jesus as his goal—

history in the strictest, positivistic sense of an assemblage of facts about Jesus—Stauffer strides into the task of telling the story of Jesus with great verve and gusto. Every vestige of theological interpretation, the Evangelists' interpretation of Jesus, the interpretation given by the dogmas of the Church, Stauffer's own interpretation, must be ruthlessly brushed aside in order to get at "Jesus as he really was." [2] So we can see that for Stauffer the story of Jesus "as he actually was" consists of a chronological sequence of not-yet-interpreted facts. It is, I think, most revealing that even the Resurrection, which is by all accounts the most inscrutable of the events recorded in the New Testament, falls for Stauffer in the category of uninterpreted fact. The Evangelists have simply stated the Resurrection as an incontrovertible fact, given immediately to human perception, and we, too, must accept it as a bare fact.[3]

A brief look at Stauffer's handling of the story of the empty tomb will help to clarify his method and his historiographical position. For him all that is at stake is the authentication of the *fact* of the empty tomb. One of the basic criteria for determining the historicity of events in the story of Jesus is that, where we can consult the evidence of both friend and foe of Jesus and they are found to agree, such agreement involves facts known to both sides. Applying this to the narrative of the empty tomb, Stauffer states first that the entire primitive Church bore witness unanimously to this fact. Nor did anyone ever contest the fact of the empty tomb, not even the Jewish Sanhedrin (Matt. 28:15). Justin Martyr mentions an official circular letter of the Sanhedrin, perpetuating the rumor that the disciples stole the body of Jesus by night from the tomb. Tertullian is also familiar with this theory as well as with the rumor presupposed in the Fourth Gospel (John 20:15) that the gardener removed the body of Jesus. Moreover, both these tales are to be found, in a number of variations, in the Jewish *Toledoth Jeshu*. Stauffer deduces from Matthew 28:12 ff. that the fabricated story of the disciples' theft was intended for Roman ears, to offset the effect the report of the empty tomb might have upon the Romans. He then finds in Tertullian and Eusebius mention of a report made by Pilate to the Roman Emperor about the empty tomb and the Jewish authorities' assertion that the disciples had stolen Jesus. But Tertullian and Eusebius are Christian sources, and that is not good enough for Stauffer. He has to ask whether there are confirmatory pagan sources. And indeed there are, for Eusebius alludes to certain "pagan records," documents of Pilate's on the subject of Jesus, certainly forgeries, and today unfortunately lost, but undoubtedly sharing with the forged Pilate-documents of the pagans' Christian enemies the assumption that Pilate had to report to Caesar on the case of Jesus of Nazareth. Further corroboration is found in the Inscription of Nazareth, preserved in Paris since 1878, and published in 1930, containing the essence of an imperial edict against grave robbing and desecration. Stauffer concludes that this inscription is possibly based on a rescript of Tiberius, the Emperor's reply to Pilate's report concerning Jesus, the empty tomb, and the rumor, circulated by the Jews, that the body had been stolen.[4]

So with the determination and the sleuthlike skill of a veritable Sherlock Holmes, Stauffer pursues the *facts* in this case, as he pursues all the *facts* relating to Jesus. His whole factual reconstruction of the story of Jesus issues of course from a certain preconception of what "history" is. Founding on the view of such nineteenth-century historiographers as Leopold von Ranke that the historian's job is simply to tell what happened (*wie es eigentlich gewesen ist*), Stauffer would eliminate every element of subjectivity on the part of the historian, and let the *facts* in their mere extrinsicality speak for themselves.[5] But can we be so sure that this is what is meant by "history"? Can "history" thus be reduced to causal sequence of merely external events? How can we be certain of *facts* which are obviously not first-hand objects of perception for us? Is "history" an exact science? Is scientific historical research always only an exercise in probabilities? Or is "history" an art, in which the historian as artist must be subjectively and sympathetically involved with his subject if he is to interpret the past for us in any meaningful way? These questions, the whole baffling problem of what is "history," have occupied the thought of our own century almost beyond all others. They need not delay us here. Only it should be said there is nothing essentially reprehensible in the attempt of the scientific historian to relate events in terms of their causality or to explain them from factors immanent in history. Man's insatiable curiosity to know *what happened* or *what happens* is the sanction of scientific historical research as it has always been the inspiration of the natural sciences.

It is, however, another matter when the selfsame posture taken in a science laboratory is adopted toward Biblical history. Then we are faced with the unavoidable question of what is the relevance to the-

ology or the use to faith of a purely photographic portrait of the outward side of events, of not-yet-interpreted facts now held up as a
spectacle. I believe we can assume that Christian faith and the Church
would only have a very restricted interest in such a presentation of
what actually took place, even if it were established with a high degree of scientific probability. For the New Testament itself, the document of the Church's faith, is precisely not interested in telling us
what actually happened in the life of Jesus (Stauffer, in his quest for
the facts, is constrained to evaluate the Gospels from extraneous
sources): it bears witness instead to "events"—Incarnation, Resurrection, Ascension—concerning which the historian *qua* historian can
really say nothing, save that a number of people came to hold belief
in these things at a certain time in the course of human history. Even
if Stauffer had proven the empty tomb beyond reasonable doubt, the
Erlangen historian would then have given us only an empty tomb and
not a risen Lord. And there would still be the possibility that, as in
the natural sciences today's assured results become tomorrow's dis-
carded hypotheses, new evidences and inscriptions might come to
light to controvert previous findings. But in any case the truth is that
in the very center of the Gospel story of the empty tomb stands the
angelic pronouncement, "He is not here, he is risen." Right at this
point the New Testament speaks "angels," and angels speak the "action of God." Into this faith-element, this supra-historical dimension
in the story, the scientific historian cannot penetrate, since he is confined to dealing with history as the sphere of the "human," with the
intraworldly nexus of causes and effects. At the most he can only leave
the empty tomb, as Stauffer has done, short of rationalizing it away, as
an inexplicable fact. Stauffer has turned his back on the convincing
arguments of Form-criticism that the Gospels are not historical source
documents for biographical facts about Jesus, but post-Easter confessions of the Church's faith in Jesus Christ as crucified and risen Lord.
I do not, of course, believe that we need to follow the most radical
line of Form-criticism and relinquish interest in the *humanity* or the
historical life of our Lord, but only that Form-criticism's understanding of the tradition has helped us to see more clearly that in approaching even his *humanity* we need the sympathy and insight of faith. A
scientific picture of the facts about Jesus "as he really was," developed
by a cold and detached historico-scientific research, would not bring
us closer, but only take us further away from the Jesus of history. For

the only means of access we have to the Jesus of history is the Gospel tradition, and the Gospel tradition is not merely a memory-picture of this man, but a memory-picture transfused with the mature knowledge of who he really was and is, that had been given to the faith of post-Resurrection believers in him.

We need not press our criticism of Stauffer's summons to a "theology of facts." The question of what is the relation to faith and the significance for theology of knowledge of Jesus mediated by historical-critical research will occupy us again in later pages. Meanwhile, what is intriguing for us is the divergent ways in which Stauffer's book on Jesus could be received in different quarters of the globe. On the continent of Europe, where the prevailing feeling is that it is impossible to return to a pre-Form-criticism evaluation of the Gospels as historical source documents or to a nineteenth-century positivistic historiographical stance like von Ranke's, it has been regarded for the most part as an anachronism. In Great Britain and America on the contrary it has been received, so far as one can gather, with scarcely any demur. I am not suggesting that Anglo-American Biblical scholars would subscribe to a position such as Stauffer's in its entirety. But, as we shall see, it does clearly enough reflect certain facets of a major trend in American Biblical scholarship particularly—the persistent tendency to view Biblical religion as a historical phenomenon on a par with other historical phenomena, and so to feel that Biblical history can be adequately and comprehensively accounted for in terms of factors immanent in the historical process, or again the readiness to put extracanonical sources on a level of equality with the Gospels as evidences for the story of Jesus.

Historical Criticism in American Biblical Scholarship

In Germany historical-critical research on the Bible grew in connection with the liberal theology. The same has been true in America. There are several reasons why we should here give some consideration to the American situation. First, it is all too easy for the theologian to complain that liberal-inspired American Biblical criticism has missed the truth by reason of its prejudice against admitting the "supra-historical": yet, on the other hand, its constant and steadfast emphasis on the concrete historical character of the revelation in Jesus and on the kerygma's being rooted in specific historical situations could be seen today as a counterbalance to current transhistorical versions of the Word or the kerygma in Europe. Second, it behooves us to put a question mark against the inclination to make liberalism in all of its manifestations everywhere synonymous with effeteness and moribundity in theology: it may safely be said that liberal theology could not have maintained its vigor in the United States had it always been so antievangelical as is sometimes supposed. Third, the dynamic survival of a strong liberal strain in American theology and Biblical criticism affords a good example of how much these enterprises can be conditioned by dominant social and cultural factors in a country.

As our first spokesman here, we shall call on a well-known American New Testament scholar, Amos Wilder:

> The Christian tradition persisted in our culture in a vital form, nourished both by the Enlightenment and by Transcendentalism, without being radically secularized by either. Thus the cultural liberalism of the twentieth century in this country was not so vulnerable to attack and criticism whether on the part of Marxism, existentialism or neo-orthodoxy as was the case in Europe. The liberal theology taught in the leading liberal Protestant seminaries in the United States after the First World War was deeply evangelical and not rationalistic or positivistic.[6]

Going back behind the years of the First World War, one could multiply instances, from the influential work of such scholars as Bushnell, Clarke, and William Adams Brown, of how the way was being paved for the continuance of this "deeply evangelical" liberal theology of which Dr. Wilder speaks. I need refer only to Brown's *Outline of Christian Theology* (1905). Here, to be sure, are the familiar traits generally associated with liberalism—the notion of the progressive establishment of the kingdom of God and the notion of the Church as the society of men and women laboring to establish that kingdom and as the agency of inspiration enabling them "to apply Christ's principles and to exemplify his spirit under all the varying conditions of our complex modern life." Yet at the same time there is discernible a genuine sensitivity to the Christological problem in its depth. Aware of the danger, on the one hand, of transforming Christianity into a philosophical speculation or mystic ecstasy by a too great concentration on the divine Christ and, on the other, of failing to see the divine significance of his person through absorption in the task of recovering the human Jesus, Brown concludes that there is nothing unreasonable in the Christian faith in a Christ who is both human and divine. The presence of an authentically Christocentric concern in the main stream of American theological liberalism has to be acknowledged. But there is the other side. The unquenchable belief in man and in the course of his history and the tendency to equate Christianity with a religion of humanism have also been deeply engraved on the American liberal outlook, not, be it said, as part of any purposefully reductionist or minimizing intention, but largely under the sway of historical circumstance and cultural influence. Out of the old frontier experience, the daily pushing out of the boundaries and the quest for wider horizons of opportunity, were begotten the activism and empiricism that seem to inhere in the American temperament. Perhaps only in America would it have been possible for a Church historian like A. C. McGiffert to declare in 1919 that a religion favorable to democracy must be a religion of faith in man. The practical, experiential attitude was given philosophical expression in the pragmatism of William James. In the sphere of religion it has meant most of all the flourishing of the "social gospel," impatient with abstractions and theorizing and imbued with the robust hope of a this-worldly consummation of the kingdom of God. It has also meant a profound concern on the part of theology for modernity, for the needs and desires of modern men.

In the late 1920's, through the early writings of Barth in particular, the impact of the new confessional orthodoxy began to make itself felt on American theological circles, and very soon thereafter, in various quarters, certain ears could hear a quivering at the foundations of liberalism's structures; insistent voices, like that of John Bennett, were raised, telling of the challenge to the whole liberal movement; Walter Horton could speak of the collapse of liberalism; Reinhold Niebuhr in his *Moral Man in Immoral Society* (1932) directed a withering attack against the prevailing liberal reliance on sociology and education as keys to the kingdom. That there was, however, to be no real collapse, the last thirty years have shown. In this period American theology and Biblical criticism have mainly been hovering between a liberal and a "neo-liberal" position, purporting to be more positive in theological outlook and more truly "modern" in the sense that it does not fail to take account of European "dialectical theology's" vehement critique of nineteenth-century liberalism. So Reinhold Niebuhr, no doubt to the surprise of some and the delight of many, has lately confessed that he feels himself to be a "liberal at heart." [7] And in some places at least, Paul Tillich's work is being claimed as a "neo-liberal" restatement of the fundamental position of Schleiermacher's *Glaubenslehre*.[8]

It would be idle to pretend that the foregoing is an adequate sketch. But just enough may have been said to expose the landscape against which is to be viewed the major movement of American Biblical criticism. The course followed by most American Biblical scholars has been shaped largely by that socio-cultural facet of American life we have just mentioned: the empiricism and activism of the American temperament, with its pride and glory in hard facts. It has, therefore, generally been axiomatic that, in the study of Biblical history and Biblical revelation, empirical considerations—historical, sociological, psychological, and philological—must be given the fullest play. Deeply suspicious of any detachment of Biblical revelation from the definite historical-cultural situations always involved in its reception, and of the description of it in categories of the timeless and transcendent, and tending to suppose that historical science can exhaust the possibilities of Biblical theology, the kerygma, and eschatology, American Biblical scholarship has been devoted principally to the task of evolving a sound and responsible historical method. It is no wonder that in these latter days "neo-orthodoxy," the theology of the Word, has been stoutly resisted as a return to the obscurantism of an outmoded Biblicism, and "existentialist exegesis" as an intrusion of alien philosophical principles that could only destroy true historical objectivity. We should remind ourselves that this opposition has deep historical roots in American soil: when the Higher Criticism, already firmly established in Germany, arose about a century later in America, an almost immediate breach was created between evangelical orthodoxy on the one hand and the friends of the "new" science of historical-critical research in the Bible on the other, who were now prone to look upon the orthodox and evangelical as unscientific, reactionary, and "dogmatic."

It seems worthwhile to illustrate the prevalent American method of scientific historical criticism in some further detail by referring to the work of Shirley Jackson Case, leading representative of the so-called "Chicago school," many of whose most able protégés have come to occupy strategic places in leading seminaries throughout the United States.

The titles alone of two of Case's books, *The Evolution of Early*

Christianity (1914) and *The Social Origins of Christianity* (1923), contain the clue to his fundamental methodological presuppositions. Sociological-cultural factors were, in Case's view, the heart and center of every phase of early Christianity: the genesis of the Christian religion could only be pictured "in terms of vital experiences and immediate social contacts on the part of its earliest advocates." [9] The "new" New Testament study advocated by Case in the 1920's was an attempt to go beyond literary evaluation of the New Testament documents to social interpretation of early Christianity's development. For this task the student of Christian origins must be oriented primarily in the life of the times which gave birth to the new Christian movement, and need deal only secondarily with the writings produced by the movement. The resistance to eclectic use of sources in the study of the whole New Testament period, the de-emphasizing of the New Testament as the sole or even primary evidence, and the resultant impression given that the Biblical canon is a somewhat fragmentary and fortuitous representation, all come strangely (we should pause to note) to the European, who is accustomed to a dogmatic and ecclesiastical tradition, which accords top priority and authority to the Scriptures, and thinks of the process of canonization as Spirit-led and Spirit-inspired. Yet these emphases remain quite typical of most phases of American Biblical scholarship. In light of them it is not hard to understand the complaint leveled by some historical critics against contemporary "Biblical-theological" treatments of the theme of the unity of Scripture, that, in the name of a search for a "theological norm," such treatments leap blithely from Malachi to Matthew, often with a blatant disregard for the history and culture of the epoch involved.[10] Whether we agree or not with this thoroughgoing "Biblical-historical" orientation, it would be churlish to withhold, in passing, a meed of praise for the brilliant and invaluable work of noted American scholars, too numerous to mention, on the history and literature of the Intertestamental period.

Returning to S. J. Case, we find that he was consciously reacting against devotion to the New Testament as containing an ultimate and timeless norm for faith, independent of all historical circumstances. For him the age-long Roman Catholic and Protestant concern with "essential" or "absolute" Christianity, defined in static terms and recognized as preserved respectively in the ecclesiastical organization, or the closed canon of Scripture, or in some speculative metaphysical system, was of the most doubtful legitimacy. Christianity could only be conceived in its development as the product of the socio-religious experience of actual people in each new generation, tackling their problems in contact with their own several worlds of reality.[11] The gospel itself is, to Case's mind, the product of the environmental and socio-cultural factors affecting the earliest Christian movement. It would undoubtedly be a mistake to see in Case's view any radical elimination of the transcendent or supra-historical element in the gospel. Rather his emphasis is on the fact that in the mediation of the gospel the responding believer does not exist in a vacuum, but in a specific social structure, of which full account must be taken. This kind of judgment, always a marked feature of the American social approach to Christian origins, furnished the later stance from which attack could be launched against dehistoricizing versions of the kerygma coming out of Europe. So C. T. Craig affirmed: "It is of the very nature of the *kerygma* that every moment of biblical religion is situation-conditioned." [12] The character of this position of hostility to the existentialist view of the kerygma is well explained by Amos Wilder (who has pleaded more eloquently than almost any other for a greater mutuality of understanding, in the contemporary scene, between existentialist hermeneutics and "Biblical-historical" hermeneutics): "From this point of view a hermeneutic based on dialectical presuppositions surrenders too easily to the task of understanding the divine operation. It fails to pursue down into the web of second causes the modes of grace and the interplay of revelation with the common life and its patterns, social and personal." [13] In other words, for very many American Biblical scholars the Bultmannian type of conception of the kerygma is too individualistic, too narrowly anthropologically oriented; it tends toward abstraction, toward removing man from the "worldly" dimension in which he is at home, from the "public" history in which he participates, from the web of social relationships in which he is involved; it is, if one may put it so, not "existential" enough.

The social view of Christian origins I have been illustrating was worked out by Case with remarkable clarity. There is yet another side of it that merits consideration. If this social approach owed much to the vigorous development of the social sciences that took place in America in the early decades of this century, it owed a great deal also to the methods and views of the *religionsgeschichtliche Schule*. American Biblical scholarship has readily allowed its insights to be fructified by such ideas from abroad as were congenial to its own frame of thought.

The conviction of Case and many others that every phase of the Biblical religion, including the kerygmatic faith of primitive Christianity, was relative to socio-cultural factors, and could be accounted for by a strictly historical method of investigation, echoes clearly enough the familiar position of the History of Religions school. For that School the application of the notion of evolution to the study of Biblical religion meant moving the center of interest from theology to the history of religions. Its members gave themselves with zeal to the task of laying Christianity alongside other faiths and studying it by the same scientific-historical method. Christianity was construed as a strictly historical evolution, but, more than that, as only one element in the wider process of the evolution of civilization. So Ernst Troeltsch believed that Biblical research must operate within the broad political, social, and spiritual history of antiquity and that the evaluation of Christianity must be made within the framework of cultural and religious history. The net results of the view that all history, including the history of Biblical religion, can be explained in terms of factors immanent in the historical process, of the causality within the nexus of things, are twofold. First, theology is surrendered to history: the emphasis is shifted from "Word," "revelation," "kerygma" to each successive generation of aspirants after religious truth, "tackling their problems in contact with their own several worlds of reality," ceaselessly striving to produce a genuine religious life at each new stage of the way, at once emulating the past and going beyond it (Case). One immediately thinks of the many modern American accounts of the Biblical religion as an evolutionary development from the crudities of primitive Semitic tribal superstition to the religious genius of the prophets, and eventually to the zenith of Christianity. Second, the restriction of Biblical study to assessment of the place of Christianity in the evolutionary process of general religious and cultural history militates against any idea of God's intervention in the world or history and precludes belief in a special and final divine revelation manifested once and for all in Jesus Christ at a definite and decisive moment in history.

It is on this last point I wish to focus attention. T. W. Manson once remarked that the acid test of liberalism, or any other theological "ism," is what it makes of Jesus Christ. Now Biblical scholarship on this side of the Atlantic has always been distinctive for its continual concern with the historical Jesus. But what has it made of him? S. J. Case's biography of Jesus was written from a thoroughly social standpoint: Jesus of Nazareth is reached and "explained" through his Palestinian environment on the one hand and through the social experience and community situation of the Evangelists on the other. The resultant portrait of Jesus is, I fear, the portrait of a discouragingly "liberal figure," not a revelation or incarnation of God, not the one in whom God was present reconciling the world to himself, but the teacher of a social ethic centering in an eschatology that is to be understood as a this-age eschatology. The thoroughgoing historicism of Case and numerous other American scholars, committed to a natural or quasi-natural understanding of revelation, could hardly go beyond humanistic delineations of Jesus, tied to this or that idealism or value philosophy. And in point of fact typical American representations of Jesus have continued to reflect Harnack's "classical" liberal evaluation of Jesus' place in and contribution to the evolving history of religion as the purveyor of a message that "may be reduced to these two heads—God as the Father and the human soul so ennobled that it can and does unite with him."

We cannot wonder that Biblical scholars in the United States who have continued to take this line of approach to Jesus have found themselves in a head-on clash with recent theological developments on the Continent. With disarming forthrightness, Dr. F. C. Grant has lately ventured an onslaught against "existentialist exegesis" and "neo-orthodoxy," both of which he regards as sinister "neo-biblicist" enemies of sound historical study. Professor Grant would regard it not as a criticism, but as a tribute, that he should be called "unashamedly liberal," both in his crusade for freedom from dogma and in his portrait of Jesus as the supreme Jewish teacher of an essentially Jewish ethic. For there breathes through his study on *Ancient Judaism and the New Testament* a wistful sigh for the return of the liberals of yesteryear and the reinstatement of the pure historical method that began to gain ground some half a century ago.[14]

I think it is fair to ask whether Dr. Grant may not have overestimated the decline of the liberal outlook and pure historical method in America. Certainly Biblical research here has never run along a single track. The picture is complex and variegated. I am hardly equal to the task of describing it. But mention might be made of the readiness of such scholars as Dr. Paul S. Minear to wrestle with the inner logic of the historical method and to ask whether history may not after all be exhausted by "chronology" but is in its very essence eschatological and personal. The resurgence of theological interpretation of the Bible in Europe has led to the appearance of a number of American studies in Biblical theology in the postwar years. Dr. G. E. Wright has assumed a *Heilsgeschichte* standpoint, from which Biblical theology is understood as confessional recital of the mighty acts of God. The hermeneutical problem has excited considerable interest in some quarters: Dr. Amos Wilder especially, with a profound understanding of both sides in the contemporary hermeneutical debate, has sought for a point of convergence between existentialist hermeneutics and the role of empiricism in interpreting Scripture. Dr. J. M. Robinson has made a number of learned contributions to the new Jesus-research instituted by the "new seekers" after the historical Jesus among the Bultmannian circle. Many more instances of this kind could be cited. Incomers to the United States, like the present writer, very quickly learn that, in regard to prevailing cultural—and particularly theological and Biblical-critical trends—here of all places generalizing descriptions are very unsafe and may be quite misleading. There is always an exception to the rule just down the street or around the corner. So, for example, in relation to current American attitudes to Rudolf Bultmann, many Lutheran schools are not at all inhospitable to his kerygma-theology, but see in it a radical confrontation, in modern terms, of modern problems with Reformation theology.

Nevertheless, there is scarcely any doubt that the objective, scientific-historical method of Biblical research, allied to a liberal theological perspective, remains a potent factor in the over-all situation. Thus Otto J. Baab's *Theology of the Old Testament* was founded on the assumption that, if only the theological truths of the Old Testament were scientifically described and defined, they would commend themselves as truths to men of all faiths and cultures.[15] In the posthumously published volume on *Religion in the Old Testament* by one of the most able of American Old Testament scholars, R. H. Pfeiffer, the author views his task as that not of theologian or philosopher, but of historian, who "searches for actual historical reality, not for normative faith and doctrine valid for all times." [16] The continuing vitality of the objective search for historical reality, in connection with

Jesus of Nazareth and the early Christian period—a search that purposively tries to steer clear of dogmatic and theological presuppositions—is perhaps best exemplified in a recent volume of essays on *Early Christian Origins* contributed by scholars associated with Chicago.[17] I here single out two of the essays as especially significant for our purpose. They seem to me to be illustrative respectively of the palpable weakness of a strictly historical approach to Jesus and of the strength of the socio-historical method as applied to the understanding and interpretation of the New Testament message over against current European ascriptions of a transcendental character to the kerygma.

Dr. Albert Barnett's paper on "Jesus as Theologian" is entirely liberal in perspective. Jesus is depicted as founder of the "theological substructure" on which the creative minds of Paul, the Fourth Evangelist, and the author of Hebrews subsequently worked: at this few would cavil. But we furrow our brows when this "theological substructure" is narrowed down to Jesus' own view of the providence of God as the doctrine which constitutes the integrating principle of every phase of his teaching and on which his whole life and message were predicated. We hear again the voice of Harnack. The gospel is reduced to a message about God that had its precedents in the Old Testament and Judaism: and the substance of the message consists of a few simple beliefs that grew out of Jesus' own religious consciousness, his own sense of dependence on God, and that he then promulgated with the most persuasive and winning power. Dr. Barnett certainly offers a winsome portrayal of Jesus' view of God's providential care of men. And certainly anyone who is not unduly skeptical about the historicity of the Gospel tradition would agree that the facts warrant our according to God's Fatherhood, God's providence, a place of the supremest importance in Jesus' life and message; the fact that he invited his disciples to call God "Father"; the fact that he himself addressed God as *Abba,* a term which in its intimacy would have been deemed irreverent by the Judaism of his day. But when this is made the basis of the whole religion of Jesus and of every theme in Jesus' teaching, without ever a mention of the outcome of Jesus' profound trustfulness in his own radical decision of obedience to God *even unto the death of the Cross,* then we have a right to feel that the Gospel materials are being handled most eclectically. When there is no word of the Gospels' tidings that in Jesus himself, in his life and in his death as a death "for us," God has drawn near to us in our history; when there is no note of the apostolic proclamation that God demonstrates his love toward us in that while we were yet sinners Christ died for us; then we are left only with the teaching of an extraordinary religious genius whose great contribution to the history of religion was the all-important truth of God's providence. And in that case it is hard to see what meaning we can give to God's providence. In terms of strict historical science, which is limited to description of the intra-worldly nexus of things and can leave no room for the irruption of God into history, not much more than this: a certain immanence of God in the process of Nature, a certain benevolence in his ordering of creation for the benefit of individuals open to the eyes of faith.[18] And what is there of saving efficacy and redemptive power in that? Little enough, and even less when we are told that the hope of creative solutions to the common problems of mankind in the twentieth century resides in *our* emulation of Jesus' piety, *our* adaptation of Jesus' view of providence.[19] No doubt common realization of "God's individualized love for persons, the worth of every person to God" could be a well of healing for the brokenness and divisiveness of human relationships today. But shall we lay hold of these things by looking back to Jesus and striving to share his view of God? Or shall we not rather grasp them only because the living God in and through the preached Jesus Christ in his grace has grasped us?

Truly the fires of the liberal approach to Jesus have not been quenched: Dr. Barnett's presentation of "Jesus as Theologian" is not uncharacteristic of certain continuing American attitudes to Jesus today. If we take issue with them, it is not because we endorse the lack of interest in the historical Jesus that the "dialectical theology" has shown in its extreme reaction against nineteenth-century German liberal theology. There is nothing wrong with emphasizing the Jesus of history. The mistake lies in the failure to recognize that the Evangelical tradition is simply not interested in giving us merely Jesus' views *about* God, or even in recording its own views *about* Jesus, but in confronting us with Jesus Christ himself. The proclaimer is at the same time the proclaimed. There is at least an implicit acknowledgment of this in Dr. Barnett's prefatory remark that what the Evangelists wrote was a form of preaching, and not history for its own sake.[20] Why then should we not take this with utmost seriousness? Why should we still take the long road back to the traditional liberal position and refuse to admit that no reconstructed picture of the Jesus of history, his views and beliefs about God, can take hold of us for our salvation, but only the whole Christian story of Jesus Christ, crucified, dead, buried, risen again the third day, and ascended into heaven, whence, by the work of the Holy Spirit in our hearts, through the witness of the Church, he comes to us again.

At any rate, if we continue to see our task now to be that of sharpening the weapons of historical objectivity simply in order to get back, in the name of escape from dogma, or if you will, Christology, to the true historical Jesus, we are really forfeiting the possibility of saying anything pertinent to the most pressing question of the relation of the proclaimer to the proclaimed, of the Jesus of history to the exalted Christ in Christian faith.

Whereas the historico-scientific method of Jesus-research can hardly give any recognition to the question of how Jesus has become the preached Christ, the Son of God and the living Lord, the socio-historical method of study of Christian origins, as it has been developed by American scholars, has an important contribution to make to the other question of how the kerygma is to be interpreted: the problem of demythologizing.

We have previously said that the historico-scientific approach to Christian origins is prone to surrender theology to history, to move the accent from "Word," "revelation," "kerygma" to socio-cultural factors immanent in the historical process. Yet we have to call attention to the fact that among representative social historians of primitive Christianity, the genuinely religious, or shall we say revelatory, element in the rise of the new religion has not been completely submerged. There is a radical divergence between the materialistic, Marxist view of A. Kalthoff [21] and that, for example, of Ernst Troeltsch. Kalthoff maintained that Christianity came to birth when the fiery revolutionary tendencies in the Roman Empire came in contact with Jewish Messianic expectations. Members of the Jewish proletariat, gripped by a Messianic-apocalyptic outlook, inflamed the communistic ideals of those who were rebellious against Roman imperialism, and the meeting of these two combustible forces set off a conflagration out of which arose the new Christian social movement. Christ became the ideal hero of this communistic, proletarian revolution, and the Gospels, purely Roman in background, its manifesto. In marked contrast with this crassly materialistic approach is Troeltsch's conviction that, in its development and dialectic, religion has an independent existence, or that the Christian religion, in its earliest manifestation, was characterized by a "formlessness" resulting from the primitive energy and explosive power contained in the new, fundamental, *specifically religious idea*.[22] Troeltsch, moreover, gave considerable prominence to the radical individualism of Jesus' message and saw it as centering in the imminent consummation of God's final victory and the conquest of demons, with which the present world order would pass away.[23]

It is of interest here that Professor F. C. Grant has followed much the same line as Troeltsch. For, while his detailed analysis of the social and economic factors involved in Jesus' Palestinian environment has led to the classification of Jesus' ethic as an "agrarian ethic," he has none the less conceded that the primary cause of the rise of the gospel was the genuine religious factor.

It is less than ever possible, nowadays, to represent early Christianity as a revolutionary social (or social-economic) movement. Although, as we insist, religion is always conditioned by the world in which it lives, including the economic factor in that world, it is clear that Christianity was from the very beginning a purely religious movement, a cult, a body of beliefs and practices centered in something else than the economic welfare or well-being of any racial, national or social group.[24]

From this background we are now in a position to consider briefly Dr. Amos Wilder's essay "Early Christian Eschatology." It contains two key points. First, there is a necessary warning against projecting back into the world in which Christianity was cradled the categories of social analysis common to the nineteenth or twentieth centuries. The ideas of "class struggle" or the "proletariat" or of modern utopianism can be utterly misleading when applied to the social factors in Jesus' setting or to his teaching on the kingdom of God. Our distinctions between "economic," "social," "political" and "religious" were scarcely made in the ancient period. Second, out of this the view emerges, in regard to early Christian eschatology, that social conditions, property, slavery, persecution, etc., form only part of the total cultural situation in which the religious heritage also comes into play. The "social" and the "religious" are thus seen to interpenetrate each other in the total way of life and world view of the ancient group. The well-known description of late Jewish and early Christian apocalyptic documents as "tracts for bad times" ought not therefore to be taken as referring exclusively to political persecution or economic pressures on the one hand or to "religious" factors on the other, but to the indissoluble union of social-political and spiritual elements in the whole situation. "The crises," writes Dr. Wilder, "were religio-cultural whether in Palestine or in the Hellenistic pagan setting. The fantasy-like but yet often healthy projection of dramatic symbol suggesting the dissolution of the usual categories of time, space and causation reflects social-cultural incoherence, anomie and loss of meaning." [25] Eschatological mood and, presumably, eschatological preaching have their background and source in a general historical crisis in which social disturbance and new religious questioning of the meaning of existence are fused together.

It would have been worthwhile looking at Dr. Wilder's paper if only to show how there is a continual wrestling with questions of the application of social-historical methodology, developed among such earlier scholars as S. J. Case, to the study of Christian beginnings, and to dispel the illusion that, on its main front, American Biblical scholarship is bound to an obsolete historicism. But there is another, and more important, reason for doing so. The insistence that the meaning of such terms as "the last things," "faith," "revelation," "the Word" was given to men of the New Testament period in the specific historical life situations in which they lived has a significant bearing on the contemporary debate about the kerygma and its interpretation.

We have seen how the existentialist hermeneutics associated with Bultmann, despite all disclaimers about his leaving room within the kerygma for the concrete historical fact of the death of Jesus Christ, runs the risk of severing the kerygma from the historical man, Jesus of Nazareth, and leaving it "suspended in thin air." Since God, being God, cannot reveal himself in the world of our objects, nor in any worldly "signs" held forth for our rational interpretation, since in the lonely situation in which man is addressed by God in the kerygma, faith cannot be founded on anything other than itself, without appeal to any outside elements, the mythological language in which the kerygma speaks about God, the world, and history must, according to Bultmann, be transposed forthwith into an understanding of man. It is just at this point that the relevance of the socio-historical emphasis we have sought to elucidate begins to appear. From the socio-historical perspective the transcendental character assigned to the kerygma by Bultmann looks very one-sided. The social historian insists on the "worldliness" of the kerygma, that is, on the historical-human factors involved in its reception and interpretation; he holds that "meaning" is inextricably bound up with the real and specific life situation, in which the event of faith or understanding takes place. Is he not right to do so? Must we not guard against that false isolation and hypostatization of the kerygma, by which it becomes a single, timeless, and absolute occurrence? It is hardly any longer a matter of dispute whether Bultmann has preserved the essentially kerygmatic character of Christianity and so differentiated it as a religion of divine grace from a philosophy of human existence.[26] The question now is whether his transcendental version of the kerygma as the agent of God's address to men takes anything like due account of the historical-human factors operative in the mediation of grace. In the "new quest" of the historical Jesus among Bultmann's pupils we see a recognition of the, fact that fuller place must be given to the concrete historical character of the revelation. In the socio-historical approach among American Biblical researchers, we see what is, I think, a valid protest against the abstraction of the kerygma from the historical context in which the believer and interpreter are situated.

Our final point must therefore be an objection to Bultmann's narrowly anthropological interpretation of the kerygma, its wholesale translation into an understanding of man. To be sure we have to allow today that the Bible's language about God, the world, and history is permeated with mythological traits, and that accordingly there is no escape from the task of demythologizing if we are to convey the gospel meaningfully to an age whose categories of thought are quite different from those of the ancient world. We ought not to discount the existentialist approach. But the questions that trouble us are these. Is the mythological language of the New Testament always only statement about human *self-understanding*? Is it always only description in "this-worldly" terms of an "other-worldly" truth that approaches us in the kerygma, soliciting our believing response and summoning us to new self-understanding? In that case, would not something indispensable for the New Testament be lost? For is not the mythological language employed by the New Testament author also seeking to bring to expression his view of *this world,* his understanding, in light of his relatedness to the world in which he lives, of God and history? The dissolution of the kerygma into that extreme and lonely frontier moment of divine summons and human response, in which faith lives only from itself, leaves the human reason imprisoned in the shadows of darkness. But the imprisonment is both arbitrary and unendurable, for the human decision to respond to the divine call is always truly historical decision, always implies the creature's exercise of perception and reason toward his creation, and so his judgment upon the world and history outside of him.

In our all too meager review of Biblical-critical trends on the American scene, we have tried at least to be just to the main-line attitudes. We have observed how a rigorously scientific approach to the historical Jesus, combined with a "liberal" distrust of dogma, forecloses the possibility of penetration in depth into the urgent question of the relation between Jesus and the exalted Christ of the Church's preaching. Yet, on the other hand, we have seen how the same empirical and pragmatic cast of the socio-historical approach to Christian origins, with its unwavering stress on the concrete historical character of the revelation and on the need to spell out the specific life situation of the recipient of the revelation, can offer a needed corrective to the existentialist theologian's tendency to elevate the kerygma to a suprahistorical, timeless absolute. I cannot think that this stress is irrelevant to Christian faith in any age or territory. For if revelation is from on high alone by the Word of a kerygma, which leaves a place for Jesus, if at all, only as an abstract, unapproachable figure, we are none the better for his having passed through this world, and the Word was made flesh to no avail.

Representative Historical-Critical Positions in Recent British Biblical Scholarship

The circumstances in which the Higher Criticism of the Bible arose in Great Britain were not the same as those which obtained in America. Victory in the battle against dogmatic orthodoxy in the churches was hastened by the fact that many of those who welcomed the new historical criticism of the Bible were devoutly evangelical theologians. There was, therefore, not the same breach created, as in America, between the uncritical evangelicals and the new critical liberals. Nor did those who adopted the new critical study capitulate with the same abandon or zeal as their American counterparts to the thoroughgoing scientific historicism already firmly established in Germany. They saw historical criticism rather as a handmaiden in the primary task of preaching and expounding the Bible in the churches. They noticed, and quite rightly, that there is nothing intrinsically anti-theological about historico-scientific research on the Bible. Such scholars as G. A. Smith and S. R. Driver were well aware that the labor of historical criticism was only the prolegomena to the main work of theological interpretation. The early wedding of scientific industry in Bible research and theological concern in some of the giants of the critical era in Great Britain has had an influence on the present mood of Biblical scholarship. I do not believe that there has ever been quite the same widespread suspicion of such terms as "revelation," "the Word," and "Biblical theology" as in America.

It would, however, be fatuous to suggest that historico-scientific study of the Bible in Great Britain was not also, over a long period of years, attended by the same defects as have everywhere been characteristic of thoroughgoing historicism. The discovery that the Biblical writers were frail mortals like ourselves and not just passive instruments of the Holy Spirit kindled the belief in Great Britain, too, that everything in the Bible could be explained from the human angle: whatever could not be humanly accounted for, revelation or the supernatural, was thrust out to the periphery. Through its intrinsic fascination, historico-scientific criticism, from being a means of clarifying the Biblical message, tended to become an end in itself. In Great Britain as elsewhere, source analysis of the Biblical documents, their dissemination into a great variety of layers of material, the tracing of environmental influences on the different writers—all this, coupled with minute philological research, furthered the process whereby the Bible was steadily reduced to an inchoate pile of disjointed fragments, with no Ariadne thread to guide one through the maze. Preoccupation with the minutiae of criticism left precious little time for theological interpretation of the Biblical writings.

The disillusionment that followed the First World War in Europe, the shattering of the old evolutionary optimism and of the humanism of liberal theology, with its faith in man and in the course of his history, produced a full swing of the theological pendulum on the Continent. The "crisis theologians," Barth and Brunner, polemicized against the attenuated theology of liberalism and so inevitably against the historicism in Biblical studies which had always been tied in with it. But the big guns of the new theological movement on the Continent certainly caused no immediate tottering at the foundations of British historical-critical scholarship. It would be safe to say that there has been hardly less distrust among British than among American scholars in these last forty years toward the "crisis theology" or the "theology of the Word." The apathy of Barth and Brunner to the concrete historical element in the New Testament, the priority given by them to the dogmas about Jesus Christ, the unrelatedness of their Christology to the work of Biblical criticism, the gap set up between God and man, all these have been continually regarded as unwelcome foes of well-balanced historical scholarship. Yet at the same time—and here perhaps we should remind ourselves that some of the early great critics in the British Isles, W. Sanday and Bishop Gore as well as G. A. Smith and S. R. Driver, were men of profound theological sensitivity and considerable evangelical fervor—more than in America there has been a real disquietude about liberal-oriented critical study of the Bible and an anxious concern to push beyond the frontiers of historicism to some adequate mode of theological interpretation. Let me cite some words written by Dr. John Lowe of Oxford in the 1940's:

In this country the uncongenial "theology of crisis" has played only a minor part. None the less there is evident uneasiness about the character of our interpretation of the Bible. It is premature to say that we have succeeded in reinstating a thoroughly theological interpretation. We do not quite know how. What we can say is that many among us are conscious of the need and are looking for guidance. It is not a matter of discarding wholesale the critical approach in which we were trained and which arrived at much that is true and valuable, but we feel that the method as practised was associated too often with underlying assumptions that need purging and that it tended to stop short of the goal. We *want* something more theological and to that extent there has been a recovery of a sounder outlook.[27]

That is a humble and revealing statement. It seems to me to point us to the middle-of-the-road position that has marked the work of the most distinguished British Biblical scholars of the last few decades. On the one hand, there has been the obvious reluctance to sacrifice the integrity of a balanced historical method of research by any return to an uncritical and authoritarian Biblicism for orthodoxy's sake. On the other hand, there has been a sensibility of the insufficiency of historical method alone and unaided to open up the permanent significance of the Biblical message, and a more genuine feeling for fundamental theological questions than was characteristic of the old liberalism. Yet withal in this co-existence of historical methodology and theological concern, I think it is true to say that the historical-critical approach has been by far the stronger partner. Consequently, the question raised for theological interpretation by the bewildering multiplicity of critical judgments among scholars surveying the same evidence with every desire to be impartial has scarcely been pressed as far as it might, any more than has the collateral question of what is the value for faith of the results of historico-scientific research. It is time, however, to be specific in support of what has just been said. I therefore propose a short investigation of the contributions of three representative British New Testament scholars, Professors C. H. Dodd, Vincent Taylor, and the late T. W. Manson.

Professor Dodd has all along been devoted to the study of historical and critical problems. But no one would care to deny his theological interest and competence, or his desire for fresh and invigorating presentation of the Christian message to our own age. "Gospels and epistles alike offer a field of study in which the labour of criticism and interpretation may initiate us into the 'many-sided wisdom' which was contained in the apostolic Preaching, and make us free to declare it in contemporary terms to our own age." [28] The Bultmannian movement has not enjoyed a monopoly of interest in translating the gospel into terms relevant to our own time. In the 1930's Dodd, out of a profound concern for the New Testament message, was calling for an end to the period of analysis (which for all its good and enduring results had led to a pitiable fragmentation of the Biblical writings), and the opening up of a new period of synthesis.[29] The sounding of the alarm was timely. The religious aridity of the discipline of criticism was stifling the breath of the Spirit.

Dodd himself gave a lead to the quest for a "new synthesis" by bringing into clear relief the original unity of the New Testament. He found the inner core or nucleus of the New Testament in the primitive apostolic kerygma, the main lines of which we see emerging primarily in the Pauline epistles and secondarily in the Acts of the Apostles, *The Apostolic Preaching and Its Developments* (1936), despite its small size, had a very telling influence on Anglo-Saxon New Testament scholarship, in bringing the kerygma to the forefront of attention.

We are concerned here with Dodd's attitude toward the question of the history contained in the kerygma. When Kähler, and later the Form-critics, underscored the kerygmatic nature of the Gospels, they intended primarily to denote that the Gospels are not first and foremost annals of past events in Jesus' ministry, but rather confessions of faith in a crucified and risen Lord. For a moment Dodd, too, appears to be on the verge of a like view of the tradition when he writes: "There never existed a tradition formed by a dry historical interest in the facts as facts. From the beginning the facts were preserved in memory and tradition as elements in the Gospel which the Church proclaimed." [30] But Dodd finds it exceedingly difficult to overcome his historicism. For, when he thinks of Mark's Gospel as kerygmatic in character, what he has in mind is that Mark wrote a form of kerygma, in other words he built upon the objective, chronological framework of the earliest kerygma, which acted as a preservative of the tradition which *conveyed the facts*.[31] Dodd's view that the principal function of the most primitive kerygma was to mediate the facts of Jesus' ministry is buttressed by his critical theories regarding the composition of Mark and the speeches given in the earlier parts of Acts.

As to the composition of Mark's Gospel, Dodd has vigorously defended the thesis that there is a connecting thread running through most of the narrative, similar to the brief summary of the story of Jesus in Acts 10 and 13. Mark had before him an earlier kerygmatic tradition, a skeleton chronological outline of the ministry.[32] The Form-critics had pointed to the "generalizing summaries" (*Sammelberichte*), with which Mark sought to knit his report together. In Dodd's view the outline used by Mark for his Gospel consisted of a continuous series of these "generalizing summaries." The fact that Mark could not actually follow through this "hypothetical" outline seemed to Dodd to indicate that it must have come to him from the tradition and was not his own creation. Now if this hypothesis of a kerygmatic chronology were shown to be implausible, one of the critical props for the factual-chronological meaning projected by Dodd on the kerygma would fall to the ground. In fact, James M. Robinson's tersely stated case against the hypothesis seems to me to carry conviction: "The case for the existence of the conjectured 'outline' really requires for its proof some such objective indication of its existence as would be provided by Mark following it in his narrative. The fact that Mark does not follow the order of the hypothetical outline certainly points to a more obvious inference than the pre-Marcan origin of the hypothetical document: namely, its non-existence." [33]

As to the sermons in the earlier chapters of Acts, Dodd was operating in 1936 with the notion that Luke exercised his historian's privilege with considerable restraint, and was following J. de Zwaan's suggestion of early Aramaic sources used by Luke particularly for the speeches in Acts 1:1–5:16; 9:31–11:18 and probably 15:1–36. "There is a high degree of probability that the author was laying under contribution an Aramaic source or sources, whether written or oral, and whether the work of translation had already been done, or whether he translated it for himself." [34] But since that time a dramatic and revolutionary change in Lucan studies has occurred. As far back as 1923 this fundamental reorientation was adumbrated in a short essay by Martin Dibelius, "Stilkritisches zur Apostelgeschichte." [35] The Luke of Acts followed a quite different working method from the Luke of the Gospel. Apart from the "travel-journal," Dibelius detected in Acts no substantial, coherent sources, but rather a number of smaller, self-contained accounts. A very large part of Acts must accordingly be attributed to the hand of Luke himself. For a while Dibelius' essay had little appreciable effect—not surprisingly, since he had removed from Acts-research its source documents and replaced them with a handful of separate stories of varying historical value, and especially since he had characterized twenty-four passages of direct speech, nearly one-third of the book, as Lucan compositions. [36] The speeches are intended to bear witness to the gospel, and, in particular, the apostles' missionary addresses probably correspond to Christian preaching of about the year 90 A.D. Latterly the wheel has turned full circle. The collection and publication of Dibelius' various papers on Acts by H. Greeven in 1951 was followed by two studies: Ph. Vielhauer's article contended that Luke, the supposed companion of Paul, was actually everywhere at odds with the apostle, that he played down the redemptive significance of the Cross, and that he abandoned expectation of the End. [37] H. Conzelmann's studies in Lucan theology demonstrated that Luke replaced primitive Christian doctrine, obsessed with the imminent End, by a historical the-

ology of salvation.[38] So Luke the historian has become to many eyes
Luke the theologian of "sacred history," and increasing support has
been forthcoming for the view that we must relinquish the idea of
Luke's use of extended sources.

In light of this distinctive scholarly trend, the burden of proof lies
heavily today on anyone who would defend the thesis of a kerygmatic
framework, consisting of a chronological summary, behind the sermons in Acts.[39] If, therefore, we cannot easily entertain the idea that
the basic content of the kerygma is a chronological sketch of the ministry of Jesus, the whole question of its meaning is thrown wide open,
as is the related question of how kerygma has passed over into narration in the Gospels, into what Luke calls *diegesis* of the things that
happened (Luke 1:1). Is the kerygma a promulgation of "facts" in
the ministry of Jesus, which in their eschatological significance as
"saving facts" can be grasped by the historian as historian? Or is it
the proclamation of a crucified and resurrected Lord, who in his hiddenness is accessible only to faith?

In his later works, Professor Dodd has touched on the problem
of how we are to understand "facts" or "events" in relation to Biblical history. The Church, he now holds, has arisen out of the death
and Resurrection of Jesus Christ: if we would wish to specify the historical reality of the "events" in which the Church originated, we must
begin with the Church and proceed from the Church.[40] Here there is
at least a tentative recognition of the inability of historico-scientific
study alone to describe and define the central "events" of the gospel.
In regard to the Resurrection, "there are," says Professor Dodd,
"events of outstanding importance in which practically nothing at all
happened, in the ordinary external sense of happening." [41] In this way
Dodd concedes the historical actuality of the Resurrection and so
guards against its being spiritualized, while at the same time acknowledging the greater significance of its "meaning" for faith. Even so, for
Dodd, both the "fact" and its "meaning" fall within the sphere in
which the historian can operate. He has never taken us much beyond
this: the new historical method to which he seems to have been
moving has remained a promise rather than an achievement. The
probable reason for this tentativeness as to hermeneutical method in
Professor Dodd's position is that his chief concern, as theological interpreter of the Bible, has been the formulation of a view of God's
absolute rulership over history, derived from the notion of the Christ-

event as a "realized eschatology," or more recently an "eschatology in process of being realized." For the rest, together with most other of his recent British colleagues, he has remained a staunch defender of the historicity of the Gospel tradition against all attacks from the continent of Europe, and of the historical reliability of its witness to the real life of a real man. But in this connection he has scarcely thought to raise the question, thrust upon us so insistently by the exigencies of our present theological situation, of whether historical scholarship can bring us saving knowledge of Jesus Christ.

Professor Vincent Taylor has devoted much of his lifework to study of the problems of Christology, not only as an exercise in New Testament exegesis, but in an attempt to bridge the gap between exegesis and dogmatics, between the particular interests of the scholar and the larger world of contemporary religion. He has never hesitated to venture out of the narrower world of criticism and declare the bearing of his critical research in the wider field of Christian belief and worship. It is significant that the last chapter of his book on *The Person of Christ* is entitled "Towards a Modern Christology." *The Person of Christ* is the third volume of an invaluable trilogy on the Christological teaching of the New Testament. The two former parts appeared as *The Names of Jesus* (1953) and *The Life and Ministry of Jesus* (1954).

Dr. Taylor's presentation of New Testament Christology seems to me to be based on a standpoint that is a curious halfway house between confidence in the ability of objective historical method to define and validate the claims made for Jesus in the New Testament and recognition of the fact that knowledge of who Jesus is is given only to the *faith* of the interpreter. "We do not first discover who Christ is and then believe in him," writes Dr. Taylor, "we believe in him and then discover who he is." [42] In light of this open confession that faith alone can know who Jesus is, it is all the more surprising that in Taylor's account of New Testament Christology the role of faith should be largely submerged in a rigorously scientific and objective mode of exegesis. When it is assumed, as it is by Taylor, that historical criticism can authenticate from the Gospels Jesus' emergent consciousness of his Sonship as a historically verifiable "fact" as the foundation of New Testament Christology, we are entitled to wonder whether the role of faith as a means of knowing has not now been canceled. Dr. Taylor is indeed still able to take the propositions that

Jesus is divine, Lord and Christ, Son of Man and Son of God, and lay
them alongside the unambiguously human elements of his earthly life,
his growing in wisdom and stature, his exposure to disappointment,
frustration, suffering, and death, as though both belonged equally to
the factual side of things, and were equally clearly offered to *historical*
perception.[43] A very high place is given in point of fact to historical
knowing and seeing: the truths about the preached Christ, the Incarnation, Jesus' filial relationship to God, are sometimes spoken about
as if they could be gathered by inference from observable facts.[44] In
the midst of his rather strictly historical approach, Taylor reminds us
from time to time that the only means of knowing Jesus is faith, the
inner testimony of the Holy Spirit in the experience of the individual
Christian. There is, however, almost no effort to discuss the relationship between historical knowledge and faith knowledge of Jesus
Christ, or to attack the question of the continuity or discontinuity
between the historical Jesus and the exalted Christ of the Church's
faith. It may not be unfair to say that Taylor the theologian would
like to break through to a hermeneutic that allows a key place to the
faith of the interpreter in the knowing and describing of historical
reality, but this is prevented by Taylor the historian. The outcome is
that he appears to regard faith or personal response to the revelation
in Jesus Christ as something simply added on to thoroughly historical
study of the New Testament teaching. When historical research is
complete, faith enters in to check, correct, or corroborate our judgments.[45] Not in this way can the gap between historical exegesis and
dogmatics be overcome.

It seems to me that, if the principle that Jesus is known only to
faith had been taken with complete seriousness and had been allowed
to become a controlling factor in the hermeneutical approach, we
might reasonably have expected the second volume of the trilogy to be
quite different from what it is. We might have expected it to deal primarily (and not less so because Taylor has been more open than
many British New Testament scholars to the possibilities of Form-
criticism) with the Resurrection as the decisive event through which
the disciples' faith in Jesus as the Christ came to fruition, and out of
which therefore, in a new and staggering way, the historical Jesus became known to them as he truly was and is and ever shall be. We
might also have expected some concession to the claim, so frequently
heard since Kähler and the Form-critics, that the Gospel tradition was

permeated from the first with the Easter faith of the primitive community, that no item in its memories of Jesus was left untouched or uncolored by its experience of the Easter event, and that accordingly, in the Gospel witness to Jesus Christ, faith and history indissolubly interpenetrate each other.

As it is, not more than four pages have been given at the close to the theme of the Resurrection, and in these the main concern is not to compromise in any way the historical actuality of the Resurrection as simply one fact among other facts of Jesus' ministry. The starting point for Taylor's reconstruction of the events of Jesus' life and ministry in their causality is a zealous defense of the essential historical trustworthiness of the Gospels as records of what Jesus actually was and said and did, and as sources from which the main sequence of his career can be traced with some degree of confidence. Taylor takes his stand not only against the extreme skepticism of radical Form-criticism but against the threat to the historicity of the Gospels implicit in the arguments of such scholars as A. M. Farrer and P. Carrington that the Gospels are structured on the most elaborate and intricate architectonic designs, involving a complicated pattern of cycles and subcycles, all determined by the Evangelists' preoccupation either with Old Testament prototypes or with the cultic and lectionary needs of the early Christian community.[46] Having argued that the Gospels do provide a reliable guide to "what actually happened," his attempt to do justice to the significance of the Jesus of history for Christology is presented in the form of a constructive life of Jesus—a very rare enterprise in this generation, but undertaken by Professor Taylor with courage, keen critical acumen, and commendable reserve in following the Gospel narrative with a minimum of conjectural interpretation. Few today would care to deny the need to stress the importance of the historical Jesus for Christology: Christology is indeed the theological doctrine of the person of Jesus Christ, the *historical and exalted* Saviour. But in view of the position we have been in recently, when theology has been greatly agitated by the problem of the relation of the Jesus of history to the Christ of faith, we cannot help doubting the wisdom of focusing upon "chronological" reconstruction of the events in Jesus' ministry. To be sure, Professor Taylor is sharply aware of the "Jesus of history"–"Christ of faith" problem; he knows that the old liberal attempt at a portrait of the historical Jesus independent of the dogmatic portrait of the Christ often resulted in a clinging to the man Jesus, in his natural humanity, and not to the preached Christ. He rightly pleads the need to keep the Christ of faith always in sight in any historical inquiry into the Gospels, precisely because "it is this Christ whose story the Gospels tell." "We cannot see the Jesus of history," he says, "if we close our eyes to the Christ of faith; we do not see the Christ of faith except in the light of the Jesus of history." All the more surprising, therefore, is the course he has taken in venturing a construction of the life of Jesus in its connectedness that is almost wholly dependent on objective historical-critical analysis. In the course of the construction some room is certainly left for consideration of the dogmatic claims implicit in the life of Jesus. But the center of attention is undoubtedly the question of how the sequence of events ran: can we draw out of our sources a chronologically coherent account of the ministry of Jesus? Thus is perpetuated the impression that the tradition is first and foremost a chronicle of "what actually happened." Our difficulty is this: is preoccupation with "what actually happened" in the ministry of Jesus in the positivistic sense the best way to carry through the sound and acceptable principle that we can only see the Jesus of history in the light of the Christ of faith, or to do justice to the twofold intention of the Gospels to be at one and the same time a monument to the memory of Jesus of Nazareth and a proclamation of him as risen Christ and Lord? To be sure the problem of forging a method that could grasp jointly both the historical and the theological reality of Jesus' life is extremely acute and probably constitutes the greatest single element of unrest on the contemporary theological front. The double nature of the problem of Jesus explains why most of those who have dealt with it have failed to satisfy either the critic or the uncritically devout, either the historian or the theologian. We remember how M. Goguel opened his attempt to retrace the origin of Christianity, beginning with the life of Jesus: "Some will charge me with failing to make use of the critical method because I have used the psychological method. Others will blame me for having tried to apply the historical method to a problem which, from their point of view, is not amenable to criticism. They are pained, and, indeed, scandalized, by what they regard as lack of respect for the Christian tradition." [47]

Our criticism of Professor Taylor (and in view of what we have just said, this has to be temperate) concerns the procedure he has adopted for the second volume of his trilogy on Christology. If we are to be true to the fact that we cannot recognize the Jesus of history unless we keep in view the Christ of faith, should we not give pride of place, not to objective historical reconstruction of Jesus' ministry, but to the indispensably prior question of Easter, and how it has affected the disciples' understanding of Jesus and colored or transformed their memories of him as these came to be collected in the tradition?

A great deal hinges upon what we mean by the "trustworthiness" of the Gospel tradition. What Professor Taylor has in view, falling as he does on the conservative side, is that it is a sufficiently accurate report for us to be able to reconstruct out of it a fairly exact picture of the course of Jesus' life.[48] But where does our factual picture stand in relation to the Gospels' twofold witness to Jesus Christ as the one whose earthly form in its pastness is remembered by the Church and who at the same time is present to the Church as risen Christ and Lord? Is it a mere abstraction? What kind of reality are we trying to reconstruct by Gospel criticism? Such questions as these have been increasingly forced upon us by criticism itself and by criticism's growing understanding of the nature of the primitive tradition. We have been brought to the place where we can now see more clearly that we have to be very careful in discriminating between the "authentic" and "inauthentic" in the Gospel tradition in any limited historical sense. For the step from Jesus in his history to *Gemeindetheologie,* the theology of the post-Easter community, may not necessarily have meant at all the distortion or falsification of the factual picture of Jesus, but rather a witness to Jesus, arising out of the event of Easter faith, that was more empiric and historic and more adequate than any factual representation of him "as he actually was" could be. Taylor holds, for example, that the Transfiguration story (Mark 9:2 ff.) has a basis in remembered fact, and to that extent can be considered "authentic." [49] As is well known, Bultmann and other radical critics regard it as a post-Easter story, created by the Church, and so historically "inauthentic." I do not suppose that we shall ever get any universal agreement about its historicity. But there is a positive factor: it is "authentic" in that its presence in the Gospel record of Jesus' earthly ministry marks the testimony of the evangelical tradition to Jesus as the Christ, its understanding of the history of Jesus in terms of his Resurrection and the experience of his glorious presence.

I am aware that I have not dealt adequately with Professor Taylor's many-sided contribution to study of the Christological teaching of the

New Testament. His position is evidently distinguished by the pragmatic middle-of-the-road attitude that has been typical of the best British New Testament scholarship. It is frequently called the "common sense" approach—by some pejoratively, by others admiringly. There is on the one hand the steady belief that historical criticism can still yield us sure knowledge of the Jesus of history. On the other there is a certain recognition of the theological "bias" in the Gospel report and of the need therefore, even in considering the historical aspect of the problem of Jesus, to keep the Christ of faith in view. Our complaint is not that there is anything essentially wrong with the middle way—the Church has taken it quite often ere now, to the preservation of the integrity of our historic Christian faith. Our chief dissatisfaction (and perhaps it is churlish, when scholars have given us so much, to complain about what they have not given us) is simply that such able critics as Vincent Taylor have assumed, rather than discussed in depth, the bearing and relevance of the facts about Jesus, gleaned from the tradition by scientific historical analysis, for Christian faith and theology.

The so-called common-sense approach is probably represented best of all by the work of the late Professor T. W. Manson, who was both custodian of the most exacting critical study of the Bible, and theologian and preacher, with a passion to communicate the gospel in a language understood by the people.

The greatest problem of Christianity is not concerned with . . . ecclesiastical questions of orders or belief or ritual, but with the historical question of a person and a life. The supreme task of New Testament scholarship is to make Jesus Christ Crucified a living reality in the *thought* of our time, to bring out all that there is of fact and meaning in these three words: and the supreme task of Christian preaching is but little different. . . . [It is] to make Jesus Christ Crucified a living reality in the *lives* of men and women in these days, to renew in them the awe and wonder, the faith and courage, which He inspired in men and women who knew Him in the days of His flesh.[50]

I have quoted these words of Professor Manson's not only because of their intrinsic value, but because they give us a good guide to the three chief emphases in his scholarly approach to the New Testament: (1) The centrality of the historical question of a person and a life. With great single-mindedness Manson devoted himself over the years to Jesus-research. (2) The necessity to bring out everything of fact and meaning in the three words *Jesus Christ Crucified*. No historical scholar has been keener than Manson to try to explain the fact of Jesus' Crucifixion by reading the history of post-exilic Judaism up to that critical point so as to measure the tensions which made the Cross inevitable; yet no theologian has been more conscious that no description of the political situation in Palestine in the first century A.D. or of the reasons for the hostility of Jesus' enemies could possibly exhaust the unfathomable meaning or significance of Jesus' death.[51] (3) "Jesus Christ Crucified," the burden of the Church's message. Manson recognized quite clearly the failure of liberalism to interpret the Bible as the Word of God; the reduction of the gospel to a few noble truths about God and man, publicized by Jesus with special force, was for him a poor substitute for the Word of the God who demonstrates his love toward us in that while we were yet sinners Christ died for us.

Impressed by Eduard Meyer's monumental *Ursprung und Anfänge des Christentums,* Manson always felt that detailed study of the historical background of the whole New Testament period was an unavoidable means of setting the ministry of Jesus in its context, and so of understanding it better. Over against the philosophico-theological concentration in recent New Testament studies, we have fortunately begun to rediscover a healthy respect for this judgment. I have spoken earlier of the renewed interest in the last few years in studies in Gnosticism and of the fresh interrogation of the findings of R. Reitzenstein and the History of Religions school. I mention here only one further example. It is the studied view, more and more accepted by scholars now that the more heady froth of the early days of the Qumran discoveries has subsided, that Christianity more than likely took its rise from the side of an apocalyptic Judaism like that of the Qumran sect. In his recent researches, Ernst Käsemann has been arguing that the apocalyptic-eschatological framework of thought constitutes the groundwork of all New Testament theology.

Manson set greater store by the importance of knowledge of background and context as a means of illuminating the ministry of Jesus than by the possibility or desirability of a biography. It is worthwhile noticing that, unlike Vincent Taylor, he never attempted any chronological reconstruction of the life of Jesus. He thought that the Gospels do not furnish us with enough material for a complete narrative of the ministry. Even so, he remained an inveterate enemy of the historical negativism of extreme Form-criticism, and particularly of all

who took the way of Wrede in impugning the reliability of the Marcan
record as an outline of things as they actually occurred in the ministry
of Jesus. "The further we travel along the Wredestrasse, the more we
realise it is the road to nowhere." [52] Manson was very fearful that
"thoroughgoing historical scepticism" might lead to the dissolution of
the real humanity of Jesus into a pale and ghostly abstraction, a
"Heideggerian Jesus," and I think we can now see there was good
reason for his trepidation. His opposition to this highly dangerous
tendency took the form not of any critique of existentialist theology,
but of a concentrated assault on radical Form-criticism. He boggled
at the presumption whereby the Form-critic thought to find in the
Gospels no material for the actual history of Jesus, but an abundance
of material for what was no better than purely conjectural reconstruction of the social and psychological history of the primitive Church.
Manson's quarrel with Form-criticism was in fact that it transgressed
its own proper limits by passing too precipitately from judgments of
"form" in regard to the New Testament materials to judgments of
historicity, and that in its judgments of historicity it attributed too
little to the credibility of eyewitnesses of Jesus' ministry and too
much to the creative imagination of the primitive Christian community. Manson's complaint has been largely vindicated by the course
of recent scholarship. The tradition surely is not to be regarded as a
de novo creation of the community. But, just as surely, the memories
of Jesus enshrined in the tradition have been worked up or modified
in light of the Easter faith and the new Christological insight that
resulted from it, in light of the needs of the community in its over-all
situation. The ability of scholarship to detect modifications in the
tradition has for long pointed to the existence of an inner core or
nucleus of material which was subjected to this process of modification. So in the case of the parables of Jesus, J. Jeremias has shown
how, with a deftness of touch, it is possible to trace our way back
with a relative exactitude through the various "community overlays"
in the parabolic tradition from the *Sitz im Leben der alten Kirche* to
the *Sitz im Leben Jesu*. Moreover, the new interest in the historical
Jesus among Bultmann's pupils in the last decade has been nurtured
by the feeling that, although the Gospels are primarily Easter confessions of the Church's Easter faith, it is not only possible but necessary
for historical research to get back into the pre-Easter history of Jesus,
in order to determine the relation between the ideas of Jesus and the

ideas of the community which took shape subsequent to Easter. The mediating position to which the latter-day heirs of Form-criticism have come would perhaps have done much to allay the hostility of the late Professor Manson. Yet we must hasten to add that the aim or goal of the new Jesus-research is quite different from Manson's. The intention of the former is to illuminate the transition from the Jesus of history to the Christ of faith, from Jesus the Proclaimer to Christ the Proclaimed: it is not interested in testing the historical reliability of elements in the Gospel tradition in order to arrive at a consecutive factual account of the life of Jesus. By contrast Manson was devoutly concerned to uphold the view that the purpose of the Gospel tradition was to present the "story" of a life, and that the fundamental historicity of that "story" could be authenticated by a sympathetic and discerning criticism. The pattern of events in Jesus' ministry adopted by Manson, as well as by Vincent Taylor, follows substantially the earlier reconstruction of M. Goguel. Like Goguel, both Manson and Taylor accept the main outline of Mark; they also accept Goguel's hypothesis that the Fourth Gospel maintains a more reliable tradition in linking much of our Lord's public ministry with Jerusalem, and favor Goguel's construction, from the evidence of the Fourth Gospel, of the last few months of the life of Jesus.

What are we to say of the devotion of a scholar such as Manson to the notion of "chronology," of a continuous "story" presented by the Gospels? I think it would be much less than just to suggest that what confronts us here is an antiquarian interest in the recovery of bare facts about Jesus for their own sake. Rather is there an eager desire to do justice to the truth that the Gospels are not first and not only testimony to the life of the early Christian Church, but to none other than the man Jesus of Nazareth. And this truth we would always wish to cherish. Nevertheless, there is this to add. Radical Form-criticism no doubt all too hastily and blithely labeled the Gospel traditions "creations of the community," "inauthentic," "unhistorical." But in reaction, Manson went too far on the other side, I think, in stressing the factual historical concern of the Gospels. It is not easy to discredit the validity of the insight of Form-criticism that, since the disciples had seen Jesus as the risen one, their recollections of the earthly Jesus were tremendously influenced by these experiences. In consequence, there is inherent in the tradition an organic unity of history and kerygma: it bears witness to the history of Jesus as the history of one who is even now present with his Church and may be understood in faith: it does this precisely because it is a response to Jesus' whole person and mission. If we need not be unduly skeptical about the ability of criticism to reach behind the tradition to the pre-Easter situation and history of Jesus, neither need we be unduly reluctant to allow that it is from the perspective of Easter that the history of Jesus is viewed in the primitive Church's tradition.[53] We do not really gain the history of Jesus by siphoning off facts from the Gospel record. No more do we lose the history of Jesus by admitting that the Easter faith has played a large and regulative part in the Gospels' telling of it. We only change our priorities. Second place is given to the question: how best can the events in Jesus' life be assembled by criticism? And first place is given to the question: how have the Gospels understood the person and history of Jesus? Here I may allude briefly to Willi Marxsen's study of the Gospel of Mark from this angle. He regards Mark not as a life of Jesus nor as a record of facts about Jesus, but as a sermon (*Predigt*). In this sermon, the history of Jesus—in his call of disciples, his table-fellowship with sinners, his preaching and teaching, his encounters with Pharisees and High Priests—and the history of the believer become contemporary: the time of Jesus coalesces with the time of the Church. Mark's sermon is not a sermon about Jesus. He preaches Jesus. Jesus is the risen and proclaimed Christ, and, for the Church, to live by faith in him means nothing else than following her earthly Master who declared his message of the coming of God's kingdom and summoned disciples to come after him. In this way Marxsen attempts to do justice to the Gospel's intention to testify to the historical reality of the person of Jesus of Nazareth as an integral aspect of the Christ in whom we believe.[54] I do not believe that even the more conservative historical critics can afford to disregard this kind of approach.

In this whole matter of interpretation of the Gospel tradition, a very great deal depends on our presuppositions about the Resurrection. Conflicting views about the Resurrection lie at the heart of the sometimes bitter differences between Continental Form-critical attitudes to the Gospel tradition and normative Anglo-Saxon historical-critical perspectives. Continental theology since Barth and Bultmann has given to Easter an absolutely central place in its otherwise restless movement and struggling. In New Testament studies, among recent inheritors of the Form-critical approach, the Resurrection has been seen not just as an event at the close of Jesus' life, even a climactic event, but as the decisive event of God's unveiling of the secret of the whole "story" of Jesus the Christ, in his earthly as in his exalted form, so that, in every layer, the tradition of the Gospels has been able to be regarded as witness both to the reality of his history and the reality of his Resurrection. I am not sure whether it is in part due to a carry-over from liberalism, or in part due simply to the empirical and prag-matic streak in the British temperament, with its love of facts, but recent Anglo-Saxon New Testament scholarship has not generally been able to give more than a very qualified recognition of the cru-ciality of the Easter event either for theology or for the interpretation of the Gospel tradition. The obverse side of this reserve about Easter has been the urgency normally accorded to the search for the "facts" of Jesus' history. It is not insignificant that, as a study of his written works shows, Professor Manson had surprisingly little to say about the Easter event. He was in fact concerned mainly to uphold its factuality. "*How* it happened I cannot tell: *that* it happened I cannot doubt. The people who report it were honest folk, and they were as sure that Jesus was alive and with them as they were sure of their own exist-ence." [55] For the rest he regarded the Resurrection in a "historical" sense as the continuation, certainly in an enlarged and intensified form, of the earthly ministry of Jesus.[56] At this very point Man-son's whole critical position suddenly seems to become luminous: the truly vital thing for Christianity is the earthly ministry of Jesus, and the critic must consecrate himself (as Manson did) to mediating from the sources, to the best of his skill and ability, the "story" of that ministry. Perhaps the very absorption in the search for the "genuinely historical" elements in the story of Jesus' life and ministry all too often inhibited the question of what kind of reality we have in our possession when we have built up our reconstruction by Gospel criti-cism. What is the relation of the factual picture of Jesus to the Christ of the Church's faith? This is precisely the question which haunts theology today, and which the New Testament critic can by no means escape: what bearing or relevance for Christian faith or theology has historical knowledge that is gained from historico-scientific research?

I believe it is clear enough that the scholars, whose work we have considered in only a few of its aspects, eminently represent the so-called common-sense, middle-of-the-road position that has character-ized the main trend in recent British Biblical studies: guardianship of painstaking historical-critical method wedded to devout theological concern.[57] If in the end they have come down rather heavily on the side of historicism, I certainly do not think that any of them could be laid open to the charge of wishing to substitute their historical reconstructions for Christological thought. There is no question here of reverting, like E. Stauffer, to "real theology" or a "theology of facts." None of these men would deny that frank recognition of the humanity of the historical Jesus should be combined with the transcendent claims of a high doctrine of the exalted Christ. Where scholars like Dodd, Taylor, and Manson have done so much to enhance our understanding of the New Testament, it is perhaps improper, as we have said, to carp at what they have not done. Yet one feels that they have not always faced as openly as they might the constraints and challenges presented to the historical and critical standpoint by the Continental theologians' critique of historicism. Native British reaction against the "extremism," in Continental theology, of the swing away from the "Jesus of history" movement has not infrequently meant a premature dismissal of the issues raised by the other side.[58] It has not always been adequately acknowledged that neither Barth nor Bultmann, for all their "extremism," has ever wished to cut the cord that binds our religion to a historical episode. Bultmann, for instance, has been engrossed, in his theological pilgrimage, with the attempt to do full justice to the paradox of New Testament preaching, namely the paradox that God's eschatological vicegerent is a concrete historical man. When Bultmann affirms that "the revelation consists in nothing else than the fact of Jesus Christ," he is affirming, in his own particular way to be sure, the Church's ancient confession *vere Deus, vere Homo.* We may not like the form in which he has given theological expression to his affirmation. But it is not a bad thing for our assumptions to be shaken by one who has it to his credit that he has wrestled, in terms of the contemporary human situation, with the problem of what we mean when we speak of our religion as grounded in "historical revelation" and has especially sounded an alarm about the danger of faith's being supplanted by historical knowledge. The challenge to those who are engaged on historical and critical tasks is just this (and German Biblical scholarship has been responding to it): when we now ask about Jesus, we must deal as clear-sightedly as possible with the phenomenon of historical criticism in its extreme sharpness.

The Question of Historical Criticism and
Its Relation to Theology or Faith

Some idealists bemoan the day Constantine was converted to Christianity in 323, because overnight, by the stroke of a pen, Christianity became respectable, so that there was no longer the same call to the old heroism and gallantry of the times of persecution. That is no more foolish than for those who take refuge in ecclesiastical dogma to bewail the rise of the historical-critical movement because it has imperiled the authority of the Holy Scriptures. For although the Church had for centuries made good stint without any elaborate armory of critical apparatus, it was not as if the rise of the historical-critical movement, with its rediscovery of the human or historical Jesus, imported something alien and deleterious into the pure essence of Christianity. Through the Copernican revolution and the great new developments in the natural sciences at the close of the sixteenth century, the old principle of unexamined authority was challenged on every side. What joy of emancipation from the old bondage to unquestioned authority the new spirit of historical inquiry brought! The Bible itself, which had been enthroned by the Reformers as the supreme authority, had to pass through this twilight of the ancient gods of authority, and was opened up in a new way. In its vitality, the new quest for historical understanding found a particularly happy hunting ground in the Scriptures. The new day of historical-critical questioning of the Bible (the medieval Church had dealt extensively with textual criticism) was no black day of disaster. We should rather be thankful for it. The Bible, with its message, can bear to have the searchlight of truth focused upon it from every direction. It survived the overthrow of the Ptolemaic system, as later it survived the Darwinian theory of the origin of species. Nor need we be fearful, for the Bible's sake, of what might be discovered on other planets in this time when the regions of the moon are beckoning American and Russian astronauts.

But at all events, the growth of the historical-critical movement (and here I am thinking of the emergence in the last two centuries of precise scientific method in handling historical evidence, especially in relation to Jesus-research) sprang from within the bosom of Chris-

tianity itself. Christian theology, external cultural factors notwithstanding, gave a remarkable impetus to scientific historical investigation exactly because of its own persistent sense of the importance of
history, and of the significance for Christian faith of the concrete historical occurrence in which it was grounded.[59] It is difficult for us,
from the vantage point on which we stand, to sense again the thrill
experienced by the nineteenth century in its rediscovery of the historical Jesus. With considerable naïveté and eager haste it imagined
itself as breaking down the baffle walls between itself and the first
century, and as standing where Peter and James and John stood, at
the feet of Jesus. It rushed into its portraits of the human Jesus all too
swiftly, scarcely taking time to test its hypothetical reconstructions
against all the evidence. Its problem was the Christ of dogma, not the
historical Jesus. We need not be hypercritical. The nineteenth century
left us one irrecusable legacy: whatever else we may say about the
Christian message, its central figure was a man. And I do not think
there can be any gainsaying that this is as vital to the Christian faith
today as it was to the ancient Church in its travail of soul amid the
great Christological controversies, in its struggle against Docetism,
Apollinarianism, and Monophysitism.

In our own century, however, everything has changed. It is the historical Jesus who has become the supreme problem. This change of
situation was precipitated both by Christian theology and Biblical
criticism. The "theology of the Word" and the "theology of existence"
barred the door against any direct knowledge of the human Jesus,
acquired by scientific historical research, as an element in the faith.
The selfsame criticism, which in the nineteenth century understood
itself as opening the way to Jesus, swept on, with courage enough to
destroy its former judgments, to the eventual discovery that the
Reformation position was in substance correct, that the New Testament documents are kerygmatic in character, confessions of faith in
the risen Jesus Christ. Today, however, we can be grateful that neither
the rarefied atmosphere of the "theology of the Word" and of "existentialist theology," nor the impasse reached by criticism, have stifled
the breath of a continuing empirical concern to investigate and shed
light on the concrete historical character of the revelation in the man
Jesus of Nazareth. They have only altered the climate in which Jesus-
research has to be conducted. While for an interval the Church and
her scholars may relinquish the quest of the historical Jesus, they will

very soon be back at it. Not for long will the questions about Jesus of
Nazareth be quenched. For one thing, at the point of our religious experience, we want to know whether we are saved in history or only
morally or metaphysically. For another thing, unless we would be content with a *fides implicita,* we cannot refrain from asking how it is that
the kerygmatic confessions "Jesus is Lord" and "God was in Christ"
can be applied to a particular historical figure. It is not any spurious
"worldly" interest on our part that keeps these questions alive: it is
the Christian message itself, with its repeated assertions that Jesus is
not a mythical but a historical figure. Herein lies the sanction for the
pragmatic, middle-of-the-road position of Anglo-American Biblical
study, with its persistent harking back to the historical man Jesus of
Nazareth. And herein also is the ground for the recent recovery of
assurance among Bultmann's followers about the theological and
critical legitimacy of Jesus-research, about the need to ask whether the
claim laid on us by the Christ-kerygma tallies with the claim implicit
in Jesus' own existence.

What then are the prospects for research on the historical Jesus?
Can we know the historical Jesus? It would be highly advantageous
for all schools of criticism today if we could reach some sort of consensus about the following difficulties and limitations in Jesus-research: (a) All historical work is at the mercy of subjectivity: the historian cannot escape his own presuppositions. The critic's assessment
of a particular saying or incident in the Gospels is more than likely to
be dependent on his own "feeling" for the situation. So, for instance,
the Form-critic's feeling that the Gospel tradition is Christological
rather than "historical" in its concern has made it easy for him to regard Jesus' predictions of his Passion as *vaticinia ex eventu.* The conservative critic's feeling on the contrary for the historicity of the tradition has led him to the defense of the "authenticity" of the Passion
predictions often out of a prior assumption about their historical integrity. If it is not possible for the critic's presuppositions to be eradicated, it may be possible for him to try to avoid making his presuppositions a criterion for the evaluation of the Gospel materials. (b) We
must confess with resolute honesty that we have no documentary evidence from Jesus' contemporaries of such an objective character that
we could, on the basis of it, build up a "neutral" portrait of Jesus. We
have in fact no sure access to the history of Jesus save in the records
of the Evangelists who had themselves already responded in faith to

him as Christ and Lord. To fail to admit this is always to run the risk of committing the "liberal error" of dissociating his history from the Church's belief in him as exalted Lord. (c) It is necessary to keep in mind the restricted scope of historico-scientific Jesus-research. Although the revelation of God in Jesus Christ is historical, yet revelation in and by itself cannot be subjected to historical criticism or scientific analysis. We must therefore beware of stretching the capacities of historical research too far. It may tell us much about the ministry and person of Jesus, but it cannot in itself lay bare the significance of the career of Jesus as the revelatory and redemptive action of God. The crowning difficulty for historical criticism is that the Gospel account of Jesus does not stop with his death, but proclaims his Resurrection. And while the critic may elucidate for us the way in which a group of people came to believe in Easter at a given time in history, he cannot uncover for us a "risen Lord." Accordingly, we can hardly dare to think that our own historical reconstructions of Jesus' life can ever usurp the place of, or become a substitute for, the Gospels' witness to him.

We have to remember these reservations. Moreover, we have, I think, constantly to recognize today that nothing at all is to be won by minimizing the extreme complexity of critical Gospel research. The horizons have widened. Literary criticism of the Gospels, with its analysis of written sources, cannot now be considered an adequate gauge of the historicity of Gospel materials—the oral tradition existed alongside the written forms, and it is always conceivable that a secondary written source may have preserved a more ancient form of the tradition. Tradition study dictates that we examine minutely every smallest unit of the Gospel tradition, according to not only its "form" but also its content and language. In particular, we are assisted in this regard by increased knowledge of Jesus' mother tongue, Galilean Aramaic, and of the eschatological frame of reference of his message. Recent studies in *Redaktionsgeschichte* cannot be discounted. Their aim has been to show, by examination of the redactional alterations made by each Evangelist to the tradition as it has come to him, how his attitude to his own composition can be elucidated; and the net effect has been to place the greatest stress on the *theological* motivations for the topographical and chronological framework in which he has set his materials. At any rate, it is improbable that we can place anything like the same reliance upon the "historicity" of the Evangelist's collection and arrangement of his materials, as upon the "historicity" of separate items in the tradition. But what I wish to emphasize here is that, as regards our question whether we can get to know the real Jesus of history, no one mode of critical Gospel research can lead to the answer, but each has to join hands with others in a concerted effort to reach the goal.

At all events we can speak with a greater surety about the possibility of a synoptic view of the historical Jesus when we realize the agreement and concord steadily attained by modern scholarship regarding the tradition's accurate preservation of Jesus' *words*. I am not here referring to the "mechanical" view of the transmission of the tradition of Jesus' words involved in Harald Riesenfeld's bold conjecture that Jesus himself paved the way for the recital of the Gospel tradition in the period between his death and the Parousia, by putting forth his teaching in a form that could be easily memorized by his disciples and recounted by them as holy Word.[60] That view seems to me to be controverted by the following facts: first, it was altogether the Easter faith in Jesus Christ that led to the preservation of the tradition of his words; second, the importance to the Church of the continuing nearness of its risen Lord kept it from treating the tradition of his words and deeds as if he were simply another Moses; and third, the passing on of what Jesus himself taught played only a secondary part in the message of primitive Christianity. Even in dealing with the words of Jesus, therefore, we are not freed from the constraint of admitting that the community of faith has not passed them on as sacrosanct and untouchable entities, but has in many ways and places given them a richer Christological coloring, albeit without necessarily falsifying their original intent.

Although we have to make allowance for the part played by the congregation in retouching the words of Jesus, it is none the less in regard to the establishment of basic criteria for determining the probably authentic sayings, and to the conviction that through these sayings we are permitted to draw close to the historical Jesus in his most characteristic features, that scholarship has steadily moved toward a consensus. There is, in fact, a presumption in favor of words of Jesus or reports concerning him that occur in diverse "forms" in the tradition, and that were therefore included in the tradition in the first instance to meet quite different needs of the community. Where such sayings and reports run across various layers of the tradition, it is likely that we are in touch with details regarding the historical Jesus that were incorporated in the tradition, not to fulfill any special requirement of the Church's *Sitz im Leben,* but simply because they were a known part of his "story." Some time ago C. H. Dodd applied this "cross section" method of investigation to nine separate passages from the Gospels, no two of which possessed the same "form" or had the same function to perform in the tradition. Yet all of them alike attested the same trait of Jesus, his love toward the outcasts of society.[61] By the same means, other traits of Jesus can be brought out: his eschatological preaching of the rule of God, his attitude toward the Law. In a recent examination of the formal structure of Jesus' message as a clue to the meaning of his existence, Dr. James Robinson has adopted a similar principle: "Particularly to the point is the fact that this structure, as can be shown, is not confined to *one* stream of tradition but occurs in the different streams of tradition in which the same logion is transmitted." [62] So may we, where this kind of convergence occurs, be gathered around the historical Jesus. And possibly most of all are we brought into touch with his person, as Käsemann suggested in his lecture inaugurating the "new quest," in those sayings in which provenance from the world of Judaism or from early Christological ideas is least apparent.

Yet Jesus' words are not all of his history. Historical research on the Gospels must look at his words in connection with his person and his deed, and will therefore inevitably turn its attention first of all to the event of his death, which is pivotal for the whole Gospel tradition.[63] It is, of course, impossible for the historian to demonstrate the truth of what the Gospels proclaim about that death, that it is for us men and for our salvation. But by recognizing how, as the tradition presents it, Jesus' whole way is determined by his triumphant negation of the world and the world's standards, culminating in a real death on the Cross, the historian can obviate erroneous understandings of the words and ministry of the historical Jesus. So long as he keeps in sight the centrality of the death of Jesus, he is not likely to fall into reductionist interpretations of his ministry, as though it were the ministry simply of a good teacher, whose execution at the hands of High Priests and Romans would, historically speaking, be an inexplicable enigma. In this regard, one might recall how misleading historically is Ernest Renan's idyllic portrait of the springtime of the Galilean ministry, and how "critically" sound on the contrary is Holman Hunt's portrait of Jesus, standing before his father's carpenter's shop, with his outspread arms casting the shadow of a cross on the wall behind.

Since the death of Jesus is presented in the New Testament not only as a divine destiny, but as a truly human death, there is much substance in the contention that a reading of the history of post-exilic Judaism forward to the critical point can clarify the total situation in which the tensions that prevailed made the Cross inevitable. On the broader scale, the enrichment of our knowledge of the historical context in which Jesus lived and died, from the increasing stock of remains of the Palestinian Judaism of his day, also means a certain enhancement of our historical knowledge about Jesus. It is not that the Qumran Scrolls have cast a direct light upon the historical Jesus: in fact, Jesus himself in his person and ministry constitutes the irreducible difference between the Qumran sect and the primitive Christian movement. What is given to us through the Qumran discoveries is the fairly extensive knowledge of an Essenic type of Judaism which, in its baptismal rites associated with repentance, in its sacred meal, and most notably in its apocalyptic mode of thought and discourse, almost certainly formed the background of primitive Christianity. There is no reason to doubt that any extension of our knowledge of primitive Christianity or of Judaism should help to illumine our understanding of the history of Jesus.[64] All in all, the signs are that we do not have to surrender to the pessimism of those who have abandoned all hope of coming into touch with the historical Jesus behind the tradition.

But it is just at this point that we are confronted with our most acute problem, one which has too seldom been considered by orthodox historical scholars in their discussions of the historical life of Jesus. What is the significance and relevance for faith or theology of the nucleus of historical knowledge obtained by historico-scientific Gospel research? Let us suppose that by dint of patient historical labors we have attained an ever so critically accurate and acceptable picture of Jesus' life and ministry. How then does this historical kernel stand in relation to the New Testament's faith-witness to Jesus Christ? Unless we would be content with our skeleton historical sketch as the bare bones of a "theology of facts," we cannot avoid this question. One customary answer of late has been that, to be sure, faith cannot be made dependent on the vagaries or uncertainties of historical research. And I think there is a sense in which we must simply

accept that. As we have said before, no description of the events leading up to Jesus' death, however historically reliable, could disclose for
us the redemptive efficacy of that death. Even less could the historian
give us any certainty of a risen Lord. In any case, Christian faith,
while not unconnected with historical knowledge, is not born of historical knowledge, for if it were, it would have become "seeing," and
so would cease to be "faith." Faith is given to us as we respond to
God's outgoing grace in Jesus Christ. Whereas, however, faith may
not be made dependent on historical research, it would be a sad day
for the Church if she became so disinterested in the person and history
of Jesus, that she declared herself independent of Jesus-research and
banned her historical scholars. For, as we have suggested already, the
justification of historical research on the life of Jesus is given in the
Christian message, with its constant references to the historical man
Jesus of Nazareth. Jesus-research, whenever and wherever it is carried on, gives conscientious recognition to the historical reality of the
revelation and to the "worldly" factors involved in the mediation of
grace. Nor is this research to be condemned because its path is strewn
with the wreckage of abandoned theories. We would not think of con-
demning medical science because it gave up the practices of cauteriza-
tion and leeching for more refined forms of treatment. The price
which history has had to pay for becoming a science is, as Troeltsch
reminded us, that its work is never done, that even its most assured
results are always liable to be overthrown by new discoveries.

But even when we accept the legitimacy of the task of trying to
recover the historical Jesus by critical Gospel study, we still have on
our hands the weighty problem of what kind of reality we want to
touch by historico-scientific research. Is it a merely factual picture of
the Jesus of history we seek? And if so, what theological bearing may
such a picture of the "facts" have? Or do we concede that what is
given to us is only an interpreted history of Jesus, so that our endeavor must be to try to see Jesus in the setting of the whole Christian
"story," with both its historical and its transcendental elements? Is it
the aim of our research then to ascertain whether the Church's faith
in Jesus Christ has any support in the historical Jesus, in the way he
has understood himself? This last question is of the utmost historical
and theological significance, for if ever it were shown that there is an
unbridgeable gulf between the historical Jesus himself and the
Church's interpretation of and faith in him, then Christian faith would

lose its historical grounding. Let us, in concluding this chapter, take these questions as a means of bringing into focus the contrast in orientation between older modes of Jesus-research and the phase of Jesus-research instituted recently by scholars of the Bultmannian fold. The orthodox critic's aim has usually been to achieve as objective a portrait of the history of Jesus as possible by *distinguishing* between him and his Church or the Church's faith in him. We talked above of how our understanding of the history of Jesus could be enriched by our knowledge of the Palestinian Judaism in which he lived. But the historical scholar has not always clearly enough recognized that the more Jesus and his history have been "explained," for the sake of an objective portrait, in terms of the Judaism out of which he has come, the more has his creative originality tended to be lost to view, and the more has the gap been widened between the historical Jesus and the Church's faith and message. The exponents of the "new quest" have sought to redress the one-sidedness of this position in which historical criticism has often found itself, as it used the critical sieve to separate the Jesus of history from the Church. The stress among the "new seekers" has been instead on the question of the connection or unity between Jesus and the Church or between Jesus and the Church's kerygma.

It has seemed appropriate to include here some brief comment on the "new quest," since no account of the problem of the bearing of historical research on faith would have been complete without it. We must, however, defer fuller discussion till later. Meanwhile, in our next chapter we shall investigate some independent attempts at a solution to the question concerning the relation between the historical Jesus and the Church's faith and message.

III

Toward a Solution of the Jesus of History— Christ of Faith Problem

It may be useful at the beginning of this chapter to look back for a moment at the road we have traversed. In each of the foregoing chapters we were moving in two different worlds of thought. In the first we discussed kerygma theology's renunciation of the question of the historical Jesus and of the Christology implicit in his person and teaching. The only historical event of any consequence for the existentialist interpretation of the New Testament is, as we saw, Jesus' death on the Cross, and even this only as it is preached and responded to in the obedience of faith. Now the de-historicizing kerygma theology may certainly have been justified as an opposition to the old quest of the historical Jesus, with its readiness to believe that Christian faith may be supported by historical proof. It is, in fact, in keeping neither with the New Testament nor with the nature of faith itself that objective scientific evidences should decide belief or unbelief. By seeking a false security in worldly signs or demonstrations, faith destroys itself and passes over to the domain of the law. In reply to Simon Peter's testimony, our Lord said: "Blessed are you, Simon Bar-Jona! For flesh and blood has not revealed this to you, but my Father who is in heaven" (Matt. 16:17). All the same, we discerned in the kerygma theology's tendency to raise the kerygma to the level of a nonhistorical absolute a distinct trend toward a Docetic Christology, which could only be checked by rehabilitation of the retrospective historical question about Jesus.

In the second chapter we transferred our attention chiefly to the

104

rather strictly historical position that has been characteristic of Anglo-American Biblical scholarship. In this milieu the typically pragmatic or empirical concern with the concrete historical nature of God's self-revelation in Jesus Christ has meant, for the most part, an unabated zeal in the pursuit of Jesus-research. We do not have to apologize for our interest in the historical Jesus. The abiding justification of critical Gospel research on Jesus is the character of the Christian message itself. Its exalted Christological titles and dignities are applied to a man. In the summons to faith this message brings to us there is laid upon us the irresistible constraint to ask about this man, Jesus of Nazareth. By repeated asking, critical research on Jesus has served to protect the historical reality of the "Word made flesh" from being dissolved into the abstract mysticism of a Christ-idea. There is nothing illegitimate in the attempt to gain a clear picture of the historical Jesus: only, in making the attempt, historico-scientific criticism comes up against a grave problem which has not always been faced frankly enough: What bearing have our historical research and ensuing reconstructions on theology or faith? Bultmann has wished theology to suppress the question of the historical Jesus; for him objectifying knowledge of the historical Jesus constitutes a destructive threat to genuine faith as acceptance of our radical insecurity before God. Ironically enough, Bultmann's standpoint has had the effect of forcing the problem of the historical Jesus upon New Testament scholarship with a fresh urgency. His own pupils have given a central place to investigation of the relation between the historical Jesus and the Church's message of the Christ.

Discussion of the "history and kerygma" problem has not of course been confined to the Bultmannian group. Numerous independent attempts at a solution have in fact been made by scholars of different countries and traditions. Some of the more important of these—we have to be selective—will be considered in this chapter.

Event-Interpretation

Efforts have been made to decide the question of the relation between Jesus and the Church on purely historical grounds. An undue prominence has indeed been given to the "chronological" problem of when the Church began. Criticism's various answers to the problem are

quite well known: it began with Jesus' call to his disciples, with
Peter's confession at Caesarea Philippi, with the Lord's Supper, with
the Resurrection.[1] One remembers Theo Preiss's apt comment that it
is a work of Sisyphus to try to establish the exact chronological point
at which the Church began: the Church came into being through
men's believing response to God's self-disclosure in the whole message and mission of Jesus Christ, crucified, dead, buried, risen again,
and ascended into heaven. If we hold, as I think we are right to do,
that the Church only clearly appeared out of the culmination of Jesus'
ministry in the Resurrection, we take it not as a calendar date but as
the regulative factor governing the Church's emergence in history.

In a broader vein, recurrent attempts have been made to show that
Jesus intended the Church as the goal of his work, that the Church
and all aspects of its life—its worship and sacraments and so on—are
rooted in the earthly ministry of Jesus.[2] But the argument that Jesus is
one with the Church and the Church one with Jesus, in the sense that
it is everywhere present in all phases of his ministry, is confronted
with a grievous stumbling-block. Refusing to yield to any excessive
skepticism, we may hold that, in order to account for the formation of
the Church and the growth of its Christology and Ecclesiology, we are
simply constrained to accept certain words and deeds of Jesus as historical, and that the critic must in any case beware of making *a priori*
assumptions about what Jesus could or could not have said and done.
Nevertheless, we are faced with a particularly sharp problem precisely at those points where there seems to be the greatest agreement
between the Jesus of the Gospels and the primitive Church, for just
there it is most difficult to be certain whether we have words of Jesus
or words adapted and worked up by the later congregation. A classic
example is the epochal text of Matthew 16:17–19, Jesus' commissioning of Peter and his granting him the "power of the keys." The uncertainty about the authenticity of sayings like this makes it hardly possible to use them as a basis for demonstrating the correlation between
Jesus and the Church. In point of fact there is a very real danger in
trying to find the clue to the intention and meaning of Jesus' person
in those words recorded of him in the Gospels which sound most like
the voice of the primitive congregation. The danger lies in the possibility of so overstressing the unity of Jesus and his Church that the
previousness of the concrete way of the man Jesus of Nazareth is
obscured and his history becomes absorbed in the Church's history.

In Bultmann's form of kerygma theology, the past way of the earthly Jesus is lost in the punctiliar here and now of the kerygma; there is another form of kerygma theology, an "ecclesiastical" form, in which Jesus tends to be lost in the Christian community.

The preceding comments may serve as introduction to a short investigation of the work of the noted American New Testament scholar, Professor John Knox, of Union Seminary, New York. Knox's theology may be justly described as kerygmatic. His emphasis is on the preached Christ. What we may know of the Christ is not dependent on any historically mediated knowledge of Jesus. The "words of Christ" are more important than what might be established by criticism as the *verba ipsissima* of the earthly Jesus. The meaning of Christ is not determined by what was present in the self-consciousness of Jesus.[3] All of this is clearly reminiscent of Barth and Brunner and Bultmann; it comes particularly close to the following statement by Brunner: "In faith we are not concerned with the Jesus of history as historical science sees him, but with the Jesus Christ of personal testimony who is the real Christ."[4] But Knox's theology is also "ecclesiastical." It is informed by a very profound sense of the Christian community, and in this regard is antithetical to Bultmann's stark individualism. Knox has been that *rara avis* among American Biblical scholars, a critic who has introduced into his interpretation of the New Testament certain philosophical concepts and presuppositions, in this case the social-process philosophy of such contemporary philosophers and theologians as C. C. Morrison and H. R. Niebuhr.[5] The significance of Knox's contribution to the problem of the historical Jesus and the beginnings of Christianity lies in his definition of the Christ-event as a triadic complex in which Jesus Christ, Church, and New Testament are most intimately interrelated in an indissoluble unity. But, within the intricate structure of the event, the chief cornerstone is the Church itself. Within its life alone does the event take place and not primarily on the stage of Jewish or Roman history.[6] The refrain that runs through all of Knox's work is quite simply that, since the Christ-event had no significant social effects whatever beyond the pale of the primitive Christian community, the Church's understanding of it constituted an integral part of the event itself and entered creatively into the development of it. The event in fact, as Knox understands it, had not fully occurred until the initial process of the Church's first realization of its meaning was complete. So the Christ who is known

of the Church, the Church which apprehends the meaning of the
Christ, and the Scriptures which grow out of the inner life of the
Church and herald "that which happened" as interpreted by it—all
three form an organic whole.

As it relates to our problem of kerygma and history, Knox's stress
on the community aspect of the Christ-event is as positively suggestive on the constructive side as it is fraught with danger on the other.
We must first try to bring into perspective what appear to be the
positive elements.

We have referred on several occasions to the fact that the historian
has access only to an interpreted history of Jesus in the Gospels. This
truth was being widely recognized around the turn of the century.
Kähler denied the possibility of getting back behind the Gospel tradition to the not-yet-interpreted naked facts about Jesus on which the
traditional distinction between the historical Jesus and the kerygmatic
Christ was founded. In his well-known book on *The Death of Christ*
(1902), James Denney observed that the death of Christ *uninterpreted*
is really equivalent to nonsignificant. "The death of Christ was never
presented to the world merely as a spectacle. It was never presented
by any apostle or evangelist apart from an interpretation." [7] In recent
years criticism has increasingly acknowledged the impossibility of
recovering the bare "facts" of Jesus' history from the Gospel records.
The Gospels are simultaneously kerygmatic and historical. I do not
suppose many will have been led up the garden path again by Stauffer's recent plea, totally unconvincing, that historical research can
reach the "facts" of the incarnate Word. To reach toward a detached
scientific picture of Jesus' history is to chase a mirage, for a neutral
picture of Jesus would not be real history at all. The New Testament
nowhere represents a neutral, nonbeliever's picture of Jesus, but is
everywhere written from the standpoint of belief in Christ.

To this truth, emphasized by us before now, Professor Knox has
given his own forceful expression. Knowledge of Jesus Christ, as he
thinks, is independent of the "facts" established by historical criticism.
It is attainable only from within the fold of the Christian community
which has remembered him in a quite particular way. The guarantee
of the historical reality of Jesus is the life of the community which has
experienced that reality and which itself forms an integral part of the
totality of the event of Jesus Christ. The Jesus who is folded up within
the Church's memory as the central element in the event can neither

be removed nor even damaged by historical criticism. Since fact and meaning, event and interpretation are seen as an inseparable unity, Knox is able to deny any discontinuity between Jesus and the preached Christ and Lord of the Church: they are always *one*. Accordingly he has found it possible, more than most Anglo-American Biblical critics, to give the fullest place to the cruciality of the Resurrection. By the Resurrection the significance of Jesus' whole life is disclosed to his band of disciples: it is a part of the "concrete empirical meaning of Jesus." [8] Since what happened to Jesus and its meaning for the community are for Knox indissolubly united, it follows that, if after the Resurrection apostles and disciples gathered their memories of Jesus together and worked them up in the light of their new, may we say Christological, insight, they were not in so doing distorting his history but only revealing it in the fullness in which they had now experienced it. So far we can agree substantially with Knox's position. The Resurrection does have a historical connection with Jesus of Nazareth, as we shall argue in a later chapter, and it is the cord which binds the whole story of Jesus together in the minds of his disciples.

We agree also that no mere historical argument, no skill of the critic can authenticate the Christian "story" to us as record of the final saving act of God by which he reconciles the world to himself. How then can we be sure of the truth of what God has done "through Christ"? The answer given by Knox seems to be the only valid one: by way of the community of the "catholic and apostolic Church" in which the decisive event of God's act of reconciliation in Jesus Christ is perpetuated, not merely as something remembered, but as a living and creative reality, which is nothing other than the living and creative presence in our hearts of the Holy Spirit, testifying to us of the truth of the "story."

So far we are in agreement with Knox's standpoint. But beyond this we have grave reservations about the way the spotlight is concentrated almost entirely upon the community and its experience of the Christ. One can hardly read Knox's works without the feeling that, within the complex whole of the Christ-event, the history of Jesus is submerged in the Church's history to such an extent that the Church's faith seems to have become faith in its own understanding and interpretation of the meaning of Jesus' history rather than faith in Jesus Christ himself. The history of Jesus Christ is all but lost in the continuing presence of the Spirit within the community. The danger in Knox's formulation is, in fact, the danger of the dissolution of Jesus Christ in the Church, in its message and doctrine. The end of the road on which Knox is traveling is reached in the position represented in Father Jean Daniélou's study *Christ and Us*.[9] Here the Christ of the Church (the Christ-Spirit experienced by the community in Knox's presentation) is the link between the Jesus of history and the Christ of faith. But so pre-eminent a place is given to the Christ of the Church that it could reasonably be claimed that Christology has become ecclesiology. The ecclesiastical and ritual institutions of the Christian tradition are so overemphasized that an institutionalized figure of the Christ, a Christ-institution, has become a substitute for the history of Jesus Christ.

Knox has, to be sure, tried to save himself from this fate of shifting the locus of revelation from Jesus Christ to the Church by upholding the "otherness" of the Church's Spirit behind and beyond its interpretation. In other words, he is ready to discover the ultimate norm of Christianity not in the community but in the "event," whose integrity and authority must at all costs be preserved.[10] Whether he has succeeded is, however, very questionable. When the Christ-event has already been defined as an organic unity of fact and meaning, of the Jesus of history and the Church's experience and interpretation of him, it is not easy to see how we can then go on and separate the history of Jesus from the Church as an inner core or nucleus, which can now be described as the normative "event" that is regulative for the community's life.[11] There is a contradiction here. And in fact, when we look at Knox's approach to the subject of the words of Jesus, it becomes evident that he has not really overcome the tendency in his hermeneutical stance to lose the independent reality of the historical Jesus Christ. He has solved the vexatious problem of the "authenticity" of the words of Jesus by getting rid of it. It is quite inappropriate, we are told, to be anxious about whether we have the words spoken by the historical Jesus or not. Only the "words of Christ" are important. "The words of Christ are the words which truly and at first hand set forth the meaning of the event, which is Christ, and therefore the meaning of the Church's true life." [12] Under this treatment we are left with no basis whatever for comparing Jesus' own person or his own understanding of his person with the Church's interpretation and proclamation. Everything has been vested in the Church and the Church's experience of the Christ-Spirit within it. Any role that historical criticism might take in distinguishing Jesus from his Church has been effectively played down. So long as we are possessed of the "words of Christ," we have enough. But do we? How is one to recognize the "words of Christ"? What is the "event" whose true "meaning" they are supposed to set forth? By what right has the Christian community read back onto the life of a particular historical man the "words of Christ"? To allow the question of what Jesus himself may have said to pale into insignificance over against the notion of the Church as the Spirit-inspired purveyor of the only true "words of Christ" is surely to come very close to allowing the history of Jesus to be swallowed up in the tradition and the Church. In short, it seems to me that Knox's stress on the primacy of the "words of Christ" must only lead us either to an uninhibited Protestant "subjectivism," which pays little regard to historical exegesis, or to the authoritarian "objectivism" of a Catholic ecclesiastical hermeneutic.

If it is true that the risen and living Christ continues to speak to his Church in and through the Spirit, it is equally true, in a full Christian sense, that no man can hear these "words of Christ" and call him "Lord" in the Spirit without being thrown back upon the days of his flesh, when he spoke human words from human lips in Galilee or Judea. To deny this is really to deny the independence of Jesus over against the Church in much the same way as Bultmann appears to have denied it over against a nonhistorical Christ-kerygma.

Our objection to Professor Knox's inability to hold on to the independent reality of the historical Jesus Christ does not necessarily mean that we would wish to reinstate the aim of the old quest to isolate the historical Jesus from the Church's message and doctrine. Rather are we fearful of any formulation of the unity or continuity between Jesus and the Church that would fail to maintain this other great truth of the New Testament: the Lord whom it confesses is one whose work was *finished* at a specific time and place. It had to be finished before the Church began; the Lord of the Church is one whose way to the Cross had to be completed before the good tidings of the gospel were preached. In his suppression of the question about the historical words of Jesus, Knox has made it largely impossible (and here he stands in the company of Bultmann and, to some extent, of Barth also) to preserve the sovereign freedom of Jesus Christ over against the Church.[13]

When the historian exercises his prerogative of examining the words

of Jesus in the context of his life and work within Judaism as himself
a Jew, "sprung from the seed of David according to the flesh," he is
able to discern how Jesus challenges the presuppositions of the community of his own people gathered under the banner of the letter of
the Mosaic Law. Bound up in solidarity with his own people, in his
word and in his work he none the less offers a radical opposition to
the way in which the whole life of this people is enmeshed in a net-
work of sacred traditions. Every pious believer among them who is
trusting, for future restoration, in the glorious past of the people of
God, every loyal follower of the Law who is laying claim to eternal
salvation because he is convinced he has fulfilled its codified demands
in worship and in life—all these are exposed to Jesus' scathing in-
dictment. The last become first and the first last (Matt. 20:16). The
tax collector hated by every Jew as the most notorious quisling is justified, while the Pharisee goes away empty-handed (Luke 18:9–14).
The old Jewish orthodoxy which held out to those afflicted by suffering and calamity, so long as they repented and wrought good works,
the promise of a just divine redress of ancient wrongs either here or
hereafter—this, too, is shattered by Jesus. For Jesus abolishes every
vestige of *quid pro quo* moralism. The reward he envisages is never a
matter of payment for services rendered, but only the nearness of
God himself to his faithful servants (e.g. Matt. 5:12; 25:14 ff.).[14]

The Son of Man is Lord also of the sabbath (Mark 2:28). Jesus
stands in lordly judgment over against all manifestations of pride
among the Jewish community of his day with regard to long-standing
institutions and traditional standards or prescriptions. He is the enemy
of all shallow religiosity. He emphatically denies the late Jewish dream
of establishing a divine community on earth, that dream which,
through the literature of the Qumran sect, is more familiar to us now
than before.

What we have been coming to is this: so to forfeit the priority of
the historical Jesus Christ that he becomes merged with the Christian
community is to lose this fact, harsh and disturbing as it is, that as
King and Head of the Church, Jesus Christ is also its Judge—Judge
of every surrender it makes to institutional arrogance or to the secu-
larized order of things. Against this peril our surest safeguard is the
continual remembrance that the Christ of the Church is no other than
this man Jesus of Nazareth, who set himself unshakeably at variance,
although assuredly with compassion and with a broken heart, to the

normal patterns and structures of the community life of his people. It may be well for us now to sum up in a few words our evaluation of Knox's "community" definition of the Christ-event. For him, just as the reality of light includes the experience of seeing it, so the reality of the Christ-event includes as an essential part of itself the responses it evoked in human minds and hearts. The Church's experience and understanding of the meaning of the event of Jesus Christ belong to the event. Now this is a valuable emphasis in so far as it exposes the fallacy inherent in the positivistic historian's search for the bare, uninterpreted facts about Jesus in order to differentiate between the historical Jesus and the preached Christ. If, however, we swing too far in the direction of focusing on the meaning of Jesus' "story" as the Church apprehended and interpreted it, we run the risk of ultimately replacing the "story" itself by some principle or truth or law of the community's life. So in Knox's case the Spirit-ruled and Spirit-guided community tends to usurp the place of the historical Jesus Christ. The "words of Christ," by which Knox means presumably the Gospel tradition of Jesus' teaching formulated and transmitted by the Spirit-led Church, are given precedence over the "words of Jesus." Accordingly, the place where revelation is located has become the Church's tradition, setting forth the meaning of Jesus' history, rather than the act and word of Jesus himself.[15] On such premises as these there would of necessity be an immediate foreclosure of the recent phase of critical research on Jesus that has arisen in Germany in the last decade, for its whole operation hangs on the possibility of differentiating between the historical Jesus in his word or deed and the Church or the Church's message, in order to compare them.

At the level of the Church's life, there is the ever present danger that, wherever the Church should fail to attribute any independent reality to the historical Jesus Christ, it would make itself, as institution, the supreme judge and arbiter of its own existence and destiny. It befits us to be mindful that the Church's Lord is the same one who, in the days of his flesh, stood over against the religious institution, cleansing the Temple and overthrowing the tables of the money-changers.

At the other pole from Knox's stress on the role of the community in his definition of the Christ-event is the inescapable priority accorded to the historical Jesus in another study of a year or two ago. In a remarkably lucid paper on the current debate concerning the problem of the historical Jesus, Joachim Jeremias took Bultmann to task for refusing to go behind the kerygma of the primitive Christian community.[16] In fact, Jeremias has so uncompromisingly stated the prior importance of the ministry and message of Jesus, and has so vehemently claimed that the origin of Christianity is not the kerygma, not the Resurrection experience of the disciples, not the Christ-idea, but the historical appearance of the man, Jesus of Nazareth, that in the end, as we shall see, he has hardly done justice to the kerygma.

Call and Congregational Response

We affirmed in the previous chapter that both the Gospels and the apostolic kerygma demand of us that we should continually return to the historical Jesus and his message. Only by avoiding the offense of the Incarnation can we dispense with the need to know who Jesus was. This is the starting point for Jeremias, as it has been the starting point for the new era of Jesus-research instituted by Bultmann's pupils.

While admitting that the dream of the possibility of writing a life of Jesus is over, Jeremias rightly contends that we can never be absolved from following along the way of the historical Jesus. The difficulty is how to avoid landing once again, like the nineteenth century, in modernizing accounts of Jesus by projecting our own theological predilections back into his life and ministry. But we need not fall heir to the old temptation to modernize Jesus, according to Jeremias, since we are so much better equipped to know him as he really was. Literary criticism has taught us to go back to the stage of oral tradition preceding the Gospels and also to discriminate between the tradition and redaction. Form-criticism has thrown light from another side on the creation and growth of the tradition. Our increased acquaintance with Jesus' Palestinian Jewish environment helps us to look at him in relation to his place and time. It is most important to notice what has happened in this regard. Whereas earlier study devoted itself to demonstrating Jesus' continuity with Judaism and so, wittingly or unwittingly, erected a fence between the historical Jesus and the Church, we have come now to appreciate much more clearly the acuteness of Jesus' opposition to the Jewish religiosity of his day. The disparity between Jesus and Judaism has been made even clearer by our greater familiarity with his mother-tongue, Galilean Aramaic.

Such words as *Amen* have been taken over by the Gospels without being translated from Aramaic into Greek. Originally, it is the response made by the congregation to a prayer uttered in their presence to denote their participation in the prayer. But now it stands at the head of Jesus' commands and prophecies as an asseveration, setting the stamp of the most immediate authority upon the words which follow. There is no equivalent to this in the literature of the rabbis. Even more significant is the word *Abba,* Father, which again, as a form of address to God, has no parallel in late Jewish devotional literature. Above all, since Albrecht Ritschl we have learned that Jesus' message is centered upon the concept "kingdom of God," and since Albert Schweitzer and Johannes Weiss that "kingdom of God" in Jesus' teaching must be interpreted eschatologically.

Jeremias has no hesitation in thinking that, if we take careful account of these various advances in critical research and knowledge, we shall not only be guarded from modernizing Jesus but shall indeed be confronted by a unique claim to authority that transcends the bounds of the Old Testament and Judaism: his unparalleled message of God's love toward sinners, his own table-fellowship with publicans and sinners, the directness with which he dares to address God as *Abba.* "If, with the utmost zeal and conscientiousness, using the critical resources at our disposal, we occupy ourselves with the historical Jesus, the result is always the same, we find ourselves in the presence of God Himself." [17] So writes Jeremias. And in view of our earlier discussion regarding the bearing of historical criticism on Christian theology, we are forced to ask whether he is not assigning to historical research, study, and criticism a weight of relevance for faith that it can hardly bear. In the modern kerygma theology there is at least this much of merit: it has hammered home to us the truth that Christian faith is not based upon historically mediated knowledge but arises through encounter with the preached Jesus Christ. Its protest against seeking a false, objective, worldly security for faith is not the product of extreme historical skepticism, but comes from a genuine understanding of what Christian faith is and from rediscovering the Pauline refusal to see Christ "after the flesh." We question, however, the right of kerygma theology to put up any sign reading, "Absolutely no entry to the historical Jesus." For not every approach of the historian to the Jesus of the Gospels is necessarily a search for an illusory security based on objectively verifiable, earthly "facts" about Jesus. If, indeed, the historian himself comes to the Gospels with the sympathy and insight of faith, far from being encouraged to cling to the world, he is called away from the world to the God who is close and near and real in every word and deed of Jesus. I cannot think, therefore, that Jeremias is wrong in telling us that faith is not taken away from us when exegesis shows us the claim to unique authority in every word and deed of Jesus. Not that this answers the problem of the relation between historical research and Christian faith. We must rather honestly confess that we seem to have been saying two different things: first, historical knowledge cannot provide a groundwork for faith; second, knowledge of the historical Jesus is not irrelevant to faith, for when God calls to faith *Jesus speaks,* and when Jesus speaks, God's call to faith confronts us. I do not imagine that the Church can ever really resolve the tension between concern with and knowledge of the historical Jesus on the one hand and the faith that is brought to life through the preaching of Christ on the other. Not without getting rid of the paradox of the Incarnation! Only by evading the offense of the Incarnation could the Church eradicate the old anguish experienced by faith, so often spoken about since the time of Lessing, the tension between the certainty of faith and the relativity of historical knowledge. I do not believe the Church need deplore this anguish and tension. It signifies the sharpness of the challenge presented to us by the mystery of Jesus Christ. Rather ought the Church to fear dictatorial scholarly solutions anent Jesus the Christ that pretend to finality and would prematurely end the Church's impatience and curiosity before the "secret" of the God-Man. Accordingly, if the objection should be made that it seems pitiable that faith should be sacrificed to a dubious and hypothetical historical research, perhaps the most fitting answer is that given by Jeremias: "God has sacrificed Himself. The Incarnation is the self-sacrifice of God, and to that we can only bow in assent." [18]

At the close of the essay we have been discussing, Jeremias raises the question of the relation between the good news of Jesus and the early Church's proclamation of faith. The reply he makes to it is of considerable interest. The message of Jesus and the Church's preaching of Christ cannot be isolated from each other. But neither do they belong on entirely the same footing. For Jesus and his message are "call," whereas the kerygma is but the congregational "response": the "call" rather than the "response" is the decisive thing. "The life, acts, and death of Jesus, the authoritative word of him who dared to say *Abba,* the one who with Divine authority invited sinners to His Table, and as the Servant of God went to the Cross, is the call of God. The Early Church's proclamation of faith, the Spirit-led chorus of a thousand tongues, is the answer to God's call." [19] I suggest that what has happened in Jeremias' presentation is this: he has located God's self-revelation completely and only in the *earthly* ministry of Jesus, no doubt in his desire to do justice to the absolute priority of the earthly Jesus. But unfortunately the whole "story" of Jesus Christ is thus truncated: the last act is the Cross; the kerygma is no more than confessional response to the earthly Jesus. It is significant that Jeremias alludes to Byzantine representations of the countless worshiping host on earth and in heaven before the gigantic figure of the Crucified. What, we may ask, of the Resurrection? Has Easter not altered the situation at all for the Church? When the Resurrection and Ascension of Jesus Christ are omitted from our purview, no adequate account can be taken of the fact that the primitive Church understood its faith and its message not simply as given to it out of the lifetime of Jesus upon earth, but out of the heavenly Lord's Easter revelation of himself. The Church's kerygma is not simply its confessional response to Jesus of Nazareth. Rather is the substance of the kerygma the whole "story" of how Jesus Christ suffered and died on the Cross for our sins, arose from the dead, ascended into heaven, intercedes for us there always, and gives himself to us through the Holy Spirit.

The problem posed for us by Jeremias' formulation of the relationship between Jesus' message and the Church's proclamation is, in fact, the problem of the extent to which a Christology is already present in the earthly life and ministry of Jesus. Whereas, as we saw, Knox tended to make the Church alone the sphere of the revelation of the Christ, Jeremias appears to indicate that the revelation of the Christ is restricted to the earthly history of Jesus. In this case, Christology is full-blown already in the life of Jesus; the significance of the kerygma is minimized, for it contains no revelation within itself and is simply and solely congregational response to Jesus of Nazareth.

A recent exegetical study of the Christological problem at the New Testament level may be said to fall midway between the two positions that we have so far considered in this chapter. R. H. Fuller's

The Mission and Achievement of Jesus falls neither on the side of a "churchly" definition of the event of Jesus Christ nor on the side of so emphasizing the historical Jesus as to underrate the kerygma.[20]

The Raw Materials of Christology in the Person and Message of Jesus

At the beginning of the century, von Harnack, sharing the Ritschlian prejudice against Christological doctrine in any metaphysical sense, and suspecting the system of Christological dogma as an alien thing that could only obscure the true teaching of Jesus, declared with some boldness: "The Gospel, as Jesus proclaimed it, has to do with the Father only and not with the Son." Although it is, of course, true that Jesus did not openly proclaim a Christology in the same sense as the Church, the day is now past for thinking of any of the Gospels as a straightforward human story unembroidered by Christology. Critical scholarship has in fact been increasingly preoccupied with the task of trying to determine whether there is a Christology in the message of Jesus and, if so, of what character it is. For long, the inquiry moved around the question of whether Jesus regarded or spoke of himself as the Messiah. In the wide scope of recent New Testament research, however, there has been a movement toward a general consensus that New Testament Christology should be approached in terms of what Jesus did rather than of what he was, in terms of his particular historical task rather than of any doctrine of his person. New Testament Christology is, in fact, to be distinguished from the later viewpoint of the early Church when, in the period of its great doctrinal controversies, it subordinated the consideration of the person and work of Jesus Christ to the problem of his "natures." "The New Testament hardly ever speaks of the person of Christ without at the same time speaking of his work . . . ," writes Oscar Cullman. "When it is asked in the New Testament 'Who is Christ?' the question never means exclusively, or even primarily, 'What is his nature?,' but first of all, 'What is his function?' " [21]

This is the standpoint shared by R. H. Fuller's monograph. The discussion as to the Christology implicit in Jesus' earthly life centers not on the question of whether he possessed a "Messianic consciousness," but on the question of such hints and presuppositions as he may have dropped in his teaching about the mission God was accomplishing in him. Now nothing has been more characteristic of research in the present century than the ever growing awareness that the whole of Jesus' teaching flows from his conviction that God is breaking into history, that crisis is impending, that the kingdom of God is near. Whoever would now compare Jesus' message with the Church's proclamation of faith must needs put his teaching of the kingdom of God at the very center of things. This Fuller has done. He accepts Bultmann's distinction between the dawn (*Anbruch*) and the irruption (*Hereinbrechen*) of God's kingdom. The kingdom of God is already dawning in the activity of Jesus, but it has not yet fully broken into history. Fuller renounces the concept of "realized eschatology" in the earlier form in which it was popularized by C. H. Dodd (the kingdom of God is already actually present in the historical ministry of Jesus) and interprets Jesus' sayings and parables about the kingdom of God entirely futuristically and his exorcisms and mighty works as proleptic or preliminary assaults upon Satan, pending his complete overthrow at the End. On the basis of a detailed exegetical study of the sayings of Jesus relating to the kingdom of God (and a futuristic interpretation thereof), Fuller concludes that Jesus' whole conception of his destiny and his whole activity are keyed up to the decisive future event of his death, through which God will bring in the final blessings of the kingdom. Turning subsequently to an investigation of the main Christological titles, Fuller finds that Jesus thought of himself as the one destined to become, by his death, the glorified Son of Man. Just as in the earthly ministry of Jesus the kingdom has not yet come, so also in his earthly ministry he is not yet the glorified Son of Man, although both the kingdom and the Son of Man "spill over" onto this side of the Cross.[22] On the other hand Jesus makes no overt Messianic claim. But that some kind of Messianic claim was at least implicit in his life is demanded by the fact that he was evidently condemned to death as a Messianic pretender (Mark 15:2, 9, 26). To the High Priest's question as to whether he is the Christ, Jesus replied: "I am; and you will see the Son of Man sitting at the right hand of Power, and coming with the clouds of heaven" (Mark 14:62). Jesus' answer denotes, according to Fuller, that Jesus considers himself to be the Christos or Messiah only in the sense that out of his present humiliation he is destined to be the triumphant Son of Man. Only after his suffering, death, and final exaltation does Jesus truly become the

Christos. Accordingly as the one who thinks of himself as Son of Man–designate and reservedly acknowledges the Messianic title, Jesus furnishes the "raw materials of Christology" for the later days when the Church will preach Jesus Christ as the decisive eschatological act of God. So the only difference between the message of Jesus and the Church's kerygma is that Jesus proclaims that God is *about to act* decisively and eschatologically in him, the kerygma proclaims that *God has so acted.*[23]

It is impossible to take up here the many finer points of exegesis in Fuller's detailed study. We must confine ourselves to taking issue (and that only briefly) first with his view of the titles "Christos" and "Son of Man" and second with his futuristic interpretation of one or two sayings of Jesus relating to the kingdom of God.

Fuller lays much the greatest stress on the title "Son of Man" as a clue to the nature of the Christological claim implicit in Jesus' life. The title of Christ-Messiah, despite various hints of Messiahship in the course of Jesus' earthly way, could be assigned to Jesus only as a result of his enthronement as the heavenly Son of Man. In Bultmann's view Jesus' life was un-Messianic, in Fuller's view pre-Messianic: for both alike Jesus entered into the full dignity of Christ-Messiah only after his Resurrection. Now in a fascinating paper, with persuasive arguments, Dr. W. C. van Unnik has recently shown that there are good reasons for doubting that the title "Christ," which is of course no different from the Jewish title "Messiah," was combined with Jesus only as the result of a transformation wrought by the Resurrection. So far as we can gather from Jewish ideas regarding the Messiah, he is always in fact Messiah *before* his death. Fuller, and here he follows Bultmann, adduces Acts 2:36 as evidence for the fact that Jesus was made the "Christ" only by his post-Easter exaltation: "Let all the house of Israel therefore know assuredly that God has made him both Lord and Christ, this Jesus whom you crucified." Obviously, however, there is no specific mention here of Resurrection-Exaltation. As van Unnik points out, this verse is the concluding appeal rather to the whole preceding argument. Jesus, as the man attested by God with signs and wonders already in his earthly ministry, could not be holden of death and is raised up (Acts 2:22–24); this man of Nazareth, witnessed to as Messiah in his lifetime not only by signs and wonders but also by David's prophecy, is vindicated and confirmed by the Resurrection (Acts 2:25–32). So by the Resurrection

God has only set the seal upon who Jesus really was, though the Jews had not recognized him and so had put him to death (Acts 2:36).[24]

If then the first followers of Jesus accepted this name as predictable of his earthly life, we are forced to ask why. Why since his life had hardly anything in common with the portrait of the Messiah in Jewish literature? Why since he possessed none of the features of the King-Messiah? Why since such Messianic hopes as he had raised were dashed by his suffering and death? Why then could the earliest Church stick to the name of Christos for Jesus? The most usual assumption has been that Jesus himself supported his Messianic claim with the title "Son of Man," and that, after his death and Resurrection, the early Church could proclaim him as the Christ, because as the Son of Man he radically transformed the notion of a political Messiah expected by the Jews, and as the Son of Man he saw himself as fulfilling the Messianic role in the "sacred history." [25] This assumption appears, however, to be based on inference rather than on the texts. For there is not a single text in which Jesus can be seen clearly to repudiate the traditional Messianic interpretation in favor of an identification of himself with the Son of Man. In regard, for instance, to the answer of Jesus to the High Priest (Mark 14:62): "I am; and you will see the Son of Man sitting at the right hand of Power, and coming with the clouds of heaven," the suggestion is almost certainly correct that the "and" ($\kappa\alpha\acute{\iota}$) with which the qualification is introduced is the Semitic adversative w[e]: "I am; *but* ye shall see the Son of Man" (cf. Matthew's "But I tell you" ($\pi\lambda\grave{\eta}\nu\ \lambda\acute{\epsilon}\gamma\omega\ \acute{\upsilon}\mu\hat{\iota}\nu$), 26:64). All the more striking therefore is the *distinction* between the "I am" of the earthly Jesus, and the third person in which reference is made to the heavenly Son of Man.

The significance of van Unnik's proposed solution to the question of why Jesus was called Christos is that it is independent of titles and Jesus' use of them. To wit, it is argued, on exegetical grounds, that Messiahship was attributed to Jesus by the early Christians, despite the lowly external appearance of his life and despite the Cross, because they saw in him the person *possessed by the Spirit* and not the outward activity of a king. As the one anointed with the Spirit, he is the Christ (Acts 4:26 f.; 10:38; Luke 3:22; 4:1, 14). Though the Gospels do not often refer to the Spirit, still for them Jesus the Christ, the one anointed with the Spirit, appears to stand behind every word and deed.

This may not be a final solution to the "Messianic problem." But it does at any rate give us pause to consider once again whether after all the dignity of the Christos could only have been attributed to Jesus Christ in light of his Resurrection-Exaltation. There was in his life a singular authority (aside from Messianic claims and titles), perhaps not least his endowment with the Spirit, that made it possible for the Church to call him the Christos in spite of all superficial appearances to the contrary. In such ways as this may we today seek support for the late Bishop E. G. Selwyn's contention that the life of Jesus is neither non-Messianic (Bultmann) nor pre-Messianic (Fuller), for "He is what He was, and He was what He is." [26]

What then, further, of the highly problematical "Son of Man" title? After many years of exhaustive investigation and animated debate, there is still scarcely more than one point of agreement. It is that Lietzmann's theory that Jesus could not have used "Son of Man" as a title, since the Aramaic *barnasha* means simply "man," and that the designation ὁ υἱὸς τοῦ ἀνθρώπου stemmed from Hellenistic Christian circles, cannot be sustained. [27] That Jesus did use the title seems to be incontestably proven by the fact that always (with the exception of Acts 7:56 and the symbolical use in Revelation 1:13 ff.), in each of its approximately eighty occurrences, it is on his own lips, and never in narration or in address to Jesus. But beyond this, agreement ends.

In the Synoptics there are three categories of saying in which Jesus speaks of the Son of Man. The first group refers in apocalyptic terms to the coming exalted and glorified Son of Man (Mark 8:38; 13:26; 14:62; Matt. 24:27, 37, 39, 44). Bultmann accepts these as authentic words of Jesus. But on the ground that nothing is said about the Parousia in the predictions of the sufferings of the Son of Man, and conversely nothing is said about death in the predictions of the Parousia, he denies that the earthly Jesus identified himself with the coming Son of Man. [28] Even if, however, we must be hesitant to speak of identification in view of the distinction between Jesus in his earthly activity and the Son of Man to come in such sayings as Luke 12:8 and Mark 8:38 and 14:62, there is none the less a close association, for what the disciples confess or deny before Jesus here on earth will determine their status and destiny in the presence of the coming Son of Man.

In the second group of sayings, "Son of Man" applies to the present work of Jesus, his authority here and now to forgive sins (Mark 2:10), his Lordship over the sabbath (Mark 2:28), his homelessness, with nowhere to lay his head (Matt. 8:20). The disagreements as to the implication of the title in this context are most interesting. Cullmann, for example, welcomes the general reaction of scholarship against understanding "Son of Man" as an expression only of the humanity or lowliness of Jesus—an understanding which has continued to be advocated by supporters of the hypothesis that both the title and its meaning were derived by Jesus from Ezekiel, where "Son of Man" suggests the contrast between the littleness of the prophet and the greatness of God.[29] More to the point is Stauffer's claim that just about the most pretentious title anyone in the ancient Near East could have used is "Son of Man."[30] However, Cullmann feels that this emphasis may be too one-sided, that the application of the title to the earthly life of Jesus does call attention to his humiliation as a consequence of the incarnation of the Heavenly Man, as in Matthew 8:20 and 11:19.[31] On the other hand, Fuller is at pains to uphold the strong eschatological orientation even of these sayings, as implying already the coming triumph of the Son of Man, as in Matthew 8:20, "The Son of Man has nowhere to lay his head," where the very use of the term "Son of Man" implies the future victory.[32] Does not this discrepancy of opinion point us in fact to another possibility: that in these selfsame places the hand of the Church has been at work in touching up the tradition? Can we really say that the incidence of the title "Son of Man" in this group of sayings proves anything about the earthly ministry of Jesus, seeing that there is ample evidence in the Gospel tradition for the interchangeability of "I" and "Son of Man" in reference to Jesus (cf. Matt. 10:32 f. with Luke 12:8 f. and Mark 8:38; or compare Matt. 16:13 with Mark 8:27)?[33]

The third group of sayings speaks of the coming sufferings of the Son of Man (Mark 8:31; 9:31; 10:33 f.). This group is most crucial of all for Fuller's thesis that Jesus understands himself as the one about to be made the exalted Son of Man by his death and Resurrection, as Son of Man–designate.

"The Son of man must suffer many things" (Mark 8:31). Here, according to Fuller, Jesus is declaring his own certainty that of divine necessity he has to suffer and die in order to enter upon the ultimate triumph of the glorified Son of Man; he is speaking, that is, as the one destined to become the Son of Man, as the Son of Man–designate. The trouble with this interpretation is that nowhere in the tradition are we

given any explicit indication as to how we are to understand the relation between the earthly activity of Jesus and his own function as the
coming heavenly judge of the world. Nor is it as though Jesus were
saying here in Mark 8:31, "I, the earthly Jesus, must suffer in order
to become the exalted Son of Man." We are in fact driven to ask
whether at this point the title "Son of Man" has lost its original force,
so that it has come to mean the lowly and humble one, the incarnation of the Heavenly Man, in which case the eschatological background of the designation would have faded from view. If that is not
so, and Son of Man here retains its eschatological meaning, we cannot fail to notice the extremely paradoxical character of the saying,
the glorious Son of Man rejected of men, a combination of ideas quite
unprecedented in the apocalyptic literature. In that instance, the
words of Mark 8:31 seem to bear less the imprint of a hope for the
future glory of the Son of Man, than of the Church's whole experience of the entire "story" of Jesus Christ, on its heavenly as on its
earthly side. In the light of his Passion and Resurrection this quite
unexpected collocation can take place, "the Son of Man must suffer,"
by which expression is given to the Church's conviction that the
exalted Son of Man, in whom it now believes, is none other than this
Jesus of Nazareth, who was rejected of men and crucified.

All this can be said without denying what we have already affirmed,
that the use of the term "Son of Man" was an original formulation of
Jesus. That he employed the title cannot be refuted: that he identified
his own person with the coming, heavenly Son of Man cannot, on the
basis of all that the tradition tells us, be ascertained with any certainty. At any rate, we can see how the fact that Jesus himself employed this designation could have led, in the process of the transmission of the tradition, to its wider and wider application to the earthly
setting of the ministry of Jesus, until, from the perspective of the
finished work of Jesus the Christ, "Jesus" and "Son of Man" have
become synonymous.[34]

Of one thing there appears to be little doubt. It is that the early
Church connected the idea of the Son of Man with the Parousia: he is
to fulfill the role of arbiter in the last judgment of the world (Luke
12:8 f.; cf. Mark 8:38). What is of the utmost significance for us is
that the old tradition does not seem to connect the eschatological
work of the Son of Man in judgment with Jesus' preaching of the
coming kingdom of God. Only in neglect of this feature of the tradi-

tion could it be contended that there is the closest connection between the notion of Jesus' understanding of himself as the one destined to be the heavenly Son of Man on the one hand and his earthly ministry and the coming kingdom of God on the other. In fact none of Jesus' sayings supports the theory of a close correlation between the apocalyptic idea of the Son of Man concealed in heaven and about to be revealed, and Jesus' preaching of the kingdom of God. For, whereas the kingdom as preached by Jesus is something in the future, in the words and deeds of Jesus it becomes present to the hearer as call to decision.[35]

We shall have something more to say in the next chapter about the Christological titles applied to Jesus. Our present brief deliberations may have shown the extreme difficulty in which critical scholarship is placed when it tries to compare the ministry and message of the earthly Jesus with the Church's preaching on the basis of the exalted titles found on the lips of Jesus in the Gospels. For precisely in the case of such Christological names of majesty as "Son of Man" is there the greatest probability that the Church, because of its faith in the resurrected and exalted Christ, may have added the titles to sayings of the earthly Lord in which they did not originally occur.[36] It is just this negative judgment about study of titles, as a means of comparing the historical Jesus and his message with the Church's kerygma, that has been turned to positive account in another direction by exponents of the "new quest of the historical Jesus." They have directed attention to those nontitular sayings of Jesus, about whose historicity we can have a greater degree of confidence.

The most significant section of the study by R. H. Fuller must therefore be said to be the earlier part, in which he seeks an avenue of approach to the Christology implicit in Jesus' life and message via his eschatological sayings, proclaiming the kingdom of God. Fuller's *futuristic* interpretation of the kingdom has to be viewed as a reaction against the widespread scholarly allegiance of the past generation to the concept of "realized eschatology," associated particularly with the name of C. H. Dodd. From the standpoint of "realized eschatology" we are asked to suppose that with the historical appearance of Jesus the kingdom of God has actually come. The popularity of this view can be gauged from the fact that its advancement was not hindered by the searching linguistic criticisms leveled by J. Y. Campbell, K. W. Clark and others against Dodd's interpretation of the verbs ἐγγίζειν (ἤγγικεν) and φθάνειν (ἔφθασεν) in such classic controversial passages as Mark 1:15 and Matthew 12:28.[37]

Over against "realized eschatology," however, there has also been an unmistakable desire in some scholarly quarters to do justice to the futuristic aspect of Jesus' proclamation of the kingdom. One recalls Bultmann's portrait of Jesus as an eschatological *prophet* who announced the impending advent of the kingdom of God, and saw his own history as the time of decision for men in the face of God's coming. Fuller objects that Bultmann's interpretation does not go far enough: Jesus was more than a prophet. So Fuller veers toward Schweitzer's "throughgoing eschatology" in maintaining that Jesus thought of his death as the necessary means of setting the eschatological process in operation.

Bultmann's understanding of Jesus' eschatological message has been opposed from another angle. W. G. Kümmel objects that Bultmann overthrows his own exegetical judgment that Jesus predicts the future kingdom of God, by wishing to refine or explain away this *future* as nothing but a part of the mythological picture of the world from which the New Testament must be freed.[38] As early as Bultmann's *Jesus and the Word,* we can in fact observe how he interprets the future predicted by Jesus as no real future *in time,* but simply as God's placing men, in this last hour, in this very moment, in the crisis of decision.[39] I think Kümmel is correct in suggesting that the tendency to rid Jesus' message of the expectation of a concrete eschatological future, whether it be by exegetical reinterpretation of the texts or by spiritualizing or demythologizing the eschatological prediction, has arisen from the zeal to make the message applicable for modern man and his moral problems.[40]

For Dodd, the New Testament knows only "realized eschatology"; it is bound throughout to the message that, in a final and absolute sense, man has been confronted *within history* by the eternal God in his kingdom, power, and glory. Accordingly, when the New Testament speaks of the Parousia in the concrete, pictorial terminology of apocalyptic, this must be understood only as *symbolizing* the truth that, in its occurrence within history, the event of Jesus Christ yet bears a supra-historical character, so that the full meaning of the kingdom of God can only be experienced by the spirit of man in the eternal order. So Dodd rejects the concrete or "futurist" eschatology because no reference to the Parousia in terms of a real, temporal future can have any bearing upon events which belong to eternity.[41]

Bultmann for his part has, of course, felt that the mythological eschatology is untenable for the simple reason that the history of the world ran on without the occurrence of the Parousia, as the New Testament expected it. We are faced, therefore, with the indispensable necessity of exposing the truth of the kerygma for men today by existentialist interpretation of the mythological expectation of the end of the world imminent in time. Now whereas Bultmann, as we have remarked, has not denied a future element in Jesus' eschatological prediction, it is nevertheless true that for him the mythological statements concerning the future have meant only that man is confronted with a decision in the here and now. As a result of this position of emphasis on the *present moment of existence,* Bultmann has been attacked from many sides for having reduced temporal eschatology— the concrete, futuristic eschatology of the New Testament—to anthropology, by no one more vehemently than by Heinrich Schlier. Schlier objects to Bultmann's rejection of concrete eschatology on the grounds that this merging of the ultimate future in the present moment, this sinking of the spread of time in a mathematically punctual instant of faith in the "now," comes perilously close to the outlook of the pneumatics or inspired fanatics in the Corinthian congregation, who felt that they had already experienced the resurrection in the spiritual blessings of the act of sacramental initiation and could experience it again and again "in the spirit." [42] W. G. Kümmel, with particular reference to Jesus' eschatological proclamation, holds that elimination of the future orientation in Jesus' message could only result in its disintegration, since "the figure and activity of Jesus would lose their fundamental character as the *historical* activity of the *God* who wishes to lead his kingdom upwards." Moreover, Kümmel quite rightly emphasizes that Jesus not only proclaims the coming of the kingdom of God in vague general terms but also, in some texts, its imminent advent within the period of the generation of his contemporaries—a fact which proves, according to Kümmel, that Jesus understood the future as a real future *in time.*[43]

Only on the basis of a quite arbitrary exegetical judgment could it be maintained then that only those sayings of Jesus about the kingdom of God are real which refer to the present, while all concrete eschatological statements are merely of "symbolic" significance as pictorial images of "eternal" truth. On the other hand, it will not do either, in reaction against the concept of "realized eschatology," to swing over entirely to the *"konsequent"* eschatological view of A. Schweitzer, vigorously revived by Martin Werner and the Bern School, that Jesus was simply the most radical of Jewish apocalypticists who expected his appearance as the Son of Man on the clouds of heaven.[44] Our reason for dismissing these various approaches as possible solutions of the problem of Jesus' eschatological message is just this: the indisputable juxtaposition in Jesus' proclamation of the kingdom of references to both the present and the future. At times the kingdom is a future happening: "Thy kingdom come," our Lord teaches his disciples to pray (Matt. 6:10). "I shall not drink again of the fruit of the vine until that day when I drink it new in the kingdom of God," he says at the Last Supper (Mark 14:25). The coming kingdom of God is described by Jesus not in terms of the apocalyptic drama; he speaks of the kingdom as "joy" (Matt. 25:21, 23), "life" (Mark 9:43, 45, 47; 10:17), "light" (Luke 16:8). Yet these blessings of the kingdom of God of which Jesus speaks are given expression not only in relation to a hoped-for future, but to a hope fulfilling itself already in his person, his deeds, his message. At times the kingdom is present. So even today, with Jesus' presence, there is joy over the prodigal's return: "It was fitting to make merry and be glad, for this your brother was dead, and is alive; he was lost, and is found" (Luke 15:32). The time of rejoicing has come already with Jesus' historical appearance: "Go and tell John what you hear and see: the blind receive their sight and the lame walk, lepers are cleansed and the deaf hear, and the dead are raised up, and the poor have good news preached to them" (Matt. 11:4–6). God's victory over the evil powers of the world has begun in Jesus: "But if it is by the finger of God that I cast out demons, then the kingdom of God has come upon you" (Luke 11:20).

This remarkable tension between present and future in Jesus' proclamation of the kingdom of God has so agitated the commentators that they have long tried to clear up the apparent contradiction by assigning the two poles of Jesus' thought and message each to a different stage in the biographical development of his ministry.[45] Some have supposed that the predictions of the near approach of the kingdom belong to the later phase of his work, others that in Jesus' consciousness there was less and less concern with the future hour of the kingdom's arrival and therefore latterly in his message a stronger emphasis on its present reality.[46] All such attempts, however, to explain away the polarities in Jesus' preaching of the kingdom by positing a development in his eschatological thinking, are dependent upon creative and imaginative combinations of texts which, in fact, exist in the Gospel tradition *only as detached sayings.*

Statements about the present and the future in Jesus' message are indeed not to be separated. His own preaching links the present of his hearers to the coming judgment of the world: by men's attitude toward him here and now in his earthly ministry will their eternal destiny be determined, when "the Son of man shall sit on his glorious throne" (Matt. 19:28–30; *cf.* Mark 8:38; Luke 12:32). Equally so does he link the future of God to the present moment. In predicting that future, he is not concerned to elucidate or elaborate the "facts" of the coming of God in the future. Certainly the much disputed "Little Apocalypse" of Mark 13 is permeated with the stock-in-trade of Jewish apocalyptic speculation—wars and rebellions, earthquakes and famines, the despoliation of Judea and the desecration of the temple. But by no means all of Mark 13:1–27, and indeed not much of it, can be ascribed to Jesus. By general scholarly consent, the bulk of the material consists on the one hand of purely Jewish apocalyptic conceptions (Mark 13:7, 8, 12, 14–20, 24–27), or on the other hand reflects the experience of the primitive Church (Mark 13:6, 9, 10, 11, 13, 21–3).[47] That is not to say that there are here no authentic words of Jesus or that he did not share apocalyptic ideas. Nevertheless, the striking thing, well attested in all the rest of the Gospel tradition concerning Jesus' eschatological message and not lost to view even here in the "Little Apocalypse," is his disinterest in apocalyptic fancy and speculation. So we hear this watchword of his: "Take heed" (Mark 13:5, 9, 23, 33–7).[48] This is the rein he holds upon all preoccupation with setting forth in bizarre detail the "geography" and "history" of the world's end. His exhortation "Take heed" is in fact a summons to the present in the light of God's future.[49]

Now the tension between present and future in the eschatological message of Jesus, as we have tried to make it clear, Fuller has recognized in his own way. He speaks about the proleptic operation of the powers of the kingdom in Jesus, about Jesus' conception that God is active in him in a way organically related to the future event.[50] Yet so much weight is given to the coming of the kingdom as a decisive event of the future that I doubt whether there is full acknowledgment of the close interrelationship between present and future, or of Jesus' presence as a real eschatological present, instead of an anticipation of the eschatological consummation. This can only be decided by reference to Fuller's exegesis of certain passages:

In the story of the Beelzebul controversy the crucial saying is "But if it is by the finger of God that I cast out demons, then the kingdom of God has come upon you" (Luke 11:20). "Finger of God," as Fuller rightly points out, is probably an allusion to Exodus 8:19, where reference is made to the plagues of Egypt wrought by the *finger* of God. So, Fuller thinks, the plagues were preliminary demonstrations of power pointing forward to the great decisive act of God, the Exodus itself, which at Exodus 15:6 is attributed to the *right hand* of God. We are then asked to believe that here we have a typology for Jesus' understanding of his own acts of exorcism. By ascribing his exorcisms to the "finger of God," Jesus is placing them in the same preliminary relationship to his own Exodus, which still belongs to the future, as the plagues of Egypt bore to the first Exodus. Of course there is no denying the prominence of Exodus typology in relation to Jesus' death in the primitive Church. The difficulty with Fuller's typological exegesis is, however, that it is impossible to sustain the view that the plagues of Egypt, wrought by the *finger* of God (as against the Exodus itself, wrought by the *hand* of God), were ever regarded as merely preliminaries to the main event, and not as an integral part of the whole. In fact, at Exodus 9:3 the plagues upon the beasts of burden and the flocks of the Egyptians were attributed to the *hand* of God. Fuller's interpretation is a far-fetched and imaginative construction: he wishes to force a reference to the future into a clause which bears upon the *present* manifestation of the powers of the kingdom. This is borne out by Matthew's interpretation of the Lucan version of the saying: "But if it is by the Spirit of God that I cast out demons, then the kingdom of God has come upon you" (Matt. 12:28).[51] (There is general agreement that, in view of Luke's tendency to introduce the idea of the Spirit into the text, the "finger of God" is probably the older version.) In the primitive Church the Spirit, like "the first fruits" (Rom. 8:23), is a technical term for the present manifestation of the kingdom of God.

I venture to suggest that Fuller's interpretation of the saying which both Mark and Matthew place in the context of the Beelzebul controversy is no less forced: "But no one can enter a strong man's house and plunder his goods, unless he first binds the strong man; then indeed he may plunder his house" (Mark 3:27 = Matt. 12:29). In this metaphorical image, Satan is clearly the strong man, and Jesus the stronger one who deprives Satan of those whom he dominates. Fuller once again takes these words to denote a preliminary assault upon Satan prior to his final overthrow at the End. He certainly seems to press things too far in suggesting, with respect to this metaphor, that the *first* ($\pi\rho\tilde{\omega}\tau o\nu$) refers to the ministry of Jesus, and the *then* ($\tau\acute{o}\tau\epsilon$) to the decisive event of the future. Jesus' acts of exorcism (with which in Mark, as in Matthew, this saying is associated) are in fact a victory already won over Satan, since Satan must already be bound if he can be robbed of the children whom he has dominated. It was a part of Jewish expectation that in the last day Satan would be vanquished: so this saying means, too, that the powers of the kingdom are already in operation.[52]

We can gather from Fuller's exegesis of these and other passages what he wishes to say and what he does say about Jesus' eschatological message. It is that it primarily points to the future. The decisive event still lies in the future. God is about to act decisively in him. In so far as he is the Son of Man—designate, Jesus' mission and message are geared to the coming events of his death and Resurrection, by which alone the eschatological process will be set in motion—even though the powers of the coming kingdom are proleptically active in his earthly ministry. It is as the one who sees himself destined to realize the eschatological future by his death that Jesus furnishes the Church with the "raw materials of Christology." Fuller's closing formulation is that the message of Jesus and the message of the Church are substantially identical—the only difference between them is that, whereas for Jesus the decisive event is in the near future, for the Church it now lies in the past.[53] This formulation is directly in line with the view of scholarship, familiar to us particularly from Bultmann, that the real difference between Jesus and Paul is the difference in their respective situations with regard to the "turning of the ages." Bultmann showed that, when at the turn of the century W. Wrede, Arnold Meyer, and others, under the "back to Jesus" slogan, set Jesus at a great distance from Paul by holding Paul up as the inventor of a mythical Christian doctrine of salvation, they were in fact misunderstanding both Paul and Jesus. For what one encounters in Jesus is the same God, Creator, and Judge, who claims man's all, that one encounters in Paul. That which for Bultmann then distinguishes Jesus from Paul is only their respective stations in regard to the shift in the ages: "Jesus looks to the future and points his hearers to the *coming* Reign of God, which, to be sure, is coming even now, is already breaking in. Paul, on the other hand, looks back and points to what has already occurred. For him, the turn of the age has already taken place, the day of salvation is already present!" [54]

It is just this distinction that has been called in question recently by exponents of the "new quest" in their attempts to establish the continuity of the kerygma with the mission and message of the historical Jesus. Taking the obvious tension between present and future in Jesus' eschatological message at face value, they have come up with the verdict that the basic direction of Jesus' proclamation is not toward the future, but is rather a pronouncement to the present, calling men to decision before God now, in the light of the imminent eschatological future. We have already seen reason to welcome this emphasis: Jesus' statements about the present and the future are not to be wrenched apart.

The new Jesus-research has, however, further sought to establish on critical grounds that Jesus' thought of his present as the present in which the powers of the coming age are already at work is based upon historical encounter with John the Baptist. The Baptist stands at the frontier of the ages and actually belongs to the time of fulfilled promise. Accordingly, since Jesus looked back to him as the one who had brought to a close the old age and ushered in the new age, in the same way as the Church looked back to Jesus, the supposed distinction between the situation of Jesus and that of the Church is canceled out.[55] Nor of course has the "new quest" stopped there. Jesus' summons to the present on the basis of the imminent coming of the eschatological event has been taken as the guide to what is constitutive of his own existence: this coming of God that makes the present of Jesus an eschatologically qualified present, calling the hearer to be ready to die in order to find life, to humble himself in suffering in order to find glory. The content of Jesus' understanding of existence, given expression in his message, is then found to be identical with the kerygma, for, when through existential interpretation the kerygma's meaning becomes transparent, it is seen to proclaim the transcendent selfhood of Jesus and so to continue his message and his claim upon men that life is to be found in death, glory in suffering. But we must ask these questions: Can the historian *qua* historian define the true historical "selfhood" of Jesus? Can historical research legitimize the Church's faith in and message of Jesus Christ by determining what was constitutive of Jesus existence? Has Martin Kähler's feeling that it is monstrous to believe that the historian can "prove" faith by discovering and describing its historical foundation been scorned or overcome at last? These and similar questions must await discussion in our next chapter, dealing with the "new quest."

Meanwhile we rest content to accept the recent scholarly stress upon the intertwining of present and future in Jesus' eschatological message as a valid and valuable counterbalance to the concept of "realized eschatology" with its elimination of the concrete eschatological future from Jesus' message, and to all futuristic interpretations which see in Jesus no more than Son of Man—designate or Messiah-designate. Some time ago the late Professor William Manson wrote: "Jesus in his characteristic words about the Kingdom of God reasons from present events and experiences to the coming of that Kingdom, not vice versa. His gospel of the End rests on the certainty of the power of God which is with him in the present." [56] Even so, Jesus can speak about the imminent advent of the kingdom of God only because it is already present in him. Its presence is given expression in everything he teaches and in everything he does, in his love for the outcasts and the sinners, in his obedience to God unto the death of the Cross. So in the earthly activity of this man, Jesus of Nazareth, this paradoxical thing has happened that in *his* lowliness and humiliation the kingdom of *God* has drawn near to men. Indelibly stamped upon the Gospel tradition, therefore, is the word about the unique authority of this Jesus, in whose ministry and message the future of God and of God's kingdom has become a present claim and a present blessing for men. There lies hidden within this authority of Jesus a Christology whose full flowering could only come through the consummation of the disciples' faith in him in light of his death and Resurrection. It is important to notice that these statements we have just made fall far short of any presumption that historical research can demonstrate the legitimacy of the Church's faith in and preaching of Jesus Christ by uncovering the constitutive ingredients of his historic selfhood. The question for the believer is not whether the his-

torian can give him assurance that the Church's understanding of
Jesus Christ matched perfectly Jesus' own understanding of himself,
but whether, in the face of Jesus' eschatological message, he can respond to the divine mission of *this* Jesus, whose word about God's
future kingdom is possible only because of God's presence with him in
the *hic et nunc* of his ministry. Only he can say "Yes" with boldness
and confidence to this question who knows that God has raised from
the dead this Jesus who was crucified.

Our survey of important recent scholarly attempts to provide a
solution to the problem of the relation between Jesus and his message
and the Church and her message would not be complete without some
reference to the *Heilsgeschichte* approach to the Biblical record that
has been an outstanding feature of modern study. The idea of "sacred
history" (*Heilsgeschichte*) is not, of course, new. It had already been
elaborated in the nineteenth century work of the Erlangen theologian,
J. Chr. K. von Hofmann. Von Hofmann considered the Scripture to
be the record of God's self-revelation in history, a self-revelation
which in its linear development becomes part of the fabric of objective history, reaching its goal in Jesus Christ. To understand this
"sacred history" one must come to it from the perspective of faith, in
which case one would discover that the "sacred history" revealed the
meaning of all events in the life and history of the world.[57]

In our own time E. Stauffer's account of New Testament theology
has followed this "sacred history" pattern. It is at once "historical"
and "Christocentric," beginning from the creation and the fall, travers-
ing the time of the Law and the promise, culminating in the event of
Jesus Christ, which itself opens up the new future of the time of the
Church, moving toward the ultimate revelation of the Christ, the
restoration of the universe, and the final glorification of God.[58] But
undoubtedly the chief modern representative of a theology based on
the idea of "sacred history" is Oscar Cullmann, and it is Cullmann's
brand of "sacred history" that we must now examine.

Christ the Mid-Point of the Line of "Sacred History"

As a younger contemporary of Barth and Bultmann, Cullmann shared
their disaffection with the nineteenth century. The way the younger
scholar was to take, however—a way pursued without deviation or

shadow of turning—was to be neither that of "theological exegesis" nor that of "existentialist exegesis." For, in fact, since his earliest article of 1925, Cullmann has consistently advocated "objective exegesis." [59] By "objective exegesis" Cullmann means that the interpreter must go beyond a merely "historical exegesis," which limits itself only to understanding the author of the religious idea and his personality, in order to lay hold of the religious idea itself. If, however, the interpreter is to grasp the religious idea in its objective reality, he must be both historian and theologian, seeking by concentrated personal effort to enter into that realm of knowing from which the original author himself has grasped the objective religious reality. So Cullmann could embrace the view of Form-criticism that the Gospels are not biographies of Jesus but witnesses to faith. The main function of the Biblical record, as Cullmann has understood it, is not to tell about events but to manifest religious reality. Certain Form-critics, however, like Bultmann, have failed to see that the religious reality and the historical events connected with it are completely woven in with each other. It is, in fact, only in the events that revelation takes place. The scandal of Christian faith is that we have to accept that God acts in time, that the divine enters the sphere of the contingent. The center of the line of time in which God acts, that is of the "sacred history," is Jesus himself, the absolute revelation of God, by which the whole of history is to be understood and judged.

Cullmann's hermeneutical attitude is well summed up in the keyword of his principal work, *Christ and Time:* all theology, as concern with God's revelation, is also "Biblical history." Cullmann's book, highly architectonic in its design, is a skillful attempt to work out in detail "the early Christian conception of time and history." "The work of Christ is primarily the mid-point of a special happening or process which extends the length of the time-line." The history of salvation, with Christ as its mid-point, is infinitely narrower, if not shorter, than general history, but even so the Christ-line furnishes the norm for judging the facts of general history. There is a cosmic extension of the historical line. It is primarily on the foundation of an investigation of the Biblical words for "time" ($\kappa\alpha\iota\rho\acute{o}s$, $\alpha\acute{\iota}\acute{\omega}\nu$, etc.) that Cullmann establishes the Bible's linear view of time, and thereafter contrasts it with the cyclical view of the Greeks. In the Christ-event God's lordship over the whole of time is revealed, over all the past and all the future. The "sacred history" extends from the Creation through

the fall, the flood, the call of Abraham, the election of the chosen people, the Christ-occurrence, the bestowal of the Holy Spirit, the life of
the Church, all moving in *temporal* progression toward the event of
the end-time. Whereas for Judaism the mid-point of the line of "sacred
history" coincides with the Parousia, for Christians it now falls in the
midst of the time before the Parousia.[60]

From every stage of the time-line the central point of reference is
the Christ. The Old Testament is preparation for the Christ-event. On
the other side the future is to be understood with reference to Christ
as a development of "sacred history." With Christ, indeed, the future
"end" has come already. The present epoch of the Church, though it
is always bound to the past work of Jesus Christ at the mid-point, is
none the less also the time of the salvation-occurrence, the time "between the times" when the Church exists under the lordship of Christ
as the one who sits at the right hand of God until his Parousia.[61] Not
only the Church, but also the individual, has his place in the history of
salvation, for, through his faith in the saving significance of the past
stage of "sacred history," the salvation-occurrence becomes effica-
cious for him in the present.

More recently in his book, *The Christology of the New Testament,*
Cullmann has approached the Christological problem in terms of the
Christological titles applied to Jesus in the New Testament.[62] But even
here he has not swerved from the pattern of "sacred history" set forth
in his earlier volume, for it is still axiomatic for him that "it is characteristic of New Testament Christology that Christ is connected with
the total history of revelation and salvation, beginning with creation.
There can be no *Heilsgeschichte* without Christology; no Christology
without a *Heilsgeschichte* which unfolds in time." [63] So the Christological titles are schematically arranged and treated according to
the following categories: first, those titles which deal with the earthly
work of Christ; second, those which relate to his future, eschatological
work; third, those which explain his present work, and finally those
which explain the work completed in his pre-existence.

In this portrait of the *Heilsgeschichte* no distinction at all is made
between the earthly and transcendental phases of Christ's work, between history and myth, or even between historical and natural occurrences, for creation is also a part of the *Heilsgeschichte.* The pre-
existent Christ, active in creation, the one who united in himself in
an unheard-of way the role of the Suffering Servant, sacrificed for

men, and the role of the Son of Man who would return at the End— it is the one Christ, "the same yesterday, today, and forever," only exercising his different chronologically or temporally successive functions in the history of salvation.[64]

Although this short description does not sufficiently indicate the wealth of scholarly knowledge or provocativeness of treatment characteristic of Professor Cullmann's work, it may nevertheless serve as a basis for discussion. Cullmann's position has been attacked from various sides. In considering the criticisms that have been made against him, it is necessary to distinguish two questions. The first is the question of whether we today need to accept the Biblical view of time or history, as he represents it, if we are to appropriate the Biblical faith. The second is the question of whether Cullmann's representation is in fact a faithful account of the Biblical point of view.

Dr. John Macquarrie takes Cullmann to task for claiming that we ourselves must inevitably hold to the Biblical view of time or history by renouncing all standards of thought, derived from philosophical or religious systems, which are incompatible with the Biblical outlook. The case put forward by Macquarrie is in effect the classic case for demythologizing: it is ludicrous to demand of us today that, in order to be genuine Christian believers, we must share Biblical ideas of time and history that no longer make sense. It is no longer possible for us, now that after a long struggle we have learned to distinguish between such concepts as "time," "cosmic process," "history," and "myth," to revert to an undifferentiated mode of thinking that takes us back two thousand years, or to conceive of Christ as the mid-point of a timeline that is coextensive with the whole cosmic process. For we now see that the "sacred history" itself is no more than a quickly passing episode within the vastness of the cosmic process. Since Cullman gives the impression that it is not possible to be a Christian believer unless one clings to the Biblical understanding of time and history, it is legitimate to complain that he is putting faith in a quite insufferable strait jacket.[65] It is difficult to accept the notion that all contributors to the New Testament, of the Palestinian Church or of the young Hellenistic Church, grasped the same unified conception of the history of salvation. It is equally difficult to imagine that the younger generation in our day, or indeed the younger Churches, in India or Japan, must be converted to a Hebrew type of mind before they can receive the gospel. It would appear that the tendency toward

absolutism in Cullmann's presentation of "sacred history," by which
Biblical theology becomes reduced to a particular philosophy of history binding upon all men, is the natural concomitant of his hermeneutic. Cullmann's "objective exegesis" presupposes that the "truth"
about Christology can be arrived at by impartial "scientific" inquiry.
"This question of scholarly investigation," he writes, "ought not to
involve theological position." [66] It does not seem to have occurred to
Cullmann that his own interpretative principle of *Heilsgeschichte* is
no less, if no more, a "theological standpoint" than Bultmann's demythologizing exegesis, controlled by the idea of the "Gnostic myth." At
all events, when, for the sake of his *Heilsgeschichte* presentation,
Cullmann does not raise the problematicality of the word "history" in
the phrase "history of salvation," but incorporates within this one
word the concepts of "time" and "cosmic process," "myth" and "history," then *in terms of his own presuppositions* he is scientifically
quite correct in everything he says. Only from this standpoint of
"objective exegesis" could Cullmann also let fall the suggestion that,
before one can be in assured possession of any authentic Christian
faith, he must believe the historical *fact* that Jesus believed himself
to be the Messiah.[67] This looks like a premature admixture of historical knowledge and faith without the question being raised concerning the relevance of historical knowledge for faith. It also seems
strange in view of the tradition's reticence about Jesus' Messianic
claim and in view of recent scholarship's uncertainties concerning it.

Whenever the problem of "history" in the words "history of salvation" is taken up, we are in fact landed in the greatest difficulties and
ambiguities by Cullmann's exposition of the "sacred history." If, as
Cullmann understands it, the history of salvation is as a whole "prophecy," is this "prophetic history" then simply an interpretative picture
of the events of world history? If not, then what is its relation to the
real events of the world historical process? [68] Are there occurrences
outside of the Biblical events that can properly be called "sacred
occurrences"—the Battle of Agincourt, perhaps, the English victory
which Shakespeare makes Henry V ascribe to the arm of God alone,
or the momentous change of climatic conditions which made D-day
possible and which former President Eisenhower in his book *Crusade
in Europe* attributes to a providential act of God? Of course we know
that, looked at from the other side of the fence, these events are
thought of as calamities. By what criteria then could we decide when

God acts or reveals himself in history? If the "sacred history" as such is to be restricted to the events recorded in the Bible, are we setting up and sealing off a unique category of events that would transcend the limits of any normal definition of "event"?

It is not easy to find a way through this maze of questions. Confronted particularly with the complex problem of the historicity of the *Heilsgeschichte,* we can do no more here than point to the vexation felt by recent scholarship over this issue. Debate on the problem has focused more upon Gerhard von Rad's exposition of Old Testament theology than upon Cullmann's "Christ-line" thesis. Von Rad, in his two-volume *Theology of the Old Testament,* sets out to do justice to the intention of the Old Testament to be a "history book." It transpires, however, that his presentation of Old Testament theology is in terms of *Heilsgeschichte,* in terms of a "prophetic history" or an "eschatologically oriented history" that has its beginning in the creation of the world and its end in the Parousia of the Son of Man, and is therefore a "history" carried through by God's Word. Von Rad's critics have not been slow to recognize that simply to recount the Old Testament "story" as a *Heilsgeschichte* is by no means to solve the problem of what it means to call the Old Testament a "history book." It has therefore been suggested that it would be better for us to relinquish the *Heilsgeschichte* version of the Old Testament "story" in favor of the account of Israel's history built up by historical-critical research, and to think of that as the locus of revelation of the God who acts.[69]

There would appear to be a twofold risk involved in the use of *Heilsgeschichte* to account for the Biblical history. On the one hand it may imply the elevation of the "sacred event" to the supra-mundane level of "divine" meaning in which lies the substance of the "sacred history," and a consequent replacement of the concrete historical event itself by some transcendent "truth" which it illuminates. The trouble with such theological coinages as *"heilsgeschichtlich,"* "supra-historical," "metahistorical" is that the stress is so apt to be laid upon the prefix in each case that the only unambiguous thing brought home to us by these terms is that we are no longer dealing with ordinary historical events. There is accordingly a sturdy common sense in John Macquarrie's question: "How could something which is at most only in part historical provide a clue to 'what history in the strict and authentic sense is'?"[70] But besides, to remove the "sacred events" of the Bible from the realm of ordinary events is to deal a disastrous blow at any sound Christian theology, which is bound to the concreteness of history by the fact of the "Word made flesh." On the other hand, there is the danger—and this is how it is with Cullmann's "objective exegesis"—of treating the history of salvation as if it were a series of historically verifiable facts that could be grasped by the historian rather than laid hold of and experienced only in faith.[71]

A possible way out of the dilemma may be found by following through assiduously the suggestion that "sacred history" as "prophetic history" is created and effected by the Word of God. The question about the relation of "sacred history" to the concrete reality of Biblical event could then be formulated in this way: where is the Word of God? If we reply that the Word of God is a transcendent mystery, belonging to the supra-mundane sphere and therefore different from all ordinary human words, then we lose this central and decisive and saving thing: that in his Word God has entered history, has turned toward us in the history in which we stand, and climactically in the "Word made flesh." On the other side, if we say that, just because God's Word must necessarily come to expression in ordinary human words, which are the only words we know, we can therefore see it and grasp it as an objective reality, then we sever the inseparable union between the Word of God and faith. God's Word and God's deed are one and the same. We can speak of them in the same breath, because the historical occurrence in which God acts has set in motion Biblical man's utterance or proclamation of God. The "sacred event" must then be allowed to embrace the totality of the event of revelation and faith-response, in which the Word of the God who acts breaks through the concrete historical occurrence and comes to speech in the language of the Bible.[72] The significance of "sacred history" would then be seen not to lie in the idea that this tiny fragment of history furnishes a ready-made explanation of the whole of history or of the whole cosmic process. Its significance would lie rather in its power to beget faith, since it is the place in which historical occurrences as God's acts (e.g. the Exodus and the death of Christ) have passed into language. This faith arises from the proclamation of what God has done and, because God's Word when it enters history always points to its goal, lives in expectation of what God will do in the future.

Now as to the specific question of whether Cullmann's version of the "sacred history" is a faithful account of the Biblical point of view, it is interesting to observe that Macquarrie, so stringently opposed to Cullmann's claim that *we* today must abide by the Biblical understanding of time and history, is nevertheless willing to concede that his exposition of these Biblical matters is probably quite accurate. But is it? Bultmann thinks it is emphatically not accurate. The main ground of Bultmann's objection to Cullmann's *Heilsgeschichte* view is that it stems from an illicit synthesizing of the differentiated elements of the New Testament's varied confessions. In short, there is no basis for thinking of a unitary New Testament understanding of time and history.[73]

The same objection has lately been made by Professor James Barr, only in this instance on strictly lexical grounds. Barr quite correctly observes that the Bible itself does not make any direct statements on the subject of "time" or "eternity" that could be understood to be the result of philosophical reflection on the subject. It may in fact be inferred from the absence of statements about time and its meaning that Biblical men were little interested in philosophical or theological speculation about time. Despite Cullmann's firm resolve to eschew all modern philosophical concepts of time and eternity in order to arrive at the purely Biblical understanding of time, his structure of the time-line is only apparently Biblical and nonphilosophical. It is precisely because the Bible itself makes no clear statements about what time is like that exegetes such as Cullmann have been constrained to draw out of the Biblical *words* for time a concept of what time means for Biblical man. Now the substance of Barr's critique of Cullmann is that to appeal to the lexical stock of the Bible rather than to the actual statements it makes is, semantically, a totally illegitimate procedure. We ought not to deduce the Biblical view of time from the lexical stock of Hebrew or New Testament Greek.

To note one or two points of detail. Basic for Cullman's thinking about the New Testament understanding of time is the distinction he supposes to exist between the words καιρός and αἰών, καιρός representing a fixed "point in time" and αἰών a "duration of time." But this difference between καιρός and αἰών cannot be maintained, since there are statements in which the words καιρός is used where it clearly means a "period of time" of some kind (Heb. 9:9; Mark 10:30; cf. numerous cases in the Septuagint of Daniel, which as an apocalyptic document would have been of special concern to early Christians). In the various

statements in which the word καιρός occurs, it may mean either a
"period of time" or a "decisive point of time." All the more misleading is it therefore to hypostatize the word καιρός as if it were a concept
or a reality existing independently of the statements in which it is
used, as if it stood for the notion of "decisive time." The idea of a
"καιρός concept" is furthered by Cullmann's habit of not translating
Greek words like καιρός into English, e.g. "the kairoi which the Father
has fixed in his omnipotence" (Acts 1:7).[74] Most damaging of all to
Cullmann's position is his interpretation of the plural καιροί in I Timothy 2:6, τὸ μαρτύριον καιροῖς ἰδίοις. It has always been open to doubt
whether the plural here is a genuine plural at all or whether it ought
not to be rendered simply, "the testimony borne *at the proper time*"
or "the testimony borne *in due season.*" Yet on this dubious plural
Cullmann has erected quite an edifice, namely his theory of a linear
series of special divine καιροί: "In the past, the present and the future
there are special divine kairoi, by the joining of which the redemptive
line arises." [75] Professor Barr now clinches the argument against Cullmann's improbable reading of I Timothy 2:6 by pointing out that
there are no syntactical contexts in which "a series of καιροί" appears
in usage.

Although we may disagree with Barr's rigid separation between
"word" and "concept," as if the Biblical words did not express concepts, the lexical evidence he produces for such words as καιρός and
αἰών and their New Testament usage is solid enough to make us hesitate to build too much in the way of a Biblical "philosophy of time"
on these words alone.[76] It is, however, only the linguistic substructure
of Cullmann's version of the *Heilsgeschichte* that is shaken by these
criticisms. The Biblical view of time and history may not be deduced
from the Biblical words for "time"; but the idea, the primitive Christian idea, of a redemptive history extending from creation to the
eschatological new creation remains an open and unscathed possibility. For quite independently of any theory derived, probably
misleadingly, as we have seen, from the lexical stock of the Biblical
words for "time," literary and theological study and analysis of the
documents may still discern an early Christian understanding of the
history of salvation, with a given beginning in the creation of the
world and a given end in the Parousia of the Son of Man. Let us
illustrate with only one example from many, in which no word for
"time" occurs. "As were the days of Noah, so will be the coming of

the Son of Man" (Matt. 24:37). The theme of the Noah cycle of stories is God's coming toward man in judgment and salvation. So here it is proclaimed that that coming of God in judgment and salvation will reach its ultimate goal in the return of the Son of Man, also in judgment and salvation. This particular example, with its suggestion of the correspondence between beginning and end, has lately been recognized by E. Käsemann as a signpost to the earliest Christian understanding of history.[77] There is scarcely a more important trend in contemporary New Testament scholarship than the rediscovery and renewal of the view, especially under Käsemann, that the chief formative influence for primitive Christian theology as a whole was the earliest Church's Jewish apocalyptic heritage, the view of the world and its history as having a given beginning and a given end, toward which history was moving through several distinct epochs, all overarched by God and God's purpose.

One speaks of a "rediscovery and renewal" of the opinion that Jewish apocalypticism was the great originative factor in the rise of primitive Christian theology because, of course, Bultmann's interpretation of the New Testament had taken as its key to New Testament theology not apocalypticism but anthropology. Whereas Bultmann acknowledged the profound influence of Jewish apocalypticism on the New Testament, he regarded it as something rather naïvely combined with the new and specifically Christian understanding of existence. Consequently, he looked upon the Synoptic Gospels as an unworthy mythological extension of the Jewish apocalyptic outlook, minimized their importance for the Christian understanding of existence, and raised the Fourth Gospel, with its background in the Gnostic redeemer myth, to the level of the norm of New Testament theology. Moreover, Bultmann detected even in Paul the beginning at least of the process of demythologizing: Christ is preached not as the mid-point of history (Cullmann), but as the end of history and of the history of salvation, so that *there can be no more history,* for history has reached its end in him.[78]

Precisely this opinion that the earliest Church believed the *end* of history had come upon it already is now challenged by Käsemann. When one speaks about a norm for primitive Christian theology, the emphasis must not fall, according to Käsemann, on the incipient Gnostic zeal of members of the Corinthian congregation who felt that all "futurism" was extinguished since the resurrection had taken place already. The emphasis must fall rather upon the prophetic zeal of those in the earliest Palestinian Church who, in the light of their imminent expectation of the Parousia as a result of the Easter event, appealed to the eschatological predictions of the Old Testament and to the work of Jesus Christ, and found in them guidance for this time in which *the end of history had begun*.[79] Since Käsemann thinks of both Paul and John as defenders of the pure orthodox faith of the earliest Church in God's direction of history toward the future coming of the Son of Man, against the fanatical enthusiasm of men of Gnostic leanings in the congregations, what this means in effect is that not only the Synoptics but also John is considered to be the outcropping of Jewish apocalypticism.

Most significant of all is Käsemann's reinterpretation of Paul's Epistle to the Romans along the lines suggested in Adolf Schlatter's *Gottes Gerechtigkeit* (1935), namely that what is involved in justification by faith is the vindication of God's rulership over our world. The history of the interpretation of Romans has of course been governed by Luther's tremendous exposition of its message as directed to the salvation of the individual soul, agonized by its feelings of sin and guilt. What is now proposed is that Paul's main interest is not in fact in the individual's salvation, but in the theme of the redemption of the cosmos, even all creatures, of the carrying through and fulfillment of *Gottesheilsplan*. Attention is called to Paul's prefatory remark in Romans 1:5: "We have received grace and apostleship to bring about obedience to the faith for the sake of his name among all the nations." Even more important is Romans 1:16: "For I am not ashamed of the gospel: it is the power of God for salvation to everyone who has faith, to the Jew first and also to the Greek."

Eduard Schweizer sets forth the thematic development of Romans thus: (a) The proclamation of the gospel to the nations occasions the eschatological outbreak of God's wrath and is in fact a proleptic last judgment upon both Gentiles and Jews. In Paul's missionary preaching the issue of mankind versus God, so frequently attested in the Old Testament, is being decided (Rom. 1:18–3:20). (b) God's grace is, nevertheless, still being bestowed. He is turning in mercy toward the Gentiles in the mission of Paul. Paul's mission is indeed the eschatological sign of fulfillment of the ancient promises of God in his ultimate victory over the world (Rom. 3:21–8:39). (c) God is at last vindicated when all the nations accept his verdict and praise his righteousness. Accepting God's verdict, all mankind is justified. At the close "the apostle is the cosmic priest presenting all nations of the earth as an acceptable thank-offering to God." The submission of the Gentiles to God's judgment is the consummation of the *Heilsgeschichte* (Rom. 12–15).[80]

This is, to be sure, an interesting rejoinder to Bultmann's anthropologically centered interpretation of Paul. We cannot linger over special points of exposition. Speaking broadly, we would put this question: Does the letter to the Romans confront us with an "either . . . or," either an overwhelming interest on Paul's part in concrete eschatology or an overpowering concentration upon the salvation of the individual? It seems to me that only a case of special pleading in the interests of a theory could rule out the fact that Paul is concerned, especially in Romans 5 to 8, with personal faith, personal life, personal salvation. On the other hand, the subservience of modern scholarship to the Lutheran understanding of Romans as dominated by the theme of the individual's justification by faith, has equally tended to obscure or minimize the importance of Paul's strictly eschatological interest in chapters 9 to 11 and chapters 12 to 15.

What, it appears, we have to reckon with in the letters of Paul is the coexistence of the personal, individual dimensions of faith and deep interest in a concrete "futuristic" eschatology, but not exclusively either the one or the other. I am sure there would be general agreement that Johannes Munck has gone too far in portraying Paul's career and activity as wholly determined by eschatology, as if Paul were completely possessed by the eschatological dogma that he was the chosen instrument of God to bring in the fullness of the Gentiles.[81] One could readily concur with the judgment of W. D. Davies: "We cannot but feel that the insistence on the centrality of eschatology tends to give a picture of Paul divested of the great depths of 'Paulinism.' We may express the point roughly by saying that while all Paul's life and thought is eschatological, eschatology is not the whole of Paul." [82] Moreover, the thesis put forward by highly reputable scholars of a diminution of emphasis on concrete eschatology in the later Paul still cannot be overlooked.[83]

Suppose then we do indeed have to reckon with the coexistence of Paul's doctrine of personal faith and his interest (derived from his Jewish apocalyptic inheritance) in concrete eschatology, in the concept of a scheme of the ages, moving toward its consummation in the end of the world appointed by God. Is there any fundamental incompatibility between them? The existentialist theologian will urge that preoccupation with the history of the world and its course can only mean surrender to the dominion of the Law, bringing us into despair, because we can make no sense out of the world's history. He will ask us to accept that faith has only to do with the here and now of our obedience to God in our concrete situation. But it is altogether too easy, in the interest of overcoming the mythical character of an apocalyptic-eschatological world view, to submit to something else that appears to be hardly less mythological, namely allowing the world and its history, past, present, and future, to collapse into a broken series of unrelated "moments" in which I am claimed by God and may respond to him in faith.

In any case, I cannot see why my personal faith that God, in addressing me, gives me a history, should insulate me from the world in which I live and to which I always stand related. Has the Law usurped the place of faith because I am concerned about the world and hope also in God for the longed-for fulfillment of its history? Though my relation with God and the world is primarily in terms of personal confrontation and response, submission and withholding, I am still creature in a creation, and my concern over it and questions about it will not be suppressed. Is there then any necessary incongruity between the belief that God creates me anew and gives me a new self in and through faith, and the belief that God will not allow the world, *this* world and its history, to end in contradiction? Theology today might, in fact, be benefited by paying heed to the recent revival among eminent New Testament scholars of the view that early Christian theology had its rootage in Jewish apocalypticism, with its rigorously historical thinking about the world and the course of its history. This might help to overcome the abstractness of much recent theology, with on the one hand its insight into the historicity of human existence leading to an acosmic emphasis, and on the other its concentration on the level of transcendent "meanings."

If we assume, as I think we should, in the light of our discussion, that the New Testament's concrete eschatology cannot be eliminated, that it does think in terms of a history or plan of salvation, moving from a given beginning through clearly distinguishable epochs to a given end ordained by God, then the question arises: what is the place of Jesus of Nazareth in the history of salvation? Returning to our starting point, Cullmann's version of the *Heilsgeschichte,* let us ask how he answers it. Cullmann is in little doubt about the matter. For him the principle of *Heilsgeschichte* corresponds to the innermost nature of all New Testament Christology, and the starting point of all Christological thought is the self-consciousness of Jesus himself.[84] Jesus knew in the first place that he must accomplish the role of the "Suffering Servant of God." He knew in the second place that his mission was to introduce the kingdom of God as the "Son of Man" who was expected soon to come on the clouds of heaven. Finally he thought of himself as carrying through the double function of the "Servant of God" and the "Son of Man" in his unique sense of oneness with God. But can we really speak with this assurance about Jesus' combining in his consciousness the ideas of the "Servant of God" and the "Son of Man"? To repeat only one point, we saw earlier the extreme difficulty in which critical scholarship is placed regarding the question of whether Jesus identified himself with the coming "Son of Man." Our own earlier conclusions about the possibility of discovering the "Christology" implicit in Jesus' life and ministry were much more tentative. We hesitated to probe into his consciousness on the basis of the titles applied to him in the Gospels, and preferred at that stage to dwell on his eschatological message as a possible clue to his "Christological" claim upon men.

However, although Cullmann may have construed the question about the historical Jesus too narrowly in terms of his "self-consciousness," one of the undeniable merits of his position is the crucial place he allows to the Resurrection. Such glimmerings of light as the disciples had on Jesus in his earthly life, now in the post-Easter time stood "in the bright light of perception, and at least a few came to understand those indirect references of his which had found no open ears during his lifetime." [85] Of this important factor we shall have more to say in later chapters.

In concluding this chapter, let us simply underscore the diversity of opinion we have encountered in our examination of recent advances toward a solution of the "Jesus of history"–"Christ of kerygma" problem: Knox's stress on the heavenly Lord of the Church; Jeremias' stress on the revelation in the historical Jesus to the minimizing of the Resurrection and the exalted Lord's revelation of himself! Fuller's view of Jesus as Son of Man—designate; Cullmann's view of Jesus as in his life Son of Man–Suffering Servant! The essentially inconclusive character of our inquiry may seem very disappointing. Can we then look to the "new quest" of the historical Jesus to clear up the obscurities and set us on a straight path of understanding? In the next chapter we shall try to find out.

IV

Features of the "New Quest"

It would be impossible to touch on every aspect of the controversy about the problem of the historical Jesus that has raged in Germany in the last decade. Fortunately there is no need to do so; as we have seen, Dr. James M. Robinson gave an admirable exposition in his book *A New Quest of the Historical Jesus.* Our purpose in the following pages is more restricted. It is to try to illuminate some of the principal features of the "new quest," and that mainly with reference to Günther Bornkamm's *Jesus of Nazareth,* and finally to assess the validity and value of the "new quest."

Bornkamm's exposition is surely the most brilliant to emanate from the post-Bultmannian group, marked as it is at once by a compelling clarity of scholarly insight into the sources and by a pervasive sense of existential urgency. In its main lines, in form, structure, and, to some extent, in content, Bornkamm's book bears a close resemblance to Bultmann's earlier work entitled *Jesus* (1926). We have spoken frequently about Bultmann's apathy toward the historical Jesus and his repeated insistence that there is no good theological reason for trying to penetrate behind the kerygma. We need all the more, therefore, to remind ourselves here that one of his earlier works was this monograph on Jesus. There already is to be found the dynamic for one of the major emphases of the "new quest," namely that the gateway to an understanding of Jesus' interpretation of his own existence is his language, his words, his teaching. In his *Jesus,* Bultmann repudiated every attempt to reconstruct the *personality* of Jesus, and was satis-

149

fied to interpret his teaching (though it is hard for some of us to see how person and word, or person and teaching, can be held apart). "Little as we know of his life and personality," wrote Bultmann, "we know enough of his *message* to make for ourselves a consistent picture." [1] Just as for Bultmann Jesus was supremely the "speaker" whose words hit us with the question of how we are to interpret our own existence, so is he also for Bornkamm. In reality, therefore, such members of the Bultmann school as Bornkamm, in seeking to revitalize scholarly concern with the historical Jesus, were trying to give a new prominence to a phase of Bultmann's own work that had been silenced latterly by his strict concentration on the kerygma—a fact which should caution anyone who might expect from Bornkamm a non- or even anti-Bultmannian orientation in regard to the writing of a "life of Jesus." I suspect that, in raising the question of the interconnection between the message of the historical Jesus and the Church's message, Bultmann's pupils imagined they might get him to bat on the same wicket. But, to judge from Bultmann's Heidelberg paper of 1959, not only did he not come in to bat, he took no part at all in the game.

In order now to clarify some of the outstanding characteristics of the "new quest," we shall begin by comparing and contrasting Bornkamm's *Jesus* with the work of T. W. Manson. We shall refer particularly to Manson's *The Teaching of Jesus,* which in its own day and in its own right was a classic of its kind and still justifiably claims the greatest respect.

Manson's Teaching *and Bornkamm's* Jesus

It would be quite wrong to suppose that a rigid line of demarcation should be drawn between such representative researchers as Bornkamm and Manson, as if Bornkamm's new account of Jesus had forthwith completely invalidated even the best insights of earlier scholarship. There are indeed some striking similarities between Manson's critical opinions and judgments concerning the Gospel tradition and those of Bornkamm.

Manson's *The Teaching of Jesus,* like Bornkamm's *Jesus,* is permeated with his strong conviction of the theological importance and decisiveness of the words of Jesus, not as an interesting addition to the ongoing history of religious ideas, or as teaching general and universal religious truths, but as the sharp sword which pierces hearers with the reality of God.[2] From his investigation of the Gospel tradition, Manson had already noted the part played in the teaching of Jesus by the audience addressed by him, the Scribes and Pharisees, the crowd, his disciples. He declares the criterion of "Jesus-audience relationship" to be the foundation principle of his examination of the sayings of Jesus.[3] The importance of the category of "encounter" with Jesus has not escaped his notice. The authority of Jesus, which immediately impresses itself upon his listeners, resides in his being the agent of God's revelation. "This authority was noticed by the people who heard him speak and the tone of his teaching struck them as being very different from that of the scribes. . . . The scribal method of definition of terms and deduction from already established rules and decisions could not but compare unfavorably with Jesus' way of piercing by prophetic insight to the heart of any moral problem."[4] Jesus puts a man in the place where he must decide for himself. All this comes remarkably close to certain of Bornkamm's own statements: "The listener is never obliged to look for premises which would give meaning to Jesus' teaching, or to recall the theory about doctrines and traditions which he would be required to know beforehand."[5] "The Gospels call the patent immediacy of Jesus' sovereign power his 'authority.' . . . In his encounters with the most different people, Jesus' 'authority' is always immediately and authentically present. . . . The encounter compels everyone to step out of his customary background. This bringing to light of men as they really are takes place in all stories about Jesus."[6]

Again Manson deals at considerable length with the parables of Jesus. He stringently condemns the familiar homiletical or allegorical use of the parables, by which they are regarded as delectable lessons, illustrating and clarifying theological or spiritual truths that are independent of them. His survey of the formal characteristics of Jesus' parabolic teaching is concluded with the observation that the parable is a work of art and also, more importantly, a test determining who are to be disciples of Jesus. The single purpose of all the parables is to show "what God is and what man may become, and to show these things in a way that will reach men's hearts if it is possible to reach them at all. And, when we come to think of it, the greatest and most effective parable of them all is his own life."[7] This is in line with the best recent scholarship on the parables, for example, Jeremias's view of them as Jesus' "weapons of war." It is in line with Bornkamm's standpoint. For Bornkamm, too, the parables reveal great art, but chiefly they are *the preaching itself* and so grip the hearer, just where he really is, with the hidden presence of the rule of God, which has to be believed and understood by him in his actual world, and not in terms of past rubrics or theories or traditions.[8]

That Manson had to a great extent broken with the fundamental presuppositions of the nineteenth-century quest is apparent from his prefatory remarks that we have no life of Jesus in the tradition, and that there are stretches of his ministry of which no detailed record has been preserved. "The material is woefully scanty both for the life and for the teaching."[9] The Bultmann school has also, of course, disavowed all "biographical" interest.

I have felt it worthwhile to draw attention to the existence of certain similarities between Manson and Bornkamm. The fact that there are not unimportant points of contact should serve to remind us that it is both unjust and misleading to classify the best twentieth-century custodians of orthodox historical-critical research in the Gospel tradition as straightforward perpetuators of the old quest. The impartial reader of Manson's book could scarcely accuse him of seeking by the historical method to verify the *fact* that Jesus' life, on its external side, followed such and such a course or sequence. The impression we have is that he is trying to let Jesus speak, that in his message men, in the very place where they are, might hear God's call to repentance and faith.

Nevertheless, such continuity as there is between the work of Manson and Bornkamm is considerably less notable than the discontinuity.

Contrasting Views of the Character of the Gospel Tradition

Despite his self-confessed uncertainty about the possibility of reconstructing a life of Jesus from the Gospels as sources, Manson continued throughout his career to defend the historical reliability of Mark's "biographical sketch." We find him in one of his latest essays still defending the historicity of Mark against Wrede's attack in *Das Messiasgeheimnis* (1901) and against the skepticism of radical Form-criticism.[10] By and large, this represents the widely accepted position of English New Testament scholarship in the last three or four decades. C. H. Dodd's feeling that the primitive Christian kerygma mirrors the skeleton framework of Jesus' earthly career has been highly influential. One recalls also Dodd's hypothesis of Mark's having in his possession a written outline of the ministry of Jesus. In 1954, after expressing grave misgiving about the project, Vincent Taylor proceeded none the less, as we noticed in the second chapter, to an account of the life and ministry of Jesus on the basis of the Marcan outline, into which are fitted at certain strategic points data from the other Gospels. The measure of T. W. Manson's confidence in the general historical trustworthiness of Mark is the way he speaks of significant chronological divisions of our Lord's life. "One of the first steps toward the understanding of the teaching will be to fit it as far as possible into the framework of the life of Jesus. The mission of Jesus, like the careers of many of the great masters in music and literature, falls into periods." For Manson, as for a great many other scholars, Peter's confession of Jesus' Messiahship at Caesarea Philippi is a crucial date in the calendar of Jesus' ministry, marking a turning-point, the close of one period in his teaching and the beginning of another.

Our reason for mentioning this is not that it is not already very well and very widely known, but simply that we might bring into clear view the contrast with members of the Bultmann school, for whom all such biographical interest is gone. Certainly Bornkamm shows how he has pushed beyond Bultmann by dealing in his third chapter with the "indisputably historical traits" of Jesus of Nazareth. But what do these amount to? His childhood and adolescence are obscure. He belonged to Galilee. His native town was Nazareth. He was a Jew, son of Joseph, the carpenter. He had brothers and sisters. His mother tongue was Galilean Aramaic. Small towns like Bethsaida, Chorazin, Capernaum were the scene of his activity. We do not know exactly how long his ministry lasted. But of his preaching, debates with his opponents, healings, and good deeds we learn a great deal. At the last he went up to Jerusalem to his death on the Cross.[11]

Very limited knowledge indeed. It is fortunate, however, that we do have much information about his preaching, debates, and good deeds, for it is precisely in his words and deeds that we find his history as occurrence. Indisputably, the Jesus of the Gospels belongs to this world and the people who meet him are completely real people. Nevertheless, in the people's encounter with him, he stands forth in his unmistakable otherness. In his word and in his deed the mystery of his own being arrests them, bearing as it does neither upon their past nor their future, but upon the instantaneous here and now of their existence. His words bring the reality of God unbearably close to those who hear. The present moment in its apparent banality is rendered decisive for those who confront him. "In the encounter with Jesus, time is left to no one: the past whence he comes is no longer confirmed, and the future he dreams of no longer assured. But this is why every individual is granted his own new present." [12] The theme of "unmediated presence" in the words of Jesus is developed by Bornkamm throughout his work. In the parables, the Beatitudes, the eschatological sayings, on the subject of the Law, the new righteousness, creation and the world, faith and prayer, reward, it is everywhere the same: Jesus in his words confronts men *now* with the reality of God.

What we see in all of this, of course, is the working out of a hermeneutic founded on the principle of a life relationship to the subject. But the curious thing, and of this we have to take careful note, is that it is not now, as with Bultmann, the Christ-kerygma that is existentialistically approached and interpreted, but the historical Jesus of Nazareth. We shall have to discuss later the combination of historical-critical research and existential openness that is typical of the "new quest."

From Bornkamm's development of the theme of "unmediated presence" in the words of Jesus, his understanding of the nature of the Gospel tradition begins to grow clear. Gone is the conviction, which has captivated orthodox historical-critical research, that our knowledge of the Jesus of history depends on whether we can so establish the connectedness of the various elements in the tradition as to arrive at a portrait of his life as a chronological sequence of events. Gone in short is the biographical concern. What then has replaced it? From Bornkamm's hearty endorsement of Wrede's theory of the "Messianic secret" in Mark, with its impugning of the historicity of the Marcan record, one would tend to think not very much that is constructive on the historical level.[13]

What we are offered on the positive side is this: Bornkamm accepts the thesis, which, since Kähler, has made such inroads into twentieth-century scholarship, that the Gospels are primarily post-Easter confessions of faith in the risen and exalted Christ. The Gospel tradition is the response of the believing community to the mission and ministry of Jesus the Christ *in its entirety*. It is witness to the history of him who is even now believed in as its Lord. What this means for us is that in every single strand and unit of the tradition we are summoned to see not a fragmentary part of his whole life but his being and his presence in its wholeness, in both the reality of his history and the reality of his Resurrection. Since this is so, it follows that, if we come to the tradition with only a passion for objective scientific historiography, we truncate his history by missing the reality of his Resurrection, which demands from us genuine existential openness.

This characteristic emphasis on the self-containedness of every single unit of the tradition, every Gospel *pericope* as, by itself and independently of its context, testimony to the totality of the person and history of Jesus, no doubt offers a rather staggering challenge to the customary biographical way of thinking. Certainly we hear in it the echo of the Form-critic K. L. Schmidt's skeptical conclusion that the Gospel tradition is like a string of pearls, of which the string has been broken. Bornkamm even remarks that the well-known pulpit device of beginning a sermon on a Gospel text with the words, "Jesus had just . . ." and a recapitulation of what has gone before, is likely to lose altogether the message of the text itself. What then are we offered in the place of any consecutive or coherent life of Jesus or instead of the traditional notion of Jesus' *life work* culminating in his Passion? As in Bultmann's *Jesus* we are invited to come to the life and person of Jesus primarily as teaching. The main body of Bornkamm's book deals with Jesus' message of the dawn of the kingdom of God, the will of God, and discipleship. Very beautifully and challengingly the theme is developed that all men "now stand in the sudden flash of light of the coming God, in the light of his reality and presence." [14] Here Bornkamm, as existentialist interpreter, tries very hard to overcome his historicism by allowing Jesus' ultimate claim upon men to shine forth so as to place *even us* in a situation of "crisis" before it.

Fatherhood and Sonship

If we choose now to contrast Manson's chapter on "God as Father" with Bornkamm's section on "God the Father and His Children," it is not because we have made an arbitrary selection, but only because this will serve especially well as commentary on another of the outstanding characteristics of the "new quest." [15]

Bornkamm, like other members of the Bultmann school, refuses to allow that the Gospels reproduce the life of Jesus in its outward progress, in its episodes and stages. Likewise, he consistently seeks to avoid "psychologizing," speaking of the inner development, the personality, the spiritual experience of Jesus. This is entirely in accordance with the fashion that has prevailed in recent German scholarship: one must necessarily attempt to differentiate one's position and the terminology one employs from the psychologism and historicism of the old quest.

On the other hand, the spiritual experience, the God-consciousness of Jesus, is the pivot of Manson's treatment of the theme of the Fatherhood of God. From a statistical survey of the texts in which Jesus refers to the Fatherhood of God, Manson shows that an overwhelming preponderance of these belong to Matthew and John, and only the merest handful to Mark and Q. How are we to explain the fact that about God's Fatherhood, which Matthew and John are ready to proclaim from the housetops and obviously regard as a vital clue to the Gospel, Jesus himself, according to the primary sources Mark and Q, is practically silent? The explanation, to Manson's mind, is that, in the ongoing life of the soul, Jesus passed through a religious experience of great intensity and sacredness in which he became assured of God's Fatherhood. His unique inner sense of filial relationship to the Father was sealed and confirmed at his Baptism (Mark 1:11: "Thou art my beloved Son; with thee I am well pleased"). This sacred and supreme reality of God's Fatherhood in his inward life did not need to be promulgated by him with much talk and argument, for it was obvious to his followers.[16] Manson of course concedes that Jesus' purpose is to make the Father real to men, but his message of God's Fatherhood is conditioned by and dependent upon the primary fact of his own consciousness of his status as the Son of God—a fact taken to be an assured conclusion of historical-critical research.[17]

The impasse into which orthodox historical criticism has come in seeking to establish the authenticity of Jesus' claim to Sonship as a prior conditioning factor giving meaning to his whole message is demonstrated by its handling of the "crux criticorum" in Matthew 11:25–30 (cf. Luke 10:21–2).[18] These verses have lately been described by Dr. A. M. Hunter as perhaps the "most important verses in the Synoptic Gospels." It would certainly be generally admitted that the question whether Jesus as a matter of historical fact thought of himself as the Son, is closely bound up with the interpretation of Matthew 11:27 (cf. Luke 10:22). "All things have been delivered to me by my Father; and no one knows the Son except the Father, and no one knows the Father except the Son and anyone to whom the Son chooses to reveal him." Even if we accept the validity of the search for what Jesus thought of himself in terms of his inward life, the variety of critical judgments about this saying, widely known as "the Synoptic thunderbolt from the Johannine sky" because of its Johannine ring or flavor (cf. John 3:35; 10:15, etc.),[19] graphically illustrates the problem of historical uncertainty with regard to the self-consciousness of Jesus. The genuineness of the saying is rejected by J. Weiss, for example, and by R. Bultmann as a "revelation word" of a Hellenistic Gnostic type. A. E. J. Rawlinson is skeptical about it even though it stands in Q. Manson himself follows the earlier suggestion of von Harnack and looks on the words "And no man knoweth the Son, but the Father" as an insertion in the text.[20] Vincent Taylor, persuaded by the appearance of Matthew 11:27 in Q, stops short of attributing it to Jesus himself, but sees in it the confession of a primitive community's faith in Jesus as Son of God, and maintains there is no reason to suppose Jesus could not have used it himself, "speaking in the language of characteristic Semitic hyperbole." "The saying is in line with the development of the prophetic consciousness carried to a higher, and indeed to an incomparable degree." [21] Now, to be sure, it is not nearly so easy to say today that Matthew 11:27 must drop out of the tradition of Jesus' sayings for reasons based on the history of religion, namely that the mutuality of relationship between the Father and the Son is a Hellenistic mystical idea that is quite alien to Judaism.[22] For Dr. W. D. Davies has convincingly shown that the kind of "knowledge" involved in the "I-Thou" relationship of Matthew 11:27 has its true parallel not in Hellenistic "gnosis" but in the "knowledge" of the Dead Sea Scrolls—"knowledge" that is always close to obedience and eschatological awareness.[23] However, it need hardly be stated that this is evidence only for a Jewish milieu for the passage and does not establish the authenticity of the saying as a word of Jesus. In fact, the texts cited in support of the claim that Jesus could have styled himself "the Son" *simpliciter* do not bear that weight of evidence: the word of the boy Jesus, "Did you not know that I must be in my Father's house?" (Luke 2:49); the voice from heaven at the Baptism, "Thou art my beloved Son" (Mark 1:11); [24] the parable of the wicked husbandmen with its allusion to the slaying of the last beloved son (Mark 12:6–8); Jesus' amazing invocation to God as *Abba* (which ought probably to be understood less as a "Christological" claim relating to his inward life or self-consciousness than as an expression of his work, his mission, to bring God near to men)—all these are of a different order from the absolute use of the title "the Son" in Matthew 11:27. The only other place in the Synoptics where this use of the word "Son" is found is Mark 13:32: "But of that day or that hour no one knows, not even the angels in heaven, nor the Son, but only the Father." Now this saying is nearly as much disputed as Matthew 11:27 in regard to its historicity. On the positive side, it is questionable whether Mark 13:32 could be altogether an invention of the Christian community, since it would have been unlikely to ascribe to Jesus ignorance of the date of the Parousia. On the negative side, the saying is a somewhat detached word in the midst of a body of apocalyptic material, which, as we have seen, clearly bears the imprint of the Church's hand; and the absence of any proof whatever that "Son of God" was used as a Messianic title in Judaism makes it the more difficult to conceive of Jesus using it as a self-designation. A way out of the difficulty has accordingly been sought in the fairly widely accepted compromise solution that there may well be in Mark 13:32 a historical kernel going back to Jesus, but that its wording has been tampered with. [25] Confronted with the problem of Matthew 11:27 and the scarcely less vexatious problem of the only other parallel passage in the Synoptics, Mark 13:32, criticism has found itself in the shaky position of having to buttress its arguments for the authenticity of the one by appeal to the other. [26] Therefore, we find it difficult, all in all, to agree with Professor A. M. Hunter's verdict that anyone who rejects the logion of Matthew 11:27 does so for no good critical reasons, but simply because he has already made up his mind that "the Jesus of history could not have made such a claim." [27] On the other hand, there is indeed a certain pathos in the extreme desire of some critics to defend the authenticity of such a saying as Matthew 11:27, as though Christian faith could only continue to live out of the fact, the historically verified fact, of Jesus' own consciousness of Sonship to God.

At all events, the reader of Bornkamm's *Jesus of Nazareth* will search in vain for discussion of such a logion as this. It is excluded as a community confession, and every effort to define the self-consciousness of Jesus as an *a priori,* authenticating his message and mission, is here avoided. When Bornkamm writes about "God the Father and His Children," he nowhere shows concern to validate Jesus' claim to Sonship as a historically demonstrated divine fact, "proving" the universal applicability of his message. Theologically speaking, this is an attempt to do homage to Bultmann's protests against seeking an objective, historically verifiable *datum* as a support for faith in Jesus as the Christ. From the critical point of view, it reflects a typical attitude of the Bultmann school: contrary to normative orthodox critical presuppositions, the message of Jesus and the kerygma of the Church cannot simply and straightforwardly be laid alongside each other. For the most kerygmatic sayings of Jesus, in which he claims for himself such exalted titles and dignities as "Son," reveal the greatest impact upon the tradition of the Church's Christological formulations and confessions, and so are the least likely to represent his *ipsissima verba.* Accordingly, new criteria have to be thought out for finding a basis of comparison between Jesus of Nazareth and the Church's kerygma.[28] It is from this standpoint that Bornkamm has recourse to the "ethical" and parabolic teaching of Jesus and, in his presentation of Jesus, avoids, for instance, in dealing with God's Fatherhood, a text like Matthew 11:27. Bornkamm notes that the idea of God as Father has a rich background both in Greek and in Old Testament and Jewish religion and is not new with Jesus. However, Jesus' use of the name "Father" for God, albeit its true import is not to be sought in terms of its inward meaning for his own self-consciousness, is peculiarly the expression of his mission, which is (as in Matthew 5:44 ff.; 10:29 f.; 6:8, 32; and in the Prodigal Son story of Luke 15:11 ff.) *to make God immediately present to men.* The Galilean Aramaic word *Abba-Father,* on Jesus' lips, is, as we have already observed, most significant in this respect. By it Jesus brings God near to men, not because it "proves" an indisputable fact of his own inward nature and personality, but only because in the word itself God's Fatherhood is encountered by those who hear, as an act of grace.[29]

The contrast between Manson and Bornkamm on the subject of God's Fatherhood may now have become clear. Manson gives pride of place to those texts which seem to verify Jesus' claim to Sonship.

Sonship as a fact of Jesus' own self-consciousness is then taken to be an *a priori* truth, to which his other teachings concerning the nature of the Father are subsidiary. Bornkamm, on the other hand, in his picture of Jesus forsakes the texts which relate to his claim to Sonship as bearing the mark of the post-Easter confessions of the Church. It is then in his teachings ("ethical," parabolic, for example, Luke 15:11 ff.) that his mission is expressed, as the concrete occurrence in which God as Father is brought near to men. The primitive Church consistently preserved in the tradition Jesus' language about the Father precisely because it looked upon God's Fatherhood and our being his children not as a fact or idea, but as a miracle of grace, present in his words and deeds.

The Problem of Messiahship

The question of the "Messianic consciousness" of Jesus has for long been a central concern of orthodox historical-critical research. When the present writer embarked on his studies in divinity in Scotland in the 1940's, he was led to assume, like most others of his place and generation, that he could accept as a commonplace of the best scholarship that Jesus looked upon himself as, and was in fact in some sense, the Messiah. The only problem to be decided was when (at the Baptism or Caesarea Philippi?) and in what sense Jesus began to think of himself as the Messiah. At any rate the prevailing trend, exemplified by such scholars as C. J. Cadoux and T. W. Manson, was to concentrate upon Jesus' "consciousness" or inner sense of vocation. Especially the Messiah–Son of Man–Suffering Servant catena of ideas from the Old Testament and the Intertestamental Literature was held to be formative and constitutive for Jesus' own belief about the nature of his vocation. Thus Manson's examination of the Gospel tradition led him to believe that Jesus transformed Jewish Messianic expectations by fusing within himself the functions of Messiah–Son of Man–Suffering Servant and interpreting his office in the light of this unprecedented combination. The ultimate stage in the development of Jesus' "Messianic consciousness" was reached when he regarded himself as the Son of Man, embodying within himself the true and faithful Remnant of Israel—true and faithful because he now saw himself to be the Servant who must suffer. "His claim to the Messiahship is a claim to be the head of the Remnant in virtue of fulfilling those ideals. And now, standing alone against the world, He *is* the Remnant. He is the Son of Man because He alone is equal to the claims of the Son of Man ideal. Son of Man and Messiah have been united in one person, his person." [30]

The attempt to explicate Jesus' history in terms of what he thought and felt about himself has continued to preoccupy historical research in some circles until now—Cullmann, for instance, has made Jesus' self-consciousness the basis of all Christology. To some extent it has been given edge in recent years by study of the Dead Sea Scrolls, which appear to testify to a certain interplay and blending of different Messianic motifs at a time prior to Jesus, and so seem to make it the more conceivable that Jesus in his inward experience could have combined the ideas of Messiah–Son of Man–Suffering Servant.[31] The methodological assumption underlying this approach has always been that, for understanding the person and mission of Jesus, the first consideration is what he felt about himself in his own consciousness and that what he felt about himself can be determined largely by expectations, traditions, concepts, and doctrines coming out of past Jewish history. This is so even of those theories which hold that Jesus did not claim to be the Messiah, but saw himself only as Messiah *designatus* or Son of Man *designatus*.[32]

Recently the familiar reference to Jesus' "Messianic consciousness" has passed out of vogue. Perhaps a more satisfactory reason for its decline in popularity would be the growing recognition that the Gospels do not give us access to the inward life of Jesus rather than Bultmann's simple "theological" decree that for faith to fasten onto Jesus' conception of himself as Messiah or Son of Man as a historical fact is to lose faith's character of personal commitment. Be that as it may, Bornkamm's approach to the Messianic problem falls under the shadow of Bultmann's now famous judgments on the Gospel tradition: that Peter's confession of Messiahship at Caesarea Philippi is the believing interpretation of the post-Easter Church; that Jesus' life cannot in any sense be regarded as Messianic; that, in the sayings on the Son of Man which can be taken as authentic, Jesus is referring to a coming figure other than himself.[33] Bornkamm purposely relegates consideration of the Messianic question to the end of his presentation of Jesus, in direct antithesis to the normal procedure of orthodox criticism, which has put it first and has emphasized its all-embracing significance for Jesus' history, construed as the inner development of his sense of vocation. What lies behind this radical change of perspective? First, there is the studied attempt to avoid psychologism, speaking about the "consciousness" of Jesus. Second, there is the critical verdict that the Messianic elements in the tradition reflect the Church's post-Easter Credo, awakened by the Resurrection, as is evident even from Mark's paradoxical doctrine of the "Messianic secret." Third, although the life of Jesus is not completely unmessianic (Bultmann), it is, for Bornkamm, "Messianic" only as a "movement of broken Messianic hopes," for Jesus altogether disappointed the Messianic expectations centered upon him. And amazingly there is no single text which gives absolute proof of his making his claim to Messianic rank the primary theme of his message. Fourth, titles and offices from the old Jewish tradition neither determine nor exhaust the meaning of his being. Fifth, these negative conclusions are not the last word; something positive can be said. The positive factor in Bornkamm's interpretation is that "the Messianic character of his being is contained *in* his words and deeds and in the unmediatedness of his historic appearance." [34]

Does this mean then that the study of the Jewish background, meaning, and implications of titles like "Messiah," "Son of Man," "Servant," should forthwith be suspended as irrelevant and valueless? Certainly not. For while we would agree that Jesus "did not make his own rank a special theme of his message prior to everything else," [35] we hold also that it seems unreasonable to suppose that his ministry and message did not carry within them some kind of "Messianic claim." Did the Church, after the Resurrection, simply transfer from Judaism and arbitrarily apply to Jesus a Messianic rank and office of which his earthly life and ministry contained no hint at all? If that were so, it would remain obscure why one who was no more than a rabbi-prophet was crucified. Also, if the title Messiah were assigned to Jesus by the community after the Resurrection without there being any suggestion whatever of a "Messianic claim" in his ministry and message, we would be forced into an extreme Judaic theory of Christian origins which by-passed the creative significance for the Church of the person and history of Jesus, and which destroyed any real continuity between Jesus of Nazareth and the Church's kerygma.[36] To say the least, "title research" has not ended. For we must continue to ask, on the basis of the Gospel tradition of

Jesus' earthly ministry, what there was in it that could have led the Church to ascribe to him Messianic titles and dignities.

We might reasonably say that what happened in the earliest days of the Church was this: in its believing response to the person and history of Jesus and under the impact of the Resurrection, the Church had to verbalize its faith in a variety of ways. So, even within the unity of its witness to the event of Jesus the Christ, the Church gave expression to its Credo in a diversity of forms—in the Synoptics, in the Fourth Gospel, in Paul. One mode of expression the Church adopted was the attribution to Jesus of such names as *Christos* and *Kyrios*.

Two crucial observations have to be made regarding these titles. First, they were not static titles for the primitive Church, but dynamic. That is to say, what they conveyed could not be confined within the boundary of their old connotation in past Jewish history and tradition. Ancient limits were transcended as the meaning of a name like *Kyrios* was filled out and enriched in the transition from Jewish to Hellenistic Christianity. In a recent monograph, E. Schweizer has shown how this took place in the development of belief in Jesus as Lord from Jesus to the Hellenistic Church.[37] In the Palestinian Church's confession of Jesus as Lord, he is the eschatological Fulfiller of all prophecies and the Redeemer from sin. In the Hellenistic context he is thought of as the One who came down from the heavenly world (cf. Paul's readiness to use Hellenistic terminology in Phil. 2:6–11), and as the overcomer of the *Heimarmene,* Fate, which keeps Hellenistic man's life in bondage.

The second essential point is that no single name or title, whether it be *Christos,* derived from the Jewish "Anointed One" (Messiah), or *Kyrios,* taking on new tones and colors in the Hellenistic milieu, continues to bear in Christian testimony and confession simply the significance it had for Judaism or Hellenism. The person and history of Jesus of Nazareth have, in fact, introduced into the titles a paradoxical meaning and content. For the Church's *Christos* (Messiah) is not the mighty leader of Jewish expectations but the one who in obscurity and lowliness goes the way of the Cross. Similarly the Church's *Kyrios*—and this is contrary to what the Hellenist could have believed—is the one who became flesh (cf. John 1:14; Heb. 4:14; Phil. 2:6 f.; I Tim. 3:16). It follows, therefore, that such titles as *Christos* and *Kyrios,* and whatever meaning for them we can draw out of our knowledge of Judaism, are not so much constitutive for the person and history of

Jesus, as his person and history are constitutive for the titles. "What the Messianic titles imply in their application to Him cannot be appreciated from the titles themselves, but only from Jesus Himself." [38] We have referred previously to Dr. W. C. van Unnik's important essay on the problem of how the early Christians could have taken over the name of Christ-Messiah for their crucified Master despite the fact that he had shown none of the characteristics of a king during his earthly life.[39] Van Unnik, most interestingly, follows out the principles we have just enunciated. He does not pursue the question in terms of Jesus' Messianic self-consciousness. That means, of course, a departure from the familiar attempt to establish that Jesus in his inward life could have fused the concepts of King-Messiah and Servant. The question asked instead by van Unnik is whether the attribution of the title "Messiah" to him rested on something in his life. He finds that "something," on the basis of such texts as Matthew 11:5, Luke 11:20, and Mark 3:21, to lie in the peculiar *spiritual power* in which he did his works and from which his words derived their special authority. From the fact that the Spirit was on him, coupled with his proclamation of the kingdom of God and his membership in David's family, he could be and was the Anointed, the *Christos*.

Van Unnik's important paper bids fair to show that "title research" is certainly not dead, especially when it is no longer assumed that we have exhausted everything we can say about Jesus and his history when we have elucidated the old connotations of Messianic names in Judaism. Moreover, it is not insignificant that a pupil of Bornkamm's lately produced a thesis on *Der Menschensohn in der synoptischen Überlieferung,*[40] in which it is proposed that the "Son of Man" sayings predicting the Passion, if not from the lips of Jesus himself, are certainly of Palestinian origin and pre-Marcan. Some of the sayings about the Parousia of the Son of Man are genuine. And, although Jesus is referring to the heavenly manifestation of a figure other than himself, he quite definitely relates men's response or lack of it to himself here and now to the destiny that will be meted out to them when the coming heavenly Son of Man appears for judgment ("For whoever is ashamed of me and of my words in this adulterous and sinful generation, of him will the Son of Man also be ashamed, when he comes in the glory of his Father," Mark 8:38). So, when the early Church developed its identification of the Son of Man with the earthly Jesus, it had a sanction from the message of Jesus himself; the proclamation was not divorced from the Proclaimer.[41]

The Eschatological Sayings of Jesus

Our investigation of Bornkamm's view of Jesus' eschatological proclamation will give us opportunity to bring together in brief summary some considerations put forward earlier on this subject.

Nineteenth-century theology, as typified particularly by A. Ritschl, understood the teaching of Jesus on the kingdom of God in Kantian fashion, as setting forth a realizable moral ideal, the goal of a human program, attainable by individual or social effort. The words of Blake's hymn, from the earliest years of that century, sum up the attitude which came to prevail in its latter part, under the impact both of evolutionism and of utopianist idealism, encouraged by an expansive political philosophy of the coming classless society:

> I will not cease from mental fight,
> Nor shall my sword sleep in my hand,
> Till we have built Jerusalem
> In England's green and pleasant land.

The work of Johannes Weiss toward the turn of the century effected a revolutionary change of outlook by drawing attention to the thoroughly apocalyptic-eschatological nature of the New Testament documents. The kingdom must and will be only the gift of God and cannot be the work of men. Since Weiss, the question which has fascinated the present century and given rise to a vast literature is the question of the relation of the person and history of Jesus to the kingdom of God which he proclaimed. The complexity of the debate on the question may be illustrated by referring only to the notorious semantic problem involved in the expressions for the "nearness" of the kingdom in Mark 1:15 (cf. Matt. 4:17) and Matthew 12:28 (cf. Luke 11:20). Broadly speaking, proposed solutions to the problem of Jesus' eschatological teaching as a whole have been developed, on theological as well as linguistic grounds, along three main lines: (a) C. H. Dodd's "realized eschatology," suggesting that in and with the ministry of Jesus the kingdom of God is already "realized" and fully present in history, has won many followers, although it should be observed that Dodd himself later became more cautious about it and would have preferred some such designation as *sich realisierende Eschatologie* ("self-realizing eschatology"). (b) Schweitzer's thoroughgoing "futuristic" interpretation of Jesus' eschatological pronouncements is distantly adumbrated in Bultmann's position, even though Bultmann could not subscribe to the notion that Jesus understood himself at the close as the one who had to die in order to end the course of ordinary history. For Bultmann, Jesus is the one who preaches the *promise* of the kingdom of God. (c) Perhaps the most widely held view of recent scholarship has been that it is only by a *tour de force* that the eschatological sayings of Jesus can be pressed into either a completely "realized" or a completely "futuristic" interpretation, and that they contain both a present and a future element (contrast Luke 10:18; 11:20; Matt. 11:5 f.; and Mark 2:15 f. with Matt. 6:10 and Mark 14:25). From this perspective a number of attempts have been made to reconcile the present and future aspects in texts relating to the kingdom of God. Explanation has been sought in the "psychological consciousness" of Jesus as matching that of the prophet, who combines both present and future within one purview. Quite common also has been the "proleptic" interpretation, such as we noted formerly in R. H. Fuller's *The Mission and Achievement of Jesus*—with Jesus the dawn (*Anbruch*) of the kingdom is taking place, not its irruption into history (*Hereinbrechen*). So the kingdom is only proleptically present in Jesus, and he conceives himself to be the one *destined to be* Messiah and Son of Man after his death and Resurrection. Again, the explanation espoused by T. W. Manson, with whom we have been specially concerned, is the biographical one. Manson acknowledges that the notions of the kingdom as a present reality and as a future consummation stand together in Jesus' teaching. But once more he thinks of each as occupying different sides of the landmark of Peter's confession at Caesarea Philippi. For before that strategic point the idea of the *coming* of the kingdom is uppermost, and only after it is this replaced by "entrance" into the kingdom, which has now become a present reality in the ministry of Jesus.[42]

Bornkamm for his part deprecates every effort to resolve or explain away the tension between present and future in the sayings of Jesus on the kingdom, and insists that they are inextricably interwoven. He is particularly anxious to emphasize the *present,* which in Jesus' preaching reveals the future as salvation and judgment. This emphasis of

Bornkamm's is also to be found elsewhere, although it is presented by him with particular power. The conclusion of W. G. Kümmel's study of the meaning of Jesus' eschatological message is that he does not summon men, after the fashion of late Jewish apocalyptic, merely to wait upon the coming eschatological consummation, but that in his person, his deeds, and his words, his presence has become a real eschatological present, confronting men with the "now" of God, which reveals the future as God's future.[43] William Manson, whose work deserves more notice in the light of the most recent developments in New Testament interpretation, had to some extent anticipated this in his affirmation that Jesus' gospel of the End rests on the certainty of the power of God which is with him in the present.[44] However, it is this theme of the indissoluble unity of present and future in Jesus' message which Bornkamm unfolds with skill and force in his chapter on "The Dawn of the Kingdom of God." We must not allow ourselves to be bemused into thinking that, in the terminology and imagery of apocalyptic, Jesus *describes* God's future (e.g. Mark 13). For, aside from the consideration that the later apocalyptic tradition of the Church has infiltrated into Jesus' message, the true direction of the message is that "God's future is God's call to the present, and the present is the time of decision in the light of God's future" (v. Mark 13:33–7).[45]

At this point we are recalled to the central motif of Bornkamm's whole treatment, namely "the unmediatedness of Jesus' historic presence." Knowledge of his person and history is not dependent on the historian's endeavor to establish the connectedness of his life in its inward or outward stages of development. Nor is it dependent on demonstrating his Messianic claim as a prior fact of his God-consciousness. The secret of his being as the one who brings God near to men is enclosed *in* his every word and deed. Thus is fulfilled Bornkamm's intention "to seek the history in the Kerygma of the Gospels, and in this history to seek the Kerygma." [46] The early Christian confessions, in all their diverse forms, in sermon or hymn or prayer, are but an answer to the word of God which had already gone forth in Jesus of Nazareth. By the events of Easter, the one in whose proclamation God had drawn near to men has himself become the Proclaimed. The interpretation put upon Jesus' ministry and message by the kerygma is inherent already in Jesus' own words. The unity of the earthly Jesus and the Christ of the Church's faith is thus assured.

The Framework of the Gospels

There is perhaps nothing more striking in Bornkamm's presentation
of Jesus than the abandonment of every thread of connectedness in
the Gospel story. We have seen how he is prepared to take each unit
of the Gospel tradition as, by itself and without commentary from anywhere else, presenting *in nuce* the gospel of Jesus of Nazareth the
Christ. But surely, it will be contended by the orthodox critic, there
is enough of a framework and sequence in the Evangelists' records
for us to be able to deduce the probable course of historical events in
the life of Jesus. Accordingly, it may not be superfluous for us to add
here that the question of the literary framework of each Gospel has
not been neglected by the Bultmann group of scholars. However, their
interest in undertaking literary investigation of the Gospel framework
is not to establish its historical probability as a biographical report of
Jesus, but to explicate and elucidate the theological or Christological
aims and intentions of the Evangelists, with the explicit assumption
that it is the Evangelist's understanding of the kerygma which has
determined the process by which his Gospel has been formed. This
approach is exemplified by Hans Conzelmann's recent study of St.
Luke's theology. The purpose of his study is not to assess Luke's
reliability as historical reporter but to estimate Luke's own comprehension of the meaning of his report. So, for instance, Conzelmann
shows that the geographical elements in Luke's Gospel are not primarily topographical, as places figuring in a biography, but kerygmatic
or religious in significance: "the mountain" in Luke 6:12 and 9:28–
36 is the place of heavenly manifestation, where "the people" cannot
come; "the plain" in Luke 6:17 is the place of meeting with the people; "the lake" in Luke 8:22–39 is the abyss of solitude. Particularly
the eschatological motifs peculiar to Luke appear in Luke's discrepancies with his sources, and it transpires that he has his own precise
theological attitude toward the problem of eschatology. In fact, Luke
eliminates the early eschatological expectation and replaces it with his
own scheme of redemptive history. Luke's framework is therefore
conditioned and formed, not by biographical concern, but by his
believing understanding of the kerygma (which for him, of course,
certainly reflects the person and history of Jesus).[47]

Critique of the "New Quest"

So far we have attempted to clarify some of the outstanding characteristics of the "new quest," with reference mainly to Bornkamm's work.
We have done so with a minimum of critical commentary. If any justification is needed for adopting this procedure, it is one's feeling that,
if some of the more radical things that such an exponent of the "new
quest" as Bornkamm is saying had really been getting through, they
would surely have raised more of an alarm and so more of a response
among Anglo-American scholars. In any case, it is time now to offer
some critical evaluation of the "new quest," taking into account other
contributions as well as Bornkamm's.

Today we can feel extremely grateful for the way in which scholars
of the Bultmann group have reopened the quest of the historical Jesus
in the last ten years. In so doing they have brought a needed corrective to bear on Bultmann's foreclosure of the question of the historical
Jesus and of the Christology implicit in his ministry and message, by
which Bultmann has been in constant danger of isolating or abstract-
ing the kerygma from any historical context. We have frequently insisted, in light of the kerygma's repeated allusions to Jesus of Nazareth, on the necessity of seeking to spell out the *Geschichtlichkeit* of
the revelation. There is an inexpugnable element of concrete historicity behind the early Church's message. And it is to the great
credit of the scholars of the "new quest" that, even while sharing the
Form-critical view of the lack of historical evidence about Jesus in
the Gospels and while aware of the undesirability of trying to "prove"
a historical basis in Jesus for Christian belief so as to remove the risk
and insecurity from faith, they have nevertheless endeavored to do
justice to the historical figure behind the kerygma. For this impulse
toward renewed interest in the controlling and determinative significance of the historical Jesus for Christian faith both New Testament scholarship and the modern Church may be thankful.

Nor, indeed, is there any question that in seeking to work out what
can be known and said about Jesus, exponents of the "new quest"
have greatly aided and abetted the critical evolution that has been
taking place in methods of research. To illustrate, one need cite only
a few of the more important emphases. In the search for criteria for

determining the authenticity or inauthenticity of recorded sayings of Jesus, there is the departure from the older normative practice of attempting to reach the historical Jesus via the Christological titles. Attention is turned instead to those logia which can the more readily be considered genuine precisely because of the lack therein of kerygmatic terminology. What this has meant in effect has been a very sharp focus on the eschatological pronouncements of Jesus as containing the clue to his own understanding of his existence. It is worthwhile recalling how J. Jeremias, who is not a member of the Bultmann group but has approved of the "new quest," included among his five basic safeguards against modernizing Jesus our increased knowledge of the eschatological character of his message. We remember also Bornkamm's determined effort to accept at face value and not to refine away the tension between present and future in Jesus' message of the kingdom of God. Hand in hand with this is the recent decisive advance in parable research, to which E. Fuchs has made his own notable contribution: the parables are no longer understood as media for conveying timeless ethical truths but as warning or exhortation to hearers in their concrete eschatological situation in the present, a present which is directed toward the future coming of the kingdom of God, depicted in such symbols as harvest, feast, etc. Of importance also is the critical reappraisal of the position of Jesus apropos the role of John the Baptist in relation to the shift of the ages. So Bornkamm looks upon Jesus' Baptism at the hands of John as belonging indisputably to the historical data of his life. Jesus connects his own vocation with that of the Baptist (Mark 11:27–33). With the Baptist, raised now above all the prophets before him, the hour of the kingdom has struck (Matt. 11:12–13). John belongs to the time in which the promise is already being fulfilled. In that case, Jesus would have understood his situation in regard to John as the Church understood its situation in regard to Jesus—as the historical occurrence in which the in-breaking of the kingdom of God had taken place.[48]

While the orthodox critic may deplore the meagerness of assured historical results in this avant-garde New Testament research, no school of criticism today can afford to neglect these and other of its findings. There can be no turning the clock back.

We have to notice that behind Bornkamm's somewhat popular presentation in his *Jesus of Nazareth* lie a number of learned technical essays expounding his methodological presuppositions and laying the exegetical foundations for his portrayal. Perhaps for this very reason, that the exegetical ground has already been prepared, there is an admirable directness and thrust in Bornkamm's delineation of Jesus. It moves us with its "preaching power." We feel that critical research has become unobtrusive, and has been shifted from being an end in itself to being a means toward letting the Gospels confront us with the message of Jesus as the one who brings God near to men. There is a supreme challenge here for all types of criticism: it is not for us, using all the historical-critical resources at our disposal, to think that more and more we can speak definitively about the life of Jesus. It is instead for us, when we have exhausted all our resources, to put ourselves in the place where he can speak definitively and decisively to us. For it is he alone who has "the words of eternal life."

I have no doubt that the real dynamic of Bornkamm's book is the prominence given to the recurrent thematic refrain that runs through it: "to make the reality of God present is the essential mystery of Jesus . . . it signifies the end of the world in which it takes place. . . . Its past is called in question, its future is no longer secure." [49] At the level of Christological thought, this emphasis on the theocentric aspect of the Gospel story seems to strike a far better balance in regard to the New Testament than did the older Biblical scholars in their preoccupation with what Jesus held and taught about himself and in their concentration on his "Messianic self-consciousness." For what strikes us about the Gospel story is that, as a man among men, Jesus claims nothing for himself as a man, but everything for the God and Father, to whom he is utterly obedient and on whom he is utterly dependent. Jesus consorts, as the records show, not with those who lay claim to godliness, but with sinners, who are thereby encouraged by his presence in their midst to do what he does, that is, fling themselves entirely on God's grace. The question about Jesus is therefore the question about God. When the Fathers of the Church, Irenaeus, Tertullian, Clement, and Origen, wrestled with the problem of whether the Logos was of the very essence of God, they were not discussing metaphysical niceties. Their most ardent concern was to ask just this: is it the Word of *the eternal God* that has been spoken in Jesus? In all this we have simply been echoing the warning, put out by Karl Barth in the earlier pages of the *Dogmatik,* against the reduction of Christology to a "Jesus-cult," which would amount to no more than the deification of a religious hero and would offer a jejune substitute for Christian faith.[50] Donald Baillie put it well: "We never find [in the New Testament] anything that could be called a Jesus-cult, or a Christology interested simply in the question of who or what Jesus was, apart from the action of God the Father. Whatever Jesus was or did, in His life, in His teaching, in His cross and passion, in His resurrection and ascension and exaltation, it is really God that did it in Jesus; that is how the New Testament speaks." [51] We would therefore heartily agree that the theocentric stress in Bornkamm's exposition of Jesus does justice to the actual documents, and is a significant and valuable counterbalance to every form of scholarly preoccupation with what Jesus thought of himself, with his "personality."

In this context we may appropriately refer to Professor Schubert M. Ogden's recent study *Christ Without Myth*.[52] Ogden sets out to affirm the ontological possibility of authentic life for any man and every man, wherever he may be and *quite apart from Jesus of Nazareth,* in direct encounter with the primordial grace and love of God. In revolt against anything that might savor of a "Jesus-cult," characteristic of certain phases of American religiosity, Ogden aspires toward a postliberal theology that will at one and the same time reveal a genuine sensitivity to the kerygma and the entire theological tradition, and also take full account of modern man's situation in the world in relation to modern philosophy and science. But the position he adopts is so radically monotheistic that he leads us into the gravest difficulty and ambiguity every time he speaks of Jesus of Nazareth. Ogden's main argument is that Bultmann's plea for radical demythologizing is quite inconsistent with his desire to impose a limit on it by binding Christian faith to the historical occurrence of God's saving act in Jesus Christ. Since authentic existence is existence in freedom and responsibility, to tie it up with a unique saving event of the past is simply to impinge upon man's freedom and responsibility. Ogden therefore finds the substance of the New Testament message to be that the only final condition for sharing in authentic life is "a condition that can be formulated in complete abstraction from the event Jesus of Nazareth and all that it specifically imports." [53] On the one hand then, Jesus seems to be expendable for Christian faith and life. But, on the other hand, Ogden, apparently succumbing to his own inconsistency, tells us that "God's saving action has been decisively disclosed in the event Jesus of Nazareth," [54] and latterly: "What has taken place in Jesus of Nazareth is nothing more and nothing less

than a definitive re-presentation of man's existence before God that
has all the force of a final revelation." [55]

What kind of shifting sand is this on which we are asked to stand?
If this is a beach-head on the postliberal shore, may the churches be
preserved from having to land on so unsure a ground! Is Jesus dis-
pensable or is he not? If he is, then we might as well forthwith surrender the ark of God to the philosophers. If he is not, is he no more
than merely "mankind's preacher," in whom the everlasting Thou
draws near? [56] If he is no more than "mankind's preacher," are we
not landed back once more in that reductionist humanizing understanding of his ministry that was characteristic of the older liberal por-
trayals of him as among the greatest and noblest of the sons of men,
but in no real sense the Son of Man and the Son of God? Is he then
the one that was to come, or do we look for another? [57]

We have turned to Ogden's book because it poses for us in a quite
graphic way the selfsame questions that arise in connection with
Bornkamm's *Jesus*. For here too Jesus appears so much only as
"preacher," only as a sign heralding the coming kingdom of God that
is detached from his person, that there is justice in Otto Piper's characterization of Bornkamm's work: "a unitary God with Jesus as his
first theologian." [58] Now to be sure, as we have said, we wholeheartedly endorse the theocentric emphasis in Bornkamm's account
of Jesus, just as we endorse Ogden's affirmation, on the basis of the
New Testament, that "God alone is the final source of authentic
human life." [59] Very well and good! That is, we feel, Christologically
sound. But while it is true that Jesus points men primarily not to himself but to God, the stubborn question is: How were those who encountered him in the days of his flesh brought into the presence of the
transcendent God? Was it through the intrinsic truth of his words, his
message about the coming God? But had not those who heard him
heard also the preaching of John the Baptist? His words were also
"true." Yet was it not something in the person of Jesus, in his gestures,
his deeds, his "loving conduct," culminating in his Passion and death on
the Cross, that gave his words their unique urgency and potency and
eschatological cutting edge? The truth is that we have to look at the
other side of the Christological coin, which such designations as "mankind's preacher" and "theologian," as applied to Jesus, cannot really
touch. That is, if Jesus claimed nothing for himself, but everything for
God, the claim is vindicated not by the spoken words that can be de-

tached from Jesus' person, but by Jesus himself in his work and in his deed. It is surely not insignificant that in the Fourth Gospel, where expression is given to the most exalted Christology, there is at the same time the greatest stress on the "I" of Jesus' person and the "I" of Jesus' deed. "And he who sent me is with me; he has not left me alone, for I always do what is pleasing to him" (John 8:29). "For this reason the Father loves me, because I lay down my life, that I may take it again. No one takes it from me, but I lay it down of my own accord. I have power to lay it down, and I have power to take it again; this charge I have received from my Father" (John 10:17–18). Here the basic function of Jesus consists in his life *work* climaxed by his Passion and death. I think we can safely say, in view of the historical sources, that, in regard to Jesus, word and deed, deed and word were inseparably allied. For, as the Synoptics represent the situation, not only a new and authoritative "word of God" was being spoken in the ministry of Jesus, but God's rule was being manifested also in deed. Acts of exorcism were being accomplished; men's diseases were being cured; they were discovering that their sins were being forgiven; the poor were having the gospel preached to them.[60] But of this more later.

The fact is that when we have said all we can say in praise of the "new quest," we still have the gravest reservations regarding it. As we proceed now to discuss what we believe to be its inherent limitations, let us begin by asking how it looks from the angle of the theologian. First a word concerning the *modus operandi* of the "new quest." On one side at least it continues to operate within the framework of objective historical-critical analysis and research. It ought to have become clear that behind Bornkamm's portraiture of Jesus lie historical-critical judgments regarding the "authentic" and "inauthentic" in the Gospel tradition. So, for example, he unhesitatingly accepts the historicity of Jesus' Baptism by John. On the contrary he detects in the "Messianic" sayings and in the materialistic apocalyptic language on Jesus' lips (e.g. Mark 13) the hand and voice of the post-Easter Church. There is therefore no abrogation of the endeavor of historical-critical research to recover the genuine words and deeds of Jesus. Nevertheless, there is laid alongside critical analysis this new thing: a concept of history, historical thought, and method, derived variously from Troeltsch, Dilthey, Heidegger, Bultmann and Gogarten —historical understanding is possible only on the analogy of our own experience and is dependent on due place being given to our own self-comprehension. I suspect that some of the "new seekers" after the historical Jesus imagine themselves as revolutionizing objective historical research by placing it now under the banner of an interpretation of history, which understands it as direct address, accomplishing a change in the self-comprehension, and not as distant contemplation from the balcony. J. M. Robinson maintains that the méthodology of the "new quest" consists in the simultaneous interaction of objective analysis and existential openness.[61] This is no doubt what Bornkamm intends also by his statement that the task imposed on us today is to look simultaneously for the kerygma in the history and the history in the kerygma. The search for the history in the kerygma involves us in inductive historical scholarship and in the evaluation of the genuineness of the tradition. The conclusions to which we come can never be certain, but only relative, and assuredly, as Bornkamm affirms, faith can never be made dependent on the relativity of historical judgments. The search for the kerygma in the history in the Gospel tradition necessitates openness for immediate existential encounter with Jesus. Bornkamm's position is indeed that we look for the history in the kerygma and the kerygma in the history not in order to separate them but only in order to show their interpenetration.[62]

The upshot is that the "new quest" has made a resolute bid to part company with the older Jesus-research, with its biographical or "psychologizing" interest in the life of Jesus, and to commit itself to the kerygma and to theological concern for the Word of God addressing us in existential encounter. Scholars of the "new quest" are, besides, sufficiently Bultmannian in orientation not to have lost sight of the danger involved for theology in trying to "prove" a historical basis for Christian faith. Their set purpose therefore has been not to establish this or that word and deed of Jesus, this or that miracle, or this or that sequence of events in his life, but rather to demonstrate the correspondence between Jesus' own understanding of his existence and the claim he lays upon us, and the kerygma's witness and the claim it lays upon our existence. But precisely here is the problem. With the best will in the world to avoid speaking objectively about Jesus or laying a concrete historical ground for faith, are we not on the verge of reviving the old biographical interest by holding up Jesus' "existence" as an objectively observable phenomenon the moment we give the impression that, by a somewhat strange amalgam of objective historical analysis and "existential openness," the historian *qua* historian can lay hold of the selfhood of Jesus? We need hardly emphasize again that to our mind this interest in the historical Jesus is in one sense at least a good thing. It comes as an invitation to the dialectical theologians to be more empirical in their concern and less aloof from the concrete historical element in the revelation. But inasmuch as the historian of the "new quest" would appear to be fusing together, or confusing, the objective seeing of historical knowledge and existential interpretation, it is not altogether surprising that such theologians as Barth and Bultmann have impenitently turned their faces against the whole enterprise. Bultmann particularly—surely not unmindful of Kähler's protestations about the absurdity of employing historical weapons to uncover the ground and content of faith—finds in Fuchs' interest in Jesus' decision and Jesus' faith a renewal of biographical concern, in Bornkamm's attempt to combine clarification of the understanding of existence enshrined in Jesus' message with elucidation of a historical picture available to objective perception an unwarranted trespass beyond the *Dass* of Jesus' life to the question of the *Wie* and the *Was,* and in Robinson's location of the meaning of the kerygma in the existence of the historical Jesus a destructive threat to the integrity of the kerygma.

Now, of course, what is for dialectical theology a gross weakness and fault is on the contrary a great merit and strength for those circles in which there never has been any inclination to doubt the legitimacy or necessity of asking the retrospective question about the historical Jesus. The question that arises then is this: How does the "new quest" look, in light of our historical sources, from the angle of New Testament criticism?

Bornkamm's portrait of Jesus is the portrait of a remarkable prophet-teacher. This is exactly what we might expect in a book which is a lineal descendant of Bultmann's *Jesus and the Word.* For Bornkamm, Jesus is, first of all and most of all and indeed almost only, the "speaker," the "preacher." How thoroughly the "speaker" theme is carried through can be judged from Bornkamm's treatment of the Passion story. The focus is not upon what Jesus does but upon what he says, even here. His reason for coming to Jerusalem is only to *deliver the message* of the coming kingdom of God in the city of God. There is no likelihood, to Bornkamm's way of thinking, that as Jesus had acted redemptively before, so he thought of himself as acting redemptively now. Everything hinges on his word. His entry with his followers into Jerusalem "would be inconceivable without his powerful claim that the kingdom of God is dawning in his word, and that the final decision will turn upon himself." [63] Why always and everywhere the *words* of Jesus? Bornkamm would, I am sure, wish to point out the radical difference between his emphasis on the words of Jesus and the emphasis of nineteenth-century "liberal theology." "Liberal theology" separated the words of Jesus from the mystery of his being, and so effaced his character as the Christ by making him a teacher purveying merely ethical instruction or religious truths. Bornkamm, however, is not unaware that being comes before speaking, for he tries to show this by reiterating frequently that Jesus' being is enclosed in his words. We may suppose that this talk of Jesus' being in terms of his words is an attempt to avoid what is conceived to be the nineteenth-century error of psychologism, talking of Jesus in terms of his person or personality. But is there not a very fine line of distinction between Jesus' "being" and Jesus' "person"? Does it not look like a scholastic subtlety? And at all events, in all philosophical naïveté it may be asked whether in fact, so long as we continue to operate within the realm of normal psychology, a man's words are the only or even the surest key to the secret of his being. The sin of hypocrisy is a perennial human failing, and it is not at all inconceivable that a man's deeds may belie his words, and his words belie his deeds.

We are aware that the contemporary interest in the philosophical and theological significance of the phenomenon of language as a most important dimension of existence is a contributory factor in the "new quest," with its stress on the words of Jesus. Pursuing this interest, Dr. James M. Robinson has recently sought to define the constitutive ingredients of Jesus' existence by investigation of the formal structure of his eschatological message. The eschatological polarity in Jesus' message, with its call to the present in view of the impending future, can be seen clearly in Matthew 18:3: "Unless you turn and become like children—you will never enter the kingdom of heaven." Jesus allows his present conduct to be determined by the coming kingdom: "I shall not eat it—until it is fulfilled in the kingdom of God" (Luke 22:16). "But if it is by the finger of God that I cast out demons—then the kingdom of God has come upon you." This logion on exorcism makes clear the superimposing of the future on the present, toward which the formal structure in Jesus' message tends, thus overcoming

the *temporal* separation that was characteristic of the doctrine of the
two ages in Jewish apocalypticism. The overlapping of present and
future as a tendency within the formal structure becomes even more
evident in the beatitudes and woes. "Blessed are you poor—for yours
is the kingdom of God"; "Blessed are you that hunger now—for you
shall be satisfied" (Luke 6:20–21). "Woe to you that laugh now—for
you shall mourn and weep" (Luke 6:25). The antithetical verbs
"hunger"–"be satisfied," "laugh"–"mourn and weep" are held by
Robinson to denote an existential dialectic that is the key dimension
of the formal structure, and is found also in the pairs of terms, "preserve"–"lose," "exalt"–"humble" in other logia: "Whoever seeks to
gain his life—will lose it, but whoever loses his life—will preserve it"
(Luke 17:33). "Whoever exalts himself—will be humbled, and whoever humbles himself—will be exalted" (Matt. 23:12). The consistent
direction of the two-member structure to the present begins to make
visible an existential dialectic that reveals an understanding of existence characteristic of Jesus. "This eschatologically qualified present,
this coming of God, is the context, the source, the constitutive ingredi-
ent of believing existence. Jesus' action consists in the actualization of
this existence. His message consists in bringing the understanding of
existence to expression." [64]

One cannot but wonder what is the need for all this expenditure of
effort, since in the midst of it Robinson is constrained to explicate
Jesus' understanding of existence in a moving summary of the situation of his life and ministry as it is depicted in our Gospels:

> God forgives the tax collectors and prostitutes; he breaks the security of
> the wealthy. The childlike are saved. The possessed are freed by the finger
> of God. Within poverty is God's reign, within hunger fullness, among tears
> joy, whereas the full starve, and laughter becomes weeping and wailing.
> The self-saving life loses itself, while he who opens himself without reserve
> even to the extent of death lives all the while from God. Those who puff
> themselves up are brought down hard, but the lowly are borne by God. For
> he counts the first last and the last first.[65]

How good it is to be brought back to the concrete language and
imagery of our historical documents! Even without and even before
any investigation of the formal structure of Jesus' eschatological message, *this* language and *this* imagery carry to us an indelible impression of Jesus as the one who throws himself entirely on the grace of

God and lets his life be determined solely by God, so that with him and in him the coming God has come. Why must we try to read off the meaning of Jesus' existence from the structure of his message and thus close up the whole life of Jesus within the capsule of "believing existence" or "eschatological existence," to the impoverishment of all the wealth of concrete details in the Gospel record? Historical research would here appear to be forfeiting its trust. For instead of seeking to eliminate all modern notions in order to understand how Jesus may have been understood by his contemporaries or how he may have understood himself, it is importing into our historical sources the categories of existence philosophy, finding Jesus in his words and so describing him more as the "Word-bearer" than as the "Word made flesh."

It is permissible to press the question whether the remarkable message of a remarkable man could by itself create in his followers the faith that he was the one sent by God to accomplish the promises to Israel and to redeem his people. Interestingly enough, therefore, another member of the Bultmann group, E. Fuchs, has found in Jesus' *conduct* the true context of his preaching. His message goes together with his action. His act or deed gives rise, in the case of the parables, to a story which sheds light on his conduct as concrete occurrence revealing the will of God. He appears therefore as the one who acts in God's place, summoning to him sinners, who without him would have to flee from God (cf. Matt. 11:19 ff.).[66] From this basic position Fuchs, sympathetic though he is to the view that our relation with Jesus Christ is a believing relation to the Christ of the kerygma, has come round more and more to a typical nineteenth-century outlook, regarding the historical Jesus as the ground of faith, as the objective foundation of salvation, as the one in whose *work* God had accomplished his plan of redemption. Not surprisingly Bultmann has reserved his sharpest barbs for Fuchs, charging him with holding up Jesus, the loving one, the faithful one, the one obedient unto death, as an objectively observable historical phenomenon. But from our own critical standpoint, it does not seem to be a matter of exposing Jesus to objective seeing, but of realistically acknowledging that the New Testament witnesses to the fact that God manifested himself in Jesus' *deed* no less than in his word. The *work* of God in the *work* of Jesus was not immediately given to fleshly seeing, for some could interpret it as the work of the devil, as in the Beelzebul controversy

(Mark 3:20–27), whereas others, endowed with the capacity for recognizing the divine self-revelation, could interpret it as the work of the
Spirit. J. A. Froude once said to the aged Carlyle that he could only
believe in a God who *does* something. In anguish the old man replied: "He *does* nothing." We can appreciate the pathos of the
answer, and we can be thankful that the New Testament, not least the
Gospels (and here we agree with Fuchs), tells us a great deal about
the God who *acts* toward men in the *act* of Jesus, turning toward them
and seeking them, even when they are disposed to flee from him.

Fuchs' stress on Jesus' *conduct* (which seems to us to be a necessary
corrective to the picture of Jesus as merely the Word-bearer), and
Bornkamm's stress on Jesus' *words* are probably not, however, so
disparate as would appear at first sight. The highlighting of Jesus'
deed by Fuchs is to be contrasted with the perspective of the "liberal theology," which detached Jesus' deeds or actions from his being
and saw his conduct as a new law or an ethical model to be copied or
imitated. But with Fuchs, Jesus' deed, interpreted by his word, is the expression of the mystery of his being. Both Bornkamm and Fuchs have
thus consistently recognized that Jesus' word or deed is that in which his
being is enclosed and expressed. In this way they have equally consistently sought to avoid "psychologizing" by penetrating into his inner life,
consciousness, personality.[67] Over against the well-known bewildering
variety of pictures of Jesus and critical opinions and judgments
handed down to us by a theoretically unbiased historical research, we
might have expected that historians, walking in the shadow of existence philosophy, would be much more likely to arrive at the same
view, committed as they are to the same *Vorverständnis* (pre-understanding) and, to that extent, looking for the same thing. And in some
degree this is true. We hear again and again the watchwords of the
movement: "existence," "being," "self-understanding," "selfhood."
Nevertheless, perhaps because the "new seekers" are, at crucial points,
really "old" and impartial historical researchers, there is scarcely a
sufficient consensus within the new school about crucial critical problems or about what the historical Jesus truly was like to engender the
belief that a final formula had at last been found for the establishment
of historical facts. Indeed, so long as we view our task as that of a
quest for the genuinely historical facts relating to Jesus, and not for
the "existential truth" of the Gospels, it is not easy to see how the new
"existentialist" concept of history can help us to solve strictly his-

torical problems, e.g. the problem of why Jesus was brought to trial and condemned, or why he could be called Messiah.

Just as in Dilthey, Heidegger, Collingwood, and Bultmann there is no unanimity of attitude concerning the character of the "existentialist" approach to history, so among the New Testament men there appears to be a prevailing lack of clarity about what the new concept of history really is that they have called in to be the handmaid of historical research. What is the category of "existential openness" as applied to Jesus-research? In Robinson it seems to be sensitivity to Jesus' being or selfhood on its inward side, in Althaus prescientific or intuitive encounter with the image of Jesus that comes to us through the Gospels, in Bornkamm the grasp that post-Easter faith has on the reality of the saving event of Jesus of Nazareth. But have "existential openness," "intuitive encounter," or "Easter faith" allied to historical research really produced a new *historical certainty* in our time by bringing Jesus in his unmediatedness right into our generation? Hardly!

Our concern here has not been with the use of existential philosophy in practical theology (demythologizing). Existential interpretation of the Christ-kerygma is one thing. The union of existential philosophy and historical research as applied to Jesus of Nazareth is another. How are we to regard this union? I believe the problem can best be illustrated further by turning once again to Bornkamm's picture of Jesus. Now we have already lauded the work of the scholars of the "new quest" on the critical side. We have lauded also the "directness" of Bornkamm's portrait of Jesus. We would not wish to retract from that one inch. But who or what is this Jesus with whom Bornkamm confronts us? Is he the historical Jesus of Nazareth as recovered by the Heidelberg historian? Or is he the Jesus Christ of the post-Easter kerygma as reflected upon by the Heidelberg theologian? Bornkamm no doubt would say he is both; at least that is what we might suppose from his methodological axiom that we are to seek the history in the kerygma and the kerygma in the history, in order to show their mutuality of relationship. It is also what we might suppose from Robinson's explanation of the distinction drawn by Bornkamm and Käsemann between the "once" of Jesus and the "once for all" of Easter: Easter was the disclosure of the transcendent selfhood of *Jesus,* and to maintain that we can encounter the transcendent selfhood of Jesus historically is only to give Easter its proper place. Toward the close of his portrait of Jesus, Bornkamm confesses that "we learn to understand that the secret of his being could only reveal itself to his disciples in his resurrection." [68] If, however, we understand Bornkamm aright, the Resurrection of Jesus Christ is something given only to faith. If that is so, how can the historian *qua* historian take hold of the transcendent selfhood of Jesus? And by what criteria can he be sure as historian that it is the selfhood of the historical Jesus? Bornkamm's *Jesus of Nazareth* seems to hover between two worlds. Now as historical critic, he appears to be interested in the historical facts about Jesus—his third chapter is an attempt to sum up what can be known historically regarding Jesus, which is not much, to be sure. So at the end of his historical tether, the historian turns theologian. The standpoint adopted by him then is so "kerygmatic," so "existentialist," so overwhelmingly concerned with existentialist interpretation of the message of Jesus, that we begin to wonder how far he really has pushed beyond Bultmann and to what extent the title of his book is not a misnomer.

I believe it is in order, therefore, to sound one or two cautionary notes about the "new quest." This wedding of objective historical analysis and existential openness can be quite misleading. It is misleading when it produces the impression that the historian has at long last overcome the problem of kerygma and historical events by holding up before our eyes what purports to be a *historically* well-established basis for the kerygma in the ministry and message of Jesus. Indeed, what the historian, in this case the "existentialist historian," is offering us is not so much a picture of historical events in the life of Jesus but rather a "kerygmatic" account of the event Jesus of Nazareth that has more to do with the response of faith and theologizing than with the question of facts of past history. So long as it is a question of fact, it is hard to understand what can be accomplished by superimposing upon scientific historical research into the life of Jesus the quest for a satisfying formulation of a theological concept of historical reality, or for what in the Gospel "story" is intrinsically or existentially true. In short, we have the greatest hesitation and reserve about this whole merger of historical research and existential openness. We still lack the assurance we would like to have that scientific historical analysis is not being overridden by a particular set of philosophical or theological presuppositions. "Historical research which is in principle not free," Johannes Munck has written, "will never achieve results contrary to its own assumptions. It can begin to run idle without realizing that it is finding only what it looks for and is establishing only what it already knows." [69]

To sum up our estimate of the "new quest." We can agree that the revived interest of the last decade in the historical Jesus came as a most timely curb on the tendency toward a Docetic Christology in Bultmann's position. For that we owe a debt of gratitude, even though we feel there was a certain inevitability about it, since the Church will not for long endure to be robbed of concern for the historical Jesus, and even though we know that in scholarly quarters outside of Germany interest in the historical Jesus had never really flagged. We can also agree that, as the "new quest" has taught us, there can be no going back to a pre-kerygmatic or pre-Form-criticism era. The historian's sensitivity to the kerygma will preserve him from thinking that he has done all and said all when, after the manner of Stauffer, he has recovered the not-yet-interpreted bare facts about Jesus behind the tradition. We agree further that the "new quest" has provided a great impetus to the search for satisfactory criteria for determining the authenticity of sayings or deeds of Jesus, that it has helped pave the way toward a consensus of scholarly opinion regarding the true character of Jesus' eschatological message, and that it has forced us to take a new look at the significance or lack of significance of the Christological titles as guides to the understanding of the historical Jesus. But we cannot agree when any exponent of the "new quest" speaks as though the one true light had at last shone, as though the problem of kerygma and history had at last been solved by the achievement of a new and absolute historical certainty concerning Jesus of Nazareth. Such assurance is premature and illusory. It arises not on any historico-scientific basis but only from the introduction of such dubious categories as "the immediacy of Jesus for me," "existential encounter with the selfhood of Jesus." I find it hard to understand what these categories have to do with the strictly historical problem of the relation between Jesus and the Church's kerygma. The one sure thing is that the debate about "faith and history" or "kerygma and history" is not ended.

It seems to me that, in connection with the question of the history embedded in the kerygma, we have to take with an ultimate seriousness Kähler's affirmation that the Gospels are first and foremost Easter confessions of faith and the now largely undisputed fact that

all we know of Jesus is presented in the light of the kerygma. Bornkamm himself indicates so much—and most of all at the end of his
work when he treats the Resurrection as the bridge between the historical Jesus and the preached Christ and examines briefly the early
Christian confessions in which the Easter faith in Jesus found expression. But if it be true that Jesus of Nazareth is only fully "given" or
"disclosed" to his disciples in the Resurrection, why should this be
appended only at the close? Should it not with greater consistency be
placed at the beginning of the book, in order to suggest that the portrait of Jesus to follow is less a purely historical-critical portrait than
one drawn by a believer who has responded to the kerygma and takes
his stand on this side of the disciples' Easter experience?

Between Jesus and the primitive Christian community stand the decisive events of his death and Resurrection. That the Resurrection in
particular was the great turning-point is obvious from the evidence of
the New Testament. But what kind of turning-point was Easter? Did
it effect a transformation in the figure of Jesus as understood by his
disciples? Or was it God's vindication and confirmation of none other
than Jesus of Nazareth, this Jesus who had walked and talked with his
disciples and had gone the way of the Cross? We can scarcely resolve
these questions by a simple fiat about the character of Easter as the
revelation of Jesus as the heavenly Cosmocrator. Investigation of the
Easter texts in some detail is required. This is perhaps especially true
for the English-speaking world, where the prevailing tendency has
been to concentrate mostly on the historical-critical possibility of
establishing the factuality of the Easter event.

V

The Resurrection of Jesus Christ

The Centrality of the Resurrection

Michelangelo once broke out in indignant protest against his fellow-artists because they were forever depicting Christ in his death on the Cross. "Paint him instead," he cried, "the Lord of life; paint him with his kingly feet planted on the stone that held him in the tomb." The artist was true to the New Testament. The New Testament, for all its emphasis on Jesus' Passion and death, will not allow us to stop short at the Cross. If the Resurrection be but an epilogue to the story of Jesus' earthly life and not an integral part of the drama of redemption, then there is no atonement. "Liberal theology," in most of its phases, made the mistake of by-passing Easter in its preoccupation with the ethical greatness of Jesus' personality or his inward life—the upper limit of its concern was the death of Jesus, in which case everything important could only belong to the historical Jesus. But the suppression of the Resurrection could only divest his death of its meaning or render it banal. The sentimentalism of Ernst Renan's famous declaration that, at the cost of a few short hours of suffering, Jesus' great soul had achieved immortality is a terrible reduction of the New Testament message. A *theologia resurrectionis* is the inescapable presupposition of a *theologia crucis,* for without Easter the Cross looks only like the tragic and premature waste of a good life.

The Christian story in its wholeness has two sides. It tells of the man Jesus of Nazareth: it tells of this Jesus as the one who after his death came to be preached as the Christ. And everywhere the tradition makes it plain that the gap between the two parts of the story is bridged by Jesus' Resurrection from the dead. The step across the bridge is neither easy nor automatic. The New Testament simply marvels and gives thanks before God that this incredible thing has happened, that Jesus has made a new beginning with his disciples after his Crucifixion. The tradition graphically portrays the disciple band straggling away from Calvary in utter dejection, brokenness, and shock. His death was really their death, the death of every dream and hope they had learned to cherish with him. Some of them were still wandering in the realm of death when they paid their visit to his tomb —"Why do you seek the living among the dead?" (Luke 24:5). Accordingly, when these same disciples banded themselves together again as the congregation of the Last Days, a short time after the climactic events that had transpired in Jerusalem, they did so not in order to put into effect any plan or program for which their dead Master had previously commissioned them; they did so first and only out of faithful community response to the certainty of his Resurrection from the dead. They were changed now. They had to be transformed from their low mood of despair after his death in order now to desire, as they did, to proclaim him as the Christ before all the world. So later, when the believing community drew together its memories of his words and teaching and preserved them, it did so not because the earthly Jesus had passed on his teaching as a "new Law" or as a "holy Word" to be transmitted in turn by his disciples, nor indeed because of their inherent merit, but simply because they were the words of its crucified and risen Lord. Sir Edwyn Hoskyns was absolutely right to state, at the beginning of his professorial lectures on the theology and ethics of the New Testament, that the only proper starting-point was the passages concerning the Resurrection.[1]

With all assurance we can say that, save for Easter, there would have been no New Testament letters written, no Gospels compiled, no prayers offered in Jesus' name, no Church. The Resurrection can scarcely be put on a par with certain other clauses in the Apostles' Creed—not if the New Testament is our guide. The primitive tradition makes only minimal reference to the Virgin Birth and the Ascension: Paul none at all. If the Easter message were excised, everything would be gone. For at the very heart of the early Church's preaching stands the word about "the Author of life, whom God raised from the dead. To this we are witnesses" (Acts 3:15). Even more emphatically does Paul confirm the cruciality of Easter: "If Christ has not been raised, then our preaching is in vain and your faith is in vain" (I Cor. 15:14). Easter, therefore, is no mere addendum to other factors in the story of Jesus Christ; it is constitutive for the community's faith and worship, its discipleship and mission to the world.

In contemporary theology the question concerning the Resurrection of Jesus Christ has become the question which decides the fate of all other theological utterances. Both Barth and Bultmann have enfolded the Resurrection in the bosom of their theologies. Barth, in fact, commended Bultmann "for displaying and emphasizing the indispensable role of the Easter event for the thought and language of the New Testament." [2] The priority of the Resurrection has lately been asserted not only by the theologians but also by the critics. F. V. Filson has taken it as starting-point and interpreting clue for Biblical theology, as the illuminating center of New Testament thinking.[3] A relatively conservative critic has recently, on the basis of an extensive examination of the New Testament's use of *testimonia* in apologetic, reached the conclusion that the "Resurrection is the vital historical fact for research into the origins of Christianity. The history of Christian doctrine begins with the debate concerning the interpretation of it." [4]

This focus on the Resurrection is at once the glory and the anguish of contemporary theology and criticism. Its glory, because in thinking on the Resurrection we are laying our finger right on the pulse of the primitive Church's life. Its anguish, because the witness to the Resurrection of Jesus Christ is linked up in our source material with the witness to specific historical events and concrete details, events and details which the historian, when put to this acid test, has seemed quite incapable of verifying. Here, where most of all we would want to know what happened and how it happened, we are the most baffled. It is not first and not only that modern man is dominated by the prevailing scientific outlook of our age and so finds peculiar difficulty in the idea of a return of Jesus from the grave—much less dominated than Bultmann imagines and much more susceptible to the unequivocal testimony of the New Testament to the event-character of the Easter revelation. Rather is it true that anyone familiar with the New Testament is immediately aware of the highly problematical nature of its witness to the Easter event, of the puzzling discrepancies inherent in the Easter stories.

We need to look only cursorily at the texts. The divergences in the various reports are serious. Nor can they be easily overlooked or removed. The geographical locale of the appearances of the risen one is, in Matthew, Galilee, in Luke, Jerusalem. Matthew closes his Gospel with the account of the risen Christ commissioning the Church with its "marching orders": he has nothing to compare with Luke's physical story of Christ eating fish and exhibiting his flesh and bones. In Luke the women visit the tomb, then Peter alone; thereafter Christ appears to his two followers at Emmaus, then to the eleven. In John, Mary visits the tomb alone, then Peter and the beloved disciple, after which Christ appears to Mary by herself at the tomb, and then to the disciples and finally to Thomas. When we set the old Easter formula reported by Paul from the tradition (I Cor. 15:3–5), with its reference to a first appearance to Peter and then to the twelve, over against the Gospels, the picture becomes even more obscure. It is made still more complex by the subsequent reference in I Corinthians 15:6–7 to appearances of the risen Christ to the five hundred brethren, to James, and to all the apostles, of which there is no trace in the Gospels. All this quite aside from the problem of the empty tomb and the question of the corporeality of the risen one!

What travail of soul there is for those who would approach the Easter narratives from the empirical standpoint, bent on learning the facts in the case! Yet to be sure there are very many who do. Critical scholarship has been almost overwhelmingly concerned with straightening out the sequence of occurrences in the Easter reports, or with establishing the factuality of the Resurrection itself, as though faith in Jesus Christ itself depended on the enterprise. The Easter texts themselves, however, severely challenge the rectitude and wisdom of a purely empirical approach. Are they no more than the record of mere empirical facts? We have mentioned the discrepancies in the Evangelists' accounts: they seem to attest that, from the beginning, Easter faith did not hinge on uniform versions of the Easter event or of the manner of Jesus' rising. Indelibly stamped upon each and every story is the faith of believers, the faith that now at last, in lifting Jesus Christ up on high, God himself had taken a hand in this sinful and rebellious world, to turn man's sighing into song and defeat into victory. From many signs in the texts it is clear that the Resurrection is not to be construed simply as an intra-worldly phenomenon that could have been observed by any casual bystander: Jesus appeared only to those who had been his disciples on his earthly way; every-where there are traces that the earliest Church connected the Resurrection most closely with the elevation of Jesus to the right hand of the Father, and surely the enthronement of Christ in his heavenly reign turns upon faith rather than fact; nowhere except only in the apocryphal gospels is the wonderful event of the Resurrection itself depicted; the risen Jesus was not immediately recognizable by fleshly "seeing," for Mary could mistake him for the gardener and he was for a while as a Stranger in the company of the travelers to Emmaus. By these many tokens it is apparent that the category of the empirical is quite ill-suited for understanding the Easter narratives. And do we need to remind ourselves that, even if the historian could verify the Resurrection as an objective worldly *datum,* he would not then have given us a risen Lord?

Certainly, however, nothing is to be gained by coming to the New Testament already strongly prejudiced against any possibility that God could have raised Jesus from the dead, as an event in our world and in our time. We have to confess that not all the mysteries of this event could enter into the heart of man: we have no right to restrict the sovereign freedom of God to manifest his reality as he wishes. But nothing is to be gained either—indeed a very great deal is lost—if we approach the Easter texts seeking only the *facts.* The men of the New Testament were not proclaiming the Easter event only as a fact: they were living in it, as Professor J. S. Stewart has reminded us, "as in a new country." [5] A new order of life had come into history, their history. Their Easter witness comes to us as a summons to share their experience, to enter into their mood, to assume their posture of faith, to widen our own theological horizons. If we would create this mood of handling the Easter theme, we have to knock down in order to build up. There has to be some clearing of the ground. So resilient has been the view that the Easter narratives are first and foremost annals and chronicles of "what happened," that we have to try to demonstrate the almost complete failure of historical criticism to authenticate and establish for us the "history" of Easter.

Attempts at Historical Reconstruction

Among modern attempts to reconstruct the "history" of Easter by harmonizing the various Easter reports into an orderly sequence of

events, should be noted especially those of Hans F. von Campenhausen and G. D. Yarnold.[6] We shall deal here only with von Campenhausen's reconstruction. He gives priority, so far as historical
reliability is concerned, to the tradition handed on by Paul (I Cor.
15:3–8), concentrates chiefly on trying to dovetail the evidence of the
Gospels with it, and suggests the following sequence:

1. After the arrest and death of Jesus the disciples remained close
by in Jerusalem (all the Gospels), but no longer ventured out in public (Mark, Matt.). We are not very well informed of their condition,
but they were downcast and ill-prepared for what would happen
(Luke).

2. "On the third day" women of the circle of Jesus' followers discovered that his tomb was open and empty (all the Gospels). No
appearances of Jesus took place here (Mark, Luke).

3. The report of the empty tomb occasioned uneasiness in the
disciples. Peter was the first, it seems, to understand the empty tomb
as the pledge of the Resurrection and to imbue the others with that
idea.

4. The disciples thereupon went, under Peter's leadership, to Galilee (Mark, Matt.), in the expectation of meeting Jesus there (Mark,
Matt.).

5. There took place hereabouts an appearance to Peter alone (Paul,
Luke), then to the Twelve (all the Gospels), then to the five hundred
brethren (Paul), then to James (Paul), and then to all the apostles
(Paul). One would have to think of these events as developing in rapid
succession. Possibly, however, the last or second last of these appearances occurred already in Jerusalem. Here are to be found later, at
any rate, Peter, James, the Twelve, and a wider circle of Galilean disciples (Paul, Acts).

6. The last appearance to Paul followed much later (I Cor. 15:8).

We cannot go into the innumerable, complex exegetical details involved in this reconstruction. The most striking feature in it, from a
historical perspective, is its correction of the traditional liberal idea
of the confusion and flight of the disciples after the Crucifixion of
Jesus: we have instead a picture of a relatively undisturbed group in
Jerusalem, rallied by Peter, and proceeding in orderly fashion to
Galilee after the discovery of the empty tomb. While the Easter re-

ports do contain a great variety of concrete details, this "amazing attempt," as Barth has called it, to combine them into a single historical account, is hardly warranted by the Easter tradition. Rather, the whole idea of a "synopsis," a "harmony," does violence to the nature and meaning of the Easter texts. If the reader will once again glance over the above reconstruction, he will see that it deals almost entirely with the followers of Jesus, with their thoughts and feelings and movements. Even so the Easter stories have been lifted out of the context to which they inalienably belong, and have been treated as if they were chronicles of a separate piece of "human history." But the fact is that they give every impression not of being primarily "chronologies" of a narrow track of worldly history, centering upon the disciples and their actions, but of being intimations and confessions of the revelation of Jesus as Lord and Christ, centering upon Jesus, or rather upon *what God has done in raising Jesus from the dead.*

Moreover, when the Easter tradition is looked at from the point of view of its development, its special character bespeaks the illegitimacy of the modern "historical harmony." The Easter narratives of the Gospels, with their numerous differences in detail, reflect a much less integrated and uniform tradition lying behind them than the Passion stories seem to have. In contrast with the continuous narratives of the Passion, telling how Jesus came to die on the Cross, *single* Easter stories would have been enough to convey the message of the risen Christ. Each unit appears to have enjoyed a vigorous independent life, gathering, as I think we must acknowledge, legendary accretions on the way. Mark's brief closing pericope (and how reserved it is and as yet unadorned with legendary material!) confirms the sufficiency of the single report as a call to faith in the risen one (Mark 16:1–8). The earliest Easter tradition certainly seems to have consisted of short lists of appearances (I Cor. 15:3–8), or individual stories. Every effort at a synoptic account of the "Easter history" therefore breaks down against the texts themselves. Indeed, it serves only to lead us away from the subject of which the texts are speaking, their central and decisive affirmation that God has raised Jesus from the dead. Recent scholarly trends in *Redaktionsgeschichte,* exhibiting the theological "individualism" of each Evangelist, corroborate further the impropriety of the "harmony." Accordingly, we cannot but wonder at G. D. Yarnold's book *Risen Indeed.* By way of preface he observes what we have already emphasized, that each narrative by itself contains the whole truth of the Resurrection and speaks from faith to faith. What can he then hope to add by piecing the various narratives together into a connected historical record? Must we not rather allow each pericope to speak for itself?

The Empty Tomb Tradition

The question of the factuality of the empty tomb does not concern us here. The case for its historicity has been allowed to rest mainly on the inferential reasoning, out of the standpoint of faith, that if Christ rose in the Body, the tomb *must have been empty,* or on appeal to the credibility of the eyewitnesses or the general trustworthiness of the Gospel records.

Our interest is in the empty tomb tradition. The texts combine two sets of stories, stories of the empty tomb and stories of the appearances of the risen Jesus. What is their relation in the tradition? I do not believe that M. Goguel's argument that the accounts of the empty tomb are a relatively late addition has ever been successfully refuted. The oldest Easter tradition, according to Goguel, contained no report of Jesus actually leaving the tomb, precisely because the earliest faith in his Resurrection was directed toward his exaltation to heaven straight from death. Goguel supports his view with formidable learning. He alludes to the materials collected by Strack-Billerbeck relating to Jewish traditions of the heavenly exaltation of men like Enoch, Moses, and Elijah; to the evidence cited by Bickermann for the prominence in early Christian legends of the notion of the assumption of the dead, to Graeco-Roman stories of the disappearance of the body as a proof of elevation to heaven, and to ancient Christian iconography of the Resurrection with the figures of the sun and the moon representing the cosmic royalty of the Christ.[7]

Most important of all is the internal evidence of the New Testament itself. Goguel makes much of the strange words embedded in Matthew's Passion narrative: "And behold, the curtain of the temple was torn in two, from top to bottom; and the earth shook, and the rocks were split; the tombs also were opened, and many bodies of the saints who had fallen asleep were raised, and coming out of the tombs after his resurrection they went into the holy city and appeared to many" (Matt. 27:51–53). We are here brought into touch, as

Goguel rightly suggests, with a very old conception, namely the conception that Jesus' Resurrection is the pledge of the general resurrection (I Cor. 15:20–23), that Jesus is the "first-born among the dead" (Rom. 8:29; Col. 1:18), and that the resurrection of the saints is the result of Jesus' victory over death. What is most noteworthy is how easily Matthew 27:51–3, which is certainly a theological reflection and not a historical reminiscence, could ignore all mention of a report that *Jesus'* tomb was empty. The same idea may lie behind the word of Jesus from the Cross to the penitent thief: "Truly I say to you, today you will be with me in Paradise" (Luke 23:43). But, apart from these passages, the Easter reports themselves and numerous confessional statements, which speak of the Exaltation of Jesus without any reference to the Resurrection, testify to the fact that in the oldest view of the Church no distinction was drawn between the Resurrection and the heavenly enthronement of Jesus (John 3:14; 12:32, 34; Acts 2:33; Phil. 2:9; Heb. 1:3–13, 8:1, etc.).[8] Professor E. Schweizer has recently amassed an impressive body of evidence illustrating that we do not need to go beyond Judaism for the notion of the exaltation of the suffering, righteous one. The thought is already present in the old Testament, e.g. Proverbs 29:23: "A man's pride will bring him low, but honor will belong to the humble in spirit" (cf. I Sam. 2:7 f., Job 22:29). The Aprocrypha and Pseudepigrapha and the Rabbinic Literature afford many examples of Jewish belief in the value of suffering and its atoning powers both for one's own sins and the sins of others. The righteous ones of Qumran effect atonement through the tribulations of the time of purification. The Wisdom of Solomon, chapters 2–5, pictures the suffering and exaltation of a righteous one, son and servant of God, condemned by men to an ignominious death. Exaltation is frequently thought of as taking place through ascension or through assumption to God.[9] Whereas it seems highly probable that this background was a regulative factor in the primitive Church's Christology, and in its Easter faith particularly, we would not wish to carry the idea too far for fear of losing what the New Testament declares with all certainty, that Jesus, raised above transitoriness and death, was not merely one of a long series of suffering and exalted righteous ones, but *the* eschatological Suffering and Exalted Righteous One.

At all events, Goguel's account of the rise and growth of the empty tomb tradition stems from the well-founded view that the Church's first Easter faith was very closely associated with the Exaltation of Jesus to the right hand of God. With the decline of the pristine spiritual fervor of faith in the heavenly Jesus, the *fonction fabulatrice* (Bergson) came into play, collectively rather than individually, and led to the invention of the materialistic story of the empty tomb as a demonstration and proof of the Easter faith. The story circulated separately for a while, and only latterly, when it was felt that it did not by itself constitute an adequate guarantee of the Easter faith, was it coupled with the reports of the appearances of Jesus. In some places, in Luke and the apocryphal gospel of Peter, the two stories have simply been juxtaposed. In others, in Mark and Matthew, they have been more consciously and definitely linked together by the angelic intimation at the tomb, of the forthcoming appearance of Jesus, so that the empty tomb has become a kind of preface to the Christophanies.

A brave venture in controverting this theory has recently been made by R. H. Fuller.[10] He proposes that the *Sitz im Leben* of the empty tomb story was the post-kerygmatic *didache* explaining to neophytes what historical happening lay behind the kerygma's assertion that God had raised Jesus from the dead. In Mark, our primary Gospel source, the revelation that God has raised Jesus is asserted, Fuller holds, in connection with the visit of the women to the tomb (Mark 16:6). The οὐκ ἔστιν ὧδε of the angelic announcement, ἠγέρθη, οὐκ ἔστιν ὧδε, defines the historical occurrence of which ἠγέρθη is the faith interpretation. Consequently Fuller maintains that in the vision pericopes his having been raised is invariably assumed. Since, therefore, the substance of the Easter event was the empty tomb, all the kerygmatic affirmations, including I Corinthians 15:3–8, must, in Fuller's view, be taken to *imply* it.

Now it is by no means inconceivable that the original setting of the empty tomb story was the post-kerygmatic *didache,* designed for neophytes. The apologetic overtones in the story are specially obvious. That its specific purpose was to denote the factual substratum on which the kerygma's proclamation of the Resurrection of Christ was founded is, however, more than doubtful. In Mark's record of the empty tomb there is no appearance of Christ but only of an angel. And the angel's words, "He has risen, he is not here; see the place where they laid him. But go, tell his disciples and Peter that he is going before you to Galilee; there you will see him, as he told you" (Mark

16:6–7); these words, far from drawing attention to the empty tomb, really point us away to the marvelous consummation of the ministry of Jesus Christ in a new rendezvous with his disciples in Galilee. Mark's intention is apparently to make the empty tomb story a signpost to something lying beyond, to a subsequent Galilean Christophany. If the empty tomb had indeed been the historical factual basis of the kerygma's affirmation of the Resurrection, we might reasonably have expected it to be used as an argument confirming the event. But in fact, so far as the tradition may have been known at all at an early date, it is not explicitly mentioned by St. Paul or anywhere else, not even in the early formula of I Corinthians 15:3–5, which, in all probability, has nothing to do with the empty tomb story, either to confirm it or to oppose it. The word τάφος, used in the Gospels, does not recur elsewhere; instead, Jesus is frequently declared to have risen ἐκ νεκρῶν.[11] Undoubtedly, as the very early formula of I Corinthians 15:3–5 itself indicates, the earliest Easter tradition consists of accounts of appearances of the risen Jesus.

We can say with some assurance, therefore, that the early Church gave top priority for its message to the disciples' experience of the risen Christ in his appearances. It is no doubt true that for the generations to come a need was felt to go beyond the disciples' experiences in order to convey the message of the risen Christ in even more concrete depiction, as perhaps in the post-kerygmatic *didache* for neophytes. But to say only so much, without further corroborative evidence than Fuller has been able to adduce against the priority of the appearances, is simply to leave open the question of whether the concrete story of the empty tomb was not the result of objectivizing or materializing embellishment of the tradition in light of certain theological tendencies. Nevertheless, even though we are not convinced that the empty tomb report possessed a historical core or was the constitutive Easter fact for the kerygma, it does not follow that we can only speak negatively of its importance. We shall come back to the positive side later.

Galilee and Jerusalem

No less vexing from the historical angle than the problem of the empty tomb is the problem associated with the Gospel records of the appearances of the risen Christ, set as they are in Galilee by Mark and Matthew, and in Jerusalem by Luke and John. Severely tested by this "geographical" divergence, historical criticism has either resorted to trying to reconcile the two accounts or moved into the defense now of the Galilean, now of the Jerusalem, theory.

Among numerous ingenious attempts to reconcile the conflicting reports, I wish to mention only two. One recalls F. C. Burkitt's well-known suggestion that Mark may have gone on after 16:8 to show how in fact Peter started on his way to Galilee, but was confronted with the risen Lord and forthwith returned to Jerusalem—a hypothesis which led Burkitt, quite implausibly, to place the familiar *Quo vadis?* legend on Easter Day. But all of this depends only on precarious conjecture regarding the contents of what, in view of recent scholarly trends, may only be called the supposed "lost ending" of Mark. More probable is the proposal put forward lately by C. F. D. Moule that the Resurrection appearances are to be seen in the light of festival pilgrimages.[12] The disciples left Jerusalem not out of cowardice immediately after the Crucifixion, but only after the Feasts of Passover and Unleavened Bread, and returned home to Galilee. Then shortly they journeyed back to Jerusalem for the ensuing Feast of Pentecost. In this case the συναυλιζόμενος, which Moule regards as the preferred reading in Acts 1:4, may be taken as referring to the festival lodging of Jesus with his disciples in the environs of Jerusalem. Professor Moule has shed an interesting light on the frequent intercommunication that must have taken place between the two regions. His proposal lends some feasibility to the idea of Jesus' showing himself to his disciples in whichever of the two places they happened to be at the time. But it really leaves unexplained the thorny problem of Mark's and Matthew's "addiction" to Galilee, or Luke's and John's "addiction" to Jerusalem (we take John 21 to be a redactional addition).

In despair of harmonizing the two firmly contradictory traditions, most critics have argued the historical priority of the one or the other. The "Galileans," to use Archbishop Ramsey's description, have usually maintained that Mark unequivocally indicates an appearance in Galilee (Mark 16:7), and that it is much easier to envisage a tendency in the primitive Church to transfer the appearances to Jerusalem as the center of Christianity, than vice versa (K. Lake, J. P. Gardner-Smith).[13] The weakness of the latter argument, as L. E. Elliott-Binns remarked, resides in the fact that it is only a little less conceivable that the followers of Jesus Christ in Galilee could have made the transfer from Jerusalem to Galilee in order to enhance their prestige against Jerusalem.[14] Supporters of the historical reliability of the Jerusalem tradition have held that the Galilean theory demands an unduly skeptical or negative view of the Lucan traditions (A. M. Ramsey), and that the words, "I will go before you to Galilee" (Mark 14:28) do not necessarily refer to an appearance there but mean rather, "I will lead you [like a shepherd] into Galilee," that is, from another place, presumably Jerusalem (J. Weiss, A. M. Ramsey).[15]

Amid so much that is uncertain, the tradition certainly invites us to reckon with appearances on the one hand in Galilee and on the other in Jerusalem. Must we accept the stark alternative, *either* Galilee *or* Jerusalem? There may have been appearances in both places. At which place the first encounter of the risen Jesus with his disciples occurred seems impossible to decide. The majority of the appearances related in the old formula handed on by Paul (I Cor. 15:3 ff.) point to Galilee. Mark most certainly does (Mark 16:7). By contrast, Luke has most consistently placed all the appearances in Jerusalem and its immediate surroundings. He has omitted the prophecy included by Mark in his Passion narrative, in which Jesus predicts his forthcoming meeting with the disciples in Galilee (Mark 14:28). He has also, it would seem, altered Mark 16:7, "But go, tell his disciples and Peter that he is going before you to Galilee," for the announcement made by the angels in Luke 24:6 is now this: "Remember how he told you, while he was still in Galilee, that the Son of man must be delivered into the hands of sinful men, and be crucified and on the third day rise." Behind this we see Luke's own conception of the "sacred history," in which the holy city of Jerusalem is the center of *Gottesheilsplan.* It has long been recognized that Luke-Acts is dominated by an ecclesiastical scheme, within which Jesus Christ is portrayed as the Anointed, the true King of Israel, and Jerusalem as the Church's capital, the starting-point from which the gospel must be preached, and the mission of the Church conducted to all the world.[16] It would appear that the Easter tradition of the Resurrection appearances in Jerusalem has been profoundly affected by theological ideas.

May we therefore also suppose that the Galilean tradition has been overlaid with theological motives? More than a quarter of a century has passed since, in his very important monograph *Galiläa und Jerusalem,* the late Ernst Lohmeyer, taking as his point of departure the alternation between Galilee and Jerusalem as the scene of the Resurrection appearances, postulated a twofold origin for primitive Christianity: a Galilean branch of the early Church, bound to a distinctive "Son of Man Christology" and to the thought of Galilee as the land of eschatological fulfillment (as attested by the Marcan tradition, and somewhat less clearly by Matthew, who stands further from the oldest stream of the tradition than Mark), and a Jerusalemite branch, bound to a "Messiah Christology." [17] Lohmeyer at the least established the probability that the primitive Church had very early roots in Galilee, in the wider sense of "Galilee of the Gentiles," extending eastward to include Peraea, northeast as far as Damascus, and north as far as Hermon. However, his theory of a fairly rigid stratification of theological outlook as between Galilee and Jerusalem has not enjoyed much scholarly popularity. If, on the scanty evidence available, Lohmeyer has not been able to prove his case, and has certainly not been able to come up with an answer to the historical question of where the first Resurrection appearances took place, he has, I think, shown clearly enough that the appearances were *interpreted* differently by persons or groups connected with different localities, mainly Galilee and Jerusalem. That these varying interpretations revolved around different understandings of the eschatological implications of Christ's victory over death for Christian mission and discipleship is what one would gather from the texts.[18]

We have barely touched upon some of the intractable critical problems confronting us in the Easter tradition—only enough to show how defiantly they resist solution. We come now to the no less acute problem of how the amazing and enigmatic *fact* of the Resurrection itself is to be understood. The eyewitness reports testify to an event in history. What happened? I do not imagine that any theologian will ever succeed in banning the question, for it is human for the Christian to wish to know. The long history of attempts to answer the burning question makes only one fact perfectly obvious: here more than anywhere else historical judgments have been conditioned by theological and doctrinal prejudices. Kirsopp Lake, of all investigators of the Easter event the most painstakingly scientific, had the candor to acknowledge that our interpretation of the historical question will be determined largely by our presuppositions—and these presuppositions, we may add, have generally been linked to the notion either of Jesus' "bodily" survival or of his "spiritual" survival.[19] All we can do here is to glance at some of the more important efforts to isolate, describe and define the factual element in the Resurrection.

The Question of What Happened in the Resurrection

Slanderous versions. The slanderous accusation that the disciples had stolen the body of Jesus and propagated the Resurrection story as a hoax was abroad in Jewish circles, as we know from Matthew 28:11–15, as early as the first century A.D., was perpetuated in the Talmud, and was revived in the modern period by Reimarus, who saw a motive for the fraud in the disciples' reluctance to return to their workaday business, once their dream of sharing in the political greatness they believed Jesus would achieve had vanished. I know of no more terse rejoinder to this view than the *coup de grâce* administered by M. Goguel: "On peut se laisser persécuter pour une illusion mais non pour une fraude."

Naturalistic explanations. Under the sway of the older Rationalism, the Resurrection had to be fitted into certain naturalistic beliefs about the world, man, and religion. In other words, every trace of the miraculous had to be drained away from it. So the theory that Jesus only appeared to have died on the Cross, subsequently revived in the coolness of the tomb, managed to hide himself from the Jewish and Roman authorities, and later confronted his disciples, was espoused in the nineteenth century notably by Schleiermacher, and developed in the present century by F. Spitta. How much further removed from the New Testament than this could we possibly be? The word of the New Testament is "Christ crucified, dead, buried, risen again the third day, enthroned *in heavenly triumph.*"

Kirsopp Lake's famous proposal that all may have developed from the strange mischance that in their agitation the women visited the wrong tomb, falls in the naturalistic category. We cannot be sure, Lake holds, that the women reported correctly: they may have gone to the wrong grave and, on being directed by a young stranger to the right one, "See the place where they laid him" (Mark 16:7—the words "he is risen" are an addition to the record), may have run away in fright.

The "human" uncertainty that attends all such rationalistic or naturalistic theories accords exceedingly ill with the joyous Easter certainty of the New Testament. Refusing to hearken to *what the texts really have to say,* they cannot really touch the New Testament attestation of the event as the event in which finally, in Jesus Christ, God has intervened in history, "the arm of the Lord" has been "laid bare," and the wickedness and rebelliousness of this sinful world have been put down.

Spiritualistic interpretations. The belief that it was the soul or spirit of Jesus that survived death and enjoyed immortality, entering into that kind of communication with his disciples that is normally associated with modern spiritualist séances, is also at variance with the evidence of the New Testament. Luke, for example, expressly rejects the idea that Jesus' existence was continued beyond death as a disembodied *pneuma* (Luke 24:37). Paul also proclaims the Resurrection of Jesus Christ *in the Body* (I Cor. 15).

The physical theory. For many centuries the orthodox within the Christian fold have been content to go along with the conviction that Jesus was raised "bodily" from the tomb and was given a new "spiritual body," no longer subject to the limitations of time and space. One could certainly say that this has been the most persistent, as indeed it is the most beautiful, picture of the Resurrection, stemming from the Easter narratives of the Gospels themselves.

In this connection Paul Tillich has held that when the Resurrection is identified with the presence or absence of the physical body, the absurd question arises about what happened to the molecules of Jesus' body, and then "absurdity becomes compounded into blasphemy." [20] Even if we would not care to go so far, it is nevertheless wise to beware of the peril of isolating and dwelling on the physical aspect of the Easter event, the peril of reducing it to something like a "nature miracle," and so of losing its character as the eschatological event, in which *God* draws near in Christ. Yet the New Testament does represent the Resurrection not as a "noumenal" or "spiritual" survival, but as *objective* and as *corporeal.* In so doing, it invites us to recognize the contingency with which the eschatological event is intimately bound up with *this* Jesus of Nazareth, with a particular moment of time, and with a particular point in space. Were it otherwise, had Easter severed the Church from the quite particular past of this man Jesus of Nazareth, it would have gone adrift on the ocean of timeless myth. As it is, the concreteness of the New Testament's witness to the Resurrection of Jesus really comes to us as a summons to acknowledge and accept the sovereign freedom of the living God, creator, redeemer, to re-create and redeem his people in their time and in their world.

Psychological theories. A long line of writers has sought to account for the Resurrection in terms of the phenomena of visions in general, and of mystical visions in particular—in terms, that is, of psychic factors in the disciples' make-up and experience.

There comes to mind Ernst Renan's somewhat cynical dictum that it was the passion of a woman in love that gave the world a risen Lord: "Ce qui a ressuscité Jésus, c'est l'amour." Of a different order and much more respectable was Theodor Keim's familiar idea of the "telegram from heaven," by which he meant that it was only through the will of God, from a sphere beyond their own lives, that the disciples were granted visions of the risen Christ. More recently the late Dr. E. G. Selwyn refused to be content with the traditional distinction that had been made in the literature of the Higher Criticism on the Resurrection between "subjective" and "objective" visions, "subjective" seeming to imply a pathological disposition in the disciples (Renan), "objective" implying that the disciples were inspired by God or by the invisible Christ to behold in faith what they did behold (Keim). But all visions, Selwyn held, are "objective" as well as "subjective," in that what is seen in them is as much an object as in normal perception. The question is whether the object imaged by the mind is real or unreal. Selwyn accordingly proceeded to a learned discussion of the appearances of Jesus and the visions of his followers in relation to the mystical experiences of the saints.[21] The critics of the mystical life drew a distinction between veridical and non-veridical visions, the former coming from God, the latter from the devil. They further recognized different types of veridical vision, exterior, imaginal (a word coined by Dr. Thouless) and intellectual, corresponding to the degree of visualization in each case. While the Easter appearances of Jesus probably differed considerably in their degree of visualization, the disciples' visions can all justly be called veridical so far as they had a uniform effect upon their lives—they were called to serve God by following Christ anew. It is a mark of Selwyn's high integrity as a scholar that at the end of his attempt to piece together the evidence of the appearances and the evidence of the empty tomb, he writes: "Reason

can estimate the evidence; but when that is done, it must make way
for other functions of the mind—for constructive imagination, for
wonder, and for faith." [22]

Not surprisingly, discussion of the appearances has lately moved
over into the realm of psychiatry, extrasensory perception, and para-
psychology. M. C. Perry, an expert in these matters, has made a
study of the Resurrection in regard to the phenomena of spontaneous
telepathic apparitions of the dead.[23] There are many points in Perry's
book, may we say, where we cannot but feel we are being led away
from and not into the New Testament. We are the more gratified
therefore at his willingness to concede that acceptance of the Christian
gospel is primarily an adventure of faith, and that there are mysteries
of the faith which can be confronted only with a reverent agnosticism.

Perhaps the classic expression of the psychological theory of the
Resurrection on the "subjective" side is that of M. Goguel, the key to
whose approach is to be found in the following words: "There is more
truth in the statement, 'They saw Jesus because they believed and
were convinced that he was living' than in that which lies behind the
tradition, 'They believed in the resurrection of Jesus because they saw
him living after his death.' The resurrection of Jesus is in reality the
resurrection of that faith in him which the disciples had had during
his ministry." [24] Goguel's "subjective" psychological explanation of
the Resurrection might well serve the thesis of Bultmann, who maintains that the historian cannot get behind the belief or faith of the disciples and so cannot verify any objective factual basis for the Resurrection. The existentialist theologian's position in this regard is well
summed up by Dr. John Macquarrie: "In all this, it is difficult to pin
down anything more objective than psychical events in the minds of
believers." [25]

We contend, however, that the Resurrection cannot be satisfactorily
explained from the inward life or nature of the disciples. There was
certainly a link between the pre-Easter and the post-Easter appearance of Jesus, and a link also between the pre-Easter and post-Easter
condition of the disciples. All the stories contain what Barth has called
"the form of the past." The risen Jesus did not show himself to everyone, to all and sundry onlookers, but only to the circle of his followers, who to be sure had previous knowledge of him in his earthly
life. But it was not that they had already believed in him in the fullness of faith, and now out of that fullness, as Goguel suggests, could

conjure up a picture of him as alive after his death. The New Testament's Easter message is the message not of believing men, but of broken and unbelieving men, now at length made whole and faithful. Their gratitude knows no bounds that all they could never be or do, in their own helplessness, God has at last wondrously done by making a new beginning with them in the resurrected Jesus Christ. In their grief and mournfulness over the death of Jesus, they could not be the ones to take the initiative and fan the flickering embers of their former believing response to his earthly person into the flame of Easter faith. They do not consider themselves to be "confederates of God and comrades-in-arms with their Lord," as Günther Bornkamm finely puts it.[26] The decisive thing in all the Easter reports of the disciples' encounters with the risen Jesus is that *God himself has taken the initiative with them,* coming near to them, conquering them and claiming them in Jesus, *this* Jesus whose company they had kept, and *this* resurrected Jesus Christ whom now they know afresh. Nowhere in this theme more picturesquely presented than in the Emmaus story. *This* Jesus was as a Stranger in the midst of the disconsolate fellow-wayfarers on the road to Emmaus. Hearts heavy from the tragedy that had befallen but a short while before in Jerusalem, they recognized him not. Only when he stooped to the pace of their slow hearts and broke bread with them in their home, were the eyes of faith opened for them (Luke 24:13 ff.). It was the risen Christ, binding together past and present, expounding for them especially the meaning of his suffering and death, who made himself known to them.

So long as it is a question of "what happened" at Easter, we do well to resort first and last to the earliest Easter text we possess, I Corinthians 15:3–8. There Paul stands firmly on the solid ground of the apostolic *paradosis,* handed down to him and in turn transmitted by him in his preaching. Not all of verses 3–8, however, belong to the oldest tradition, which is almost certainly restricted to verses 3–5. Balancing each other in the parallelism of these three verses are the verbs "dead"-"buried," "raised"-"appeared." The essence of the Easter event is to be found here. It is not a word about the disciples. It is not even solely a word about Jesus. It is a word about the act of God in Jesus. For Christ "died according to the scriptures" and "was raised on the third day according to the scriptures," so that now were fulfilled in him the *promises* that *God* had made of old to Israel. I want to call attention chiefly to the term "appeared," used already in the old formula. "He appeared [ὤφθη] to Cephas. . . ." The same term is picked up again in the following verses with reference to the other encounters with the risen Jesus that are listed: "He appeared to more than five hundred brethren at one time" (I Cor. 15:6); "He appeared to James, then to all the apostles" (I Cor. 15:7). I do not think that this ὤφθη really invites us to any modern psychiatric or "clinical" approach to the Resurrection. Rather is it the very term employed by the Septuagint translation of the Old Testament to tell of heavenly appearances, "epiphanies." It tells of something breaking from the side of heaven, from the side of the living God. With this ὤφθη there is no question of the reality of the one who appeared: it speaks in the first place not of the disciples' subjectivity or consciousness, but of *Jesus of Nazareth*. But neither is there any question that his appearing is not an objective *fact* that can be viewed as a spectacle by anyone at all: rather it can be grasped as God's dealing with the world only by believing seeing.

In all the Easter texts there is scarcely any more significant fact than that Paul is able to tie in his own experience of the risen Christ with the encounters of the first disciples. "Last of all, as to one untimely born, he appeared also to me" (I Cor. 15:8). At the outset we opened the question of what is the appropriate mood or posture in which we should approach the Easter texts. I believe that Paul himself has given us our surest clue. For when we think of what happened to him on the Damascus road, we are not confronted with a "serial story," first the appearance of the risen one, which the latter day historian could verify as a fact, second the apostle's conviction of the reality of Jesus' appearance, and third his decision to believe on the basis of the fact: we are confronted rather, as Gerhard Ebeling says, with a "single indivisible event: Paul falls down in faith before the overpowering reality of the Crucified One." [27] Even so historical criticism's repeated attempts to compartmentalize the Easter event by isolating the factual element from the message or faith with which the history is bound up, have constantly tended to reduce the Resurrection itself to a bare fact that is only recollected from the far away and long ago, and not experienced here and now as a vibrant present power and reality.[28] If it is true that, in regard to the Resurrection, historical criticism cannot take us very far and we are forced to take hold of the dimension of faith that is imprinted on all the Easter stories, does it follow that we can afford to sit lightly to the historical element in the tradition? Are we to take the way of Bultmann, whose passionate concern with the meaning of the Resurrection has seemingly made him quite apathetic to the historical aspect? It is necessary for us to consider Bultmann's view of Easter.

Bultmann's Understanding of the Resurrection

In *Die Geschichte der synoptischen Tradition,* Bultmann classifies the Easter narratives as "Tale or Legend." The report of the empty tomb and of the appearances, as well as stories embodying material proofs of the Resurrection or describing Jesus' call to mission, are among those elements of the Gospel tradition which possess a religious rather than a historical character. The Easter accounts occur in a context relating either to the life of the religious hero (in which case they can be designated as biographical legends), or to the faith and cultus of the community (in which case they can be designated as cultic legends). Both categories give expression to the Church's Easter faith, and, although they were first related in the Palestinian community, they were transformed in the transition of Christianity from the Palestinian to the Hellenistic sphere and received their form in the Hellenistic community. Legendary as they are, therefore, the Easter stories really do not tell us anything about how the Easter faith arose in the disciples.[29]

From this critical basis Bultmann subsequently expounded his conception of the Resurrection. The Easter event is not an event on the plane of history, but is itself an article of faith, and must consequently remain invisible and hidden from us. The Resurrection has an entirely soteriological function for the New Testament, being intimately connected in Paul's thought with salvation (I Cor. 15:21 f.; II Cor. 4:10 f.; 5:14 f.). "Belief in the resurrection is simply and exactly the same as belief in the Cross as 'salvation-event,' in the Cross as the Cross of Christ." So the Resurrection is not an event separate from the event of the Crucifixion, but constitutes together with it the cosmic eschatological saving-event. Jesus Christ then does not rise in the world; the idea of the resuscitation of a corpse is sheer myth; his rising again cannot be established as an objective fact. The risen Christ is therefore simply the preached Christ. He is present in the kerygma. The Easter faith has become, with Bultmann, faith in the

Word of preaching as the Word of God. It is not for anyone to question the legitimacy of this Word of preaching: it comes to the hearer only as personal challenge: "If he heeds it as the word spoken to him, adjudicating to him death and thereby life, then he believes in the risen Christ." [30]

In short, the Resurrection means for Bultmann that the Cross has come to be interpreted as God's act of grace opening up the possibility for men of a new self-understanding and so a new existence. Beside this, for Bultmann, all speculation concerning the mode of the appearance of the risen Jesus, all narratives of the empty tomb, and all Easter legends, pale into insignificance.[31]

At the beginning of this chapter we spoke of the decisiveness and cruciality of the Resurrection—without Easter there could be no such thing as the Word of God's grace and reconciliation. And this is precisely what Bultmann seems to be saying: Easter and Good Friday constitute one indivisible salvation-event, in which God's grace is disclosed to men, bestowing on them a new life: "We love, because he first loved us." The present writer (if a personal note may be introduced) was nurtured on the works of James Denney. Now no one saw more clearly than Denney that the first and last and dominating element in the thought of the New Testament was the Resurrection or the good news thereof. Yet also no one saw more clearly than Denney that what Easter revealed was the Cross standing at the heart of everything, the death of Jesus Christ as a saving death, and the Word of the Cross as a matter of life or death. The religion of the New Testament is, more than any other religion, as Denney put it, "a form of the absolute consciousness, and deals not with a sliding scale but with the blank, unqualified antithesis of life or death, weal or woe, salvation or perdition, heaven or hell." [32] In his own way, as one now sees, he was prefiguring certain emphases that have appeared in Bultmann. "To receive the reconciliation, or not to receive it—to be a Christian or not to be a Christian—is not a matter of comparative indifference; it is not the case of being a somewhat better man, or a man, perhaps, not quite so good; it is a case of life or death." [33]

From this background, we do not find it hard to agree that, if the proof of a theology is in its preaching, Bultmann's understanding of the proclamation of Christ crucified and risen as a summons to men to die to the world with Christ in order to live unto God is near the heart of the true evangel. The essence of the message is that in and through the Cross, where all human hope is silenced and all human dreams are vanquished, God speaks the Word of life in death. The cost to God of rending the veil between himself and us, and drawing us to him, is the death of Jesus Christ. It is difficult no doubt to formulate a philosophy of the Cross of Christ. Our profoundest theories of atonement look poor and faltering before the mystery of it. All the more credit to Bultmann, therefore, that he has called this generation of preachers not to be cravenly apologetic about centering the message in the death of Christ. He has called us to recognize that the Word that creates life is the same Word that intimates death, Christ's death and our death. Only in the renunciation and extinction of our earthly hopes and helps may the divine hope and help dawn for us. His Word, as Luther puts it, is a Word that slays and "destroys what is in us before He bestows on us His gifts." Before the song lies the sacrifice, before the glory of the Resurrection life lies the death of the Cross, before God's help lies our helplessness. Perhaps only those who, out of their longing, have encountered God in the preaching through the darkness of death, will not ultimately be cast down by anything that may transpire in a ruinous and dying world. Perhaps only they will be able to go into their societies to bear the light of divine hope when the shadows gather and to steady and rally the fearful and fainthearted when the world and worldly things are failing them.

Granted the power and relevance of a preaching centered upon the great act of God's surrender in Jesus Christ crucified and risen, we are nevertheless still perplexed. We are perplexed because we wonder whether Bultmann's establishment of the kerygma as the proclaimed Word of God can be convincing so long as this "risen" is understood as no more than the interpretation of the meaning of the event of the Cross. According to Bultmann, the Cross is the last Word of God, his ultimate activity. The Resurrection in that instance possesses no independent status: it is simply the release of the message of the Cross as the eschatological event; it has to do with the attitude and understanding of Jesus' disciples after his death and not with God's history with the world. It therefore remains unclear (seeing that in Judaism the idea of the expiatory power of the suffering righteous had been developed) how and why the disciples could have interpreted *this* particular death, the death of Jesus Christ, as *the* eschatological event. In other words, it remains unclear what the Resurrection really is, if it is understood to be nothing more than the rise of this interpretation of the Cross. On what basis was it possible for the disciples to decide afresh concerning the death of Christ, especially if, as Bultmann has it, he were crucified merely as a rabbi-prophet? Whence that grace wherein the disciples came to stand? Whence the birth of Easter faith? We cannot believe that these questions are as inconsiderable as Bultmann supposes.

Now it is true that Paul, for example, quite deliberately affirms the centrality of the crucified one for his preaching: "I decided to know nothing among you except Jesus Christ and him crucified" (I Cor. 2:2). But it is equally true that he makes that affirmation not from the side of the earthly history of Jesus, culminating in the Cross, but from the vantage point of one for whom the risen one is a living and present reality (I Cor. 15:5–8). "It is one thing," says Professor James Stewart, "to preach the Cross as the last word of divine revelation. It is quite another thing to preach it as the road traveled once for all by One now known to be alive for ever." [34]

The problem we have been discussing may best be brought into focus by considering one or two points in Bultmann's condensed treatment of the Resurrection in the first volume of his *Theology of the New Testament*. Bultmann invites us to think of the Cross, as we have seen, as the *end* of the activity of Jesus and so the *end* of the activity of God, in him, toward the disciples. Through his death on the Cross, the disciples were faced with a new crisis of decision, and, through the rise of the Easter faith in them, Jesus, the teacher and prophet, was metamorphosed into the Messiah. "They understood Jesus as the one whom God by the resurrection has made Messiah." [35] A severe break, a radical transformation, is thus presumed between Jesus and his history and the so-called Christ of the Church's Easter faith. The favorite texts adduced for the fact that Easter made Jesus Messiah are Acts 2:36: "Let all the house of Israel therefore know assuredly that God has made him both Lord and Christ, this Jesus whom you crucified," and Romans 1:3–4: "The gospel concerning his Son, who was descended from David according to the flesh and designated Son of God in power according to the Spirit of holiness by his resurrection from the dead, Jesus Christ our Lord."

The "therefore" of Acts 2:36 denotes the concluding appeal of the whole preceding argument. Jesus of Nazareth was a man approved of God by the signs and wonders wrought through him (Acts 2:22). His death was predetermined by God (Acts 2:23). His whole earthly mission was God's activity and his death a part of God's plan of salvation, which had to be completed by his Resurrection, because he was the one who could not be holden of death (Acts 2:24). As the Christ already, "he was not abandoned to Hades, nor did his flesh see corruption" (Acts 2:31). This Jesus, "killed by the hands of lawless men," the Messiah, attested by mighty works and signs as well as by David's prophecy (Acts 2:25–28), is vindicated by being raised from the dead. In the Resurrection, who he really was is now confirmed.

Dr. W. C. van Unnik's explanation of Romans 1:3–4 seems to me to be convincing. There is clearly a parallelism between the phrases "Spirit of holiness" and "according to the flesh." The whole sentence is a description of the Son, "concerning his Son," who is both of the lineage of David and also "Son of God." It is not that he is made the "Son of God" only by the Resurrection: rather he is "Son" already as a descendant of David. If he became "Son of God" only by the Resurrection, it is hard to see what is the sense of the words "concerning his Son who was descended from David," and, further, the words "in power," which break the parallelism we have just mentioned, would be redundant. As it is, the phrase "designated Son of God *in power* according to the Spirit of holiness" may be taken to indicate that this Jesus who is already the "Son" is powerfully corroborated as such by the Resurrection.[36]

So we are disposed to believe that the risen Christ of the Church's faith and the historical Jesus are in continuity and identity. This is further borne out, cumulatively, by the many references in the Easter stories to the disciples' "sight" of the risen Jesus, and by Paul's linking his own encounter with the risen Jesus to those of the first disciples. This Jesus appears after his death for renewed activity with his disciples. In his earthly appearance and in his Easter re-appearance God's history with the world is carried through and completed. In the totality of the concrete history of Jesus, God in his freedom provides the foundation for the possibility of man's deciding and the occasion for faith. Out of the immediately past history of Jesus, consummated now in his Easter manifestation, the faith of his disciples is born. Over against this, Bultmann's indifference to the concrete historical element in the Resurrection brings him to what may not unfairly be called an entirely self-sufficient view of Easter faith: it arises only from itself and lives within itself. So Bultmann's word about Easter is simply this: "The Church had to surmount the scandal of the cross and did it in the Easter faith." Even more mystifying is this word when it is tied to the apparently contradictory sentence that directly follows it: "The rise of the Easter faith made necessary *a way of understanding the cross* that would surmount, yes, transform, the scandal of the curse which in Jewish opinion had befallen the crucified Jesus." [37] What of this "had to" (*musste*)? Does it not place us with the disciples in a meaningless world in which justice and righteousness, truth and love are laid in the grave with the crucified Jesus? Out of this wasteful and senseless world, in which death reigns supreme, the disciples are forced, by some inward compulsion, to make sense, out of darkness light, out of death life. Faced with this "had to," we are somehow reminded of Heidegger's category of man's "being towards death": the shadows of "Nordic gloom" lie heavy on the scene: on the one hand there are only the Cross, the death of Jesus, and the grave, and on the other only the disciples in their loneliness, compelled to overcome this nothingness. Confronted with the death of Jesus, they are confronted also with death as the limit of their own existence, as the disturber of the whole of life. For Bultmann, man does not have the possibility through his own resources of conquering death. Even so, through the Cross itself, revelation becomes the occurrence that abolishes death and brings new life.[38] But exactly at this point it is difficult to square the thought of the Cross as revelation-occurrence with this "had to"— "The Church had to surmount the scandal of the Cross and did it in the Easter faith." Could these men, in their emptiness, have had such a hand in surmounting the Cross and its curse? Was their subsequent Easter joy no more than the anxiety that motivates men, now in a specific modification "overcome"? [39]

It seems to me that, if Easter has nothing to do with any new beginning made by the crucified Jesus toward his disciples, then there is really no word of death defeated or justice and love vindicated by God —certainly no word of God's just and loving control and guidance of this his world and its history toward the End purposed by him. Only if Easter is the disclosure of Jesus himself can the Church make its Easter confession with the joy and gladness that are instinctive to the New Testament and are of the essence of its life—steady assurance and astonished gratitude that God has been beforehand with men in the concrete history of Jesus of Nazareth, creating the possibility of deciding and the occasion for faith. Just as we said before that there is no rejoicing in the Resurrection unless the Cross is kept at the center of things, no song without the sacrifice, so now we can add that there is no preaching of the Cross as God's victory over sin save from the standpoint of encounter with the risen life and continuing activity of Jesus.[40]

We have reached the place where we can give account of what we believe to be the appropriate mood in which to approach the Easter texts. Whereas the Easter stories are not annals or chronicles but carry within them the dimension of faith, and whereas historical criticism is unable to isolate or verify the factual element in the Resurrection, we cannot discount the concrete historical character of the tradition as witness not simply to the origin of faith or the kerygma but to the history of Jesus as God's dealing with men. We may now turn to a short examination, out of the great abundance of materials relating to the Resurrection in the New Testament, only of the main Easter reports.

I Corinthians 15:3–8

Bultmann has held that Paul is here trying to prove the miracle of the Resurrection by adducing a list of eyewitnesses. In Bultmann's view, Barth has involuntarily shown what a "dangerous procedure" this is by arguing that the list of eyewitnesses was inserted not to prove the fact of the Resurrection but to show, by way of defense of Paul's apostolic credentials, that his preaching of Jesus as risen Lord was in line with the preaching of the first apostles.[41] In opposition to Bultmann, Hermann Diem contends that we must take I Corinthians 15:3 ff. at face value, as authentication of the faith that Christ is risen. And why should Paul not affirm the Resurrection as a historical fact, since, if it really happened, it had eyewitnesses too? [42]

But is it necessary to suppose that what is involved here is proof, legitimation? Much rather should we say that it is here made plain that the Easter faith and message are indissolubly linked to the Easter testimony of the original disciples, and so are bound to a fixed and circumscribed place in history and not to any hazy mythical realm. As we noted previously, I Corinthians 15:3–5 is a well-patterned kerygmatic formula, couched in rhythmic form, that takes us back to a time very close to the event it describes.[43] What we have before us, therefore, is not a casual fragment but a creedal summary of the most im-

portant points in the earliest Church's faith. Nor can we fail to notice
the realism with which that faith is tied to events: "died"-"was
buried," "was raised"-"appeared," all introduced by the same "that"
(ὅτι), and all uniformly attesting something that happened to Jesus. On
death, the interpretative comment is added "for our sins according to
the scriptures," and on Resurrection the comment "on the third day
according to the scriptures." All the information we are given about
the Resurrection is the exact indication that it happened "on the third
day according to the scriptures." The formula would therefore lead us
to expect the existence of proof texts of certain classical Old Testament passages that could be shown to find their fulfillment in the death
and Resurrection of Jesus Christ.

However, the trouble is that, whereas the thought of his atoning
death clearly brings to mind such passages as Isaiah 53, no Old Testament text, prophesying the Resurrection of the Messiah "on the third
day," immediately occurs to us. Various possibilities have accordingly
been suggested: (a) Matthew 12:40 explicitly connects the Resurrection with Jonah's three days and nights in the whale's belly (Jonah
1:17). But it is unlikely that I Corinthians 15:4 alludes to Jonah 1:17,
since this interpretation of the Jonah passage first appears in Matthew
and is therefore late in the New Testament—it does not appear in
Paul, Q, Mark, or Luke. (b) The suggestion has been made that the
reference is to Hezekiah's recovery from illness as related in II Kings
20:5. No reference to this passage or its context, however, is made in
any layer of the New Testament. (c) The most popular approach has
been to find the Old Testament passage alluded to in Hosea 6:1–2:

Come, let us return to the Lord; for he has torn, that he may heal us; he
has stricken, and he will bind us up. After two days he will revive us; on
the third day he will raise us up, that we may live before him.

Although in rabbinic exegesis Hosea 6:2 is connected with the resurrection,[44] it speaks of the restoration or revival of the nation Israel and
is not mentioned in Paul or anywhere else in the New Testament. If
I Corinthians 15:4 were linked to a basic proof text like Hosea 6:1–2,
why then was the text lost, or why did it fail to become a great text
in the dogmatic thinking of the early Church? Father Barnabas Lindars has lately attempted to overcome this difficulty by the following
arguments: (1) The prophecy of rising "on the third day" in the Passion narratives of the Gospels goes back to Jesus himself (e.g. Mark

14:58: "I will destroy this temple that is made with hands, and in three days I will build another, not made with hands"). Jesus had the Hosea passage in view, and was referring, as it did, to God's restoration of a new people. In that case, "in three days" means simply "in a little while," "in the near future" (compare the Hebrew idiom t⁰môl shilshôm = heretofore, formerly). (2) While the Hosea passage was understood metaphorically as denoting restoration of the people Israel "in a short while," *the actual appearance of our Lord "on the third day"* had all the more dramatic effect and led to the *literal* interpretation of the Hosea text. (3) If Hosea 6:2 were subsequently neglected by the Church, it was simply because it was the words of Jesus in Mark 14:58, based on the prophecy of Hosea 6:2, rather than the prophecy itself that the disciples continued to grasp (cf. Mark 16:7, "there you will see him *as he told you*"). The fact that his appearance took place "according to the scriptures" was not forgotten, even though a greater interest now attached to the fulfillment of the words of Jesus than to the fulfillment of any particular text. The literal fulfillment of the prophecy thus became a theologumenon of lasting importance in the presentation of the kerygma.[45]

The case presented by Lindars is an intriguing exercise in probabilities. It begins from the very questionable assumption that the words of Mark 14:58, in the exact form in which we have them, go back to Jesus himself.[46] Nor is it any more than a conjecture that, if Jesus did in fact utter the saying about the destruction of the old temple made with hands and the building of a new one not made with hands "in three days," he had Hosea 6:2 in mind. It is very much open to question whether we can interpret the kerygmatic formula of I Corinthians 15:3–5 in the light of the concrete depictions of the later Easter narratives, dating the first appearance of the risen Jesus on the first day of the week. If we are willing to let ourselves be guided by the formula itself, then we must acknowledge that the first appearance of the risen Jesus is as yet *undated*—"He appeared to Cephas." In all probability therefore the phrase "on the third day" should hardly be taken as an accurate piece of historical information: it is parallel to the phrase in the preceding line "for our sins," which is of course not a historical reminiscence but an expression of faith in Jesus' death as an atoning death.

If it is not a historical note and if we cannot establish with any certainty a particular proof text lying behind it, how then has this "on the third day" arisen in the Church's Easter testimony? Out of the Jewish belief that the soul hovered near the corpse for three days and departed only on the fourth day, when death finally supervened? Out of the notion that corruption was believed to set in on the fourth day after death (cf. John 11:39), and so out of the prediction of Psalm 16:10 that God would not allow his holy one to see corruption? Out of the fact that in the ancient Near East "three days" constituted a temporary habitation, while the "fourth day" implied a permanent residence, so that, as Professor Bruce Metzger has proposed, by the "third day" the Church meant to convey that Jesus was only a temporary visitor in the house of the dead? [47]

It is impossible to substantiate any of these hypotheses. What I think we can say with some assurance (and we can say it independently of our success or failure in demonstrating a specific Old Testament proof text for I Corinthians 15:4) is that, by the phrase "on the third day" embedded in all the Easter reports of the Gospels as well as in this very early kerygmatic formula, the primitive Church has clearly marked out a date for the Resurrection of Jesus Christ in the calendar of the world's time and so has directed us not to the vague realm of myth but to an immediately past history. Consequently, one could say that "on the third day" is historical in the profoundest and most significant sense.

The twice repeated words "according to the scriptures" in all surety carry the same implication. The plural ($\kappa\alpha\tau\grave{\alpha}$ $\tau\grave{\alpha}\varsigma$ $\gamma\rho\alpha\phi\acute{\alpha}\varsigma$ = according to the scriptures) seems to bear the same sense as the singular and to refer to the Old Testament scriptures as a unitary whole rather than to several *particular texts* of scripture. Accordingly, when the Church declared that Jesus' death and Resurrection occurred in accordance with the scriptures, she was stating her conviction that the promises of God *as a whole* in the Old Testament had been brought to fruition at last, that God's age-old plan of salvation, initiated in the call, redemption, and renewal of Israel, had reached its climax in the deliverance of Christ from death.[48] To speak in modern language, they were eschatological events. Agitated above all by the problem of her sins and of how she would stand in the hour of God's judgment, the Church answered in her creed: Christ died for our sins and God accepted this by raising him from the dead. Sin and death had therefore been deprived of their power: the eschatological day had dawned. By proclaiming also that Christ died "according to the scriptures" and was raised "according to the scriptures," the Church exhibited her understanding that she stood in temporal succession to the old Israel of God, that the consummation she had now experienced brought to fulfillment what God had intended in beginning and carrying through his historical activity toward Israel. Throughout the Old Testament there sounds a twofold theme. On the one side there is Israel's affliction and distress, the sore burden of her guilt, her waywardness. On the other side is her faith in the sovereignty of her God, just and faithful, righteous and merciful, toiling with men, showing patience and withholding judgment, steadfast in his mercy even when administering judgment, working for a life of blessing for men despite all of men's guilt. The history of salvation, wrought with Israel and in Israel from of old by her God, has reached its goal in the death and Resurrection of Jesus Christ. The Old Testament must henceforth be viewed as the indispensable preceding context from which alone the Christ-event can be comprehended as the eschatological act of God; the Christian Church must continue to live out of the Old Testament. For, while God's eschatological work in Christ summons the Church to live in waiting for the imminent coming of God, it also has a past which illumines the Church's interim present situation. "Listening to the OT insures the true historicity of Jesus Christ," says W. Zimmerli, "in that it makes visible not only the *kairos* of a 'today' but also a yesterday, and with it a tomorrow as well. Christ is 'the one who is to come.' " Listening to the Old Testament prevents us moreover from falsely isolating the Church's message of Christ and the Church's faith in Christ as though they belonged to the instantaneous now in which past, present and future are merged.[49]

The Old Testament emphasizes that *God,* no other than Yahweh, the God of Israel, is acting in Jesus Christ. Yet on the other hand what is emphasized in I Corinthians 15:3–8, as elsewhere in the New Testament, is that God has now acted uniquely and finally in the concrete history of *Jesus.* There is an undeniable emphasis in the formula of I Corinthians 15:3–5 on the death and burial of Jesus, closely connected, in parallelism, with his being raised and his appearing. The testimony is plain. The one who was raised is the same Jesus who hung on the Cross and lay in the grave. It is not some miraculous new "being" who has been manifested in the Resurrection; knowing the risen one is, for the first followers, knowing the Jesus who had been known before; *Jesus* appeared to Cephas and the rest. The same is true also for Paul, who points to himself as the last link in the apostolic chain: "Last of all he appeared to me also, as to one untimely born" (I Cor. 15:8). This passage probably reflects the polemical situation of Paul in relation to the original apostles and the controversy regarding his apostolic status in Galatia and Corinth. A conflict of opinion about the nature of the apostolate seems to underlie Paul's invective against "those who have the reputation of being pillars" (Gal. 2:9) and his gibe at the "superlative apostles" (II Cor. 11:5; 12:11). Does Paul then, in opposition to the Jerusalem leaders and their view of apostleship, as determined by eyewitness of the earthly Jesus, move out from the primitive tradition of I Corinthians 15:3–5 to broaden the basis of apostleship along charismatic lines, so as to include those who, like himself, had received their call and commission directly and only from the risen Lord? [50] To be sure we have to reckon with Paul's reserve toward the Palestinian traditions of the earthly words and deeds of Jesus, and his almost monumental stress on his relation to the crucified and resurrected Christ. We have to reckon also with the text which is frequently taken as the foundation of Paul's particular conception of the apostolate: "Even though we once regarded Christ from a human point of view, we regard him thus no longer" (II Cor. 5:16).

However, even if the situation reflected by the evidence appears to be one of contrast between Paul, as witness only to the Resurrection of the Lord, and the closed circle of the μάρτυρες, associated with the earthly Jesus, and so constituted the true apostolic body, as expressed by the Church in Acts 1:21–2, we must not succumb to the danger of misunderstanding Paul in a Gnostic sense—as though Paul's encounter with the risen Christ were a new communication or special revelation, of a different order from earlier encounters, a communication or revelation of the heavenly Christ. The special point of Paul's defense of his apostolic prestige appears in fact to be that he stands in the succession of the first apostles precisely because he has encountered like them the revelation of *Jesus himself:* "He appeared also to me" (I Cor. 15:8). Paul serves notice of his interest in the temporality of the resurrected Christ. Nor is this interest contradicted by his declaration in II Corinthians 5:16 that it is no longer a question of knowing Jesus "after the flesh" (or better perhaps, "from a human point of view"), for what is here implied is not repudiation of the historical

Jesus, but rather that direct experience of the risen one is the gateway to life-giving or saving knowledge of Jesus Christ. Bo Reicke has suggested, not implausibly, that Paul is here, in I Corinthians 15:3–8, attacking a docetizing Gnosticism of Judaizing character, as it manifested itself in the "Christ party" in Corinth (I Cor. 1:12). This faction was concentrating on the exalted heavenly Christ, with whom communion was possible through a true *gnosis*.[51] With them the Cross and the earthly existence of Jesus had been neglected, and there was a one-sided eucharistic celebration of the Lord of heavenly life. W. Schmithals, who believes that Paul's opponents at Corinth were Gnostics, sees in the party cry "I am Christ's" the watchword of the Corinthian Gnostics, who understood themselves to be *Pneumafunken*, or, in substance, parts of the heavenly Christ.[52] The real character of the "Christ party" at Corinth remains obscure. Nevertheless, whether they were Gnostics (Baur, Lutgert, Schmithals), Judaizers (Schoeps), or Judaizing Gnostics (Reicke), there is certainly evidence in the Corinthian correspondence of a circle in the Corinthian congregation who were in the grip of an extravagant "spiritual" enthusiasm or fanaticism—enough evidence to warn us of the extreme danger to the primitive Church if it had, in the post-Easter situation, relinquished the preaching of the *theologia viatorum* and the *theologia crucis* and had surrendered to the conviction of the Corinthians that they had already attained, had already passed beyond earthly travail and temptation, and had already been elevated to the status of angels.

As Paul's resounding proclamation in I Corinthians 15 as a whole makes plain, Easter was the climax of the history of the crucified Jesus Christ—a history, which thus consummated in his Resurrection (I Cor. 15:3–5), preceded (and alone makes intelligible) the eschatologically conditioned history of the Christian community, living in the critical interim between the finished ministry of Christ and his coming again in the Parousia (I Cor. 15:23). So the apostolic preaching of the Christ as the firstfruits of the resurrection is bound up with the witness of God's past action in him (cf. Rom. 10:8–10; Luke 1:1; Acts 1:21–2; 5:32; John 15:27). Attestation of the Easter event, confirmed by many witnesses who were still alive, and proclamation of the transcendent reality complement each other. Paul does not seem to be aware of any dialectical tension between the word of the witnesses of the Resurrection and the Word of the risen Christ. If Christ be not risen, if this amazing thing that has happened be called in question or rejected, then Christian faith is futile and Christian preaching vanity (I Cor. 15:14).

Mark's Easter Witness

The historical information conveyed by the kerygmatic formula of I Corinthians 15:3–5 is scant enough. As a creedal confession it is quite bald: "dead"-"buried," "raised"-"appeared"; of the empty tomb there is no mention; of the event of the Resurrection only this "appeared." As we pass therefrom to Mark's Easter report, we enter the world of concrete portrayal. We should not be overly reluctant to step across the line, for none of the Evangelists' Easter accounts is merely a "legend empty of concern." How reserved and reticent is Mark's story, told with bated breath and quite free of the often bizarre details incorporated in such later apocryphal gospels as that of Peter! The astounding event of the Resurrection itself is not depicted. Everything centers on the angelic announcement at the tomb: "He has risen, he is not here" (Mark 16:6). The intimation comes as a reply to the question engraved on the whole of Mark's Gospel: "Is this the one through whom will be inaugurated the kingly rule of God?" Short and sharp is Mark's Easter record; it shows every sign of having been compiled with care and exactness. Its simplicity belies its subtlety: its concreteness belies its depth of theological meaning: its apparent unreflectiveness belies its allusiveness to Easter faith and Easter message.

We observed earlier how Willi Marxsen has characterized the Gospel of Mark as a *Predigt,* a sermon.[53] One could say that, homiletically, it is a brilliant and arresting construction. Especially does the close perfectly match the opening, bridging the gulf, on which Bultmann insists, between the historical Jesus and the resurrected Christ. This view is confirmed in R. H. Lightfoot's impressive exposition of Mark.[54] At the beginning Mark plunges us immediately in medias res. The Prologue (Mark 1:1–13), which can be likened to the Prologue of the Fourth Gospel (John 1:1–18), brings us at once to the very threshold of the New Age now breaking in, where John the Baptist points to the one stronger than he, the one designated forthwith as the beloved Son, the Messiah (Mark 1:11). Mark's highly condensed introduction ends as abruptly as it had begun: the Messiah, mightily tempted, endures victorious. "And he was with the wild beasts" (Mark 1:13). We hear an echo of Genesis 3. The first man, Adam, unable to withstand the tempter in the garden of Eden, was banished and lost his Paradise. But now Jesus Christ is set to restore the world to its pristine incorruption and purity.

The story of restoration and victory told by Mark is not an ascending "psychological biography," not an account of the growing conviction of Jesus about the nature of his vocation, nor of the disciples' deepening perception of who he was. Rather is it the austere, paradoxical record of the crucified Messiah. The tragedy of the Cross is the end of the Son of God, but it is a tragedy divinely ordained, as the inexorable "must" (δεῖ) of the latter part of Mark's narrative shows. Into the period of the obscurity, suffering, and rejection of the Messiah, however, shines the majesty of his impending triumph, for Jesus himself proclaims the coming of the kingdom with power. We have a glimpse of the ultimate victory of the Messiah and a promise already in his resistance to Satan (Mark 1:13). But still the one who is to be Victor has to die. And after his death, Jesus was buried and a stone rolled before his grave. Then follows the astonishing discovery of the women and the angel message at the tomb: "He has risen, he is not here; see the place where they laid him. But go, tell his disciples and Peter that he is going before you to Galilee; there you will see him, as he told you" (Mark 16:6-7).

On the ground that Galilee is to be understood as the land of eschatological fulfillment and that, in the Gospels and Acts, ὤφθη, and not ὄψεσθε, is used for Resurrection appearances of Jesus, Lohmeyer held that it is the Parousia, and not a Resurrection appearance, that is spoken of in Mark 16:7. But his view rests on nothing surer than the prominence of Galilee in the Marcan record, and, as Lohmeyer himself concedes, Paul and John do employ ὁρᾶν for "seeing the risen Lord" (I Cor. 9:1; John 20:18, 25, 29).[55] Mark's Transfiguration story (9:2-8) and the pericope of the descent from the mount that comes immediately after (9:9-13) may offer some guidance as to his conception. The Transfiguration story, often taken to be an Easter story, certainly appears as such in II Peter 1:16-18 and in the Ethiopic Apocalypse of Baruch.[56] But the presence of Moses and Elijah, the cloud, the voice, and Peter's words in Mark 9:5 make it unlike any other appearance story in the Easter tradition of the Gospels. Probably therefore the story has two main themes: first, the attestation of Christ's Messiahship and, second, the promise or pledge of the Parousia.[57] Moses and Elijah appear as the *dramatis personae* of the time of the inauguration of the kingdom of God, as the preparers of the way of the Messiah. But the dominant theme is that the veil of the flesh is temporarily withdrawn and the three most intimate disciples are permitted to see Jesus as he really is, in the form of the heavenly Son of Man in the glory of his Parousia. In what follows, however, in Mark 9:9–13, there is no mention of the Parousia, but the limit prescribed by Mark for the disciples' silence about his glory is the Resurrection.[58] "He charged them to tell no one what they had seen, until the Son of man should have risen from the dead." The mention of the Resurrection comes somewhat startlingly, and the disciples are puzzled about the meaning of this rising from the dead (Mark 9:10). In the next three enigmatic verses concerning the question about Elijah, this much stands out clearly enough, that the Resurrection must be preceded by the suffering and rejection of the Son of Man. Does Mark then, influenced perhaps by the delay of the Parousia, mean the Church to understand that in the Resurrection, Jesus of Nazareth is vindicated and exalted, as an earnest of his coming again in glory in the Parousia, a glimpse of which has now been given beforehand in his Transfiguration? At all events Dr. A. M. Ramsey's pronouncement that the Resurrection in Mark "is in truth the Parousia" may be too bold.[59] And R. H. Lightfoot's comment about these verses is apposite: "We may perhaps see the Church striving to construct some kind of a philosophy of history, in the light of its convictions about the person and office of its Master, and of his work and its results." [60]

Father Gabriel Hebert describes his recent paper on "The Resurrection-Narrative in St. Mark's Gospel" as a midrash on R. H. Lightfoot's treatment of Mark.[61] Probably too imaginatively midrashic! For I imagine that many will find his exegesis of Mark 16:4, "the stone was rolled back, for it was very large," somewhat fanciful. A few manuscripts and versions combine the observation "for it was very large" with the women's question in verse 3: "Who will roll away the stone for us from the door of the tomb?" [62] But the best manuscripts place it at the end of verse 4: "And looking up, they saw that the stone was rolled back; for it was very large." Placed there, it can hardly mean, according to Hebert, simply that the stone was too heavy for the women to move, but rather only that what was humanly impossible, God alone could accomplish (cf. Genesis 18:14). The background for the "removal of the stone" in Mark's account is therefore to be found in Mark 11:23, where Jesus says: "Truly I say to you, whoever says to this mountain, 'Be taken up and cast into the sea,' and does not doubt in his heart, but believes that what he says will come to pass, it will be done for him." This logion stands in its true context in Mark (contrast Matt. 17:20 and Luke 17:6), and is to be connected with the prophecy of the cleaving of the Mount of Olives in Zechariah 14:4.[63] So Jesus is expressing the conviction that with his going up to Jerusalem, the phenomena of the Messianic Age are about to be fulfilled. Accordingly the stone in Mark 16:4 is the whole structure of Pharisaic legal righteousness, which is to be "cast into the sea." Only God could uproot this offense, only God's Christ could take away the sin of the world, including the sin of its false religion (cf. John 1:29). Hebert appeals to the antiphon on the *Magnificat* in the Vespers for Easter Day in the Latin rite: "And when they looked, they saw that the stone was rolled away; for it was very great, alleluia." I do not quite see how this "alleluia" supports Hebert's particular exegesis, rather than simply voicing the congregation's praise that in the wonder of the Resurrection of his Son, God's great might and majesty have been revealed.

More likely to commend itself is Hebert's suggestion regarding Mark 16:2: "And very early on the first day of the week they went to the tomb when the sun had risen." "Very early" (λίαν πρωΐ) must mean "before daybreak." Consequently the phrase "when the sun had risen" cannot refer to time at all. The allusion is to the Septuagint version of Malachi 4:2: "And there shall rise for you that fear my name a Sun of righteousness, and healing in his wings; and ye shall come forth and leap like calves released from bonds." Though the world is still in darkness, and though the women are unaware that the darkness has been dispelled, nevertheless their Sun has risen. It has to be allowed that, in his presentation of Jesus, Mark does depict him as engaged in a life and death struggle with the powers of darkness that reaches its climax in the black and eerie night of his Passion. And now is the darkness overcome: the Sun has risen.[64]

Father Hebert has done us the useful service of confirming Lightfoot's view of the "theological completeness" of Mark 16:1–8. Despite all controversy about the hotly disputed "ending" of Mark's Gospel with the words, "And they said nothing to anyone for they were afraid" (ἐφοβοῦντο γάρ Mark 16:8), the Easter message is here present, in its wholeness and integrity, in these few short verses, so characteristic of Mark's story-telling art—the day decreed by God for the salvation of the world has now come with the Resurrection of Jesus Christ. At the dawning of this day of the Lord, the women's "amazement" and "fear" are understandable and their silence but a foil to the resounding news "he has risen." The *silent* dread, with which Mark's record closes, need not be taken as an editorial insertion on Mark's part ("they said nothing to anyone") to account for the lateness of the empty tomb tradition, nor yet as an implied condemnation of the women's craven-heartedness. It is instead a sign of the awe and reverence of those for whom "the sands of time are sinking, the dawn of heaven breaks," for whom the old world has run its course and the New Day of God been actualized through the death and Resurrection of Jesus Christ. If the purpose of Mark's sermon (*Predigt*) is to encourage and exhort a Church in the throes of persecution to the gallantry of Christian faith, one could not imagine a more fitting conclusion than this, in which, with a brevity that yet says everything needful, the Resurrection of Jesus Christ is held up as the pledge of God's breaking into history to end his people's night of sorrow.

Matthew's Easter Witness

B. W. Bacon's theory of the composition of Matthew's Gospel has wielded considerable influence. Rightly discerning that the figure of Moses underlies Matthew's portrait of Jesus, Bacon held that he meant his Gospel to be regarded as a new Pentateuch, and that his work is divided into five "books," each containing a narrative introduction and a discourse, and marked off by a formula of transition (Matt. 7:28; 11:1; 13:53; 19:1; 26:1). This new Pentateuch is contained within chapters 3–25, and chapters 1–2 are prologue, chapters 26–28 epilogue.[65]

All we would say here on the subject of structure is that, at the level of theological understanding of the Gospel, to think of chapters 26–28 simply as epilogue could be very misleading. For we discern in Matthew's Passion narrative and in his Easter tradition in particular the key to his whole picture of Jesus. It is not only that his special themes appear therein. Rather, the risen Christ in Matthew points back to his earthly work and words: "Go therefore and make disciples of all nations . . . teaching them to observe all that I have commanded you" (Matt. 28:19–20). The words of the Teacher in the Sermon on the Mount are not to be divorced from the work of the crucified and risen Messiah. The Teacher is indeed no other than the crucified and risen one (a fact which by itself ought to make us cautious in adducing parallels between Matthew and the Dead Sea Scrolls). We have already observed how Matthew is able to allow the time of the risen and exalted Christ to coalesce with the time of the earthly ministry and suffering of Jesus by the inclusion in his Passion narrative of the apocalyptic fragment heralding the emptying of the graves of the saints *at the moment of the death of Jesus* (Matt. 27:52–3).

The Matthean tradition of the empty tomb, with its reference to the earthquake, the rolling away of the stone by the Lord's angel, and the fainting of the guard (Matt. 28:2–4) is much more elaborate than Mark's. In language which has an Old Testament ring, Matthew explicitly presents the empty tomb as the miracle by which the God of Israel and the God of Jesus has brought his great divine plan and saving purpose to completion. Neither the treachery and resistance of the Jewish leaders to Jesus, which God has foreseen and which the prophets had announced (Matt. 13:13–15), nor the connivance of the representative of Rome is able to withstand God's mighty work (Matt. 27:62–6). God has carried Jesus through the gates of death without the help of men and despite the world. Every precaution of men to have done with Jesus or to make him at most a fleeting memory has gone awry.

The story told by Matthew, after the report of the empty tomb, in which he describes the subterfuge of the Jewish elders, their bribery of the guard to spread the rumor that the disciples had stolen Jesus' body (Matt. 28:11–15), reveals a development of the tradition to meet the needs of Christian apologetic.

But everything in Matthew's record moves toward the final manifestation of the risen Jesus in Galilee (Matt. 28:16–20): [66]

Now the eleven disciples went to Galilee, to the mountain to which Jesus had directed them. And when they saw him they worshiped him; but some doubted. And Jesus came and said to them, "All authority in heaven and on earth has been given to me. Go therefore and make disciples of all nations, baptizing them in the name of the Father and of the Son and of the Holy Spirit, teaching them to observe all that I have commanded you; and lo, I am with you always, to the close of the age."

Matthew describes the Easter appearance of Jesus to his eleven disciples in the form of a theophany on a mountain in Galilee. Galilee is the land in which Jesus first called his disciples to "follow" him: it is the land of mission: it is now to be the land of a new "following" and a wider mission. The mountain, which has its prototype in the mountain of God on which Moses received the Torah, is for Matthew the place of the revelation of Jesus (Matt. 5:1; 15:29; 17:1; 24:3), the second Moses, the Leader and Teacher of the new people of God.

But Matthew's concluding pericope, decisive for the understanding of his Gospel, succinct and concise though it is, contains more than the record of a Resurrection appearance. J. Jeremias, following O. Michel, points out that in verses 18–20 we have a good example of a "triple-action coronation text": (1) the assumption of all authority by the risen one in verse 18; (2) the command to proclaim his authority among all nations in verses 19–20a; (3) the word of power in verse 20b. That Matthew's emphasis is on the heavenly enthronement of the risen Jesus is apparent from the fact that he refers to his Easter appearance only in a participial clause, "and when they saw him" (καὶ ἰδόντες αὐτόν, Matt. 28:17).[67] Moreover, the "doubt" to which Matthew alludes here in the phrase "but some doubted" is not like the doubt of the disciples in the Lucan account (Luke 24:41), where it is the bewilderment of men who cannot believe their eyes at the appearance of the risen one, and where their suspicion is overcome by clearer sight and by Jesus' own invitation to eat. The "doubt" recorded by Matthew seems to reflect the questionings of the later Church about a new Easter certainty and conviction.[68] And in fact, in Matthew's report, the doubt is vanquished by the following words of the risen and exalted Christ, announcing his sovereign heavenly Lordship. The words of the Christ that dispel doubt are in the first instance a pointer to the future. The resurrected one hardly assumes immediately all authority in heaven and earth. But the consummation can be confidently awaited, for with the "close of the age" will come the eschatological kingship of Jesus Christ over the world ("Lo, I am with you always, to the close of the age"). The assurance and guarantee of that future lie, however, in the presence of the exalted Christ with his community even now—with his risen presence the eschatological time is already inaugurated, the beginning of the End has arrived. Professor C. H. Dodd would appear to be correct in describing Matthew 28:18–20 as a "kind of proleptic Parousia." [69]

But more still, the community, conscious of the nearness of the risen and exalted Christ and so moved with expectancy toward the future, is committed in its missionary task to allegiance to the *past* ministry and message of Jesus of Nazareth. The believing community is to teach *all things that Jesus has commanded them.*[70] The Church's own way into the future is to be controlled and governed by the way Jesus has already gone and the message he has already proclaimed. So the resurrected Christ directs the Church back to what has been established in his history—and, despite Matthew's stress on Jesus' reinterpretation of the Law, the decisiveness of his history and person resides not only in his teaching, but in the healing and redeeming mercy he brings, for one of his commands is the command at the Last Supper "to drink of the cup, all of you, for this is my blood of the covenant, which is poured out for many for the forgiveness of sins" (Matt. 26:28). Does not the baptism in the triadic name, which is enjoined upon the Church in its mission (if it be not a later liturgical addition to Matthew 28:19),[71] also recall his death as the agent of God's forgiveness for sins?

Just as there is the closest link between the risen and exalted Christ and the earthly Jesus, so also in Matthew there is a most realistic historical connection between the pre-Crucifixion and post-Easter disciples of Jesus Christ. "Galilee" seems to symbolize this unity for Matthew. Whereas the disciples of the earthly Jesus responded to his call to "follow" him by leaving their boats and nets and customs tables in Galilee, so now in a new way certainly, albeit still under the guidance of his *past* history, the community is to conduct its mission from Galilee to all the world. In and through the mission to the nations Christ will finally come again as sovereign Lord.[72]

Quite obviously, for Matthew, the missionary preaching of the Church is most intimately allied with the presence of the exalted Christ: "Go therefore and make disciples of all nations . . . teaching them to observe all that I have commanded you; and lo, I am with you always to the close of the age." I do not believe we should restrict ourselves to saying that Matthew simply means to indicate that through the preaching the presence of the exalted Lord is actualized in the community.[73] O. Michel has observed that "I am with you" is a Biblical mode of expressing the assurance of divine protection.[74] And indeed, as at the beginning of Matthew's Gospel, the revelation that is brought with Jesus is the revelation of Emmanuel, "God with us" (Matt. 1:22–23; cf. Isaiah 7:14), so now at the close there is the promise from the exalted Christ of the same nearness and the same comfort. Accordingly, as the Church carries its message to the world, in the resultant hardship it enjoys the protection and guidance of its Lord, a protection and guidance that go back to the history and person of Jesus of Nazareth. Can we go still further, and add this? After the Resurrection the Gentiles are now no longer strangers: to them also God is turning in his mercy: they too have become heirs of the kingdom of the Son of Man. Now, as the judgment scene of the Son of Man in Matthew 25 shows, the Son of Man himself is present to every man and is indeed concretely identified with him: "Truly, I say to you, as you did it to one of the least of these my brethren, you did it to me" (Matt. 25:40).[75] Even so, the fullness of the presence of the Christ makes possible the movement of the missionary Church into the world, acts as the medium of communication between it and the world, and alone assures the success of the preaching of the Gospel. On one side the Church may manifest its acknowledgment of Christ's Lordship only by carrying through the mission to all nations. On the other side the presence of the exalted one himself is the inspiration of the mission, until that day of the incorporation of the nations in the disciple body of Christ, awaiting fulfillment in the Parousia.

Luke's Easter Witness

Luke's narratives of the Resurrection reveal him as "the odd man out" among the Evangelists. It is not only that his Easter account is much more extensive, but also he alone has composed, as a sequel to his Gospel record "of the things which have been accomplished among us," in the earthly ministry of Jesus (Luke 1:1), a second volume, containing the story of the expansion of the primitive Church, prefaced by his report of the Ascension of Jesus in physical terms.

Nevertheless, Luke is clearly not so far "out" that he has given up working with traditional materials. Like the other Evangelists, he too introduces the climax of his Gospel with a record of the discovery of the empty tomb (Luke 24:1–7). Apparently he has somewhat drastically edited Mark's record. Now two angelic beings, in place of Mark's one, appear at the tomb (Luke 24:4)—perhaps a sign of Luke's fondness for "double witness" (cf. Acts 1:10 f.). But more important is Luke's deliberate alteration of the Marcan picture in regard to the content of the angelic message. For, whereas in Mark the angel indicates an appearance of the risen Jesus in Galilee, here the angels refer to a prophecy, made by Jesus in Galilee, regarding what would take place in Jerusalem, his Passion and Resurrection there (Luke 24:6). We are thus introduced to one of Luke's special "themes": the "sacred history" must be consummated in Jerusalem and nowhere else; the promises of God to his people Israel must be accomplished in the holy city; Jerusalem must be the center for the mission to the Gentiles (cf. Luke 1:5, 25; 2:25–38; 9:51).

As Luke has it, the women (who, according to Jewish practice, are unable to bring legal testimony and whose role as witnesses has been played down in the tradition, Mark 16:8; John 20:1–10) return from the tomb, bringing the tidings to all the disciples. The disciples, however, are incredulous and unconvinced: "these words seemed to them an idle tale" (Luke 24:11). If verse 12 is genuine, Peter also, having come to see for himself, departs from the tomb still unsure and debating with himself. In forceful language Luke has given expression to the view, common to the other Evangelists, that the empty tomb cannot be made a proof of the Resurrection. In Mark, the women run from the tomb and say nothing to anyone (Mark 16:8). Matthew expressly mentions a viable alternative interpretation of the empty tomb, namely that the disciples may have stolen the body of Jesus (Matt. 28:13). And in his own way Luke has shown that the empty grave can in no wise by itself establish faith in the risen one.

In Luke's report of the empty tomb another note is sounded. It is that there is a contrast between what men can think or say or do and what God can do and has done. "Why do you seek the living among the dead?" the angels ask of the women (Luke 24:5). The crucified Jesus is in the realm of the living: it is his disciples who are in the realm of the dead. His followers, bereft of hope, haunted by thoughts of the grim finality of death, are still wandering in a darkened world. In such a world neither human memory and reminiscence, nor the logic of the human mind, nor the imagination of the human heart can smite death with Resurrection. So it is that Luke moves us inevitably toward the central and joyous Easter message: *"God* has raised this Jesus."

Luke's Emmaus story (Luke 24:13–35), justly described, together with the whole narrative up to verse 53, as "a treasury of Luke's Septuagintal style and vocabulary," [76] is a highly finished literary and artistic creation, bearing unmistakably the imprint of Luke's own hand, which offers the most articulate and comprehensive "philosophy of the Resurrection" in the New Testament. Whether or not Luke had before him a written source, containing an original historical nucleus, is extremely difficult to prove. More surely can we say that the Emmaus story has certain affinities with Greek tragic literature or even with Graeco-Roman mythology. Of decisive importance in Greek tragedy is the moment of the *anagnorisis* or "recognition." So Luke's tale reaches its denouement in the travelers' recognition of the Stranger in their midst. On the other hand it is reminiscent also of certain old stories of the appearance of God himself on earth, and perhaps particularly of Abraham's encounter with the three men at Mamre (Genesis 18). Eduard Lohse has recently suggested, however, a formal parallel with the Graeco-Roman myth of the visit of Jupiter and Minerva to a town in which they found all doors closed against them. Only one old couple in the entire neighborhood were pleased to open their door and offer hospitality to the unknown wayfarers. They waited on them as best they could. Miraculously the wine did not go to the dregs. The gods thereat made themselves known to the old people and bade them follow them to a hill above the town. Then they saw beneath them how the town had been wiped out: only their own house was left standing in its place, but changed now into a temple of the gods.[77]

Now whereas Luke's narrative most probably contains legendary traits, his thoroughly "Christianized" story is really in marked contrast with Graeco-Roman myths, which are designed to illustrate a universal truth or timeless principle. For Luke is concerned with history, with the historical figure of Jesus of Nazareth. And his story is a wonderfully moving account of how the event of faith in Jesus of Nazareth, the Christ, takes place. Faith does not arise out of dependence on any ancient tradition or institution, not even from authoritative Scripture: while hearts burned at the words of Scripture (Luke 24:32), faith was not yet born. Nor does faith arise from any objectively observable phenomenon such as an empty tomb: the travelers to Emmaus tell the Stranger by their side of how, subsequent to the women's report, certain followers went to the tomb to find out for themselves, *but yet did not see Jesus* (Luke 24:24). The eyes of faith are opened and the Stranger is recognized only when at length he himself mercifully takes the initiative with them and, in the breaking of bread, offers himself to them, as Jesus had done once before in the past. Even as, in the breaking of bread, Jesus emerges as a "form of the past," familiar to them, and yet in such a way as to reveal for the first time the meaning of his life, so the meal at Emmaus could hardly fail to bring to mind for Luke's readers the Church's Eucharist, with its remembrance of his Passion and death and its celebration of his continuing, yet hidden, life.

Enshrined in Luke's Emmaus story are other special features of his Easter message. The "fulfillment of prophecy" motif is evident in the appeal of the risen Jesus to Scripture: "Was it not necessary that the Christ should suffer these things and enter into his glory?" (Luke 24:26). "And beginning with Moses and all the prophets, he interpreted to them in all the scriptures the things concerning himself" (Luke 24:27). Reflecting on the ministry of Jesus, Luke has evidently understood that he was not only the consummation of the entire Scripture but the mediator of its meaning as a whole. As the mediator of the Scripture, Jesus occupies for Luke the center of the line of "sacred history," going back to Israel and forward to the epoch of the Church. The things concerning Jesus of Nazareth, which took place in Jerusalem in those days, are the culmination of God's history with Israel. The good news that Christ has really risen (Luke 24:34) means that the promises of God have now come true: God has accomplished the climactic act of deliverance of his people.

In what follows the Emmaus story, Luke first of all makes very plain the identity of the risen Christ with the earthly Jesus. The risen one is no disembodied spirit, but Jesus himself (Luke 24:36–43). Thereafter Luke directs us to a new period of the "sacred history," the period of the Church. The epoch culminated by the fulfillment of Scripture in the death and Resurrection of Jesus Christ must now give way to the preaching of repentance for the forgiveness of sins to all nations "in his name," beginning from Jerusalem (Luke 24:44–7). The apostles are now ready for their great task of witness, armed with the authority of those alone who have encountered the risen

Christ (Luke 24:48). The enabling power of the Spirit sent from God on high will confirm them in their work (Luke 24:49).

The very last scene of all is an act of worship. The risen Christ lifts his hands in High Priestly blessing over his people, and his people respond in the attitude of *proskunesis* before him (Luke 24:50–53).[78] As Luke's Gospel begins in the temple, so now it ends. The time ushered in by the angel's intimation to Zacharias of the birth of a son named John to Elisabeth, his wife (Luke 1:13), has now run its full course and is triumphantly completed in the Resurrection and Exaltation of one mightier than John. As the prelude to Luke's Gospel resounds with hymns of praise, so now the Gospel ends with songs of praise and adoration. From worship before the risen and exalted *Jesus,* the disciples turn to blessing *God* in the temple continually. They were not thereby repudiating the monotheistic faith of their fathers, for, as Dr. A. M. Ramsey has so admirably put it, "to worship Jesus is to affirm that all that is true of God is true of Him." [79] From that day of his Resurrection and Exaltation onwards the Church has worshiped him as Lord. Neither the "creative imagination" of the earliest community nor such ideas as it might have borrowed from the surrounding world were more fertile sources of the development of Christology that took place in the Apostolic Age than its primitive worship of Jesus.[80] Nor should we allow ourselves to forget today, in the midst of our historical concern, that our inability to define historically what occurred "on the third day" is no impediment to the adoration which as Christians we are glad to render now.

In the close of Luke's Gospel, the Resurrection of Jesus and his enthronement as the heavenly King coincide: both belong to Easter Day. By contrast, in the preface to his account of the rise and expansion of the primitive Church in Acts 1, the Ascension is separated from the Resurrection by the "forty days" of the Resurrection appearances (Acts 1:3), and the Ascension is portrayed in terms of time and space as a separate event (Acts 1:9–12). Dr. P. A. van Stempvoort has recently pointed out a clear connection between the demarcations of the *annus ecclesiae,* as formulated by Palestinian bishops after the *Pax Constantina* in the fourth century A.D., and the Lucan "chronology": they found in Luke's "forty days" the sanction for that exact calendrical chronology by which they inserted Ascensiontide into the great season of Pentecost on the fortieth calendar day.[81] The modernday historian has consequently been inclined to see Luke in the light of the calendrical precision of the much later "Church year." So long in fact as Luke has been regarded as "historian" in the unqualified sense of the Harnack era, it has been easy to think of him as preoccupied with items of "chronology," and the seeming discrepancy between the end of his Gospel and Acts 1 has constituted a painful "thorn in the flesh" for scholarship. Moreover, of course, the primitive cosmology implied in Luke's physical record of the Ascension in Acts 1:9–12 is most troublesome for the "modern man," who knows that heaven is infinitely distant and that our earth is not the center of the cosmos.

However, as we observed previously, a dramatic change has lately taken place in Lucan studies. For many, Luke, "the scientific historian," has now practically been ousted by Luke, "the theologian of sacred history." At any rate, the present climate of Lucan scholarship allows us to feel freer than heretofore in approaching Luke from the angle of the theology bound up with his "history."

One important result of the recent departure from the "chronological" view of Luke has been that such scholars as van Stempvoort and E. Haenchen have become much less reluctant to accept the integrity of the longer text of B and C in Luke 24:50–53 and to allow the admittedly disturbed text of Acts 1:1–12 to stand as also original with Luke.[82] In that instance, we are faced with two apparently contradictory records of the Ascension, the one placing it on Easter Day (Luke 24:50–53), and the other placing it "forty days" later and depicting it as a separate "physical" event (Acts 1:1–12).

As to the former, while we discern the hand of Luke in Luke 24:50–53, he has evidently worked upon traditional materials, and has known from his sources what is assuredly the oldest tradition of all, that in the first faith of the Church the Resurrection of Jesus and his heavenly enthronement belonged together. We have confirmation of this indeed in Luke's account of Pentecost, in which the Resurrection and Exaltation of Jesus and the gift of the Spirit are all most intimately combined (Acts 2:32 f.). Through the Resurrection, the Christ has already entered into the glory of his reign at the right hand of God, into the heavenly order, with all that this implies for the universality and transcendence of his Lordship. Quite fittingly can this be described as the "doxological interpretation."

However, it is when we turn to Luke's second interpretation of the Ascension in Acts 1 that we encounter his own "new" and singular contribution. Here alone in the New Testament is a specific duration ascribed, rather than implied, for the post-Easter Christophanies (Acts 1:3). Here alone are concrete details given regarding the Ascension (Acts 1:9–12). Luke's whole Ascension narrative, we have to note, re-echoes a series of Hebrew traditions relating to the "assumption" or "translation" of living persons, such as Elijah or Enoch or Moses, Ezra, and Baruch in the Pseudepigraphical literature. Again the "forty days" of Acts 1:3 ("appearing to them during forty days") has a Hebraic background. "Forty" has sacred overtones in Israel's history and religion: Moses' "forty days" on Mount Sinai and the "forty years" of the Israelites in the wilderness. And, in fact, Luke had a parallel nearer to hand in the previous appearance in Mark's record of the "forty days" of Jesus' temptation. May we not say then that the "forty days" is for Luke a "holy number" rather than a mathematical cipher? It possesses first of all a theological significance, representing for Luke the holy interval in the "sacred history" in which the apostles must be prepared for their task of witness in the period of the Church after the Ascension of Christ and the bestowal of the Spirit.[83] Indeed, with Luke, it is less as private individuals than as the official representatives of the Church that the first disciples have experienced the Christophanies (Acts 1:3, 8), and now are confirmed for their mission to the world.

The special import of the "forty days" would seem to be not so much that it marks the *terminus ad quem* for the Ascension as that it delineates a specific and limited time for the Resurrection appearances. The Christophanies did have their own unique and unrepeatable place in the history of God's dealings with men. After this, Luke's narrative of the Ascension comes, as C. F. D. Moule states, "like a declaration of acted finality." We should not be satisfied to refine away the apparent crudities of Acts 1:9–12 by a typological exegesis that explains the Ascension simply in terms of earlier "assumptions" of Israelite heroes or of the Shekhinah cloud of God's glory, valid though such exegesis is. Even less so should we be content to dismiss Luke's Ascension story as simply a myth, a false objectivization, betokening the petrifaction of the Church's first dynamic experience of the transcendence of the Christ. Rather may we see Luke, pondering the introduction to his volume on the history of the primitive Church, wrestling quite realistically with *historical* questions. Thinking on the situation of the Church up to his time, Luke signifies by the Ascension

that Christ may no longer be "seen" as he was by earthly companions
or by eyewitnesses of his Resurrection, but must "appear" to faith
from the mysterious distance denoted by the word "heaven." With the
Ascension, the time of Jesus has given way to the time of the Church
and the Spirit. There is no word in Luke comparable to Matthew's
"Lo, I am with you always." Even so the Church must live now not
out of the historical presence of Jesus but out of the energizing presence of the Spirit, vouchsafed from God in heaven. The Ascension,
the heavenly enthronement of Jesus, through which is inaugurated the
period of the Church and the Spirit, is for the Church also the pledge
and the promise of the Parousia (Acts 1:11: "This Jesus, who was
taken up from you into heaven, will come in the same way as you saw
him go into heaven"). Yet our concluding observation must be that,
for Luke as well as for the Church, the time of the Church and the
Spirit and the longed-for Parousia would be utterly inconceivable
without that history that had already taken place, *the history of Jesus
of Nazareth,* which occupies its own fixed location in the "story of
salvation."

John's Easter Witness

John's account of the empty tomb is reminiscent of Mark and Matthew, the rest of his Easter tradition much more reminiscent of Luke.
His sources, therefore, can hardly be restricted to *one* of the Synoptic
Gospels. Whether he had the narratives of all three Synoptists before
him, or whether his sources were traditions lying behind the first three
Gospels, he seems to have employed the method of taking from his
sources a nucleus on which to build his own structure. So he records
a visit to the tomb, but of Mary Magdalene by herself (John 20:1–2),
then of Peter and the "other disciple" (20:3–10), and finally an
appearance of the risen Jesus to Mary Magdalene at the tomb (20:11–
18). As in Matthew and Luke, Jesus thereafter appears to his disciples, but here in John they are assembled behind closed doors in
Jerusalem, and here alone does Jesus impart to them, already on
Easter Day, the gift of the Holy Spirit (John 20:19–23). John's Easter
witness then reaches its climax in the singularly compelling story of
Thomas, peculiar to the Fourth Gospel (John 20:24–8).
    Leaving aside for the moment the Thomas story, let us look at two

outstanding themes that belong uniquely to John. When Jesus appears
to Mary in the garden, she first mistakes him for the gardener (John
20:15). The moment she does recognize her Lord, he says to her: "Do
not hold me (μή μου ἅπτου), for I have not yet ascended to the Father;
but go to my brethren and say to them, I am ascending to my Father
and your Father, to my God and your God" (John 20:17). In the
Fourth Gospel the way of Jesus is, from the first, the way to the
Father, a way that has to be traveled through suffering and death toward *"that day"* when he will have attained to his heavenly glory by
the Father's side and the Father will be able to bestow his power and
blessing on men (*v.* especially John 16:26 and 20:19). And so here
the risen Christ entreats Mary not to hold or "cling to" him, for his
journey to the Father is as yet incomplete. It is hardly enough to maintain that what is implied is John's own renunciation of all tactual or
visible evidences for the Resurrection. The word "cling" (ἅπτου) is
the only significant word in the story of the appearance to Mary
(John 20:11–18) that does not occur elsewhere in John or in the
Synoptic witness to the underlying source.[84] Therefore its use is the
more striking. It is, however, familiarly employed in the Synoptic
accounts of healing miracles in reference to sick people laying hold of
Jesus for the healing that is accompanied by the forgiveness of sins,
for salvation. So here it is implied that no remembered fact from the
past of Jesus of Nazareth, no cherishing of his earthly appearance can
by itself bring salvation. Saving faith can only come to life out of the
one indivisible *kairos* of Jesus the Christ, out of the whole message of
his life, death, Resurrection, and Exaltation to the Father.[85]

Closely connected with this theme is the following pericope (John
20:19–23), with its report of Jesus' bestowal of the Spirit on the disciples, creating them anew—even as God first formed man by breath-
ing into his nostrils the breath of life (Genesis 2:7)—and empower-
ing them for the mission of bringing the forgiveness of sins to men.
But this great day of new power and new life could never have dawned
for men apart from the consummation of the way of Jesus—himself
the Way, the Truth, and the Life—by his journeying through death
to Exaltation with the Father. Earlier in his story John has made this
perfectly clear: "As yet the Spirit had not been given, because Jesus
was not yet glorified" (John 7:39).

Despite the emphasis in John's Easter tradition on his own particular theological themes, the gift of the Spirit stemming not from any

one "moment" of the total divine *kairos* of Jesus the Christ, but only from his whole way to the Father, he is none the less hardly less interested than the other Evangelists in the historical connection of the Resurrection with Jesus of Nazareth. John's account of Mary's visit to the tomb recalls Mark's account of the women's visit. John goes out of his way to stress the detail of the "other disciple's" entry into the tomb and his resultant "seeing and believing." In John's story of the appearance to Mary the "form of the past" occurs once more, for in the instant when a familiar voice out of the past says "Mary," she recognizes her Lord. As in Luke's record of the appearance of Jesus to the disciples, so in John, when the risen Jesus confronts his disciples in Jerusalem, he identifies himself with the crucified one by showing them his hands and feet.

Now Bultmann has refused to countenance any element of the past whatever in John's witness to the Christ. For Bultmann, John has solved the problem of the nonoccurrence of the Parousia by testifying solely to the *Christus praesens,* the Christ present in the Word which proclaims him, whence the Now of the Church's existence derives its eschatological character.[86] So because John has perceived that the true meaning of the Synoptic message of Jesus is that it is the negating of the world's understanding of itself, he no longer participates in the transmission of the historical tradition about Jesus. The Church's testimony is the testimony of the Spirit, and that is not an evocation of the past but only a call to the believer, in the light of the eschatological occurrence in Christ, to understand the present moment. John therefore conveys nothing, by way of historical reproduction, of the concrete content of the life or history of Jesus of Nazareth. Jesus in the Fourth Gospel reveals nothing except that he is the revealer, the starkness of whose demand for faith shatters all human norms and calculations. Whereas it would be untrue to say that, for Bultmann, Johannine theology is completely divorced from history, nevertheless in the Johannine Church, as Bultmann understands it, history is swallowed up in eschatology.

In accordance with his view that, in the Fourth Gospel, the process of demythologizing is already well under way, Bultmann not surprisingly asserts that the Resurrection cannot here be an *event* of any special significance. For John the hour of Christ's Passion is already the judgment of the world (12:31; 16:11), and already before his death and Exaltation, he is the lordly giver of Life (11:25; 14:6).

The Easter promise, "I will see you again" (16:22) coincides with the promise of the Parousia (14:18) and with the coming of the Spirit (14:15–17; 15:26; etc.). So in John the Resurrection is indeed identical with the Parousia and the pouring out of the Spirit (20:19–23).[87]

Why then does John include Easter stories in his Gospel? They are for John, as Bultmann believes, like the miracles, "signs" given to faith for which there ought to be no need, but which have been granted as concessions to man's weakness. We must suppose therefore, especially from what Bultmann considers to be the reprimand of the risen Jesus to Thomas, "Blessed are those who have not seen and yet believe" (20:29), that John incorporated the Easter stories in his Gospel in order to expose the error of desiring objective and tangible demonstrations of the revealer.[88]

If this interpretation is correct, we are constrained to ask why John has bothered to include an Easter record at all. Since in the body of his Gospel the Evangelist has dealt very freely with the tradition, it would seem unlikely that in relation to his Easter narratives he should simply *follow the Synoptic tradition,* only at the end to overthrow the validity of its concrete depictions by correcting them in the Thomas story. If he had thought of the Easter tradition as expendable, he might easily have omitted it. Or he might have concluded his Gospel with a kerygmatic epilogue comparable to his prologue instead of riveting our attention to a concrete Easter tradition akin to that of the Synoptists.[89] We can hardly overstress the fact that John, like the Synoptists, has written a Gospel and not a dogmatic treatise.[90]

The popular conception, or rather misconception, of the Thomas story as the story of "doubting Thomas" lends a certain credence to Bultmann's position. But in fact when we look closely at the account, we discover that correlation of "seeing" and "believing" that is part of the intricate correlation of record and confession implicit in the whole Gospel. For John, objective "seeing" is inadequate unless accompanied by inward faith experience (2:23; 4:47 ff.; 7:5; 14:8–9; 20:29).[91] It is the Spirit that quickens and interprets to men the truth disclosed in history. Yet the Flesh cannot be discounted for "the Word became flesh" (1:14). So the risen Lord invites Thomas to touch him *and* to be believing, invites him, that is, to a "believing seeing or touching" (20:27). And Thomas, who is certainly not charged with being faithless *because he has seen,* answers, without ever "touching" Jesus, with the sublimest confession of faith possible for the Evangelist, recalling as it does the prologue (1:1), "My Lord and my God" (20:27–28).[92] However, future generations are unable to participate in this kind of "seeing" or "touching." They must be reliant solely on the action of the Holy Spirit to bring God's revelation in Christ to them ("Blessed are those who have not seen and yet believe," John 20:29). Yet they too will have before them the tradition and the witness of Easter, reported by John as by the other Evangelists, to remind them of that *history,* the history of Jesus of Nazareth, whose meaning is perceived through the operation of the Spirit.

Salient Easter Motifs

It is time now to draw the threads of our inquiry together by underscoring what seem to us to be the predominant Easter motifs.

The "form of the past" and faith. Paul Tillich's "restitution theory" of the Resurrection implies that the Easter event, in and through which has come to birth the Easter faith of the disciples, is conceivable only in view of that incipient and dimly comprehending "faith" which they had had in him in his earthly history—something so decisive happened in the Resurrection that the disciples discovered that the power of the New Being was and is present in Jesus the Christ. A "restitution theory" would appear to be faithful to what the texts are saying.[93] Just as all the texts we have studied denote the closest identity between Jesus of Nazareth and the risen and exalted Christ, so almost invariably do they denote a strong link between the pre-Crucifixion and post-Easter disciples. By virtue of Jesus' making a new beginning with his disciples in the Resurrection, his work has now reached its goal in their Easter faith in him as the Christ of God. The risen Christ reveals the mystery of his whole person and history, so that faith in the Resurrection is not something that is simply added to or can be taken away from the story of Jesus at random: it is the fullness of faith in *Jesus.*

In this context, the story of the empty tomb, whatever we think of its origin or place in the tradition, or however theologically illegitimate it may be to take this enigmatic fact as the basis of Easter faith, can be said to have a positive theological significance. As the grave in which the crucified one is laid, the tomb becomes, in the witness of all the Evangelists, a signpost to what the Easter manifestation really is,

to wit, the appearance of *the crucified Jesus.*[94] The Christ of the
Resurrection is no new and otherworldly Being, but rather the same
Jesus with whom the disciples had walked on the way. For *this Jesus,*
by virtue of his Resurrection, the highest dignity heaven affords cannot be too high, since Easter faith is faith in his heavenly enthronement and reign and glory with the Father. When we go to the texts
to ask about Easter event and Easter faith, we are in fact met, and
nowhere more clearly than in Matthew and Luke, with the worshiping
response of many tongues in praise and adoration of the risen and
exalted Lord.

Fulfillment. In the post-Easter time, the community early sought to
understand its situation by turning to the eschatological predictions
of the Old Testament. So it recognized that, when God vindicated
Jesus of Nazareth by raising him from the dead, the promises of God
of old to Israel and the history he had initiated and carried through
with Israel have been brought to their consummation at last. Mark
thus bears witness to Easter as the coming from the beyond of the
promised Day of the Lord; Matthew to the Passion and Resurrection
of Jesus Christ as the inauguration of the End, in which the graves of
the saints are emptied and they proceed to the holy city; Luke to the
risen Christ as the mediator of the meaning of Scripture in its entirety. Nor has John altogether neglected the Old Testament background, for in his Gospel the fathers and prophets of Israel derive
their greatness from the fact that they are witnesses to Christ (e.g.
John 12:41). "The fathers, the prophets, and the Scriptures point [for
John] to something beyond themselves; whoever heard the word of
God in their testimony would be open to hear and see, to believe and
rejoice, when he met the revelation of God in Christ, full of grace and
truth." [95] Even so, listening to the Old Testament, as we affirmed
earlier, assures the true historicity of Jesus Christ, "in that it makes
visible not only the *kairos* of a 'today' but also a yesterday, and with
it a tomorrow as well." A tomorrow! For Mark the today of Easter
and the tomorrow of the Parousia are indissolubly tied up together.
Matthew's closing pericope is "a kind of proleptic Parousia"—only
the Church's accomplishing its mission to all nations lies between
Easter and the "close of the age." For Luke, the period of Jesus,
climaxed in the Passion, Resurrection, and Ascension, is the indispensable prerequisite of the period of the Church's mission to the
world, carried through in the radiant hope of Christ's coming again

(*v.* Acts 1:11). Although John places the greatest stress of all on the *finality* of the revelation in Jesus Christ, proclaiming that with his Resurrection and Exaltation the End has come and "eternal life" is here, the eschatological task of the Church is still to be carried through. The Church's eschatological mission to the world must be conducted, as Sir Edwyn Hoskyns said, so as to preserve Christ's words in such a way that the world hears his voice (John 14:26; 16:4, 17:20, 21).[96] Living waters are to flow from Christ to the disciples and from them to the world. But, while the Church is gifted with the glory of Jesus (17:22), it may not be taken "out of the world": rather must it suffer as he suffered, be hated and persecuted as he was (7:7; 15:18, 19, 20–21; 16:2–3).

We may not say then that Easter or the Easter message brings the *end* of history, so that past, present, and future are swallowed up in the Now in which the Word is proclaimed. They lift the curtain for the Church on the beginning of the end of history and open up that critical interim, in which discipleship and mission are the order of the day, and in which the community looks back not only to the "old" history of God with Israel but to the past of Jesus of Nazareth himself (cf. Matt. 28:20), and, in the light of his presence, looks forward to his Parousia with great expectation.

Discipleship and mission. In a way quite different from any rabbi, Jesus had called disciples to "follow" him. The hopes awakened in the disciple band who "followed" were shattered by Good Friday. But when Easter Day overcame the breach and discontinuity created by the Cross and called his followers into the community of the new people of God, they understood his call to decision afresh as the eschatological call of the Messiah of God who was to come. How realistically the historical link between the pre-Crucifixion and post-Easter disciples could be construed is most evident from Matthew and from the redactional twenty-first chapter of John, which, with its detailed report of a *Galilean* appearance and a new call to discipleship to Simon Peter, looks like a lengthy embellishment of Matthew's Easter witness.

The community's "new" obedience and following of the risen Christ (and here the Gospels speak with one voice) harks back to that first historical "following," the "following" of Jesus of Nazareth.

There is, we must add, a rich and complex variety of materials relating to the Resurrection in the New Testament on which we have not even touched. Let us say that even in I Corinthians 15 alone Paul makes plain what we certainly should not fail to emphasize, that the Resurrection is no isolated "individual" event but a "communal" event, inasmuch as the risen Christ who is the "firstfruits" cannot be separated from those who belong to him, his congregation of the faithful (I Cor. 15:23). This is borne out further by the First Epistle of Peter, which purports to address itself to a group of strangers. To such a group of strangers is the word held forth: "Blessed be the God and Father of our Lord Jesus Christ! By his great mercy we have been born anew to a living hope through the resurrection of Jesus Christ from the dead" (I Pet. 1:3). In the midst of the tribulation they suffer as a result of their obedience to Christ, they are endowed, through what God has done in raising Jesus Christ from the dead, with a hope that outlasts all worldly hopes, and are constituted a fellowship guarded by the power of God (I Pet. 1:5).[97]

However, the chief purpose of our inquiry into the Easter texts in some detail has been to show that the Resurrection was not a radical transformation, a radical break with the past of Jesus of Nazareth, but God's vindication and confirmation of *this Jesus*. No matter how exalted were the dignities conferred on Jesus Christ by the Church in the post-Easter development of its Christology, it was always and everywhere still speaking of Jesus. By the certainty of the Resurrection, Jesus of Nazareth, the Proclaimer, passed into the message and became himself the Proclaimed, the preached Christ. The heart and center of the kerygma is therefore the Resurrection. And, if it be true that the Church's kerygma confronts men with the *Christus praesens,* nevertheless this "present" is a "present" in which the past of Jesus is not devoured but is given to faith as the specific locus of God's dealings with men. To the extent that mythological traits have entered the New Testament materials relating to the Resurrection, they may be seen as corroborating this truth that, in the quite particular history of Jesus of Nazareth, God's history with the world has been carried through and God's plan of salvation brought to fruition.

VI

Earthly Suffering and Heavenly Glory

The Resurrection is the center of the kerygma. Easter diffuses its light both backward and forward, backward on the earthly history of Jesus and forward on the Christological affirmations of the primitive Church. After the Resurrection the apostles and disciples gathered together their memories of Jesus of Nazareth, but these memories were now supplemented and indeed re-formed because at Easter Jesus himself had made a new beginning with them and had finally disclosed the "secret" of his history, the "secret" of who he was and is and ever shall be. When eventually they left their accounts of Jesus of Nazareth, based on memories of Jesus colored by experience of the risen Christ, at the disposal of the congregation, these accounts inevitably contained the "secret" that had been divulged in the Resurrection. Their accounts therefore assumed the form of *Gospel,* "good news" of this remembered Jesus, whom God had vindicated and confirmed by raising him from the dead, so that he became far more than merely a memory. The Gospel "story" of Jesus could accordingly be re-counted henceforward only, so to speak, as a "kerygmatic history."

Likewise, by the light of the certainty of the Resurrection and the faith in Jesus' Exaltation that accompanied it, the early Christians were able to accord to him the highest and most honorific titles, "Christ," "Son of God," "Son of Man," and "Lord." But when they did so, in the varied forms of their confessions of faith, in liturgical formulae, in sermons, hymns, and prayers, they were simply expressing their conviction that God had already acted mightily for men's

241

salvation in the historical man, Jesus of Nazareth. Consequently, the Christological confessions of the New Testament are confessions of *Jesus* the Christ.

We are constrained to recognize today that when we compare the Gospels with the other New Testament writings, it is not a case of the purely historical versus the purely kerygmatic. Rather we have to do, in the Gospels as well as in all other New Testament confessions, with an indissoluble amalgam of the historical and the kerygmatic. Certainly the Gospels emphasize the earthly obscurity, lowliness, and suffering of the Christ. Certainly also, on the other hand, the Epistles and the Apocalypse emphasize the Exaltation and heavenly reign of Jesus. But all alike are making statements about *Jesus* the Christ, and God's action in him. The old historians of Jesus committed the error of blotting out the "secret" in the Gospels, and in their search for a nonkerygmatic or plain and factual biographical portrait of Jesus, indulged in a purely speculative exercise, as Kähler showed very clearly, and really betrayed their sources, which were all written down from the standpoint of Easter faith and belief.[1] In this way they lost sight of the Christ character of Jesus. On the other side the modern theologians, who owe allegiance to existence philosophy, have been at fault, with regard to the New Testament's confessions of faith, in de-historicizing the kerygma by minimizing or almost entirely effacing the name of Jesus with all of concrete history that it implies.

Our intention in this chapter is to try to do justice to the unity of the historical and kerygmatic standpoints in all the New Testament writings. In other words, our theme is that intermingling of earthly suffering and heavenly glory that seems to us to be of the essence of all New Testament confessions of faith in Jesus the Christ. We shall begin with the Gospels and their stress on Christ's earthly ministry. Now it is hardly any longer a matter of debate that the Gospels do not afford us materials for a biography of Jesus. Criticism itself has brought us to the place from which we can see that, if we wish to elucidate the decisiveness of Jesus of Nazareth for the primitive Church's faith, it will not be by attempting a neutral or detached scientific picture of the facts about Jesus. Rather do we believe that this end can best be achieved by seeking to show how the Evangelists have understood and presented the history of Jesus.

The "Secret" of the Messiah

According to the normative interpretation of Mark's Gospel in the nineteenth century, its author was understood as objective biographer of Jesus concerned with history only as a series of events tied together in the chain of cause and effect. In the first five years of the present century, the works of W. Wrede and J. Wellhausen, dramatizing the nonhistorical character of Mark, opened the door on a new era of Marcan research: Mark wrote not as objective historian but from the standpoint of Christian faith.[2] The breakthrough acted as heady wine for those who, like Arthur Drews, were ready to pounce on any chance to attack the historicity of Jesus, and to demonstrate, on the ground of Mark's "mythological" record, the mythical character of Christian origins.[3] In a more sober vein, from the standpoint of scholarly respectability, were the new expositions of the Marcan attitude to Jesus Christ and history which later sprang out of the Form-criticism movement. M. Dibelius, for instance, did not altogether neglect the role of Mark as the one who collected materials, hitherto circulating in the context of the Church's life, into a presentation of Jesus. Nevertheless, Dibelius' greatest stress was on the Hellenistic influences operative in the Marcan tradition, for he characterized the Gospel as a "Book of secret Epiphanies of the Son of God," the θεῖος ἀνήρ ("divine man") of Hellenism.[4] Bultmann also considered Mark to be more mythical than Matthew and Luke, and, whereas he did not deny that the Gospel reflected the historical figure of Jesus, he thought of it as molded to the Hellenistic pattern of an "epiphany of the Son of God."[5] Only recently, J. Schreiber has once again emphasized the conformity of Mark to the Hellenistic type of kerygma. The focal points of his treatment are (a) the view, adapted from Kähler, that Mark, like the other Gospels, is a "Passion narrative with extensive introduction": in the center of the Hellenistic kerygma stands the Cross as the altogether decisive "sacred event"; and (b) the "Messianic secret" in Mark is conditioned by the Hellenistic kerygma, according to which (Phil. 2:6–11; I Cor. 2:8) the redeemer appears on earth, in obscurity, as a man and is crucified by the worldly powers who do not recognize him. The conclusion of Schreiber's study is accordingly that Mark's Christology is of the Gentile-Christian-Hellenistic type, belonging to the Pauline sphere.[6] This emphasis on the Hellenism of Mark's conception of Jesus Christ calls attention to one of the most intriguing facts in the New Testament, namely that the earliest of the Gospels bears on its tradition the imprint of Hellenistic religious ideas. We may perhaps see the Church, represented by Mark, feeling its way toward a proclamation of the gospel in a language that the wider Graeco-Roman world could the more readily comprehend.

But there are good reasons for believing that Mark has certainly made no unconditional surrender to Hellenism. The special "feel" of the Marcan tradition is still Jewish. The debates or controversies of Mark's Gospel still belong to the world of Jewish thought. There is a sufficient number of Semitisms in the sayings of Jesus as well as in the narratives to tell against any theory of the corruption of the tradition by Hellenistic influences. Most important of all is the fact that Mark, who according to the testimony of Papias was the secretary of Peter, shows in his record that the disciples, gathered around Jesus, understood their Master only slowly. The principle of the "Messianic secret" that permeates Mark's Gospel has two main facets. First, it indicates Mark's conviction that the reality of the Son of God, "Christ," is present already in the historical way and appearance of the Son of Man, "Jesus." Secondly, inasmuch as the reality of "Christ" is provisionally concealed in the earthly way of "Jesus," and neither Peter nor the other disciples are idealized as in any full sense believers in the "Christ," Mark's interest in the "secret" is a sign of his undoubted respect for the history of Jesus of Nazareth. Mark confronts us as one who desires to narrate history. And nothing could be more significant than that he begins his history not with Good Friday and Easter, but with John the Baptist, standing at the threshold of the public ministry of Jesus. His record should not be taken therefore as evidence mainly or only for the early Church's faith in Christ, understood in the light of Hellenistic religious ideas and ideals. Rather does Mark tell us of that history of Jesus by which the "time of salvation" has been brought in, and which lies at the root of the Church's history, of the Church's present life and worship of its heavenly Lord. From this point of view we welcome such explications of Mark's Gospel as that of Willi Marxsen, who regards it, as we have seen, not as a *Historie* nor as a *Vita,* but as a *Predigt* (Sermon). Quite realistically Mark brings his hearer face to face with Jesus in such wise that the hearer's own history and situation in the Church of around A.D. 66–70 coalesce with the history of Jesus, and in such wise that the concrete features of the historical appearance of Jesus are seen to be an inseparable aspect of the Christ in whom the hearer believes.[7]

The "Messianic secret" itself is the clue to the Marcan understanding of history as embracing within a unified whole both the history of Jesus and the history of the Church. By the "secret" Mark has apparently tried to maintain a schema of the time of Jesus' earthly obscurity followed by the time of his glory and heavenly Lordship over the Church. Silence has to be enjoined on the evil spirits who recognize him (1:25, 34; 3:11 f.), on those who have been healed by him (1:44; 5:43; 7:36; 8:26), on Peter (8:30) and the disciples (9:9). The disciples indeed, in his earthly presence, must be puzzled and bewildered and without true understanding (6:52; 7:18; 8:17 f., etc.). Meanwhile Jesus must remain the *Christus absconditus*. The day of his post-Resurrection glory must be attained before he can finally become the *Christus revelatus*.

Paradoxically, however, the "secret" is not completely hidden. The evil spirits, on whom silence is imposed, are even then aware that through his earthly ministry their rule is coming to an end. Those who are healed by him experience his power. The disciples, for all their obtuseness, wish to proclaim him Messiah. Beyond that, he appears in his ultimate glory to Peter, James, and John in the Transfiguration (9:2 ff.). Who he really is can scarcely be suppressed. He is *anointed* with precious ointment (14:3 ff.). In the night trial before Caiaphas, he declares himself, and warns Caiaphas that, by a startling reversal, he shall become in the day of his glory the Judge of his present judges (14:62). So the "secret" keeps coming out, disclosing Mark's notion that the earthly activity of Jesus is already the locus of revelation, the matrix of the "time of salvation," that the risen Christ who is proclaimed is identical with the Jesus who is the originator of the gospel.

In his own way Mark sets down beside the history of Jesus the Church of his own day, living still in the anguish of the tensions of the present age in which the conflict between the Spirit and Satan is continued. Set down beside Jesus, the believer can see how Jesus' fate of suffering and rejection is the divinely ordained precondition of his triumph (8:31). And as it is with Jesus, so it is with his disciples. The disciple must lay down his life in order to find it (8:34 ff.). Service and self-sacrifice, baptism into death, are the sole guarantee of the coming glory (10:35–45). Likewise the Church itself must pass through a dire period of distress, the pain of facing hostile courts, the suffering of international wars, the danger of being led astray by Messianic pretenders, before entering on its final blessedness (13:3 ff.). The one thing which the Church most surely has in common with the person and history of Jesus is that it too *must suffer* in the world, until that day when the conflict between the Spirit and Satan is ended and the goal of history is reached. The goal of history! For whereas Mark is concerned with the past of Jesus of Nazareth chiefly as a history of lowliness, rejection, the uttermost limit of diabolic involvement and death, from the standpoint of faith in the resurrected Christ, he also turns toward the future and sees in that same history the given pledge of the End and the one sure gateway to final glory.[8]

The highly condensed concluding pericope of Mark (16:1–8) leaves us in considerable uncertainty, as we noted in the last chapter, as to whether he alludes to a Resurrection appearance of Jesus in Galilee or to the Parousia of the Son of Man itself. Even if, however, we are right in thinking that Mark's Gospel is terminated with the Resurrection, we are not left entirely in the dark as to the futuristic element in his perspective on the combined history of Jesus and history of the Church. For Mark, the kingdom of God is already breaking into history in Jesus' earthly ministry (1:15 and 9:1), and the coming unveiling of that which has been hidden is promised (4:22 and 9:9). Just as the historical appearance of Jesus, his baptism with the Spirit and his temptation by Satan in the wilderness present for Mark a new kind of history, different from all history preceding John the Baptist, so Jesus' preaching of the nearness of the kingdom opens up a new kind of future, a *real future,* to wit, the event of the Parousia. Mark's eschatology, which implies that the Church's historical situation in the critical interim between the death and Resurrection of Jesus Christ and the Parousia is but a continuation of the type of history enacted in Jesus' earthly ministry, has a strong apocalyptic flavor. Beyond the woes and supernatural portents and the gathering of the elect before the Last Days, Mark looks further into the future, to the Parousia itself, which will usher in the expected consummation (13:14–23). The concreteness of the Marcan eschatology, as applying both to Jesus and to the Church, prevents us from thinking of Mark as enunciating abstract truths about history or as reducing the faith and life of the Church to timeless mystical experience.

With an almost naïve realism Mark then preaches Jesus. Jesus confronts the hearer just where he is as the one in whose ministry of suffering and obscurity the hidden and coming glory of God is already present. Mark's Sermon is a Sermon of both challenge and comfort to the Church in its own history. The challenge is the challenge to endure with fortitude, even as Jesus himself endured, the toil and travail of a world in which the warfare between the Spirit and Satan goes on. The comfort is the comfort of knowing in faith that, precisely because, as with Jesus himself, the coming glory of God lies concealed amid the toil and travail, it will surely come, when the God-appointed goal of history is attained.

The "Meek King"

Very prominent in Matthew, as compared with Mark, is the Jewish pattern of prophecy and fulfillment. Point by point Matthew endeavors to show that in the life of Jesus the Scripture of the Old Covenant is brought to its accomplishment. It may suffice here to mention his allusion to Isaiah (7:14) in the introduction of his Gospel (1:22–23): "All this took place to fulfill what the Lord had spoken by the prophet: 'Behold, a virgin shall conceive and bear a son, and his name shall be called Emmanuel' (which means, God with us)." Moreover, in Matthew's great collection of the words of Jesus in the Sermon on the Mount, Jesus stands forth as the Teacher who undertakes a radical reinterpretation of the Law of Moses: "You have heard that it was said to the men of old . . . but I say unto you" (Matt. 5:21–2, 27–8, 31–2, 33–4, 38–9, 43–4). The continuity of the words and deeds of Jesus with the events of Israel under the Old Covenant is assurance of Matthew's interest in the historical reality of what he is recording concerning Jesus of Nazareth.

Nevertheless, the words and deeds of Jesus could not for Matthew be explained or understood solely from the past of the Old Covenant. Rather their true implication could be comprehended only from the viewpoint of the apostolic congregation as enlightened by post-Easter Christology. Matthew has not eliminated the Marcan principle of the "Messianic secret." He has indeed retained some of Jesus' injunctions to secrecy upon those who have been healed by him (Matt. 8:4; 9:30; 12:16). So far he appears to agree with Mark that the mystery of who Jesus is could be manifested only through his death and Resurrection. But Matthew has modified the "secret," for with him it is a much more open "secret." The result is that Matthew's Christ is less *aloof* from history than Mark's Christ, who simply comes into the world in his own history-creating power. This is apparent in the Matthean account of the Baptism, where he interpolates into the Marcan narrative the discussion of John the Baptist with Jesus, in order to show that John already recognized him as the sinless Messiah for whom no baptism could possibly be necessary (Matt. 3:13–15). There is no hint of John's acknowledgment of Jesus as Messiah in Mark, where Jesus comes to John among the crowds as the unrecognized Messiah, the Son of God, the Beloved, with whose "hidden" coming the time of God's salvation is inaugurated among the people gathered together by John (Mark 1:9–11). Matthew's Christ, recognized by John straightaway, is much less completely isolated than Mark's.

There are many more tokens of Matthew's modification of the "secret." For him Jesus is already in his historical ministry the Son of David, in whom are fulfilled the prophecies of the Old Testament. His supernatural birth (1:22), episodes from his early life (2:5, 15, 17, 23), his Galilean ministry (4:14), his betrayal (26:24) and his arrest (26:54, 56) have all been foretold in the Scripture. Frequently, in Matthew, Jesus is quite openly addressed as Son of David.[9]

Matthew is also at pains to establish the closest relationship between the earthly Jesus and the coming Son of Man. The contrast between Mark 13:4 and Matthew 24:3 bears this out. In the former, after Jesus' saying about the destruction of the temple, the disciples ask: "Tell us, when will this be, and what will be the sign when these things are all to be accomplished?" In the Matthean parallel the words "of your coming" are inserted into the disciples' question: "When will this be, and what will be the sign of your coming and of the close of the age?" Apparently with some deliberateness Matthew connects the one who is to come at the end of the world with the earthly Jesus. Once more, in Matthew's picture of the Son of Man in Judgment (25:31–46) the titles "Son of Man" and "King" are equated (25:34, 40). The name of "King" is favored more by Matthew than by Mark or Luke (Matt. 2:2; also Matthew's quite frequent use of the title in his Passion narrative, 27:11, 29, 37, 42). Yet for Matthew this "King" of the Last Judgment is no other than the "meek King" who rides into Jerusalem on an ass to meet his death (Matt. 21:5).

Matthew further betrays his special intention to identify the earthly Jesus in his history with the exalted Christ of the Church's faith in his alteration of the Marcan perspective on the attitude of the disciples to Jesus. In Mark, to the very end, the disciples do not yet see who Jesus is. In Matthew there is a pointed contrast between the unbelieving disposition of the crowd and the Jewish leaders toward Jesus and the believing understanding of the disciples. The Jewish people's rejection of Jesus is for Matthew part of the divine plan and the fulfillment of Old Testament prophecies (13:13–15). They have scorned Jesus' mighty works (11:20–24), have demanded external signs (12:38–42), have attributed to Beelzebul what was really the work of the Spirit (12:22–37), have spurned the true revelation of God for their own human traditions and religious formalism (15:10–20; 23:16–28; etc.). All this resistance of the Jews to Jesus is but the inevitable outcome of their past crimes recorded in the Scripture (23:34–7). The disciples of Jesus on the contrary are blessed because they both see and hear (13:16–17). They have the capacity to know the secrets of the kingdom of heaven (13:11), and to them the parables are not obscure (Matt. 13:51; cf. Mark 4:13).[10]

In Mark's story of Jesus' walking on the water, the only response of the disciples, because of the hardness of their hearts, is that of dumb incredulity (Mark 6:51–2). In Matthew, however, they confess him as the Son of God and worship him (Matt. 14:33). Matthew's account of Peter's confession is also significantly different from Mark's (Matt. 16:13–23; cf. Mark 8:27–33). In Mark the confession of Peter is followed by a stern rebuke from Jesus: "Get behind me, Satan! For you are not on the side of God, but of men." Mark's account might more appropriately be entitled "the repudiation of Peter's confession," whereas, in Matthew, Peter's confession has become the ground for his being designated the rock on which the Church is to be built (Matt. 16:18).[11]

Grave suspicion still attaches to the epochal text of Matthew 16:17–19, and it seems unlikely that, in the form in which we have it, it goes back to Jesus himself. Certainly the undoubted Aramaic coloring of the language of Matthew 16:18, with its pun on the name Cephas, which could be rendered only in Aramaic, points to a very old tradition. The possibility has to be left open, therefore, that an authentic saying of Jesus may lie behind this verse. Otherwise there are several obstacles to accepting the words as they are as words of

Jesus. Is it probable that Jesus would refer to the new and true Israel of God as "mine," "my Church"? The word "Church" itself occurs only here in the Synoptic tradition in the sense of the totality of the Church; in Matthew 18:17 it denotes simply an assembly of the Church. So important is the saying of Matthew 16:18 that it is hard to imagine why Mark and Luke should have omitted it if it had been known to them. There is besides very little sanction for assuming from the teaching of Jesus on the kingdom of God, as it is recorded elsewhere in the Synoptics, that he there has in view any such clearly defined community as is envisaged by the term "Church" here in Matthew 16:18. For, while the word "Church" in Matthew 16:18 has profound eschatological overtones, implying the primitive Church's understanding of itself as the true Israel of God, the elect congregation of the Last Days, the institutional form of the community reflected in Matthew 16:18–19 is at variance with Jesus' message of the imminence of the kingdom of God. The Church would now appear to have arrived at a stage of institutionalism, properly belonging to an epoch considerably later than the Resurrection, in which both office and order have become very important for it—the monarchical office of a particular apostle, and the order associated with the vesting of ecclesiastical authority in the community over doctrinal and legal matters, represented here by the "binding" and "loosing" (Matt. 16:19). The genuineness of the saying of Matthew 16:17–19 is consequently open to great doubt.[12]

However, not all that can be said about this text is negative. In Matthew the words about the Church do fall from the lips of *the historical Jesus*. Highly significant also is the consistent future tense throughout the passage: "I will build my church"; "the powers of death shall not prevail against it"; "1 will give you the keys of the kingdom of heaven"; "shall be bound in heaven"; "shall be loosed in heaven." May we not find here a guide to Matthew's point of view? The future tense of these verbs points to a period beyond the Resurrection; the Church arises after Easter through the response of believing men to the whole way of Jesus culminating in his death and Resurrection. For Matthew, Easter has created the Church, not as an exact chronological point in the calendar, but as the final unleashing of the call of God that has gone forth, in all its rigor and decisiveness, in the history of Jesus of Nazareth. So the earthly ministry of the historical man Jesus of Nazareth contains within it the seed of the future of the new people of God: "I will build my Church" (Matt. 26:18). So also the existence of the post-Easter Church under the Lordship of the exalted Christ is controlled and regulated by a quite particular past, the past of Jesus: "Go and make disciples of all nations . . . teaching them to observe *all that I have commanded you*" (Matt. 28:19–20). Matthew is thus able, in apparent defiance of chronology, to make the time of the Church under the rule of the resurrected and exalted Christ and the time of the historical Jesus overlap.

This is further borne out by Matthew's version of Jesus' stilling of the storm (Matt. 8:22–7), as Günther Bornkamm has shown. When we compare Matthew's story with those of Mark (4:35–41) and Luke (8:22–5), we discover certain touches that are peculiar to Matthew. He alone introduces the *terminus technicus,* ἀκολουθεῖν: "And when he got into the boat, his disciples followed him" (Matt. 8:23). Only in Matthew does the request of the disciples to their Master become a sudden fervent prayer: "Save, Lord: we are perishing" (8:25). The notion of a "nature miracle" does not exhaust the meaning of the story for Matthew. The presence of Jesus in the boat with those who have *followed* him in fact strongly suggests the presence of the exalted Lord with his Church in its littleness and loneliness amid the turbulence and chaos of the world.[13] Even more explicitly Jesus' words to the disciples sound forth like Christ's words to the Church: "Where two or three are gathered in my name, there am I in the midst of them" (Matt. 18:20).[14] The same power of God, by which the presence of the resurrected Christ is vouchsafed wherever a handful are assembled "in his name," is active already in the earthly Jesus. Is it not the same also with Jesus' stilling of the storm-tossed sea? The same power of God at work in the risen and exalted Christ's guidance and protection of his Church is at work in the wondrous works and deeds of Jesus of Nazareth.

Yet in his special way Matthew bears witness to the supreme paradox that the mighty works and deeds of Jesus are the works and deeds of the obscure and humble one, who appears in the form of the Servant among men.[15] In Matthew 12:14–21, the passivity of Jesus' withdrawal from the Pharisees, his healing of all the people, and his injunction to silence are explained as manifestations of the activity of the Servant of God of Isaiah 42:1–4. These are the marks of Jesus' lowliness and humiliation. In the *Reflexionszitat* or "formula quotation," incorporated in Matthew 12:18–21, Matthew shows us by his free rendering of the Isaianic prophecy that what Jesus has done is the token of his humiliation as the Servant of God of Isaiah 42.[16] Another "formula quotation," from Isaiah 53:4, occurs in Matthew 8:17: "This was to fulfill what was spoken by the prophet Isaiah, 'He took our infirmities and bore our diseases.'" Here the healing work of Jesus is linked with that amazing condescension whereby he has identified himself utterly, as the Servant of God, with men's infirmities and sicknesses. E. Lohmeyer has correctly observed that no early Christian writer has so much as Matthew preserved in its purity the notion of the righteous, obedient, suffering Servant of God.[17]

In the story of the "triumphal entry" into Jerusalem, Matthew has made a rather striking change (Matt. 21:5) in the quotation he offers from Zechariah 9:9. In the latter we read: "Lo, your king comes to you; triumphant and victorious is he, humble and riding on an ass, on a colt the foal of an ass." Matthew has omitted the words "triumphant and victorious is he" and so has allowed the paradox of the "meek King" to occupy the very forefront of the picture. In Matthew, the Kingship of Jesus resides exactly in his renunciation of lordliness and authority, in the submissiveness and obedience with which he travels the *Via Dolorosa*.

Not for one moment, as we gather from Matthew's closing pericope (Matt. 28:16–20), is the community of believers permitted to detach itself from the history of Jesus, the history of the "meek King." As the community moves into its mission to the world, its experience of the exalted Christ cannot be spoken of in abstract or mystical terms, as though some new universal truth or principle had now dawned upon it only from the side of heaven. For, even as the Church participates in the eschatological sacrament of baptism for the forgiveness of sins "in his name," in fervent expectation of the coming of the Lord, and even as, one might add, it partakes of the Lord's Supper in the glad hope of the Lord's return, the light of that great future shines for it only because it is also committed to the *past* way of Jesus of Nazareth and the events reported about him. Nothing, neither the present nor the future, neither the gospel nor the mission, holds good apart from him and the pathway of his history. The road Jesus traveled, a road in the first instance through lowliness and humiliation and death, is prior to the Church and is determinative for the believer in the Church after Easter. He will be involved, like the follower of the earthly Jesus, in the insecurity and distress that result from the repudiation of the world and the world's standards: "He who does not take his cross and follow me is not worthy of me. He who finds his life will lose it, and he who loses his life for my sake will find it" (Matt. 10:38–9). In the very act of repudiating the world the disciple may learn who Jesus is, may learn that, as the meek one who goes to his death on the Cross, he is at the same time, and precisely in so doing, the King. His way therefore, when it is shared by the disciple, contains for the disciple as for Jesus himself, the pledge of the coming kingdom of God and the promise of exaltation to God's glory.

The One Anointed with the Spirit

Luke explicitly tells us immediately in his preface that, as others have done before, he will seek to present the truth about the historical Jesus. His intention is to *narrate* the events that happened among men in accordance with the testimony of eyewitnesses and servants of the word (Luke 1:1–3). Not that he is a modern historian, a purveyor of such biographical facts as could be scientifically accounted for by historical criticism. But even more expressly than the other Synoptists does Luke affirm his conviction that his subject is "historical." The history he has to narrate is both the continuation and consummation of the history of God's dealings with Israel. As his narrative begins in the temple with the priestly ministrations of Zechariah, so it ends in the temple with men's praise to God for all that He had done in raising Jesus Christ from the dead. And throughout the Gospel, Luke has richly developed the prophecy-fulfillment theme.

Yet Luke, whose avowed intention is to narrate, introduces into his presentation of Jesus Christ more of what we may call "kerygmatic" material than the other Synoptic Evangelists, and in such a fashion as to convey the impression that he is very often holding a number of sermonic threads in his hand at one time. Out of the wealth of "kerygmatic" material in the work of Luke, who seems to sense no inherent contradiction between the historical element in his narration and the kerygmatic, we shall deal only with some primary features. We may take our point of departure from the principle of the "secret," which, as we shall see, is certainly not absent from Luke, but which is a "secret" disclosed from the first in his Gospel. The birth stories form a prologue in which we learn who this one really is whose history is

to be told. His birth is surrounded with glory and miracle, and he is
designated as Messiah, Lord, and Son of God. He is further sealed as
the Son of God at the Baptism, and his glory shines forth in the Transfiguration. As in Matthew, Jesus' disciples (to whose preparation and
training Luke, with the thought of the Church and the Church's mission in his mind, devotes a great deal of attention) are able to discern
the effects of his Messianic power and authority, operative already in
his historic appearance: "Blessed are the eyes which see what you see!
For I tell you that many prophets and kings desired to see what you
see, and did not see it, and to hear what you hear, and did not hear
it" (Luke 10:23–4).

But the openness of the "secret" in his Gospel notwithstanding,
Luke has preserved the lowliness of the way of Jesus. In contrast with
the leaders of Judaism, who have turned away from the outcasts of
Israel and have annulled their opportunity to serve as agents of God's
purpose by rejecting the way of the Christ, Jesus himself is depicted
by Luke as turning toward the social outcast and failure and the
despised foreigner. "A scribe of the gentleness of Christ," Dante called
Luke. As the one who turns toward the sinner, Jesus must be involved
in suffering, rejection, and death, as an indispensable prelude to his
exaltation to heavenly glory. From the standpoint of Easter, Luke de-
velops one of his principal themes: through death to heavenly glory.
Immediately after the anticipatory unveiling of his glory in the Transfiguration, the time of Jesus' *analempsis* (his "being taken up") begins:
"When the time drew near for him to be received up, he set his face
to go to Jerusalem." There seems to be an allusion here to the steadfastness of purpose that characterizes the Servant of Israel: "For the
Lord God helps me; therefore I have not been confounded; therefore
I have set my face like a flint" (Isaiah 50:7). And the death of Jesus
is latterly quite explicitly connected with the suffering of the Servant:
"I tell you that this scripture must be fulfilled in me, 'And he was
reckoned with transgressors'; for what is written about me has its fulfillment" (Luke 22:37; cf. Isaiah 53:12). The period of his *analempsis*
is an inexorable movement toward Jerusalem and his death on the
Cross, and yet at the same time toward his own ultimate "perfection"
in the Resurrection: "Behold, I cast out demons and perform cures
today and tomorrow, and the third day I finish my course. Nevertheless, I must go on my way today and tomorrow and the day following;
for it cannot be that a prophet should perish away from Jerusalem"

(Luke 13:32–3). True to his own prediction, it is finally as the one who goes through death that he is raised up by God to glory, a glory consummated by his Ascension to a seat at the right hand of God, in fulfillment of the prophecy of Psalm 110:1 and of his own declaration to the High Priest: "But from now on the Son of man shall be seated at the right hand of the power of God" (Luke 22:69).

The "through death to heavenly glory" theme is very prominent also in the speeches of Acts. Whatever theory of the composition of the speeches we may hold, we may safely take them as illustrative of the gospel's meaning for Luke. For even if, in opposition to recent trends in Lucan studies, we think of the speeches in Acts as reflecting the primitive Jerusalem kerygma, Luke would scarcely have been so theologically insensitive and so historically scientific as to proffer versions of the gospel which were in discord with his own point of view in his own day and place. Now in the climax of his speech on the day of Pentecost, Peter declares: "Let all the house of Israel therefore know assuredly that God has made him both Lord and Christ, this Jesus whom you crucified" (Acts 2:36). Taken by themselves, these words might seem to indicate that Jesus of Nazareth, a *man* attested by God with mighty works and wonders and signs (cf. Acts 2:22), was exalted, and only through the radical transformation wrought by the Resurrection, implied if not expressly mentioned here, was made "Lord" and "Christ." We should then have a suggestion of an adoptionist point of view on Luke's part. But such an understanding of the text finds its rebuttal in the body of Peter's speech. This Jesus of Nazareth, attested by signs and wonders and by the accomplishment of David's prophecy (Acts 2:25–8), was the Messiah, carrying through God's action all through his history. As such, "he was not abandoned to Hades, nor did his flesh see corruption" (Acts 2:31). "His flesh" is a substitute for "thy Holy One" in the Davidic prophecy (Acts 2:27). The Resurrection was but the confirmation of who this Jesus was and is, namely both "Lord and Christ." [18] There is, therefore, no incompatibility between the Christological content of Peter's Pentecost speech and the Christology implicit in Luke's Gospel, where the "secret" of Jesus' Messiahship is not laid up until only after his death and Resurrection, but is divulged already in every phase of his earthly life, indeed even in his birth as the infancy stories demonstrate. The divine glory is about him on his way through suffering and death. We need only add at this point to what we have previously said about the disclosure of the "secret" of who Jesus is already in his earthly history that Luke appears to place a special emphasis on Jesus' being hailed as "King" on his entry into Jerusalem (Luke 19:38).[19]

Both the Gospel and Acts attest Jesus as the bearer of the Spirit. In the Nativity report Luke has demonstrated the connection between the Christ and the Spirit: "The Holy Spirit will come upon you [Mary], and the power of the Most High will overshadow you; therefore the child to be born will be called holy, the Son of God" (Luke 1:35). According to Luke's Gospel, Jesus is at the very outset visited by the Spirit (3:22), impelled by the Spirit (4:1), empowered by the Spirit (4:14). His ministry opens with an extensive declaration in the synagogue of Nazareth, where his quotation from Isaiah 61:1–2, that has now come to pass, as he proclaims (Luke 4:21), specifies both the nature of his task and his special equipment for it: "The Spirit of the Lord is upon me, because he has anointed me." In his account of the episode at Nazareth, Luke would appear to draw attention to the interrelation between Jesus as the bearer of the Spirit and "the prophet." His hearers are amazed at the words of grace that proceed from his mouth (4:22). And Jesus tells them: "No prophet is acceptable in his own country" (4:24). In the following pericope, the people are amazed by the authority and power of his word, through which the unclean spirits are exorcised (4:31–6). The supreme vocation of Jesus, according to the words recorded of him in Luke 4:43, is to preach the good news of the kingdom of God. It is probably denoted here that he is sent as a prophet to Israel. Luke, in fact, lays great stress on the prophetic aspect of Jesus' ministry. Now "prophet" and "Spirit" are closely associated. In the Damascus Document II, 12, the prophets are represented as "those anointed with the Spirit."

Of especial significance for Luke is the notion of the "prophet like unto Moses," deriving from Deuteronomy 18:15: "The Lord your God will raise up for you a prophet like me [Moses] from among you, from your brethren—him shall you heed." This text, cited by Philo and the Pseudo-Clementine *Preaching of Peter,* figured largely in the rise of the Jewish faith in the eschatological prophet, a faith further attested for us recently from the literature of the Qumran sect, whose *Manual of Discipline* reveals the hope of the coming of a prophet together with the expectation of Messiahs of Aaron and Israel.[20] While the Deuteronomic prediction of a "prophet like unto Moses" does not appear to have been given a Messianic interpretation in the first century, in Lucan usage it has come to be quite clearly connected with the work of Jesus, since it is expressly mentioned in the speeches of Peter and Stephen in Acts as part of their testimony to Jesus (Acts 3:22; 7:37). Moreover, after the fashion of Moses, in the terms of Luke's Gospel, Jesus appointed the Twelve and the Seventy and bequeaths to his successors the Spirit with which he himself was endowed.[21]

The "Spirit" bears a relation to the "prophet." O. Cullmann observes that the concept of the "prophet" lends itself to combination with other significant Christological concepts applied to Jesus, and leads particularly to the idea of the Suffering Servant.[22] This seems to be true for Luke, who raises the curtain on Jesus' ministry with Jesus' application to himself of the words of the prophet of Isaiah 61, anointed with the Spirit, and probably to be identified with the Suffering Servant to whom God has given the Spirit. As the one possessed of the Spirit, therefore, Jesus is the Servant-Prophet.

If the Spirit is found in relation to the "prophet," it is found also in relation to "anointing" and to the "King." Van Unnik has lately called attention to the fact that, in the Old Testament, "Spirit" and "anointing" are closely combined, and with particular reference to kings. So after being anointed, Saul prophesies because "the Spirit of the Lord comes mightily upon him" (I Samuel 10:1 ff.; 9 ff.). Even more striking is the connection in I Samuel 16:13: "Then Samuel took the horn of oil, and anointed him in the midst of his brothers; and the Spirit of the Lord came mightily upon David from that day forward." In the Psalms of Solomon 16:32 the king, the "anointed of the Lord," is described in this way: "For God will make him mighty by means of [his] Holy Spirit and wise by means of the spirit of understanding, with strength and righteousness." In II Corinthians 1:22 Paul associates God's "anointing" with the gift of the Spirit. A rich background, therefore, lies behind Luke's emphatic witness to Jesus as the "anointed" bearer of the Spirit, nowhere more explicitly affirmed than in the brief summary of his life in Acts 10, where we read "how God anointed Jesus of Nazareth with the Holy Spirit and with power; how he went about doing good and healing all that were oppressed by the devil, for God was with him" (Acts 10:38).[23]

Jesus' possession of the Spirit seems to be, for Luke, the regulative factor relating to all the activity of Jesus as Messiah-Servant-Prophet and to afford the clue to the meaning of Jesus' history. We may see in it also the chief clue to Luke's understanding of the connection between the differentiated but not unrelated epochs of "salvation history." We noted earlier how "modern" Luke is in the sense that he wishes to distinguish between the epochs on the line of "sacred history," the epoch of Israel, of Jesus, and of the Church. The Ascension, which looks like "a declaration of acted finality," not only demarcates the close of the epoch of Jesus, but symbolizes the distance of the Christ, now enthroned in heaven, from the Church in its own new time. The past of Jesus is *past* in relation to the Church of Luke's generation. There is in fact a remarkable contrast between the Matthean and Lucan conceptions. In Matthew, the risen Christ promises his disciples his abiding presence: "Lo, I am with you always" (Matt. 28:20). In Luke, the risen Christ refers his followers to the words he spoke during his earthly ministry: "While I was still with you" (Luke 24:44).

Nevertheless, the exalted Christ is for the Church no remote, "unknown" Being. The Ascension is followed by the pouring out of the Spirit in power at Pentecost, to which the indispensable prelude is the activity of Jesus of Nazareth, in his history himself the bearer of the Spirit. Thus the Spirit, through whose coming the Church lives in its own period, harks back to the time of the earthly Jesus.[24] That time, as it is recorded in Luke's Gospel, is a time of preparation for the greater mission that is to come. In it Jesus calls disciples to follow him and commissions them to "catch men." Later, in the context of his own journey through death to heavenly glory, he instructs his disciples in the continuity of their mission with his own, saying to the Seventy, "He who hears you hears me" (Luke 10:16). Toward the close, at the Last Supper, he covenants the kingdom to his disciples and points up for them sharply the contrast between all worldly power and the authority of the disciple of Christ, which resides only in his voluntary acceptance of lowliness and service (Luke 22:14–30). And after the Ascension, during its mission to Israel under Peter's leadership and its expansion to Rome under Paul, as related in Acts, the Church in truth, in its own existence under the Spirit, recapitulates the experience of Jesus, his mighty works and wonders, his suffering and bringing of salvation, his call to repentance and forgiveness of sins. The Church's pathway of mission to the world is a pathway of trial and hardship, and through it all it is linked by the Spirit with the way of the lowly and yet exalted one.

In the last chapter we sought to show that the Resurrection does not denote a radical discontinuity with the history of Jesus, but is indeed connected with Jesus of Nazareth. In the present chapter, up to this point, we have attempted to explicate the unity of historical and kerygmatic elements in the reports of the first three Evangelists. Now we are well aware that the historian who is devoted to literary criticism of the documents will object that we have only dealt with the form of the Gospel traditions as they have come down to us and, consequently, have been able to say precious little about the Man of Nazareth in his historical actuality. Can the historical scholar rest content with this state of affairs? Must he not endeavor to reconstruct the historical Jesus as he actually was? Is there any assurance that the Evangelists' kerygmatic interpretations are not falsifications of the true history of Jesus? We have many times of course reiterated the theological legitimacy of the question about the historical Jesus—in the face of the message of the "Word made flesh" we are unwearied in asking it. Yet the sufficient answer to the questions just posed seems to be that any non-kerygmatic portrait of Jesus we might build up by historical research will be merely *our* portrait, and not that of the Evangelists, for whom the unity of history and kerygma is everywhere of decisive importance.

Confessedly the hand of each Evangelist, or the Church he represents, is revealed in the traditions recorded by him. Matthew and Luke, for example, as editors of Mark, are unlike Mark in that they devote a great deal more space to the words or teaching of Jesus. But they certainly do not stand over against Mark as presenting us with the life of a Teacher, since for them the words of Jesus are worthy of preservation precisely because they are the words of the crucified, risen and exalted Christ. We stressed Luke's particularly forceful witness to Jesus as the bearer of the Spirit. But this is no isolated development or "heightening of Christology" resulting from Luke's creative imagination, for Matthew also testifies in his first chapter that Jesus is born of the Holy Spirit (Matt. 1:18, 20), and Mark too tells of Jesus' baptism by John and the descent of the Spirit on him (Mark 1:9–11). In fact, despite the varied nuances in their presentations of Jesus the Christ, a straight line can be drawn from Mark through Matthew and Luke. All alike proclaim that the living God has intervened in the heart of Judaism at a specific period of history in the words and actions and death of Jesus; all discern in his history the fulfillment of Old Testament prophecy; all declare that, in the events that have taken

place in and around Jesus, God has acted mightily, His kingly rule
has dawned, and that those who turn toward Him experience the remission of sins, are released from the powers of evil, and are become
heirs of the promise of the age that is to come. None of the Evangelists is a fanciful innovator, creating *de novo*. All have one plan, one
picture in mind. It is a plan and a picture that have come to them all
in an already interpreted tradition, containing within it the unbreakable unity of the historical and kerygmatic. "Neither Mark, nor Luke,
nor Matthew, is interpreting a mere series of facts," wrote Hoskyns
and Davey many years ago, "still less are they imposing a Christology
upon an undefined human personality. The interpretation is given
them in the material which comes to them from various sources, and
it is the same interpretation which is being presented to them throughout." [25] In spite of the contention of many scholars that the earliest
traditions were thoroughly historical, there does not appear to be any
layer of the Gospel tradition in which the historical is dissected from
the kerygmatic, so that it is very doubtful whether even at its earliest
stage the tradition of Jesus of Nazareth was void of Christological
interpretation.

Advocates of the "new quest" of the historical Jesus will argue
that to attempt merely to demonstrate the overlapping or unity of the
historical and kerygmatic in the Gospel tradition is not enough to meet
the demands of the contemporary theological situation. Certain of
their number have indeed gone much further. In dependence on his-
torical-analytical procedures fortified by the new weapon of "existence
philosophy" or "existentialist historiography," they have thought first
to sift out the sayings of Jesus that can be considered "authentic" or
unaltered in the tradition (relying mainly on the findings of Bultmann's
History of the Synoptic Tradition), and then to lay hold of the "existence" of Jesus of Nazareth, his selfhood, his intention, his meaning, as
these are latent in the sayings. Their aim is to test the right of the
kerygma to appeal to Jesus, by asking whether Jesus' own existence
matches the type of existence of which the kerygma speaks. Now this
grasping of the existence of Jesus only arises on the basis of a previous
determination by historical-critical research of what can be regarded
as trustworthy historical material in the tradition of Jesus' words. To
that extent the "new quest" has nowhere been more misleading than in
giving us to think that, by its supplementary use of "existence philos-

ophy," it has overcome the critical problems and has arrived at a new certainty about what the historical Jesus really was like. And yet we are made to feel that it is via the historical route that the nearness of God in the words and deeds of Jesus is being established and demonstrated.[26] In fact, the historian cannot go so far without transgressing the limits of historical inquiry. And the suspicion is created that the exponent of the "new quest," in which historical research is bound up with a particular brand of philosophical understanding, is selecting from and finding in the traditional materials relating to Jesus only what he is looking for, only what accords with "existence philosophy." Entirely relevant, therefore, to the situation of the "new quest" are the words of the distinguished scholars just cited above: "Critics have wished their work to be immediately fruitful, and have desired to present assured results which they think may be acceptable to the modern world, or may relieve the tension between the Church and Modern Thought. The moment the critic surrenders to such a desire he ceases to be a historian." [27]

The question we have to put to the "historian" of the "new quest" concerns what sort of historical reality he is actually seeking to reconstruct. Is he trying to read back into the earthly Jesus his own existentialist understanding of human existence? Or does he desire, in a manner not very different after all from the old quest, to find Jesus "as he truly was" in his historical being? If the latter be true, were it not in the long run better and less confusing to acknowledge that we must remain satisfied to live with the tension between faith's certitude of the Christ and the incertitude of our critically reconstructed portraits of Jesus? At any rate we do not believe that the attempts of the "new seekers" to disengage the historical from the kerygmatic in the Gospel tradition are foolproof or infallible. Rather is it their philosophical standpoint of "existential openness" toward Jesus that has produced the impression that the goal of Jesus-research has at last been reached. It would accordingly seem to us that the historian, so long as he remains historian, has no other option but to try to accept and assess with as little prejudice as possible that state of things whereby history and kerygma are united in the New Testament presentation of Jesus.[28]

We spoke earlier about the straight line that can be drawn from Mark through Matthew and Luke. We have now to ask whether the same line extends to the Fourth Gospel.

The Humiliated-Exalted One

It is, on the face of things, a far cry from Mark's rather austere message of the crucified Messiah to John's Logos Christology, his doctrine of the Incarnation and Exaltation of the Christ. The picture that has grown up around the author of the Fourth Gospel is one that paints him as interpretive theologian, schooled in Greek ways of thought, eager to communicate the gospel in concepts and language understandable and relevant for Greek man. So he has become known as the Evangelist of profound mystic tendency, and, apparently living himself in closest communion with God through the working of the Spirit in him, as the "spiritualizer" of the gospel, zealous only to transmit the message of the *Christus praesens* to his hearers.

There is in fact, in John's delineation of the Christ, an inescapable emphasis on nouns describing Christ and on sentences in the present tense, as in the great "I am" sayings: "I am the way, the truth and the life" (John 14:6; cf. 6:48; 8:12; 8:58; 10:7, 9, 11, 14; 11:25). John's chief concern is evidently to communicate that testimony of the Spirit which makes present the eschatological occurrence, and so to challenge men to faith here and now in the Christ, the Son of God (20:31). We may think of him closing the gap between the past events of salvation and the contemporary Church, the constitutive principle of whose existence is its life in the Son and the Son's life in it. John constantly shows us the Christ on the God-ward side: he comes as the pre-existent Logos; he is the bringer of eternal life and the present Lord of the Church. The hour of Christ's Passion and the hour of his Exaltation are more completely and perfectly blended together by John than by any other Evangelist (3:14; 7:39; 8:28; 12:16; 12:32–4; 13:31; 17:1–5), and the Church is placed by him in the present time in confrontation with the message of the humiliated-exalted Christ.

John has thus advanced further than the other Evangelists in regard to the "kerygmatic" character of the story. Nevertheless, while this Gospel offers little information about the historical Jesus, who is seen throughout as the "Christ of faith," John intends nothing essentially different from Mark or Matthew or Luke, since he too follows a form and a program that is definitely "historical." It is of the utmost significance that he casts his message in the shape of a gospel, for he thus lays his own work alongside those others which relate Christian faith to the words and deeds, the Passion and Resurrection of Jesus. In John 21:24, which is admittedly a part of what is most likely an editorial epilogue, the whole Gospel is described as μαρτυρία (testimony). H. Strathmann has shown that in profane Greek μαρτυρεῖν denotes both "witness to facts" and "affirmation of beliefs or truths." Luke uses the noun "witness" apparently with this double connotation (Luke 24:48; Acts 1:22).[29] Nor is the importance of eyewitness, probably in this double sense, neglected by John. In the first place, the climax of the prologue declares that something quite decisive has occurred in history, to which witness can be made: "And the Word became flesh and dwelt among us, full of grace and truth; we have beheld his glory, glory as of the only Son from the Father" (John 1:14). To the "Word become flesh" John the Baptist bears witness (1:14, 32–4). The disciples bear witness to Jesus (3:11). The Samaritan woman bears witness to Jesus (4:39). The Scriptures of the Old Testament bear witness to Jesus (5:39, 46). It is true that for John the Scriptures testify to Christ in the present much more than to a history of salvation in the past, which possesses a significance of its own. It is true also that the Scriptures cannot be judged, as the Pharisees imagine, "according to the flesh" (John 8:13–18). The Jews, as John understands it, have indeed, by seeking to take Moses, the Scriptures, the fathers of Israel, and even God Himself as their own religious possession, forfeited the possibility of knowing the one true God revealed only in the Son, to whom the Scriptures in their wholeness point, and from whom alone they receive their meaning and authority (5:39). Yet it is a fact of some theological significance, as N. A. Dahl has recently insisted against Bultmann, that John has not altogether ignored that there was a history even before Christ, a history which reached its peak in Christ.[30]

The Spirit also bears witness to Jesus, recalling the critical importance of his words and teaching, even as he bears witness to himself: "If anyone hears my sayings and does not keep them, I do not judge him. . . . He who rejects me and does not receive my sayings has a judge; the word that I have spoken will be his judge on the last day" (12:47–8). The testimony Jesus bears to himself it will be the work of the Spirit to bear also. For whereas the Spirit will be the disciples' guide into the future, the Spirit will simultaneously take them back to

Jesus' words, bringing to their remembrance everything he had said to them (14:26).

While the distinctive emphasis of the Fourth Gospel is on the presence of the Christ with the Church, its author has not wholly lost sight of the difference between the time of Jesus and the time of the post-Easter Church, as is evident from the temporal adverbs employed by him, "now" and "afterward" (13:7, 36), "hitherto" (16:24) and "henceforth" (14:7), "before" and "when" (14:29). Most significant of all perhaps is the "not yet" that belongs to Jesus' ministry. "My hour has not yet come" (2:4; 8:20); "my time has not yet fully come" (7:8). So the ministry foreshadows and moves toward its completion in the death and Resurrection of the Christ, when victory is achieved ("It is finished," 19:30), and the new creation is inaugurated with the bestowal of the Spirit on the disciples, even as at the first creation God breathed the breath of life into men's nostrils (20:22).

The "not yet" of the ministry of Jesus is implicit in John's development of the "discipleship theme." The impetuous Peter is ready to follow Jesus forthwith and even to lay down his life for his sake. But he is forcefully reminded of the crises that must come to pass before he will be fit for true discipleship (13:36–8). Jesus must go the entire way through suffering and death to Resurrection and Exaltation, before his disciple can be empowered by his presence in the Spirit to follow him. Whereas, for John, "following" Jesus in the post-Easter period is more or less synonymous with "saving belief" in him as exalted Lord (8:12; 12:46), it is none the less only possible for disciples to "follow" him at all because his own way is completed and behind them as that which he has "once" accomplished. He must be "lifted up" from the earth before he can draw men unto him (12:32). Not until the destination of his journey is reached in the Father (16:28) and in the heavenly dwelling-places (14:2) can he bring his disciples with him (14:2). No one can come to the Father, therefore, save through Jesus (14:6). But in view of what we have said, this "through Jesus" should not be too spiritualistically conceived as mystical communion with him, but includes the idea that Jesus himself and the way he has traveled are prior to the disciples. Now the way of Jesus is, for John, quite concretely the way of perfect obedience to the Father (10:17–18; 12:24–8; 13:20; 14:10–11; etc.). As the humble and obedient Son of the Father, he has in turn commands to give to those who would be his disciples. And only to the obedient "follower," in fact, is Jesus manifested for who he really is (14:21–4).[31]

The Fourth Gospel is an interpretation of the history of Jesus, whose meaning has finally been disclosed only by his death and Resurrection, under the guidance of the Spirit. Even though, however, the history of Jesus can only be interpreted by the Spirit, it is not deprived of its character as history. The accepted view that the Fourth Gospel, with its numerous allusions to the humanity of Jesus, is permeated with a strong anti-Docetic strain, is well justified, and finds added support in the first Epistle of John. The Epistle addresses itself to a situation (reflected also in the probably nearly contemporary writings of Ignatius, Bishop of Antioch), in which the integrity of faith as faith in *Jesus* the Christ is in grave jeopardy from the rise and growth in the congregations of a "spiritual romanticism" that tends to discount the "flesh" of the Son: "Every spirit which confesses that Jesus Christ has come in the flesh is of God, and every spirit which does not confess Jesus is not of God" (I John 4:2–3). Against this spiritualizing "refinement" of the faith the Epistle campaigns at nearly every point. The message is sounded forth that the Church rests not upon spiritual experience, but upon the ministry and death of the one who came as the Word of Life and Love, that Word which has been seen and handled by witnesses (I John 1:1) and which provides the only true dynamic for Christian behavior (3:5 f., 16–18; 4:9–11). Whereas there is the same emphasis as in the Gospel that there is no salvation in trying to seize the facts of history in their objective or material aspect, but only in the spiritual comprehension of the historical (6:63), nevertheless the historical is asserted. "There are three witnesses, the Spirit, the water and the blood; and these three agree" (5:8). Spirit first, to be sure! But on the other hand, as Denney wrote: "There is no such spiritualising as would leave to the historical merely a position of vanishing or relative importance. There is no sublimation of Christianity into 'ethical' or 'spiritual principles' or into 'eternal facts,' which absolve us from all obligation to a Saviour who came in blood." [32]

Neither does the Gospel of John intend to preach an abstract idea or a timeless Revelation Word devoid of specific content. It intends, without surrendering the tradition to speculation, in its own way to bring the historical Jesus, the son of Joseph (John 6:42), near to the Church. Like the other three Gospels, the Fourth Gospel refers the

faith of the Church to the man Jesus, who had been known and loved
by such men as Peter, and himself had loved others. This is corroborated by the explicit references in the Gospel to an eyewitness, to wit,
the beloved disciple, who is said to have understood Jesus more intimately than the rest (19:35).

All the Gospels alike, written from the standpoint of faith in the
resurrected and exalted Christ, none the less apply this faith to Jesus,
as the one in whose sayings and deeds, in a quite particular past history, the Word of God had already gone forth. In their testimony
therefore, history and kerygma are found inseparably united.

To be sure it does seem strange that the post-Easter Church should
find a steady and controlling point of reference for her faith in the
earthly history and ministry of Jesus, especially since now she was living in the certainty of the presence of the risen Christ and was standing
on tiptoe toward the future when he would come again. Yet what we
see in the Gospels is precisely this: the Church gathers herself around
her earthly Lord and counts herself among his contemporaries. She
hears again his utterly decisive word to his disciples to "follow" him.
She listens to his message of the coming kingdom of God and watches
his wondrous works. She sees him turning toward the outcasts and sinners. Above all, she teaches herself to stand at the place where his way
still lies ahead to the Cross and Resurrection, which have "not yet"
come, the way through rejection and suffering to glory. Standing beside her earthly Master, the Church, in the midst of the expansion of
her faith in Christ into the heavenly order, refuses to succumb to any
kind of spiritual fanaticism that would take her out of this world and
allow her to lose herself in the splendor of God's world, as if it had
already fully come.[33] From the nonhistorical Gnosticism of the second or third century we can readily visualize into what ranges of
shapeless religiosity the Church, humanly speaking, might have fallen,
if ever she had divorced herself from the governing influence of the
historical revelation in Jesus.

At this juncture we are confronted with a most pressing question of
the New Testament. How do the Gospels relate to the "kerygmatic"
writings, the Epistles of Paul, the Epistle to the Hebrews, and other
documents? Granted that the traditions embodied in the Gospels are
transfused with the light of Easter faith. Granted also, therefore, that
the message they convey is the message of the crucified and risen Jesus
Christ. Yet they do intend to narrate the words and deeds of Jesus of

Nazareth. And they do intend to apply Christian faith to him. The apostolic kerygma on the other hand, the kerygma of Paul, for example, seems to confine itself to the proclamation of the crucified and resurrected Lord, and to be relatively unconcerned about the history of Jesus. What has happened in the transition from preaching to a preaching *that wishes also to be narration*? Have the Evangelists carried through a correction of the primitive Christian kerygma? Or have they misunderstood it and to a large extent corrupted it by their mythicizing and materializing depictions? Or is it much less a matter of radical opposition, misunderstanding, or correction than simply a matter of two different emphases, the Gospels stressing the earthly ministry of the Christ and so affording us materials for the Incarnation, and the "kerygmatic" writings stressing the Exaltation of Jesus? We do well to think in terms of the last possibility, as we shall try to show in the following pages.

Confessions of the Exalted Jesus Christ

As is well known, all details of the ministry of the earthly Jesus recede into the background in the letters of Paul. The apostle evidently maintained an attitude of great reserve toward the Palestinian traditions of the sayings and deeds of the historical Jesus. That this was his position is scarcely controverted by such echoes as there are in the epistles of the *verba Christi,* the "Halakha" decisions of Jesus regarding the indissolubility of marriage (I Cor. 7:10–11; cf. Mark 10:7–12) and the rightful claim of the Christian evangelist to be supported by his flock (I Cor. 9:14; cf. Matt. 10:10; Luke 10:7–8).[34] In fact, if Paul were our only source, we would know nothing of Jesus' parables, the Sermon on the Mount, or the Lord's Prayer. Paul does not appear to have thought of himself as a disciple of the historical Jesus, but as a man commissioned by the risen Lord and laid under obligation not to transmit the traditions of the historical Jesus but to preach the Christ. Hence his insistent appeal to his startling Damascus experience, in which he received the gospel by direct revelation of Jesus Christ, as the constitutive factor for his apostolic authority (Gal. 1:11–12).

Out of the immediate personal experience that apostolic men like Paul had of the risen Christ came the far-reaching affirmation "Jesus is Lord," an affirmation which appears in the earliest confessions of faith attested by the apostle (I Cor. 12:3; Rom. 10:9; "Christ Jesus the Lord," II Cor. 4:5; Col. 2:6; "Christ Jesus is Lord," Phil. 2:11). At least in the first instance, we do not need to hurry off, like the History of Religions School, to the religious ideas of the Graeco-Roman world to discover and explain the source of the title "Lord" that came to be assigned to Jesus Christ. Many scholars have rightly emphasized the importance of the very early Aramaic formula, *Maranatha* ("our Lord cometh"). To the Greek-speaking Jewish Christian the term "Lord" could only have meant one who stood on the side of God, inasmuch as "Lord" is the very name given to Yahweh, the God of Israel, in the Septuagint. And indeed, following the elemental principle that all preaching should be relevant in language and content to the situation to which it is addressed, the earliest Church proclaimed Jesus Christ to Jewish man as the Fulfiller of the prophecies and promises of the Scriptures, as the one by whose death and Resurrection the power of sin and death was broken, so that in him the *Heilsgeschichte* reported in the Old Testament reached its final goal (I Cor. 15:3–5). Yet at the same time the title "Lord" made contact possible with the religious syncretism of the wider world of Hellenism, for Hellenistic man was familiar with its usage in reference not only to the cultic heroes or gods of his pagan Mystery religions but to the highest secular authorities.

In the picture he draws of the "Lord Jesus Christ," Paul unquestionably makes use of mythological concepts prevalent in the Hellenistic milieu. Christ is presented as the pre-existent supernatural Christ, who comes down from heaven to earth in the lowliest guise and is exalted to the rank of Cosmocrator, with power over all celestial and earthly beings (Phil. 2:6–11). Under the influence of the History of Religions School, modern scholarship has therefore very often regarded Paul, unlike the Evangelists, as orientated not by the historical figure of Jesus but by the exalted Christ of the Spirit, construed in terms of the "divine man" or "son of God," who reveals himself as *soter* or "savior" to the devotee initiated with appropriate rites and ceremonies into the Hellenistic "mysteries." On this theory the movement of the gospel into the pagan world has brought with it new Christological formulations that constitute a radical departure from the Jewish Christianity of the infant Church at Jerusalem, and an all-embracing acceptance of the thoughts and imaginations springing from the Hellenistic myth of the heavenly redeemer god, whose contact with earth and history is very slight. So Paul's Christ is a heavenly being, the pre-existent Son of God and God's agent in creation, in whose exalted divine status the historical Jesus is all but wholly absorbed. In coming from heaven to accomplish his redemptive mission, he barely touches our earth at all.

In light of recent research, we are no longer so ready to grant the validity of the generalizing conclusion, based on the work of R. Reitzenstein and others, that Paul was extremely dependent on the Mystery Religions and more narrowly on a pre-Christian Gnostic redeemer myth. We have to think twice before regarding the apostle as simply an innovator in Christology, drawing upon soteriological myths that already lay to hand in the world of Hellenistic syncretism. Nor, in regard to the heightening of Christology in the so-called kerygmatic writings of the New Testament, can we afford to neglect the facts of the situation for apostolic men like Paul and the churches addressed by them. New conquests were constantly being made, new converts won, new communities established in Christ's name. New facts were becoming available to the Church through its experience, under the leading of the Holy Spirit, of Christ's ever-expanding sovereignty and power over the Church and over the world. There is, however, no denying that, in according to Christ the highest dignities of heaven, Paul used such mythological concepts to get his message across as the pre-existence of Christ and his agency in creation.

The problem here, then, in view of Paul's tremendous emphasis on the exalted Christ, is to find out whether his allusions to the history of Jesus occupy only a peripheral or incidental place in his theology. That, for Paul, Jesus was no mythical figure but a real historical fact is beyond question. And while Paul disclaims the relevance for his theology of historically mediated knowledge of Jesus (II Cor. 5:16), he bears ample testimony to Christ's coming "in the flesh." We learn from the apostle that Jesus was born under the Law as a Jew (Gal. 4:4), was of Davidic descent (Rom. 1:3), was betrayed (I Cor. 11:23), was crucified by the powers of this age (Gal. 3:1; Phil. 2:8; etc.), was buried and resurrected (I Cor. 15:4; Rom. 6:4). Are these historical reminiscences of a person and a life merely momentary concessions to history and tradition on the part of one like Paul whose religious experience was otherwise dominated by Hellenistic mythological categories of thought? Or do they possess foundational significance for the apostle's gospel?

Let us take I Corinthians 15:3–8 as a point of departure. Here Paul refers quite expressly to the fundamental facts connected with the Resurrection of Jesus and reminds the Corinthians of how he had preached these facts. Although the apostle is here concentrating on the question of the Resurrection so that there is no mention of the life of Jesus, it is none the less a matter of certain facts of the past, confirmed by eyewitness, that are of inescapable importance for preaching in the present. So, even in this context, there is an unbroken line from the historical Jesus to the kerygmatic Christ.

For Paul the Resurrection is quite unlike the *deus ex machina* of Greek drama, nor does it have an analogy in the Hellenic idea of an eternal dying and rebirth in nature. On the contrary, it has a historical connection. God's mighty act in lifting up Jesus, "descended from David according to the flesh," and declaring him to be "the Son of God in power" (Rom. 1:3–4), is the ratification of Christ's obedience and the promulgation of the mystery that underlay his life all the time. The *Christus patiens* is now disclosed as what he always had been, the *Christus victor*.

The obedience of Jesus Christ! Paul does not proclaim the Cross as a bare, unapproachable fact, as though it could be separated from the public ministry of Jesus or as though it were a matter of indifference whether we understood it simply as natural occurrence, the result perhaps of political misunderstanding, which is about all, on the historical side, Bultmann will say about it. We are not left in the dark by Paul as to who died on the Cross or as to how that death could be understood as God's great redemptive act for men. For the death of Christ on the Cross is the culmination of a human life lived out, by one who might have sinned, in perfect righteousness and obedience. "As one man's trespass led to condemnation for all men, so one man's act of righteousness leads to acquittal and life for all men. For as by one man's disobedience many were made sinners, so by one man's obedience many will be made righteous (Rom. 5:18–19).

The formula reported by Paul in I Corinthians 15:3–5 makes it quite clear that from the very earliest stage in the Church's history the death of Christ was understood as a death "for our sins according to the Scriptures." Nor is Paul, for all the creativity of his thought and his opening up of new horizons of meaning in the event of Jesus Christ, at all eager to depart from the tradition. Frequently he repeats its own terms, referring to Christ as a propitiation through faith by his blood

(Rom. 3:25) and to his death as a death for the ungodly (Rom. 5:6), as a work of reconciliation (Rom. 5:10), and as a costly death (I Cor. 7:23).

Paul was certainly no mere traditionist, and we could not here deal with his many-sided and enriching interpretation of the death of Jesus. We want only to treat a little more fully an outstanding emphasis, just mentioned, on Christ's death as the climax of a life of obedience. We recall how the late Professor T. W. Manson supported the notion that Paul worked under the influence of the great Jewish festivals, most notably the Passover.[35] That he wrote I Corinthians with the Passover in mind is a feasible proposition, given weight by the reference to the "firstfruits," a familiar part of the Passover ritual, in I Corinthians 15:23 and by the declaration in 5:7: "Christ, our paschal lamb, has been sacrificed." It is certainly in harmony with this that, in his account of the Last Supper, Paul places a singular stress upon the death of Jesus as the inauguration of the New Covenant ratified in Jesus' blood (I Cor. 11:23–6). The point we have been coming to is very clearly made by Dr. W. D. Davies. He adduces evidence from the Old Testament (e.g. Exod. 19:3 f.), the Apocrypha and Pseudepigrapha, and the Rabbinic literature to show that the other side of God's steadfast love in the covenantal relation with His people is their *obedience* to Him, that indeed covenant is equated with the laws commanded by Yahweh. Obedience to the commands of Yahweh meant inevitably for Israel in the course of her history enduring the hardships that arose from the conflict between the requirements of the Torah and the demands of worldly authorities. Through periods of suffering and persecution, Judaism in her later stages had to reckon and did reckon with the thought that the supreme manifestation of obedience to the commands of Yahweh was the martyr death of the righteous. In the Assumption of Moses, which is probably to be dated between A.D. 7 and 30, Taxo and his seven sons elect to submit to death rather than transgress the commandments of the Lord God.[36] Against such a background as this Paul probably thought of the death of Jesus in terms of the suffering righteous one's obedience to the demands of God even unto death. If we are right, what is important for us is that Paul is interested in the death of Jesus not merely as a *nudum factum* but as the climactic expression of a life of obedience.

From this angle we may approach the hymn of Philippians 2:6–11, a hymn of praise to Christ who, "though he was in the form of God, did not count equality with God a thing to be grasped, but emptied himself, taking the form of a servant, being born in the likeness of men. And being found in human form he humbled himself and became obedient unto death, even death on a cross. Therefore God has highly exalted him and bestowed on him the name which is above every name, that at the name of Jesus every knee should bow, in heaven and on earth and under the earth, and every tongue confess that Jesus Christ is Lord, to the glory of God the Father." Nearly all scholars now agree that we have here a pre-Pauline hymn to Christ in two or three stanzas. Details of the hymn present many complex exegetical questions. Our problem is to try to discover how completely the content of Pauline Christology at this point is conditioned or determined by the categories of the Hellenistic myth of the descent of the heavenly man to earth on his mission of salvation and his ascension once more into heaven.

Let us say in the first place that the incidence in the hymn of the words "servant," "obedience," "death," far from moving us toward the notion that the humiliated Christ has become a slave of the powers of nature in the Hellenistic sense,[37] seems to call us back to the sphere of Jewish ideas regarding the obedience unto death of the suffering righteous one. To be sure there is here a remarkable extension. For the humiliation of the Christ is projected back to the *pre-existent* stage, when, although in the "form of God," he emptied himself and took the "form of a servant." On the other side, exalted by reason of his obedience unto death, he is given the new name of "Lord," and before him all the powers of the cosmos worship.

The germ of this extension of Christology may be said to lie in the traditional statements of the primitive Church. For when it is reported in the Gospels that Jesus called disciples to "follow" him, it is understood that in this call everything decisive has happened and God's grace is present, so that Jesus could be spoken of as the one who has been "sent" or who has "come" from God. On the other hand the victory of the exalted Christ over all cosmic powers in the Philippians hymn is, shall we say, anticipated in the Gospel witness to Jesus' subjugation of demoniacal forces even in his earthly ministry. But also behind the primitive Church and behind the New Testament there stood a whole series of Old Testament and late Jewish speculations concerning Wisdom as the personification of God's outgoing Word or Spirit, a Wisdom which was pre-existent (Prov. 8:30 f.; Eccles.

1:4; 24:9), which was with God (Eccles. 1:1) and seated with him on his heavenly throne (Wisdom of Sol. 8:3; 9:4). That Philippians 2:6–8 represents a marked advance on these Wisdom ideas we do not doubt—we are mindful of H. J. Schoeps' recent warning that the myth of the hymn can be connected with Judaic-Hellenistic Wisdom speculations "only by ingenious contrivance," and that not even Philo, the Septuagint, or the Hellenistic rabbis could have entertained the notion of the *real divine sonship* of some man or of the expected Messiah.[38] Nevertheless, certain New Testament texts do seem to establish a link between Jesus and the Wisdom of the Old Testament. In I Corinthians 8:6 Jesus is portrayed, like Wisdom, as the Mediator in creation; in I Corinthians 10:4 he is described in words applied to Wisdom. John's affirmation that the Logos was "with God" (John 1:1) re-echoes Wisdom notions. From such facts as these we may therefore legitimately infer that Wisdom speculations played some part in the growth of declarations regarding the pre-existence of Jesus Christ.

In the end, however, what is most important is the presence in the hymn of the Jewish motif of the obedience unto death of the suffering righteous one. The hymn has not infrequently been regarded as combining within itself the themes of the Second Adam and the Suffering Servant.[39] As to the former, suffice it to say that it is not nearly so explicit here as in Romans 5. As to the latter, there is, we believe, much to be said for E. Schweizer's contention that what is involved is not *the* Servant of God, since then the emphasis would be on his special status in distinction from all men as the one foretold by the prophets, and not on his total self-identification with men as *a* lowly servant among them. The one who emptied himself is not described as "the servant of God," but as taking upon himself the "form of a servant." What seems to be meant is his status of lowliness on earth among men, a status which results from his own act of self-humiliation, in contrast to the heavenly status of God. Precisely because he has moved amid the ranks of men and has entered the depths of involvement in the order of history through his own obedience unto death, even the death of the Cross, he is exalted and given the name that is above every name.[40]

Let us grant that the setting of the hymn to Christ is mythological. In the opening the pre-existence of the Christ is expressed in mythological terms, as is his Exaltation in the end: neither belongs to history nor to the earthly way of the servant, yet both indicate the whence and whither of a historical life of obedience and service, culminating in death on the Cross.[41] Even so the hearer of the message of Jesus Christ encounters neither a mythological figure nor yet merely an ethical teacher, but a person and a life and death in which God Himself has come to meet men. Thus in the hymn of praise to Christ in Philippians 2:6–11 is established the sure priority of the historical way of Jesus as a way of humiliation and suffering involving obedience unto death—it is the way of God with men. To this way of the lowly one, exalted by his obedience, the Church is tied. For here we come upon a Church, as Schweizer states, "in which mankind finds its fulfillment in obedience, in which such obedience is as a matter of course realized in humiliation even unto death." [42]

But for Paul's own religious experience also Jesus' life of service and obedience, climaxed by his death on the Cross, and ratified by the Resurrection, was both pre-eminent and decisive. In the death, Jesus made a victorious renunciation of the world and the world's claim, out of loyalty to God. And in the Resurrection, God set His seal upon and vindicated that loyalty. So Paul tells the Philippians that he too is ready to renounce all previous gains in order to know "the power of Christ's resurrection" (Phil. 3:10), that is, to experience that very same power by which God raised Jesus on the third day. Yet inseparably woven in with the experiencing of that power is the willingness to continue in one's own life and to imitate (Paul uses the word himself in I Corinthians 11:1) the action of Jesus in obediently accepting death, the willingness to "share the fellowship of his sufferings" (Phil. 3:10). From what Paul has said to the Philippians we may judge it to be quite intentional that he should place the hymn to Christ in the context of this statement: "Have this mind among yourselves, which you have in Christ Jesus" (Phil. 2:5). The humiliation and death of Jesus are both a finished act and example. They are both and more than both, for what is true for the community "in Christ Jesus" is now to be realized by them in their day-to-day dealings with one another.

So far it is clear that for Paul the death and Resurrection of Jesus, which happened once for all in Palestine, are utterly decisive in their significance for the religious experience of men. Nor is it otherwise with the controversial passage on baptism into the death of Christ in Romans 6:1–11, despite the fact that Paul's interpretation of baptism here has often been understood to originate from the Hellenistic Church and to have its analogy in the initiation sacrament of the Mystery religions, the meaning of which is that the initiate shares in the fate of the mythical cult god who has suffered death and awakened to life. There is, as we think, a great deal of merit in the view that a different world of thought from this forms the background of the passage, that in it there are at work distinctively ethical, communal, and realistically historical considerations which are foreign to the Mystery cults. That Paul's teaching moves here in the moral or ethical sphere is plain from the text. The solidarity of the Christian man with his Lord, "dying with Christ" and "living with Christ," has the most searching ethical implications, since it means that his life is laid under the constraint of a death which was a triumph of righteousness over this sinful world, a righteousness authenticated by all that God had done in raising Jesus from the dead. So penetrating and profound is this constraint that the Christian is re-created by it: it kills and makes alive at once. "So you also must consider yourselves dead to sin and alive to God in Christ Jesus," writes the apostle, and then he continues: "Let not sin therefore reign in your mortal bodies, to make you obey their passions" (Rom. 6:11–12). Further, we have already noted Paul's concern with the Jewish festivals, especially with the Passover. Does not this Romans passage also echo the liturgy of the Jewish Passover, in which the member of the Jewish community is summoned to recapitulate in his own history the historical events of Israel? Thus W. L. Knox comments on Romans 6:

In Romans 6 . . . the death and Resurrection of Jesus replace the Exodus from Egypt. The proselyte through circumcision and the proselyte's bath was enabled to come out of Egypt and pass through the Red Sea into the promised land of Israel. . . . Paul transfers the argument to the death and Resurrection of Jesus. Those who share in it through faith pass through the waters of Baptism, are delivered from the old Egyptian bondage to sin and pass instead into a new slavery to righteousness which results in sanctification. Here the union of the Christian with Jesus is stated in terms of an exchange from one slavery to another on the strength of the Christian conception of the passion and Resurrection as the new Passover.[43]

Martin Noth has recently shown with particular clarity how in the Jewish cult the great events of Israel's past history were actualized (*vergegenwärtigt*) and appropriated through a re-living of them. The use of the Psalms in the cultus of the temple in Jerusalem no doubt brought home to the worshiping congregation their solidarity with the Hebrew people past and present.[44] The paraenetic sections of Deuteronomy clearly reveal the same trait, e.g. Deuteronomy 6:23 with its use of the first person pronoun: "And he brought us out from there, that he might bring us in and give us the land which he swore to give to our fathers." May we suggest then that Paul's interpretation of baptism in Romans 6, with its stress on union with Christ in his death and Resurrection, falls within this orbit of ideas? [45] May we suggest also that that most characteristic and fundamental of Paul's concepts, "in Christ," which has given rise to theories of what is commonly called Paul's Christ-mysticism, should be viewed in close connection with other texts in which the preposition "with" is richly suggestive (e.g. Rom. 6:4, 6, 8; 8:17; Gal. 2:20; Col. 2:12; 3:1)? No doubt "in Christ" implied for Paul the most intimate kind of personal communion with Christ. Yet how problematical is the term "mystic" in relation to Paul and how limited should be the use made of it was shown by M. Dibelius in his short study *Paulus und die Mystik* (1941).[46] To suffer with Christ, to be crucified with Him, buried with Him, risen with Him, here is the unfolding of what is involved for Paul in being "in Christ." "The union of the individual with Christ," says Dr. W. D. Davies, "is such that the experiences of Christ are re-enacted in the experience of the individual Christian. The life, death, resurrection and glorification of Jesus cease to be mere external facts of history but living realities in the Christian's own life. The latter appropriates to himself the past events of the historical and risen life of Jesus so that they become his own." [47]

Since the question of the appropriation of the event of the Cross by the believer is at the heart of the Bultmann debate, it might be well for us to look at it for a moment from that angle. There has been heated controversy concerning Bultmann's position on this matter. Bultmann himself has repeatedly maintained that we can go no further than the mere *that* of Jesus' Crucifixion. Now it has been argued that Bultmann has not in fact consistently stuck to the *that* of the Cross, since he has pointed to the existential decisiveness of Jesus' message, Jesus' proclamation, as demanding a decision relative to his person.[48] Dr. J. M. Robinson has resolutely contended that there is an "undercurrent" in Bultmann's writings, in which it emerges that he sees the original meaning of the Cross in the context of Jesus' *message and person*.[49] On the other hand, certain "left wingers" in the Bultmann discussion have replied that Bultmann is interested solely in the possibility of a new understanding of existence offered in the message of Jesus, and that the question of whether, in going to his death on the Cross, he actualized the possibility is no part of Bultmann's theology.[50] But we have no wish to enter the lists of the debate on the interpretation of Bultmann's theology. Let us say quite simply that if it is a matter of "hearing" the apostolic testimony rather than of listening to the demands of modern "existence philosophy," the Word of the Cross that comes to us is the Word not of a bare and utterly unapproachable *fact* but of a Life, a Life given unto death. It is the act of *righteousness* of one man that "leads to acquittal and life for all men" (Rom. 5:18). It is through the *obedience* of one man that "many will be made righteous" (Rom. 5:19). It is the Life that saves, not a denuded *that.* The words of Denney from another day, when the old issue of an "objective" theory of atonement was very much at stake, are apposite even yet: "The love which is the motive of his death acts immediately upon the sinful; gratitude exerts an irresistible constraint; His responsibility means our emancipation; His death our life; His bleeding wound our healing." [51]

From this standpoint we feel ourselves in sympathy with exponents of the "new quest" who have consistently related Christian faith to Jesus' life, person, intention. So Fuchs has spoken about man's decision of faith as an entering in upon Jesus' own decision. So also Robinson has held that the death on the Cross ought not to be understood as a purely biological occurrence, as if it were accidental or involuntary, but as a genuinely historical event, as Jesus' own existential act of accepting his death.

Dr. John Macquarrie, who may be said to occupy a position to the conservative "right" of Bultmann, insists that we must try to get "inside" the event of the Cross. When viewed from the outside merely as a worldly spectacle it has no atoning power. Only by being "crucified with Christ," that is, by thinking ourselves into the event, by participation, does the character of the event as an atonement become clear to us. Macquarrie takes Barth to task for asserting that the Cross is an event "significant in itself," that it has completed and not just begun a process, that it atones apart from any existential relation to the event itself. How can this be? What is meant by "significant in itself"? For an event to be "significant" at all it must be "significant to someone." So Macquarrie concludes: "An event which is 'significant in itself' and need never be 'significant to someone' would seem to be no different from an event which is without significance at all." We can

agree with Macquarrie that for the Christian it is necessary to get inside the event, to participate, in the sense of "taking up his cross and
following Christ" (Mark 8:34).[52] Canon C. E. Raven's observation is
pertinent: "The heart of Christianity is a Cross, and I suspect that the
price to be paid for knowing what it means is taking up and bearing a
cross oneself."

Nevertheless, we are in grave danger of distorting the New Testament emphasis whenever we give the impression that there is a lack or
incompleteness in Christ's work of reconciliation that can only be
made up by our appropriation or participation, as if it were a work
directly wrought only in the souls of men. We need only refer again to
the hymn of Philippians 2:6–11, with its undoubted stress on the absolute pre-eminence of the work of Jesus Christ. Here any substitution
of man's insight, man's understanding, man's religious participation
for God's work in Christ is stoutly resisted. Here everything depends
on the fact that *he* came from God in heaven to our world, that in
him heaven and earth were united. Another and most intriguing aspect
of the hymn should be mentioned: there is no mention in it of the
Christian believer. To be sure the existence of the believer is assumed,
for it is he who sings the hymn. To be sure also, if the work of Christ
is absolutely pre-eminent, it is only through first-hand personal experience in the face of that work that we can know what redemption
is. Yet here we come upon the Church in the act of singing her praise
to God in the mythological language of the cosmic drama of Christ's
self-humiliation and Exaltation. The fact that the Church sings at all,
and in this language, shows that she is the community of those who
know that God's dominion has been established in this our world, that
in the finished work of Christ heaven and earth have come to be *at
one*.[53] The awesome sense of indebtedness to Christ for his work in
redemption, which is a uniform characteristic of New Testament life,
finds expression here in a cosmic form of speech that will not be
translated into the singer's own understanding of existence, but tells of
the outreach of the world round about him, of the glory and activity of
God in it, and of the homage of all cosmic powers before Him. The
scope of the transaction of redemption is extended to include the
whole creation and all creatures within it. Such language, in many
other early New Testament hymns as well as this, militates against
that separation of man's existence as a moral, personal being from his
life as part of the physical cosmos that was characteristic of second-

century Gnosticism, and has been no less characteristic of recent narrowly anthropological interpretations of the Christian kerygma. Some
time ago H. Wheeler Robinson wrote: "The modern emphasis tends to
fall on salvation from the power of moral evil in present experience.
The New Testament, without, of course, denying or excluding this element as an accompaniment or even a condition of salvation, finds its
center of gravity in a cosmic event." [54] That man's redemption is
linked up with the redemption of the whole cosmos is the truth expressed in Paul's portrait of the creation groaning and travailing in
pain until now (Rom. 8:22). From this perspective, the world in
which New Testament man is placed, to which he is related, and in
terms of which he understands his existence cannot be treated as an
indifferent factor—the apostolic message ought not to be detached
from the quite particular historical setting in which it emerged and
held up as if it were but a timeless corollary of human existence.

It has not been our intention to examine all the Pauline passages in
which it appears that, to Paul's mind, redemption has been wrought out
in the figure of Jesus, in his life's act of righteousness and obedience,
culminating in his death on the Cross. We have sought mainly to show,
on the basis of some typical texts, that for all Paul's stress on the resurrected and exalted Christ, there is none the less in his testimony an unbroken thread of connection running from the historical Jesus to the
preached Christ. His witness in its integrity is witness to the one who
took upon himself the form of a servant and humbled himself even
unto the death of the Cross, whom God also has highly exalted. The
controlling and regulative significance of the Pauline kerygma's identification of the humiliation and exaltation of Jesus Christ for believers
becomes apparent in the paradoxes with which the apostle describes
their life: "as impostors, and yet true; as unknown and yet well known;
as dying, and behold we live; as punished and yet not killed; as sorrow-
ful, yet always rejoicing; as poor, yet making many rich; as having
nothing, and yet possessing everything" (II Cor. 6:8–10).

The paradox of joy in suffering is pointedly expressed in the First
Epistle of Peter. And here once again Christian conduct is rooted and
grounded in the whole way of Jesus Christ. After a preface sounding
the appeal for ethical steadfastness in I Peter 3:15–17, the whole context of Christian baptism is unfolded as the suffering and death of
Jesus "in the flesh," his descent to preach to the spirits in prison, his
Resurrection, and his enthronement at the right hand of God in heaven

(I Pet. 3:18–22). As in Philippians 2, the confession reaches its climax in the declaration of Christ's victory over all cosmic powers as an accomplished fact resulting from his Passion and Resurrection. And here too the Church that makes the confession knows that what was true for her Master is true also for herself. Looking up in faith to her exalted Lord, she recognizes that only as she continues her own way through suffering with courage and with obedience is she able to lay hold on the promise of participation in Jesus' exaltation to glory. The faith in God which the community has through Jesus Christ (I Pet. 1:7–9; 1:21) is the inspiration of that *imitatio Christi* so much emphasized in the epistle: "To this you have been called, because Christ also suffered for you, leaving you an example, that you should follow in his steps" (I Pet. 3:21; cf. 4:1). The Passion of Jesus is held up as a paradigm for Christian believers, as a means of exhorting to patience and constancy those who are having to undergo the trials and hardships of a day of persecution. Yet it would be unworthy of the epistle to believe that the obedience and suffering of Jesus unto death are no more than proffered as a model to be copied by those who are far from him. Not in that sense could we ever imitate him. The pre-eminence and uniqueness of his way are well established. He has been and done what we could never be or do. He is sinless; we are not (I Pet. 2:22–4). What is offered in the epistle is the profounder interpretation that behind and before all genuine *imitatio Christi* is the "living hope" and resultant joy in suffering which have come to men through the Resurrection of Jesus Christ from the dead (I Pet. 1:3) and by which he is most intimately present. It is not merely that the new order, instituted by Christ's victorious completion of his way through suffering to glory, is shortly to be revealed, but that it is even now so near and so real as to transfigure the sufferings of the disciple and to enable him to see his earthly pilgrimage amid the turbulence of the world through new eyes (I Pet. 1:3–9). Through the sufferings of Christ and the subsequent glory, predicted by the prophets, the disciple is made valiant for his daily task (I Pet. 1:10–12). As Bacon's old aphorism has it: "Prosperity is the blessing of the Old Testament; adversity is the blessing of the New, which carrieth the greater benediction." [55]

Turning to the Epistle to the Hebrews, we would draw attention to two facets of the document that are vitally significant for our inquiry: (a) its importance as a counterpoint to the recent restrictively anthropological concern of existentialist interpretation of the New Testament message, and (b) its presentation of the atoning death of Jesus in the light of the High Priest concept as a demonstration of what O. Cullmann has lately called "the true New Testament dialectic between deepest humiliation and highest majesty." [56]

The exclusively anthropological interest of the contemporary type of hermeneutical stance dominated by existentialist categories, reminiscent as it is of the sharp Kantian distinction between "the starry heavens without" and "the moral law within," relates the message of Jesus Christ directly to the essentially inward life of the self, to the individual man defined only in terms of free, personal selfhood. From such a stance the Word of God is understood to appeal only to the will of the individual man—the hearing of the Word and the response of obedience to it belong merely to that center of personal life which is shut up "within." [57]

Now the author of the Epistle to the Hebrews is fully conscious that the Word addresses itself to the *now* of man's existence and comes with all urgency as a summons to decision in the inward places: "The word of God is living and active, sharper than any two-edged sword, piercing to the division of soul and spirit, of joints and marrow, and discerning the thoughts and intentions of the heart" (Heb. 4:12). However, the epistle as a whole shows that the writer does not think of the Word as a timeless form of divine address only to the inward life of man's will. The relationship of man to the Word is not confined to inward hearing and the will's obedient response. For the fundamental aim of the writer is to appeal also to the "eye," to lead his listeners to a new "seeing" or "vision" of the work of the crucified and exalted Christ through which time and eternity, earth and heaven are merged together.[58] So, in carrying through his intention, he draws upon the symbolism and imagery of his time and place and interprets the Word in a cosmic mode of speech that is calculated to kindle the flame of thought and imagination in his hearers as they contemplate the world and its structures around them. Here most vividly is the life of the new order described not solely in terms of personal selfhood and inwardness, but in terms of entry into the heavenly "inheritance" which has dawned on earth through the finished work of Christ, in the concrete language of apocalyptic: "You have come to Mount Zion and to the city of the living God, the heavenly Jerusalem, and to innumerable angels in festal gathering, and to the assembly of the first-born who are enrolled in heaven" (Heb. 12:22–3). Not man "within himself," but man in the world; not man in his loneliness abstracted from the world, but man in community; that is the theme. The new order is the communal order of the "city": "Here we have no lasting city, but we seek the city which is to come" (Heb. 13:14). The hortatory message of the epistle is in fact the challenge and the comfort and the promise of a new *citizenship* in the world. Only by a drastic impoverishment could the language in which the Word is here proclaimed be reduced to the narrow category of human self-understanding.

As to the "dialectic between deepest humiliation and highest majesty" of which we have spoken, it should be noted that the Epistle to the Hebrews offers a stringent rebuttal to the attitude of those modern theologians who are reluctant to think of the Cross as a genuinely historical act issuing from the righteousness and obedience and moral perfection of Jesus, for fear of relapsing into the liberal view. The author of Hebrews, as Cullmann has written, "had the courage to speak of the man Jesus in shockingly human terms." [59] While there is hardly anywhere in the New Testament a greater stress than here on the deity of the Son, who can be described not only as the mediator of creation (Heb. 1:3), but even as the Creator (Heb. 1:10), it is none the less of the very essence of the author's faith and life that Jesus, at the cost of an agony accompanied with "strong crying and tears" (Heb. 5:7), *voluntarily* chose the "shame" of the Cross (Heb. 12:2) and the "reproach" involved in it (Heb. 13:13).

The writer's conception of Christ as the great High Priest ministering perpetually at the heavenly altar, naturally points us primarily to Jesus' Passion and sacrifice on the Cross. But the mere *fact* of the Cross is not nearly enough for the author of Hebrews, for the exaltation of Jesus to his heavenly Priesthood is grounded in the various stages of his earthly life of consummate obedience, leading up to his death on the Cross. [60] In his voluntary acceptance of suffering, Jesus was "faithful" to the Creator, even as Moses was faithful (Heb. 3:2, 5). It was through everything he suffered that he "learned obedience," "was made perfect" and "designated by God a high priest after the order of Melchizedek" (Heb. 3:8–10). While the notion of his being made perfect has strong sacramental and cultic overtones and hints at his completed act of sacrifice on the Cross, [61] the fact that it occurs in conjunction with his learning of obedience suggests that the idea of his moral perfection is not to be excluded. Accordingly, the saying of Psalm 40:7–8, "Lo, I have come to do thy will," is transferred to Jesus and is considered to be fulfilled in the offering of his body on the Cross (Heb. 10:9–10). The epistle therefore offers us a considerable bulk of materials for the Incarnation. Moreover, the decisiveness for the writer's faith of the earthly life of the incarnate one is most explicitly substantiated in such pivotal texts as 4:15: "We have not a high priest who is unable to sympathize with our weaknesses, but one who in every respect has been tempted as we are, yet without sinning." The significance of the words "who in every respect has been tempted as we are" can hardly be overemphasized. We must distinguish, as Cullman rightly notes, between this total self-identification of Jesus with the lot of men in his submission to the selfsame temptations as beset us just because we are men and the temptations recorded of him in the Synoptic Gospels after his baptism by John. For in the latter the temptations are the temptations of the Messiah or the Christ, and set him apart from men in his Messianic distinctness and uniqueness.[62]

It may seem as though our stress on Jesus' having become equal in every respect to those whom he came to help leads us back to the quite unfashionable thought of his personality, his "self-consciousness." Be that so, if only we understand that what is decisive for us, as for the author of the epistle, is not any unlimited "psychologizing" but simply acknowledgment of the fact that his utter likeness with men in their temptations is the mark of the real humanity of the incarnate one, and the measure of the perfection of his obedience in going to his death on the Cross.

The Christological picture presented in the epistle moves between the complete humiliation of the earthly Jesus and the glorious majesty of the exalted Christ. A document of the "shame" of Jesus, it is no less a document of the heavenly glory of the Christ, to which the words of the hymn well apply:

> The highest place that Heaven affords
> Is His, is His by right,
> The King of Kings and Lord of Lords
> And Heaven's eternal Light.

Jesus' coming to do the will of God is pushed back to the advent of the pre-existent Christ from heaven (Heb. 10:5–10). Right at the beginning, Jesus appears as the effulgence of God's glory and as the upholder of the whole universe (Heb. 1:3). He is so much superior to the angels because he has inherited a more excellent *name* than they (Heb.

1:4–5)—here Psalm 2:7 is related to the Exaltation of Jesus.[63] Yet the unique divine status which Jesus enjoys, he does not enjoy merely by a celestial decree or by his possession of a divine nature. It is something won by his struggle as a man among men. In the thought of the author this is the one altogether crucial thing, that the Exaltation of Jesus is inseparably connected with his whole earthly life as an act of obedience, completed in his Passion (Heb. 2:9: "crowned with glory and honor because of the suffering of death"). His perpetual priestly ministry in the heavenly tabernacle is the outcome of his once-for-all sacrifice on earth (Heb. 9:11–28). In Hebrews 4:14 the notion of Jesus' passage through the heavens as our great High Priest seems almost to have acquired a relevance of its own for faith. But in Hebrews 9:11–28 the entry of Christ into the heavenlies finds its analogy in the earthly priest who, having made the sacrifice, goes behind the veil and appears in the inner sanctuary before God. What is involved therefore is primarily the beginning of Christ's intercession for his people at the throne of God.[64] Only because he has offered for all time a single sacrifice for sins has Christ been able to pass through the veil and make this intercession (Heb. 10:12).

The concept of Christ's High Priestly work has of course received extensive interpretation in the theology of the catholic tradition. And frequently in the doctrine of the Eucharistic sacrifice the "once-for-all-ness" of Christ's finished act of obedience on Calvary has been depreciated, even if only by the fact that the mass is designated a "sacrifice." The epistle is certainly full of the idea of the continuance of Christ's work on the Cross in the heavenly realm. But the reiterated stress on the uniqueness and finality of Christ's earthly self-sacrifice, which annuls forever the Old Testament priesthood with its repeated sacrifices, cannot be effaced (Heb. 9:12; 10:10).[65] Whenever, in the Church's worship, there is a tendency toward reproduction of the event of the Cross, the "once-for-all" is minimized and the scandal of the gospel's particularity obscured. One detects a movement in this direction in Evelyn Underhill's noble book on worship, where the great creations of the Christian liturgy, and notably the Eucharistic liturgy, are described as "sacred dramas, in which the mystery of salvation is re-enacted and re-experienced by the worshipping group." [66] Must we not guard against the temptation to think of the "mystery of salvation" as belonging most properly to the beauty of the holy place and the poetry of the liturgy, rather than to the obloquy and ugliness and horror of the death of the man of Nazareth on the Cross?

The recent vogue in "kerygma theology" has been to apply a rigid distinction between *Historie* and *Geschichte* to the New Testament message, as if the event of the Cross, as a genuinely historical act on Jesus' part *in its pastness,* were as nothing, and the kerygmatic repetition of the Word of the Cross, actualizing it for the life of the hearer, were everything. I think the Epistle to the Hebrews gainsays any such distinction when it is too rigorously drawn. The author is, to be sure, devoutly interested in the continuing and present activity of Christ at the heavenly altar. But for him, in the most realistic sense, it is the past of Jesus that is made forever present; it is his manhood that is exalted; it is the person he was, and the life he lived and the death he died on earth, to which we are brought near in the message and in worship. "He whose faith in Christ is endangered by Christ's completely human features," writes Cullmann trenchantly, "shows that he has not understood what the New Testament means by 'faith in Christ.' [67] The essence of faith in the New Testament is faith despite the scandal of humanity."

The Epistle to the Hebrews is one of our surest warrants for opposing the view that, in the Church's message and worship, Jesus is made contemporary only as a *nudum factum* recollected and remembered, or as an empty name hidden within the kerygma, or as being assimilated to our existence in something like the same manner as the Gnostics erroneously equated Christ with the divine essence concealed in the human soul.[68] Rather is Jesus present in the Word and in worship as the one who is most truly "the same yesterday and today and forever." He is the one who "ever lives to make intercession for us," continually "touched with the feeling of our infirmities," precisely because he has stood where we stand, has entered into our trials and temptations, and has shared our experiences. One is reminded of these relevant words in Browning's poem "Saul":

> 'Tis the weakness in strength that I cry for! my flesh, that I seek
> In the Godhead! I seek and I find it. O Saul, it shall be
> A Face like my face that receives thee: a Man like to me,
> Thou shalt love and be loved by, for ever! a Hand like this hand
> Shall throw open the gates of new life to thee! See the Christ stand!

It has to be noted that the Epistle to the Hebrews does not make as explicit to us as the Pauline epistles how it is that the once-for-all act of Jesus on the Cross becomes effective for men. Certainly the author allows the faith of the individual to enter into the horizon of his thinking, and for him faith plays its necessary part in the attainment of salvation (Heb. 10:22, 37). In the famous eleventh chapter, "faith" is defined as "the assurance of things hoped for, the conviction of things not seen" (Heb. 11:1). The unseen world becomes as real to faith as the visible world is real to sight. And the answer to our question is involved in the truth that, in that unseen world, the central and decisive place is held by Christ, in his continuing ministry for us, as our great High Priest. Having entered into the honorable and glorious office in which he ministers everlastingly in heaven, because of the suffering of death (Heb. 2:9), Christ has blazed the trail for men. Jesus is introduced in Hebrews 2:10 as the "Pioneer" (ἀρχηγός) or "Leader" of a new humanity. While the meaning of the term "Pioneer" or "Leader" is much debated, it does seem clear enough that the inescapable priority of the way of Jesus through humiliation to glory is established as the only way that the saved can follow. If that is so, it would be a mistake to conceive the relationship between Christ and the brethren, as depicted in Hebrews 2:11, in any Gnostic sense as a physical relationship, or as an identification by which Christ and the Christian are made one person. Long ago, Denney lamented the inclination of Seeberg, in his essay on the death of Christ in Hebrews, to put the Christian on a par with or in complete unity with the Christ, and took vehement exception to such utterances as this: "The thing Christ has done (*die Leistung Christi*), though it has not been done by the sinner, is yet a thing which he might or would fain have done, and is therefore in principle his doing." "This," said Denney, "is not wrestling with mysteries, or sounding great deeps; it is trifling with words, or trying to say Yes and No in the same breath." [69]

Whereas it is true that Jesus the sanctifier and the many sons who are brought to glory and sanctified "have all one origin" (Heb. 2:11), the epistle as a whole leaves us in no doubt that Jesus' Sonship is something unique (Heb. 1:1–4). As the "Leader," therefore, it is he who has taken the initiative and done everything needful, indeed only he who could have done so, in calling the brotherhood into being. While he has fully taken upon himself our human nature, he so far stands out above everything men can think or say or do that he has destroyed the power of death, released men from its thraldom, wrought expiation for the sins of the people, and by his own suffering and temptation has become able to help those that are tempted (Heb. 2:14–18). If then we would speak of the believer's having to take the way shown by the "Leader," we must emphasize that he can do so only by holding fast to what has been done and what has been revealed in Jesus.

That Jesus and his way are forever prior to men is further corroborated by the designation that appears in Hebrews 6:20, where he is called the "Forerunner." In this context what is stressed is, as we have seen, Jesus' entry into heaven from earth, in consequence of his once-for-all act of sacrifice on the Cross, to make intercession for men, after the analogy of the earthly high priest who, when he has offered the sacrifice, passes beyond the veil to make intercession for Israel. I do not believe the epistle justifies the notion that it is Christ's atoning sacrifice rather than his ministry of intercession that is repeated in the heavenly realm.[70] But also, inasmuch as the epistle makes it plain that it is most of all from the fear of death that men need to be delivered (Heb. 2:15), there would appear to be considerable merit in Cullmann's suggestion that the "Forerunner" here is thought of as the one who draws his faithful ones with him into his Resurrection and its consequences, and that the very expression "Forerunner" ($\pi\rho\acute{o}\delta\rho o\mu o\varsigma$) has an affinity with Paul's view that through the Resurrection Jesus has become "the first-born of the dead" ($\pi\rho\omega\tau\acute{o}\tau o\kappa o\varsigma$ $\tau\tilde{\omega}\nu$ $\nu\epsilon\kappa\rho\tilde{\omega}\nu$).[71] There is no question here that the way of Jesus is altogether pre-eminent, that faith finds its sure foundation for confidence toward God only by looking to his work as a finished work.

This has to be borne in mind when we come to Hebrews 12:2, where Christ seems to be held forth as the great exemplar of faith, toward whom the eyes and hearts of the Christian community, living under the hardships of this present time, are to be lifted up, and where the Church's service and obedience seem to consist in an *imitatio Christi:* "Let us run with perseverance the race that is set before us, looking to Jesus the pioneer and perfecter of our faith, who for the joy that was set before him endured the cross, despising the shame, and is seated at the right hand of the throne of God." If we give to the "once-for-all" of Hebrews the central place that it deserves, we shall not readily misconstrue the Church's service and obedience in terms of her need or capacity to do over again what he has already achieved *for us.* Never in that sense could we imitate him. Rather the faithfulness of discipleship is possible for the Church only because he has done uniquely and finally what he has done. "This becomes more obvious in Heb. 13:12 f.," E. Schweizer writes, "where following

Jesus is described as going forth unto *him* who went without the gates of Jerusalem not only as the first One, but as the One who sanctified the people. Therefore it should be implied in the expression 'Pioneer and Perfecter' that *he* first creates the Church and that *he* perfects her." [72]

The Epistle to the Hebrews accordingly provides a very vivid illustration of how constitutive for the Church's faith and life, on her road through the trials and temptations of this world and under the burden of everything that daunts the soul, was the way of Jesus himself through earthly humiliation to heavenly glory. For the Church knew that the majesty of her Lord in his perpetual ministry in the unseen heavenly world, which becomes real to faith, was rooted and grounded in an earthly life climaxed by his unique act of obedience and sacrifice on the Cross. And knowing this, she could bear up under the misfortunes and discouragements of this present time.

If we have devoted a larger space to this epistle than to other books of the Bible, our reason is simply this: Hebrews' development of the High Priest Christology is not peripheral in the New Testament. It has a close affinity with the thinking of Paul, who himself builds everything upon the continuing ministry of the exalted Christ as based upon his once-for-all act of obedience and righteousness on the Cross: "The death he died he died to sin, once for all, but the life he lives he lives to God" (Rom. 6:10). Moreover, the author of the Gospel of John is familiar with the High Priest concept, as is clear from what has become widely known as the "High Priestly prayer" of chapter 17, which forms part of the farewell discourses of Jesus. Here once more (John 17:17–19), as in Hebrews 2:10 ff., the way of Jesus as the one who has been sent by God into the world and who is, in a unique sense, the sanctified is the indispensable pre-condition of the sanctification of his disciples and of their mission to all the earth. The farewell discourses from chapter 14 on develop the theme that Jesus himself has gone ahead of his people as the "Forerunner," and, only because his journey through earthly humiliation and suffering (in which, for John, the glory of heaven already resides) to the side of the Father is complete, are those who belong to him and are his own able to follow him without flinching in the face of the world's hatred and persecution.

The unbroken and unbreakable continuity between the continuing gracious work of the exalted Christ and the finished work of the earthly Jesus is to be found even in the Book of Revelation, which occupies a singular place in the New Testament. As we might expect in a document belonging to the apocalyptic literary genre, there is a preponderance of symbols and images stressing the celestial dignity and majesty of the Christ. Nevertheless, even here the decisiveness of the past work of Jesus, in the days of his humiliation, is assuredly not overlooked. We propose to illustrate this principally by reference to the opening doxological confession and to the figure of the Lamb in the Apocalypse.

Interwoven with the Seer's address to the seven churches is his sudden song of praise: "Grace to you and peace . . . from Jesus Christ the faithful witness, the first-born of the dead, and the ruler of kings on earth. To him who loves us and has freed us from our sins by his blood and made us a kingdom, priests to his God and Father, to him be glory and dominion for ever and ever. Amen" (Rev. 1:4–6). The title "faithful witness" re-echoes the witness borne by Jesus before Pilate (Mark 14:53 ff.; John 18:36–7) and can be regarded as an epitome of his earthly life. But more than that, this designation represents the bond of unity between Jesus and his disciples. As the supremely "faithful witness," he has suffered under Pontius Pilate and submitted himself to death, only to come to life again in the Resurrection, as the first-born from the dead (Rev. 1:5; 2:8). Here once more Jesus is presented as the "Forerunner" of his people. Here once more what he has done is determinative for the faith and life of his followers: they too can lay hold of the promise of the crown of life, if only they are faithful unto death (cf. Rev. 1:5 and 2:13; 2:8 and 2:10; 2:26–8 and 12:5).[73] Jesus Christ, "the faithful witness," "the first-born of the dead," "the ruler of kings on earth" (Rev. 1:5)— since the last phrase of the threefold description alludes to the exaltation and cosmic authority of the Christ, we are confronted here in this highly condensed formula with a summation of the whole way of Jesus through death and Resurrection to heavenly glory, on which the very existence of the Church depends.

The following ascription makes it plain that, if the Church, as the Seer knows it, can count on the everlasting sympathy and love of its Lord and Christ ("to him who *loves* us"), it can count on it only because of the liberating work already accomplished by Jesus in the past ("*has* freed us from our sins," Rev. 1:5). The statement of Revelation 1:5 is, in fact, the statement of a Church that knows she is constituted the new people over whom God reigns and enjoys the privilege of standing in God's sight in worship only through the fact of Jesus' costly Passion and sacrifice on the Cross, out of which grace has come to the community of believers.

The most prominent Christological image, occurring no less than twenty-eight times in the Apocalypse, is that of Christ as the Lamb. The figure of the Lamb, first introduced against the magnificence of the celestial throne and the unimaginable splendors of its surroundings (Rev. 4–5:6), applies primarily to the exalted Christ. It is the Lamb who, by his triumph, is empowered to open the sealed scroll (Rev. 5–6), who from the midst of the throne leads the redeemed like a shepherd (7:17), who achieves the final victory (17:13 ff.; 19:11 ff.), and who dwells with the saints in light (21–22). "The author of Revelation," says Dr. C. K. Barrett, "was able to presuppose the useful cryptic equation, Lamb = Messiah, and could therefore say about the Lamb anything that could be said about the supernatural Messiah." [74]

Merged with the idea of the Messianic Leadership of the glorified Christ in the Apocalypse is the idea of the Lamb as it had been slain, of Christ as a sacrificial and redemptive offering. The writer does not appear to be conscious of any antinomy between the two ideas. There are at least three passages relating to the Lamb where the thought expressed in the opening doxology, that he has freed us from our sins at the cost of his own blood (Rev. 1:5), is repeated and combined with Christ's exalted status, namely 5:6–14; 7:14; 12:11. Looking only at the first of these, we notice that, although the Lamb is alive and has his place by the throne of God, he carries within himself the virtue and power of his death, for the new song sung by the saints deems him worthy to control the whole future only because he was slain and by his blood did ransom men for God.[75]

To appreciate what the idea of the exalted Lamb that had been slain could have meant for the Church's own understanding of its historical situation, we may most profitably turn to the crucial text of Revelation 14:4, where we read of the chaste ones that "it is these who follow the Lamb wherever he goes; these have been redeemed from mankind as first fruits for God and the Lamb." The picture we have here is of a Christian community protected, guarded, and guided by the exalted Lamb, who in his never-ending ministry is always ahead of the Church on its every step through the tribulations of this world. It seems more probable that this following of the Lamb "wherever he goes" alludes to the Leadership of the exalted Christ rather than to the way of Jesus through death and Resurrection to heavenly glory and so to an *imitatio Christi* on the Church's part.[76] But at the same time, it is certainly made clear that to follow Christ at all is only conceivable or possible because the power of his Passion has descended into the heart of the community and because it has experienced the redemptive effects of his death. Only on the ground of his death, and the purchase of men for God accomplished by it, is the Christian life able to begin and go on.

I feel it is necessary to conclude our account of "the dialectic of lowliest humiliation and highest majesty" in the New Testament by referring, however briefly, to two of the most distinctive facets of New Testament life and thought, the Lord's Supper and the idea of the Church as the Body of Christ.

The Lord's Supper

It is a well-known fact that many critical problems connected with the various formulae of institution of the Lord's Supper in the New Testament still await definitive solution. There is, for example, still no general agreement regarding the date of the Last Supper. Did it take place, as the Fourth Gospel suggests, before the Passover, or was it held as a Passover meal, as Mark, Matthew, and Luke suggest? One could perhaps say only that, despite the question of chronology, there has been an increasing readiness to acknowledge that the Supper has strong Paschal overtones.[77] Further, the protracted debate about the respective claims to historical priority of the different accounts of the Supper in the Synoptic Gospels and in I Corinthians has focused especially upon the Marcan and Pauline formulas. It is familiar that Paul's record differs from Mark's chiefly in that he has substituted for the Marcan "This is my blood" (Mark 14:24) the words "This cup is the new covenant in my blood" (I Cor. 11:25) and has added the command to repeat the rite, "Do this in remembrance of me" (I Cor. 11:24–5). While the view that the form presented by Mark is the most Semitic and ancient has received weighty support,[78] the discussion as to whether the Pauline formula represents a modification of Mark, or whether it is the other way round, cannot be said to have yielded any very sure conclusion. Is each account therefore simply an independent and original variation on the same theme? [79]

Amid the prevailing uncertainties, there is no reason to doubt that this much of genuine history is reflected in the texts: Jesus of Nazareth, filled with the certainty of his approaching end, celebrated the last meal with his disciples. Nevertheless, in trying to determine which account of the Supper most faithfully echoes the thought and words of the Master, and in trying to get behind the texts to the exact procedure at the last meal, historical criticism has experienced the most serious difficulties. It is widely recognized that the cult and liturgy of the later Church, in its celebration of the Supper, has profoundly influenced the tradition of the texts relating to it. Moreover, Schweitzer pointed out many years ago how acute is the problem of reconciling what appears to be Paul's doctrine of the glorified Christ and the Christian's communion with the glorified Christ with the reported words of Jesus about the bread and wine as his body and blood. "To speak of the body and blood of Christ is an absurdity from the point of view of the apostle's doctrine. As regards his Eucharistic doctrine he is unable to adjust the historical words with his own Christology and yet he must do so. The compromise he attempts remains obscure to us." [80]

A great deal has been seen to hinge on the problematical observation with which the apostle prefaces his formula of institution: "I received from the Lord what I also delivered to you" (I Cor. 11:23). The Greek terms for "received" and "delivered" correspond to the Rabbinic words, *qibbêl* and *mâsâr*, which apply to the "reception" and "transmission" of a tradition. Many scholars have accordingly held that Paul is here speaking of tradition that had been handed on to him by the Church in the period after his conversion. But, as Dr. W. D. Davies has noted, the Greek παραλαμβάνειν (and the underlying *qibbêl*) properly refers not to the indirect but to the direct reception of a specific tradition.[81] Consequently, even though H. Lietzmann's view that Paul is alluding to a direct visionary revelation from the Lord as to what took place at the Last Supper has not met with much approval, we ought not hastily to dismiss the possibility that first-hand apostolic experience of the resurrected and exalted Christ has exercised a governing influence on the tradition and its transmission.[82] It is important also on the other side that, as Davies again has remarked, the term "deliver" ("I delivered to you," παρέδωκα ὑμῖν) need not indicate a precise reproduction of the *ipsissima verba* of Jesus, but may denote an interpretive version of what was received. We therefore have to leave room for the fact that Paul may have been "moulding what he had received in such a way as to reveal its inner meaning." [83] There is, however, no question of a complete departure on Paul's part from the tradition of the Lord's Supper. Not only is the meaning of Paul's formulation quite close to Mark's, but also the apostle seems to be conscious of passing on at least the substance of what was simply a datum for him as for the primitive Church, handed down along with Easter and Pentecost. Yet this does not alter the fact that Paul has made his own reinterpretation.

The thorny question is the question of what direction the apostle's reinterpretation takes. On this score quite opposite views continue to be held. Davies, for instance, has argued that the prominence given in the Pauline formula to the idea of the New Covenant instituted by Christ's blood, together with the explicit emphasis on the command to repeat the rite, betokens the activity of a Rabbinic mind which thought of the Supper as matching the Passover of Judaism. In that case the background for Paul's stress on the *community* aspect of the rite is to be found altogether within the pale of Judaism.[84] On the contrary H. J. Schoeps, following fairly closely the lead of the History of Religions school, has lately held that the Pauline version of the Supper presents us with what is essentially a piece of Jewish-pagan syncretism. He maintains that the apostle has modified the Marcan, or rather the Lucan, tradition (Luke 22:19), and has brought the Last Supper into line with the cult practice of the Hellenistic Mystery brotherhoods by adding the thought of the sacramental communion of the celebrants with their Lord and of their being welded, through participation in the bread and wine, into a "body," the Body of Christ (I Cor. 10:16–17; 11:23–6).[85]

It would be folly to pretend that any of the complex critical questions we have mentioned could be decided or even adequately discussed in a page or two. Our intention is to deal quite narrowly, in regard to the Last Supper, with the humiliation-majesty motif. In this connection, Günther Bornkamm has recently cut the Gordian knot of several of the historical problems that have vexed the critics in an interesting attempt to elucidate the indivisible unity of Supper-Death-Resurrection.[86]

Bornkamm appeals to the first of the Arnoldshain theses on the Lord's Supper: "The Supper which we celebrate is founded in the institution and order of Jesus Christ, the Lord, who was delivered unto death for us and rose again." There is no reference in the thesis to an objective historical datum; it does not say, for example: "Jesus Christ instituted the Lord's Supper, which is celebrated by us, on the night of Maundy Thursday." If then the statement has been cautiously formulated, the reason is to be sought in the view of Form-criticism that it is very doubtful whether we can get back behind the texts in their present form, reflecting as they do the liturgical tradition and cultic practice of the primitive Church, to chronologically or historiographically verifiable data concerning the actual institution of the Supper. Bornkamm therefore affirms that the Supper was inaugurated not merely by the historical Jesus but by the risen Christ and Lord, breaking through the chronological events in his person and saving action. In this way the worshiping Church, celebrating the Eucharistic meal and experiencing the meaning of the death of Jesus, in the light of Easter, in ever new depth, formed from the beginning an integral part of the event of the institution. If the unveiling, through the Resurrection, of the redemptive significance of Jesus' death entered into whatever meal he may have instituted, it follows that such historical references as "on the night when he was betrayed" and "do this in remembrance of me" (I Cor. 11:23–4) are of secondary importance for the understanding of the Supper.

According to Bornkamm, three stages in the development of the Lord's Supper are to be traced: (1) a meal Jesus celebrated with his disciples, which later awakened sacred memories in them because it was the last meal they had had with him; (2) the death of Jesus on the Cross; (3) the post-Easter interpretation of the meaning of his death as applied to the Last Supper. In this final stage the community of faith, advancing, under the guidance of the Spirit, in its understanding of what transpired in the event of God's presence in Jesus of Nazareth and especially of the meaning of his death, transformed the last meal into the Holy Supper.

Bornkamm's main purpose is to defend the notion that the truth about the Last Supper, with which is interwoven the redemptive post-Easter history of Jesus as the Christ, cannot be confined to an objective history of facts. But, while for Bornkamm it is the risen Lord who is the real author of Holy Communion, the decisiveness of the second stage in its development, the death of Jesus on the Cross, is not neglected by him; rather does he lay due emphasis on the need to ask whether the Church's celebration of the meal was an adequate representation of the significance of Jesus' death.

That for the early Christians the Eucharistic rite was quite centrally linked both to the Passion and the Resurrection; that the light of Easter, with all that it increasingly revealed of the meaning of Jesus' death, shone in the Supper; that our ability or inability to reconstruct what actually took place in word and deed in the Upper Room may not be the most crucial thing in the understanding of the meal—with all of this we can readily agree. Nevertheless, many historical critics, we dare say, will find little to rejoice over in Bornkamm's presentation. His stress on the risen Lord's authorship of Holy Communion and on the believing community as belonging from the beginning to the event of the institution, and his apparent disregard of chronology involved therein, might seem to them to connote the subjugation of "history" to "theology." However that may be, we certainly believe that the relegation to a place of minimal importance of such a historical reference in the Pauline formulation as "do this in remembrance of me" may be contested. It is of course true that historical criticism has been hard put to it to defend the originality of these words as a command of the historical Jesus. J. Jeremias' interpretation of the command to repeat the rite seems hardly less startling when one reads the recent edition of his work *The Eucharistic Words of Jesus* than when one first encountered it: "this do in remembrance of me" can be taken to go back to the historical Jesus, Jeremias has contended, because it refers not to the community's remembrance of his death, but to God's own remembrance of His Messiah, by which is meant God's acting in grace to fulfill His promise by bringing about His kingdom in the Parousia.[87] Failing acceptance of this exegetical reinterpretation, we are faced with the somewhat dubious *argumentum e silentio* that, although Mark and Matthew, like Paul, found the command to repeat the rite in the tradition received by them, they felt no need to record it because they could assume that no one doubted it.

If we cannot with any assurance trace these words back to Jesus in the Upper Room, we can notice the significance that may be attached to the fact that Paul has given them explicit expression. For Paul or for the Church represented by the tradition he reports, the death of Jesus has come to mean the renewal of the divine covenant entered upon at Sinai (Exod. 24:8) or the foundation of the New Dispensation, the New Community (I Cor. 11:25). And just as in the *Passover Haggadah* the Jewish community participates in the recitation of the act of redemption from Egypt, out of which it was created as a people, even so the "in remembrance of me" (εἰς τὴν ἐμὴν ἀνάμνησιν) of the Eucharist brings vividly into the present experience of the New Community the historical act of Jesus' death on the cross in which it originated. If therefore, in the Eucharistic rite, the Church is constituted one body by her common sharing in the life and power of her risen Lord, the *anamnēsis* also dramatically brings home to her that the one who appears under the sign of the bread and wine for ever renewed activity and blessing and challenge to decision is the same Jesus who on a fateful night in history was betrayed and who was crucified on the Cross.

In I Corinthians 11:26 Paul has added to his formula of institution an explanatory comment: "For as often as you eat this bread and drink the cup, you proclaim the Lord's death until he comes." It will be agreed that in this note there is no suggestion of the believers' absorption in the mystical body of the exalted Christ after the fashion of the initiates' incorporation with the cult god in the sacramentalism of the Hellenistic Mystery cults. Rather the Eucharist, as Paul here interprets it, is the proclamation of what has already been accomplished, of the historic act of redemption by which the Christian community has been established. There is no question here of any such merging of the Church with the Christ that the Church takes his place, and the priority of what he has done "for men" is lost; rather does the community show forth what he has already achieved. Here also it becomes clear that, although the Pauline formulation brings into greatest prominence the idea of Jesus' death as the ratification of the New Covenant, the apostle has not omitted from his own understanding the strong eschatological emphasis that is a feature of the Synoptic reports. Indeed, the death of Jesus is placed by him in the light of the coming eschatological fulfillment: "until he comes." So it is in Mark, where the formula of institution is followed by these reported words of Jesus: "Truly, I say to you, I shall not drink again of the fruit of the vine until that day when I drink it new in the kingdom of God" (Mark 14:25). There, too, the death of Jesus is placed in the light of the coming kingdom of God, and his destiny is distinguished from that of his disciples: "*I* shall not drink again." [88] Thus in Paul's interpretive comment in I Corinthians 11:26 the priority of Jesus and his destiny, over against the Church, is upheld and his death and coming glory in the Parousia, with which the death is most closely linked, stand out in bold relief as the true dynamic of the community's life and fellowship "in him."

If there is any substance in what we have said, we should look with disfavor on any attempt to interpret the Last Supper without reference to Jewish background, and, in particular, holding that in I Corinthians 10:16 ("the fellowship of the blood of Christ") the thought, as the context shows, is of the establishment of the Christian community in its solidarity through the sacrificial death of Christ, we should hesitate to ascribe to the Pauline doctrine of the Eucharist the "mystical" idea that, through feeding on his body and blood, the Church *becomes* the very life and body of the exalted Christ.[89]

The Church, the Body of Christ

It goes without saying that in a few paragraphs we cannot deal thoroughly with the rich and varied complex of ideas relating to the concept of the Body of Christ. As to the longstanding controversy about the external sources of the doctrine (Stoic, Gnostic, Rabbinic speculation on the Body of Adam?) J. A. T. Robinson very fitly pointed out, in his monograph *The Body*, that in the prevailingly syncretistic thought of the hellenized Judaism of Paul's day, the apostle may have been influenced, almost without knowing it, by any of these sources.[90] Bishop Robinson's own eminent contribution was to show that the content with which the term "body" was filled by Paul, in application to the Church, derived from his own reflection on the oneness of the Lord Jesus Christ as he had seen him in his risen body.[91] The apostle's problem therefore was to explain how the many, the members of the Christian community, can be *one*—he may have been assisted in elucidating this by the Old Testament notion of corporate personality. So he takes as his starting point, in his fullest treatment of the Church as the Body of Christ in I Corinthians 12:12–31, that the unity of Christ is like that of the human body: "For just as the body is one and has many members, and all the members of the body, though many, are one body, so it is with Christ" (I Cor. 12:12).

In his subsequent lengthy development in this passage of the idea of the mutual interaction of the various members of the human body, there is not wanting the thought of the interdependence of the many members of Christ's Body, the Church: "God has so adjusted the body . . . that there may be no discord in the body, but that the members may have the same care for one another" (I Cor. 12:24–5). Nevertheless, the all-important thing is that, just as all the members of the

human body, despite their number and diversity of function, form a
unity or one body, so the members of Christ's Body are included in
and constitute the *one* "in Christ" (cf. Rom. 12:5; Gal. 3:28). Do we
have here the description of a living organism drawing its life from a
single source, or, as some would hold, a more externally conceived
relationship of ethical obedience on the part of the Church toward
Christ? So realistic is Paul's thought of Christ as a new Body, so much
does he pile up compound verbs with the preposition σύν, "with," even
inventing one like συνεσταύρωμαι, "I am crucified with" (Gal. 2:20; cf.
Rom. 8:17) to express the oneness of the Church in the oneness of
Christ's Body that it is difficult to escape the view that for the apostle
"body" is no *mere analogy,* metaphor, or figure of speech, but implies
a real organic unity of the Church "in Christ." [92]

If, however, we were to leave the matter there, we would be in
danger of simply equating or confusing the Church with Christ, of
blotting out the priority of Christ over his Church, and so of losing
the apartness of the Word of God from man. And that would be to
ignore the distinction that is made in the teaching of the New Testament, notwithstanding its insistence on the oneness of the Christian
community with Christ, between the Church and Christ as Head of the
Body. The notion of the Headship of Christ, first implied in I Corinthians 11:3, "the head of every man is Christ," is brought to clear
expression in the Epistle to the Ephesians, written most probably by
a disciple of Paul's (Eph. 1:23). It is of the utmost significance that the
idea of the Church as the Body of Christ, so maturely developed in the
latter part of Ephesians, is in the former part conceived to be rooted
and grounded in everything God has already done in Jesus Christ, in
His gift of grace in Christ's once-for-all sacrificial act of redemption
(Eph. 1:7–8), by which reconciliation has been achieved for men,
peace proclaimed, access gained to the Father, and inclusion as citizens
of the household of God made possible for those who were hitherto
but strangers and sojourners (Eph. 2:16–19). Markus Barth has observed, justly, we believe, that whenever in the New Testament Christ
is thought of as identifying himself with the Church, it is not the divine
character of the Church, but his grace and mercy and power that are
duly praised.[93] The Church is utterly dependent on him. He is not in
the same sense dependent on the Church. By what he has done he has
brought the Church into being. It is the gift of God and could only be
received by those whom he, in his freedom, calls to be his people.[94]

It is instructive to compare the situation in the Fourth Gospel. The Fourth Evangelist does not of course use the terms "Church" or "Body of Christ," but his language concerning Christ as the vine and the disciples as the branches has an affinity with Paul's affirmation, in his development of the notion of the Body of Christ, that we are σύμφυτοι with Christ (Rom. 6:5), "grafted onto his stock," as well as with the affirmation in Ephesians that "we are to grow up in every way into him who is the head, into Christ" (Eph. 4:15). It may not be amiss then to think of John as having his own concept of the nature of the Church, and as seeking to convey that concept through the representation in his Gospel of Christ's intercourse with the disciples. In that event, the image of the vine and the branches expresses once again the notion of the organic oneness of the Christian community with him who is the sole source of its life. But once more we should be wary of going too far in the direction of a purely "organismic" or "mystical" interpretation. For with John the uniqueness of Jesus Christ or his priority, so to speak, over against the Church is well established. If he identifies himself with the Church, the Church is not thereby constituted his equal. Rather he alone has seen the Father and declared Him (John 1:18; 6:46). Only he has descended from and ascended into heaven (3:13), and only through the completion of his whole way is God's offer of salvation made and discipleship rendered possible (13:36–8; 20:17). The Shepherd, who is the Lord of the Church, goes ahead of the flock (10:11–16).

John's view of the Church hardly allows of the idea that the members can be so lost in mystical absorption in the Christ that all individual ethical responsibility is suppressed, for what is expected of them is a life comparable in the power and quality of its love to the love that was active in the Cross (10:14–15; 12:32–3; 15:12–13).[95] The believing community is sent by Jesus, as Jesus was sent by God (17:18; 20:21); the community is commissioned to be the bearer of the Word, just as Jesus gave his Word to the Church (cf. 17:20 with 15:15; 17:8, 14). The Church and the Church's solidarity in Christ is, in Johannine terms, simply a gift, the gift of Jesus' very own glory (17:22). It is an exceedingly costly gift, costly for both giver and receiver. For just as Jesus' glory resides in his suffering, rejection, and death, so the Church can lay hold of the promise of glory for her only through sharing in his suffering: as he was hated and persecuted, so will the Church be (7:7; 15:18–21; 16:2–3).

When in the third century A.D., in his *Exhortation to Martyrdom,* Origen, the greatest of the early Church Fathers, spoke of the sufferings of the martyrs as being taken up into, or merged with, the sufferings of Christ, he was not superimposing upon the New Testament a new and fanciful idea. He was expressing a thought that is present in the New Testament: that the sufferings of Christ and the sufferings of his followers are somehow most closely connected (Col. 1:24). And we would be doing not only John, but also Paul, as well as other New Testament writers a great disservice were we to see the notion of the organic unity of the Church "in Christ" in such a blinding light as to miss the other truth that, under the Headship of Christ and in the light of the unmistakable priority of what he once accomplished, the Church has a *representational* function to perform, and that it can perform this function only through loving response and loyal obedience to its Master in carrying its own share of his suffering for the world.

Recent scholarly emphases on the Church as the *missionary* Body of Christ in the New Testament are to be welcomed. The insight that, for Paul, the preaching of the gospel to the Gentiles is an eschatological event of first importance allows us to notice that, although in such a chapter as Romans 12 the Body of Christ idea is not explicitly expressed, the apostle is nevertheless showing how the members of the Church are rendering their services to the whole world and not only to one another. There are to be found here, as E. Schweizer has lately convincingly demonstrated, "theological concepts pregnant for further development." And the development is carried through in such passages as the hymn of Colossians 1:15–20, confessedly much disputed. In these verses there is, as Schweizer thinks, a combination of two elements. The background of the Colossians letter as a whole and the content of the hymn itself suggest that Pauline thought has here been reinterpreted in the direction of the well-attested Hellenistic concept of the world as a living and divine body, governed by God as its Head or permeated by God as its soul. Only now it is Christ, and not Zeus or Ether or any cult deity of the Mystery religions, who is the Ruler of the cosmos: "In him [Christ] all things were created, in heaven and on earth, visible and invisible, whether thrones or dominions or principalities or authorities—all things were created through him and for him. He is before all things, and in him all things hold together" (Col. 1:16–17). The message that Christ is the Creator of the cosmos and the Reconciler of earth and heaven (Col. 1:20) would have been most meaningful to Hellenistic man who understood him-self as irretrievably separated from heaven or alienated from a life with the gods. But, on the other hand, the author of Colossians has refused to allow the Church's praise to Christ as Lord of the cosmos to degenerate into the notion that his Rulership over the world is simply a *physical* phenomenon that can be taken for granted, and has offered his own correctives to bring the hymn into line with the authentic Pauline understanding. For all the emphasis in the hymn on the exalted Christ and the oneness of earth and heaven in him, it is emphatically declared that reconciliation is not, in the first place, the reconciliation of nature but is effected only by Jesus' historic act of redemption on the Cross, by which peace is offered solely to those who have made the personal decision of faith (Col. 1:20, "making peace by the blood of his cross"; cf. Col. 1:22–3). It is not only the Spirit of the exalted Christ that is accomplishing this marvelous work of the reconciliation of earth and heaven. For now in retrospect, from the standpoint of the fellowship of the redeemed, it can be seen that their very existence as the Body of Christ depends on the fact that his death on the Cross was God's offer of a new beginning to men, if only they would come and accept it, and that in that redeeming death lay the "secret" of their new community and its extension in the world.

The idea of Christ's Headship, not over the cosmos, but over the Church, is permitted to occupy the center of the hymn: "He is the head of the body, the Church" (Col. 1:18). And both from what goes before (Col. 1:5–6) and from the commentary that follows the hymn (Col. 1:24–9), it is made plain that the Body of which Christ is the Head is growing and must grow, permeating the whole world, through the Church's promulgation of the "mystery" laid up for countless ages but now revealed, through the proclamation of the gospel and through the anguish and hardship inescapably involved in the task. "Thus it is in the preaching to the world and in the suffering for the world that this lordship of Christ over the world is established," E. Schweizer writes, "Christ, through his body, is searching and find-ing the world, permeating it, blessing it, rendering it obedient to him-self." [96]

The Church cannot be satisfied to remain a "remnant," practicing an esoteric cult of souls. Rather, as the Body of Christ, it gladly renders its bodily obedience to its Lord and, in claiming the bodily obedience of all men through the preaching of the message and its suffering for the world, it manifests its concern for their material and social well-being. So the Church must be forever restless until, in its passion of high belief that God has already done everything needful for the salvation of men in Jesus Christ and through its own representation of Christ to the world, mankind truly becomes "one Body" according to the eternal purpose of God (Eph. 4:13–16).

This emphasis on the missionary aspect of the idea of the Body of Christ in the New Testament is certainly not new. But it is good that it is being recaptured by contemporary exegesis. It is good because it may serve to give us pause before surrendering wholly to the liberalizing type of Christianity advocated recently by such existence philosophers as Karl Jaspers, who calls upon us to recognize that we can be true to our own faith without denying that others may have found God in different ways. In the same vein Arnold Toynbee has written: "The missions of the higher religions are not competitive, they are complementary. We can believe in our own religion without having to feel that it is the sole repository of truth. We can love it without having to fear that it is the sole means of salvation." [97] So also John Macquarrie, under the aegis of existence philosophy, has argued that, in a restricted way, only for Western man, under the factual conditions of his existence, does Christianity possess an "inescapably definitive character." Whereas at the beginning of this century Western culture was bidding fair to become a world culture and Christianity to assume a definitive status for all men, it is now apparent that, through the vigorous new life of African and Asian nationalism, the association of Christianity with Western imperialism, and the re-awakening of Islam and Buddhism, we must expect to live for a long while yet with other world religions on the face of the earth.[98]

That there is reason and merit in these points of view no one will deny. Yet it is not too much to say that, when pressed too far, they could be subtly destructive of the Church's one true charter of existence as it is set forth in the New Testament. When all due allowance is made for the cultural and racial differences between an African Muslim or an Asian Buddhist and Western man, it is not easy to see how a religion of historical revelation, that has *definitive* status for me, as human being, and is able to confer on me a new self-understanding, should not also possess *definitive* status for *all human beings*. Further, to be sure, there is every reason to deprecate the dogmatic prejudice, bigotry, and narrow exclusiveness that have unhappily all

too often been characteristic of the attitude of Christian believers toward men of other faiths. Yet it is not necessary to be bigoted and bit-
terly exclusivist in order to believe that through his Body, the Church,
Jesus Christ is claiming, and searching, and finding *the world*. On the
contrary, since its most primitive age, the Church, wherever and whenever it has been truly the Church of Christ, has conceived itself to be
the nucleus of a new humanity, ruled by the spirit of divine love not
only internally toward its own members but toward all men. And, as
the growing Body of Christ in the world, as Donald Baillie very well
put it, "it will transcend all barriers of class and race and nation, because from the standpoint of the Community of the Cross there is no
difference: all are sinners and all can be saved. This new and universal
community was created by what God did in Jesus Christ, and is based
on nothing else: and through it God draws other men into community,
and so saves the world." [99]

   With this word we conclude our investigation of the "dialectic between lowliest humiliation and highest majesty" in the New Testament. We have attempted to explicate the indissoluble unity of history
and kerygma in all layers of the New Testament witness. On the one
hand, while the Gospels intend to narrate, and do provide us with
materials for, the life of the Incarnate, they are at the same time
"kerygmatic" confessions of Jesus as risen Christ and Lord. On the
other hand, while the so-called kerygmatic documents of the New
Testament lay great stress on the presence of the resurrected and
exalted Christ in the Spirit, the form of kerygma they present none
the less carries within itself, as it were, the "form of the past"; they
incontestably bear testimony to a history, a person, and a life; they
are everywhere speaking of Jesus of Nazareth and what he has done.
When, therefore, we look at the New Testament as a whole, I think we
find, according to the varying emphases of different sections of the
Canon, that Jesus Christ is presented as both Teacher and Teaching,
as both Interpreter of the Law and himself the New Law, as both the
Lowly and the Glorious, as both the Crucified by the powers of the
world and the Victor over the powers that hold men in thrall, as both
the Victim and the one true Priest, as the Sacrificed and the one true
perfect Sacrifice.

   It will be objected that in all this chapter nothing whatever has been
proven about the existence of Jesus of Nazareth. If that is so, it is not
because we share the view that no facts concerning Jesus are recover-

able, but only because, when we have used all the historiographical
means at our disposal toward factual reconstruction of the history of
Jesus, we feel very unsure, in relation to New Testament life and faith
and theology, about what kind of reality we then have in our possession. Exponents of the "new quest" for their part will maintain that it
is incumbent upon us, allying scientific historical analysis with "existentialist historiography," to test whether the writers of the New Testament have not indeed deformed the figure of the historical Jesus by importing into it their kerygmatic ideas of the Christ. If we have not
taken their way in trying to grasp the selfhood, the meaning, the intention of the historical Jesus, it is not only because we feel unhappy
about the alliance they propose, but also because, inasmuch as we
cannot be absolutely certain as historians that it is the selfhood of
Jesus and not of the "kerygmatized" Jesus Christ we have grasped,
we lean toward Bo Reicke's conviction that "it is only by vivisection
that history may be separated from kerygma in the Gospels; but it is
highly doubtful that such a difference ever existed." [100]

In particular we have said very little about the words of Jesus, his
parables, his ethical teaching, his message as a whole. It is not that the
decisive significance of his words can be discounted: he alone has "the
words of eternal life." But some counterbalance is needed to the contemporary desire to read off the meaning of Jesus' existence from his
words alone. It could be true that recent German New Testament
scholarship, in reaction against Bultmann's denigration of the Synoptics and his setting up of John and, secondarily, Paul as the norm of
New Testament theology, has tended to go too far in according to the
Synoptics a place of supremacy over against the other New Testament writings. It could be true also that it would be beneficial for us
to renew in ourselves with fresh zeal the sense that the Synoptics are
bound together with the rest of the New Testament by the fact that all
alike testify to the unique *act* and *deed* of a unique person and life.
There is much in favor of Dr. Leonard Hodgson's view: "The divine
revelation is given in acts rather than in words and is received by those
whose eyes God opens to see the significance of what he does. The
eyes of the Biblical writers were opened to see the significance of certain events as the key-feature for the understanding of the universe." [101] And as a corollary of this, from the perspective of the
Christian life and in face of current restrictive stresses on the spoken
word and the kerygma, there come to mind the memorably simple

words of T. W. Manson: "It is still true that the best propaganda for genuine Christianity is genuine Christians; and the New Testament is full of declarations of the convincing power, not of the spoken word, but of the lived life." [102]

The unity of history and kerygma, about which we have been speaking, in all New Testament confessions, the kerygma's identification of the humiliated and exalted Jesus Christ, can be and has been described in a variety of terminologies. In the jargon of the day, we may say that *Historie* has been taken up and absorbed in *Geschichte* so as to become a permanent possibility for *Geschichte,* through Christ's Resurrection and Exaltation.[103] Again, in his admirable exercise on New Testament Christology, *Lordship and Discipleship,* E. Schweizer has shown, with persuasive exegetical arguments, that the early Church consistently knit together the "for us" of the earthly Jesus' life and death and the "with us" of the presence of the exalted Christ. I may be permitted to quote part of his concluding statement, because it seems to me to be especially relevant to our contemporary theological situation:

> Both assertions [the "for us" and the "with us"] have come from the same source. The picture of Jesus who called the disciples to follow him and walked with them on the roads of Palestine has retained its force. It has guarded the Church against lapsing into a merely academic acceptance of a *doctrine* of atonement and into an enthusiastic Gnosis, thinking in purely physical terms. It has also saved her from a corruption of the message into an ethic determined by an example, or a morality exemplified in the figure of a teacher. It has determined her preaching through all the changing stages of development. . . . Thus the exalted Lord accompanies his Church through decades and through centuries, as he accompanied his disciples when he walked on earth.[104]

May we not say, in the simplest language, that the Lord of the Church, and the one who, the Church believes, is and will be the Lord of the world, has human features? His visage is "marred more than the visage of any man." The *humanity* of the Church's Lord is vividly symbolized in an episode recounted by Sacheverell Sitwell: on visiting the temple of Christ Pantocrator in Athens, he experienced an irresistible longing, he tells us, to climb into the dimly-lit dome and strike matches in order to see more clearly the lines of agony on the face of the all-conquering Christ. In a talk entitled "Why I Believe," given shortly before his death, Dr. John White, distinguished Scottish churchman, declared quite simply: "In believing, I met *a Man*." The essence of faith in the New Testament is that it has to live with the scandal of humanity. Faith is inextricably linked, as all confessional statements affirm, with the historical Jesus of Nazareth. And that is so even though the concrete events, to which faith is anchored, cannot be exactly recovered and even though historical data for the reconstruction of his earthly life are lacking, for their character as events is not thereby altered. We need look only, for instance, at the notion of Christ's continuing ministry of intercession "for us," as it is graphically portrayed in the Epistle to the Hebrews: one could wish it were more regarded and studied by present-day theologians. If ever the theology dominated by existence philosophy, with its disinterest in and unconcern for the completely human features of our Lord, were to infiltrate the life of the churches in any strength, would they not very soon go hungry for want of the humanity of the Son of God?

Conclusion

In the preceding chapter I have not thought to try to penetrate behind
the testimony of the Gospels and the other New Testament documents
in order to recover the historical facts about Jesus of Nazareth as they
actually happened. It is not that I believe, like many today, that the
question of what actually happened can be or ought to be stifled,
almost before it is asked, in the interests of a sound theology. Despite
all difficulties inherent in the nature of sources in which history and
"kerygmatic" interpretation are indissolubly united, I do not think it is
either theologically unjustifiable or critically hopeless to seek for historical knowledge. Faith is most closely associated with a concrete history, a person and a life, and is therefore naturally interested in attempting to see more clearly the historical reality that lies behind the
tradition. The historian who sets himself by all available critical
means to get at the facts does not seem to me thereby necessarily to
be taking the way of unbelief or playing truant to genuine faith by
seeking false security in worldly knowledge. He commits no crime,
when, as part of his desire to give a "reason for the faith that is in
him," he devotes himself to a profounder understanding of the history
of God's presence in Jesus of Nazareth, out of which faith has come
to life.

Although the facts behind the New Testament tradition are very
hard to come by, the facts are there. Nor is the wish to uncover them
so reprehensible as the extravagant anti-historical bias of recent theological trends would make out. Indeed, it is not easy to comprehend

307

why, in our generation in particular, the facts of the past should be so despised and the realm of "meaning" prematurely thrust to the forefront. It is not permitted to the average citizen of our day to set eyes upon any stockpile of nuclear weapons. Yet the weapons are surely there as one of the grimmest facts of our situation in the world, and the future historian will have to take account of this fact, threatening and fearful to everyone, in dealing with our time. In an analogous way this is also true in the area of the New Testament. Even if in this sphere the underlying facts are not immediately open to the historian's view, they are there, and I do not think they should be ranked as low as they have been lately. There is need for us to urge, in regard to the tasks of exegesis and preaching, the importance of the empirical-historical over against the existential-historical. Professor Vincent Taylor recently described his career as historical-critical researcher as a period of unremitting labor in "the basement of the temple of faith." It is good for us to remember at this stage that, even if the crown of faith may not be won for us through what can be established by our historical researches, nevertheless the basement of the temple of faith is very close to its foundations.

In spite of what we have said, we can hardly fail to recognize that, while the course of historical criticism itself, with its unabated zeal for the establishment of the facts and its development of ever new skills over a long period, has greatly enriched our understanding, it has also made us see that our historical knowledge of the facts about Jesus of Nazareth has become more and more uncertain. It is no longer possible to imagine that, with anything like the abandon of our predecessors, we can plunge straight into the Gospels and come up with indisputably historical information concerning Jesus. In view of what we now know of the nature of our Gospel sources, it may be that the greatest gains for the future are to be made from what might be called "indirect" Jesus-research. By this I mean that we are called upon to apply ourselves with all vigor to garnering such knowledge as we can from the religious, social, cultural, and political history of Jesus' day in order to shed light upon the life of Jesus itself by shedding light upon the circumstances that surrounded it. As we suggested in an earlier chapter, the death of Jesus is, and must remain, a most crucial point for historical inquiry. Whereas it is not within the historian's province to demonstrate the truth of what from the first the Church believed, that in that death God Himself had sacrificed Himself, he may yet, by constant and repeated investigation of the nexus of events that led up to and surrounded the Crucifixion, bring us the perennial reminder that the road on which faith holds God's history with men to have been worked out is a road of shame and offense on the human plane. Paul Winter's recent book on *The Trial of Jesus* [1] is a remarkable example of what can be done in this field.

Beyond that, new and exciting possibilities have been opening up for the revision of old knowledge and the acquisition of fresh knowledge in regard to the historical matrix within which Jesus lived and died, within which the Church arose and the faith was cradled. Earlier pretensions about the direct bearing of the Dead Sea Scrolls on our historical knowledge of Jesus "as he actually was" have given way to much more cautious and reserved scholarly estimates; but, clearly, enough has been gleaned already from the increasing stock of remains of Judaism that have of late come down to us to dispel some of the hitherto darker spots on the map of the Intertestamental period and to offer us surer guideposts to the links between Judaism and the early Church's life and worship, faith and tradition. The importance of all this for a better understanding of the life of Jesus is not to be underrated. Studies of the Gospel tradition emanating from Scandinavian sources bid fair to introduce a new era of interrogation of the axioms of Form-criticism. Birger Gerhardsson's recent work entitled *Memory and Manuscript: Oral Tradition and Written Transmission in Rabbinic Judaism and Early Christianity* is an outstanding case in point.[2] His purpose is to renew the question of the *Sitz im Leben* of the Gospel tradition, and he discerns it in an institution in the primitive Church analogous to the transmission of the oral tradition in contemporary Rabbinical Judaism. The first part of his thesis is given to an intensive examination of the process of the handing on of both written and oral torah in late Judaism. Our attention is drawn to the provisions made for the accurate preservation of the written torah in the organizations of the School of Scribes, the elementary school, and the synagogue, as well as to the stress placed on correct memorizing of pivotal texts, in the transmission of the oral torah, through repeated verbal recitation by both teacher and pupil. In regard to the oral torah, two sources can be detected: a sayings-tradition passing on the words of the great rabbis and a narrative tradition whereby the deeds of the rabbis could be remembered as models for imitation. The second, and more controversial, part of Gerhardsson's thesis is an attempt to trace

in primitive Christianity, on the basis of the writings of the early
Church Fathers, of Luke, and of Paul, an institution similar to that
which guarded and governed the transmission of the tradition in late
Jewish life. His argument, as it affects the New Testament, has three
main facets. First, the apostolic collegium in Jerusalem, comparable
to the general session of the Qumran community and the rabbinic
academies, acted as the custodian of "the word of the Lord," which in
Acts appears almost to be an independent entity and is synonymous
with the tradition concerning Christ (Acts 6:7; 12:24; 19:20). In
Acts 15 the collegium of the apostles can be observed disposing cases
and making judgments in rabbinical fashion. Second, Paul leaves us in
no doubt, if only by the rabbinical terms reflected in the Greek words
he uses for the "reception" and "transmission" of tradition, that he is
aware of constituting a link in the chain along which is passed the
Christian "word" or tradition (I Cor. 11:23 ff.; 15:3 ff.). Moreover,
he seems to offer decisions on special problems or cases after the manner of the rabbis (I Cor. 7:1 ff.; 9:1 ff.; 11:2 ff.). Third, while the
primitive Church saw in Jesus much more than simply a teacher, and
indeed worshiped him as risen Lord and Christ, it always remembered that he had taught and had replaced the oral torah of Judaism
with a radical reinterpretation of his own, a reinterpretation that consisted not only of his words but of his deeds. In the two decades after
the Resurrection the apostolic collegium in Jerusalem found itself
engaged in multifarious activities that called for the remembrance and
application to whatever exigencies arose in the Christian community
of Old Testament texts and of sayings and acts of Jesus. As a result
of this process, the Jesus-tradition was transmitted orally by the collegium in Jerusalem in a quite methodical way.

Gerhardsson's presentation, in its wealth of detail and constructive
arguments, may well create for many a new presumption in favor of
the historicity of the Gospel tradition, or at the least a new questioning,
as we have said, of the verdicts of Form-criticism. But the question of
the existence in the earliest Church of an institution bordering on the
nature of a Christian rabbinate will be much discussed. And, even if
the hypothesis of such an institution were more surely established than
it has been through the evidence adduced by Gerhardsson, there would
still be no final guarantee of sure access for us to the *ipsissima verba et
acta Jesu*. For it may be felt that insufficient consideration has been
given to the influence of the Church's Easter faith on the shaping of

the tradition through the notably "kerygmatic" interpretation or theological formulation that has affected many of the sayings of Jesus.
While any new historical assurance we might win on the idea of an
unadulterated transmission of the Jesus-tradition would still leave the
problem of the relation of historical knowledge to faith or theology
delicately poised in the balance, the importance of such studies as
Gerhardsson's is not only that they lead us to the re-examination of
old hypotheses, but that they may enhance our understanding of Jesus
and his Church by enhancing our understanding of the world of their
environment.

On the other side, studies in the Mystery Religions of Hellenism and
in Gnosticism in particular are bound to occupy a strategic place in
the next generation. Already Günter Wagner has extensively examined
the "Mystery Religions hypothesis" in regard to the notion of baptism
into Christ in Romans 6:1–11 and has sought the sources of Paul's
thought elsewhere.[3] Carsten Colpe has been subjecting to the closest
scrutiny the generalizing conclusions that became current coin on the
basis of the researches of the History of Religions schools and particularly of R. Reitzenstein, who posited a pre-Christian Gnostic redeemer
myth that had a profound impact upon the primitive Church in its
expressions of its Christology. Colpe has, in fact, been suggesting an
inverse order of influence.[4]

Much more could be added. In a great many ways efforts are being
made to wrestle with the facts of the world of the surroundings of
Jesus or of Paul and the early Church. It is to be hoped that the rather
select group of scholars who are engaging in a lively debate on Biblical
hermeneutics, with their philosophical interest in the phenomena of
language and their appeal to the later Heidegger as an aid to the understanding of Biblical hermeneutical problems, will not allow their
philosophical preoccupations to take too much pride of place over
empirical concern for and sober historical study of Christian origins.
Sober historical study of the matrix within which Christianity arose,
that is not necessarily articulated along any single modern philosophical line, may best serve to illumine the concrete human factors
operative in the mediation of grace and the decisions involved for
faith.

I do not suppose that many will cavil at our plea for the significance
of "indirect" Jesus-research. It is, however, in relation to "direct"
Jesus-research, to the historians' attempts at factual reconstruction of

the life and history of Jesus for the Gospel tradition, that the "history
and faith" problem has been most acutely felt by our generation. In
the foregoing pages we have frequently raised the pressing question of
what kind of reality we have in our hand, when with the help of all
the historical-critical apparatus at our disposal, we have drawn from
the tradition our factual portraits of Jesus. The truth is that the once
straightforward word "facts" has itself become problematical and
ambiguous. Champions of the "new historiography" have been telling
us insistently that genuine historical inquiry into the facts must be and
is inquiry into what is exposed in the facts.[5] And thereby hangs a tale.
Such theologians as Bultmann and Brunner have implied that, inasmuch as the critical historian applies himself to the rediscovery of
"Jesus as he actually was," he approaches the subject with his mind
and not his will, and in concerning himself with Jesus as a figure who
can be described by a cold and detached scientific criticism, he fails to
relate himself existentially to the past. Now the critical historian must
certainly confront the evidence before him with as much impartiality
and as little prejudice as possible in order to attain to such objectivity
as he can. But, since history is the sphere of the "human" or the
"personal," he may not become a mere statistician or chronicler of
dry-as-dust facts, conducting his researches at a purely impersonal
level. Even so, in the field of the New Testament, the "photographic"
kind of portrait of Jesus developed by a detached scientific criticism,
as envisaged by the theologians, would not, as Donald Baillie remarked some years ago, be real history at all.[6] Here more than anywhere else the historian needs the gifts of sympathy, understanding,
and imagination, and the insight of faith.

As I understand it, the "new quest" of the historical Jesus has
sought to fructify historico-critical method with "existentialist historiography" in a determined endeavor to convince the theologians
that by "existential openness" the historian can grasp the meaning of
Jesus' person, his selfhood, and his intention and that "history" and
"faith" need not be too sharply set against each other. But the prominence given to the "new quest" and the adverse criticism of the "old
quest" that has been a salient feature of our time should not blind us
to the fact that several of the most doughty practitioners of the latter
have been profoundly concerned about "meaning," about the divine
claim implicit in Jesus' life. Thus A. E. J. Rawlinson wrote: "It is the
historian's part to interpret the evidence, to attempt simply to under-

stand the New Testament, and to present an historical portrait. . . .
The portrait of Jesus, fairly presented, upon the basis of a legitimately
critical study of the evidence, turns out to be of such a kind as to involve and to imply a supremely staggering claim, and to challenge a
decision in terms either of faith or unfaith." [7] In his important paper
on the contemporary debate concerning the historical Jesus, J. Jeremias said much the same thing. C. H. Dodd, seeking to define historical event as "occurrence plus meaning" declared some time ago
that a series of events can only truly be apprehended when it is "apprehended in some measure from within the series and not from an entirely detached standpoint." [8] In his essay in the first volume of
Kerygma and Myth, J. Schniewind argued that there is the closest connection between historic encounter with a person and the science of
history, by which all the peculiarities of the person's life are elucidated.[9] Lastly we recall T. W. Manson's pronouncement that the greatest need of the time is for us to wrest all that we can both of fact *and
meaning* out of the three words, *Jesus Christ crucified.*

I have cited these diverse cases to show that, quite apart from
the "new quest" and its devotion to "existentialist historiography,"
there has been the frankest scholarly recognition that the historian of
the New Testament must go far beyond the collecting and cataloguing
of mere facts. The integrity of the much condemned "old quest" in
this respect ought to be more openly acknowledged than it frequently
has been lately. If, however, the "new questers" have the more relentlessly pursued the question of "meaning," it may be because they have
been the more passionately concerned to overcome the inconclusive-
ness and uncertainties of orthodox historical-critical research and to
take hold of Jesus of Nazareth with all certainty in an age of great
doubt.

The notion of the possibility of direct encounter with the person of
the historical Jesus is not, of course, a new thing. In our first chapter
we saw how, in the closing years of the last century, Martin Kähler
affirmed that the man of sensitivity, in his contact with the Biblical
narratives and quite apart from the exercise of scientific historical
criticism, can enter sympathetically into the life of the clearly defined
personality of Jesus. On a different tack, Kähler's opponent at the turn
of the century, the Ritschlian theologian, Wilhelm Herrmann, made
the impact of the inward personality of Jesus upon the minds and souls
of his disciples the very heart and center of all Christian theology. For

him the experience of the power and grace of God hinged upon the soul's encounter, definite and historical, with the concrete reality of the person of Jesus, as that reality is set forth in the New Testament. "The appearance of Jesus can become for us the expression of God's forgiveness as soon as we perceive in Him, as nowhere else, the nearness of God. It is not through long-winded dogmatic reflections that we reach the sense that we receive the forgiveness of God through Jesus; that comes into our consciousness as soon as we understand religiously, or lay hold of as a work of God upon us, the fact that the Being of this Man is part of our sphere of existence." [10] Of Herrmann, H. R. Mackintosh once wrote: "In a sense he was a 'one-idea'd' man; he was determined to know nothing, as a pathway to God, but the Person of Jesus. On this he dwelt with prophetic insistency; and whatever be the defects of his argument, from the standpoint of a fully systematic thinker, it was this which stamped his message as—in a rare degree and in the great sense—evangelical." [11] One may be pardoned for sighing a little wistfully, amid the complexities of the contemporary discussion about the historical Jesus, for this kind of evangelical simplicity.

It is instructive to compare the disposition of the "new quest" with Herrmann's stance. We observe in both the same deep concern for immediate encounter with Jesus. The "new questers," however, have resolutely sought to dissociate themselves from "psychologizing" interest in the inward personality of Jesus and to speak about his *person* and the meaning of his person in the language of "existence." Whether they have succeeded and whether Jesus' person and personality can be held apart are questions left very much open. But beyond this, the most distinctive trait of the "new quest" has been the conviction that by a consciously articulated historical methodology—the proposed alliance of "existential openness" and objective analysis—firsthand encounter with Jesus, in his unique right and authority to enunciate God, is possible. Thus Bornkamm speaks of men's confrontation with the immediacy of God's presence in the words (and deeds) of Jesus, J. M. Robinson of encountering in Jesus the actualization of eschatological existence, Fuchs and Ebeling of experiencing in Jesus the ground of the Word of God.

An obvious question arises at this point. How far can the historian *qua* historian go? When is he making historical-critical judgments and when dogmatic or theological pronouncements? The historian, in working with the Gospels, can, as I believe, show us how the historical evidence implies God's act and presence, but nothing save faith itself can grasp the implication. "No man can say Jesus is Lord, save in the Holy Spirit." The "new quest," however, in channeling into a consciously devised existential-historical method the sympathy and understanding and imagination that we have said are necessary for the historian in dealing with Jesus' life, seems to have gone beyond the limits of what the historian as historian can demonstrate about Jesus. For, whereas on one side the "new quest" seems simply to coalesce with the "old quest" in asking purely historical-critical questions, on the other it gives every impression of passing over quickly, when it has reached the end of its historical tether, into the realm of dogma and theology, and of taking the believing stand of Easter faith or of response to the kerygma, while at the same time continuing to suggest that it is really proffering us assured historical results. At any rate, the new historical movement has not succeeded in effecting the desired *rapprochement* of historical method with theology. Both Barth and Bultmann have found its desire to validate the presence of God in Jesus by historical means totally uninviting. At the opposite pole, orthodox historical critics, in so far as they have tried to understand the "new quest" at all, have probably been both puzzled and disturbed by its tie-up with existence philosophy and its tendency to fasten onto only the statements in the Gospels which confirm its own special existential view of Jesus' self-understanding.

But it would be quite unfair to begrudge the "new quest" the praise it deserves for what it has achieved. It has served to arrest the Bultmann trend toward a Docetic version of the kerygma. It has brought the historical Jesus again to the forefront of discussion, and, as some of us believe, he is still the supreme mystery and central figure of our historic religion. It could also help, if only there were real openness to the enterprise, to purge certain phases of historical criticism of their theological or "kerygmatic" insensitivity. Yet withal, if one may venture a prophecy, the "new quest," in the form in which it has lately been presented to us, scarcely seems likely to have a great future ahead. Whatever the theologians may think of it, it does not appear to provide us with a stable enough position for further advance in the historical-critical sphere of Jesus-research.

How then, we ask, can Jesus be known by us? For my part, I am forced to acknowledge that he may only come to us of a surety through

our receiving and responding to the apostolic testimony within the
context of the community's life and faith and worship. Does that mean
that one could camp down altogether happily with the dialectical theologians, who forbid us to penetrate behind the witness of the New
Testament or behind the Christ-kerygma? I do not think so. Not so
long as we respect the validity and relevance for theology of the type
of historical research on Jesus that is not bound up with any particular
modern set of philosophical presuppositions. As we have quite frequently remarked in these pages, the message of the Word made *flesh*
commits us to diligent study of a particular track of history. Not that
faith can be made dependent on the variable conclusions of even the
most diligent historical study, nor that the historian can ever place the
facts about Jesus, or indeed what is exposed in the facts, in our possession with such assurance that faith is made easier or removed from
its insecurity in the world and before God. The historian can neither
prove the Incarnation, nor show us an empty tomb, nor bring us a
risen Lord. What the historian can do by his devoted labors is this: he
may constantly protect the Church's theology from relapsing into
a-historical speculation, or into myth; he can preserve, if not authenticate, the truth that our faith and our religion are rooted and grounded
in a particular history and person and life; he can clarify the scandal
inherent in the Christian message and, by arresting us with the completely human features of our Lord, far from making faith more easy
for us, he may expose the offense with which faith must live and the
inward battle which it must continually wage in the world; renouncing
modern philosophical categories and avoiding the temptation to furnish us with theological judgments and dogmatic statements as if they
were historical proofs, he can throw some light on how Jesus' contemporaries understood him and even, to some extent, on how he may
have wished to be understood.[12]

There is, to be sure, a limit to what the historian can do: he is not
able to give us Jesus in the fullness of the mystery of his person. How
then does he come to us? The traditional answer of the Church has
been that, within the life of the community of faith and in and through
the documents of faith, the Spirit testifies to him—in the Spirit he
appears, through the preaching and under the signs of the bread and
wine of the Eucharist, for ever-renewed historical activity. It is a good
answer. Over against the extreme "individualism" of recent theological understandings of the kerygma, we need to stress today that

first and last through our membership in and place in the community of faith, the Church which is his Body, Jesus is most surely known of us. When we look back to the people of God of the Old Covenant, there, in her cultus, Israel remembered her holy past and in the spoken recital the past was made present. There also, within the community of faith, to which the individual inwardly belonged and whose shared history was the foundation of his life, men could truly *know* Yahweh, their God, and confess him as the Lord of history.[13] Even in this way to the question "Who was Jesus?" the Church answers with her praising confession. She adores her God in singing the honor of Jesus: "He lives, he lives; Christ Jesus lives today." But her most worthy praise does not end with the song of the sanctuary. There is another great truth to be added. Not only in the temple (nor indeed only in the scholar's study nor on the spectator's balcony) but on the road, Jesus comes to be most truly known. Albert Schweitzer was, I think, right when he declared that no generation of men can really be related to Jesus of Nazareth that is not genuinely concerned for the world's weal and woe.[14] Indelibly stamped on many pages of the New Testament is the word that only the disciple can know who Jesus was and is, only the follower who is already on the highway of most loyal obedience to God in the service of men.

As the Gospels relate, in his agony in Gethsemane, Jesus was bereft of the comfort and companionship of those whom he had called to follow him. "Could you not watch with me for one hour?" They could not yet share his destiny, for they did not yet "know" him. And in his final suffering on Calvary, they were still not "with him." Only later, when through their certainty of his Resurrection from the dead, Jesus himself made a new beginning with them, did they "know" him as he was and is. They were "with him" now in truth, and their knowledge of him manifested itself in the shape and direction of their lives. Making their amends for former failures, they gladly rendered him their bodily obedience and shared with him in his sufferings for the world even unto the death of martyrdom. Sharing the destiny of the humiliated one, they also shared for certain the glory of the exalted one, in the inheritance, incorruptible and undefiled, laid up for them.

We cannot miss the relevance of that for today. In a world that appears to be perishing of its own worldliness, men on every hand are asking "Where is God?" How fearful, in the face of that question, would the betrayal be, if the Church were to be found so conformed to the world as to be seeking her own comfort only from the little gods of the crowded market place! It could be that the most urgent order of the day for the Church is that she should learn to make herself expendable in obedience to the one God, through sharing in Jesus' sufferings for men. It could be that, most of all, the Church should learn, through looking up in faith to him who, as the Forerunner of all his disciples, has passed through the death of the Cross to glory, to bear on her Body the marks of the Master's Passion for the world and so to actualize his redemptive power for men that they may find in her the hidden majesty of God and thus take heart from grace. Perhaps only in learning this can we be united in the communion of true knowledge with the man, Jesus of Nazareth, whose history has been pinned down to a specific date and place in Palestine, but who is "the same, yesterday, today, and for ever."

Notes*

Introduction

1. G. von Rad, *Theologie des Alten Testaments;* Band I, *Die Theologie der geschichtlichen Überlieferungen Israels,* 2nd ed., München, 1958. Band II, *Die Theologie der prophetischen Überlieferungen Israels,* München, 1960. The first volume has been translated by D. G. Stalker, *Theology of the Old Testament,* Edinburgh and London, 1962.

2. W. Eichrodt, *Theology of the Old Testament,* Vol. I (transl. by J. A. Baker), Philadelphia, 1961, pp. 516–17. Cf. R. Rendtorff, "Hermeneutik des AT als Frage nach der Geschichte," *ZTK,* LVII (1960), 27–40. Cf. also J. M. Robinson, "Basic Shifts in German Theology," *Interpretation,* XVI (Jan. 1962), 76 ff. Robinson appeals to the view of the later Heidegger that "truth" does not lie in the categories of thought set up by the "subject," but rather in the object or, better, subject matter, breaking through from its hiddenness and unveiling itself to thought and so evoking expression in language. The notion of *Lichtungsgeschichte* or "clearing-history" is applied to the Old Testament as a means of bridging the gap between "salvation-history" and actual historical occurrences. "*Heilsgeschichte* is to be approached initially as the linguistic expression evoked by a given subject matter: the God who acts. Israelite history as God's act emerges from forgetfulness into the clearing of thought through the event of language."

3. We say so-called Jesus of history–Christ of faith problem, first, because there is a sense in which the name Jesus is "kerygmatically" employed in the N.T., as in "Lord Jesus," and, second, because on the other side it is a crucial point of discussion whether the title "Christos" properly applies to the historical

---

* Abbreviations are used for the following periodicals: *ET, Expository Times; JBL, Journal of Biblical Literature; JTS, Journal of Theological Studies; NTS, New Testament Studies; SJT, Scottish Journal of Theology; TLZ, Theologische Literaturzeitung; ZNW, Zeitschrift für die neutestamentliche Wissenschaft; ZTK, Zeitschrift für Theologie und Kirche.*

Jesus and not only to the exalted Lord of the Church's faith. *V.* W. C. van
Unnik, "Jesus the Christ," *NTS*, VIII (Jan. 1962), 101 ff.

4. M. Kähler, *Der sogenannte historische Jesus und der geschichtliche,
biblische Christus*, Leipzig, 1892. New ed., München, 1956.

5. W. Wrede, *Das Messiasgeheimnis in der Evangelien*, Göttingen, 1901.

6. A. Schweitzer, *The Quest of the Historical Jesus* (Engl. transl. by W. A.
Montgomery), 2nd Engl. ed., London, 1922.

7. J. Weiss, *Die Predigt Jesu vom Reiche Gottes*, 2. Aufl., Göttingen, 1900.

8. The view that R. Bultmann's existentialist approach came out of the negative conclusions of his historical researches is countered by H. Thielicke, who
holds that the existential interest has been a "constant" with Bultmann from
the first; *v.* "Reflections on Bultmann's Hermeneutic," *ET*, LXVII (Feb. 1956),
154. Cf. J. Macquarrie, *The Scope of Demythologizing*, New York, 1960, p. 65.
For the view that Bultmann deliberately courted negative conclusions from historical research in order to remove all worldly supports from faith, *v.* Hermann
Diem, *Dogmatics* (Engl. transl. by Harold Knight), Edinburgh, 1959, p. 90.

9. P. Althaus, *The So-called Kerygma and the Historical Jesus* (Engl. transl.
by David Cairns), Edinburgh and London, 1959, p. 42.

10. R. Bultmann, *Theology of the New Testament*, Vol. I (Engl. transl. by
K. Grobel), London, 1952, pp. 63 ff.

11. R. Bultmann, *Primitive Christianity in Its Contemporary Setting* (Engl.
transl. by R. H. Fuller), London and New York, 1956, pp. 196 ff.

12. R. Bultmann, *Jesus and the Word* (Engl. transl. of the German work,
Jesus, 1926), New York, 1960.

13. H. Thielicke, "The Restatement of New Testament Mythology," *Kerygma
and Myth*, Vol. I (Engl. transl. by R. H. Fuller), ed. H. W. Bartsch, London, 1953,
pp. 138 ff.

14. K. Barth, *R. Bultmann, Ein Versuch ihn zu verstehen*, Zürich, 1953.

15. E. Käsemann, "Das Problem des historischen Jesus," *ZTK*, LI (1954),
125–53.

16. J. M. Robinson, *A New Quest of the Historical Jesus*, London, 1959.

17. *Der historische Jesus und der kerygmatische Christus*, ed. H. Ristow and
K. Matthiae, Berlin, 1960.

18. J. M. Robinson, op. cit. p. 94.

19. E. Fuchs, "Die Theologie des Neuen Testaments und der historische
Jesus," *Zur Frage nach dem historischen Jesus*, Tübingen, 1960, p. 404; *v.* also
"Das Zeitverständnis Jesu," pp. 304 ff., and "Was ist Sprachereignis? Ein Brief,"
pp. 424 ff.

20. G. Ebeling, *Das Wesen des christlichen Glaubens*, Tübingen, 1959. English
transl. by R. Gregor Smith, *The Nature of Faith*, Philadelphia, 1961.

21. J. M. Robinson, "Neo-Liberalism" (Review of Ebeling's *Das Wesen des
christlichen Glaubens*), *Interpretation*, XV (Oct. 1961), 484 ff.

22. K. Barth, *The Humanity of God* (Engl. transl. by J. N. Thomas and
T. Weiser), Richmond, 1960, pp. 32–3.

23. R. Bultmann, "Das Verhältnis der urchristlichen Christusbotschaft zum
historischen Jesus," *Sitzungsberichte der Heidelberger Akademie der Wissenschaften*, 1960, pp. 19 ff.

24. K. Barth, "How My Mind Has Changed," *Christian Century*, LXXVII
(Jan. 20, 1960), 75.

25. H. Ott, "Die Frage nach dem historischen Jesus und die Ontologie der
Geschichte," *Theologische Studien*, Heft 62, 1962. For a valuable summary of
recent views, *v.* J. M. Robinson, "Basic Shifts in German Theology," *Interpretation*, XVI (Jan. 1962), 76 ff.

26. W. C. van Unnik, "Jesus the Christ," *NTS*, VIII (Jan. 1962), 101 ff.
27. Schubert M. Ogden, *Christ Without Myth*, New York, 1961, p. 143.

Chapter I

1. A. von Harnack, *History of Dogma*, Vol. I (Engl. transl. by Neil Buchanan), New York, 1958, p. 77.
2. A. Schweitzer, *Geschichte der paulinischen Forschung*, Tübingen, 1911.
3. M. Goguel, *The Birth of Christianity* (Engl. transl. by H. C. Snape), London, 1953, p. 1.
4. E. Käsemann, "Das Problem des historischen Jesus," *ZTK*, LI (1954), 141.
5. E. Hoskyns and F. N. Davey, *The Riddle of the New Testament*, New York, 1931, p. 14.
6. It is interesting to observe that an article entitled "Jesus or Christ?," written by Rev. R. Roberts and published in the *Hibbert Journal* of Jan. 1909, stirred quite a controversy. The outcome was a special supplement of the *Journal*, containing contributions from British and Continental scholars on this theme "Jesus or Christ?" The editorial preface states: "What is here under discussion is the whole problem of the relation of the Jesus of History to the Christ of Religion."
7. A. Schweitzer, *The Quest of the Historical Jesus*, p. 396.
8. A. Schweitzer, op. cit. p. 348.
9. Ibid. p. 369.
10. Ibid. pp. 309 and 401.
11. Ibid. p. 369.
12. Paul Althaus, op. cit. p. 16.
13. F. Buri, *Die Bedeutung der neutestamentlichen Eschatologie in der neueren protestantischen Theologie*, Zürich, 1935, pp. 170 ff.
14. F. Buri, "Entmythologisierung oder Entkerygmatisierung der Theologie," *Kerygma und Mythos*, Vol. II, ed. H. W. Bartsch, Hamburg-Volksdorf, 1952, pp. 85 ff.
15. K. Barth, *The Epistle to the Romans*, 2nd ed., London, 1921.
16. K. Barth, *Church Dogmatics*, Vol. IV, Part 2 (Engl. transl. by G. W. Bromiley), Edinburgh, 1958, pp. 149–50.
17. K. Barth, "How My Mind Has Changed," *Christian Century*, LXXVII (Jan. 20, 1960), 75.
18. K. Barth, *Church Dogmatics*, Vol. IV, Part 2, pp. 156 ff.
19. C. W. Hartlich and W. Sachs, "Kritische Prüfung der Haupteinwände Barths gegen Bultmann," *Kerygma und Mythos*, Vol. II, 1952, p. 120.
20. For example, R. R. Niebuhr, *Resurrection and Historical Reason*, New York, 1957, pp. 74 ff.
21. R. G. Collingwood, *The Idea of History*, London, 1946, p. 10; Raymond Aron, *Introduction à la philosophie de l'histoire, Essai sur les limites de l'objectivité historique*, Paris, 1937.
22. M. Kähler, op. cit. pp. 3 ff.
23. Ibid. pp. 78 f.
24. Paul Althaus, *The So-called Kerygma and the Historical Jesus*. Althaus has here attempted to revive this aspect of Kähler's position as a counterpoint to Bultmann's separation (as he holds) of the Christ of the kerygma from the historical Jesus. He reasserts the need to "hark back" to the historical Jesus as the originator of the Kyrios-Christology.
25. M. Kähler, op. cit. pp. 62 f.
26. W. Herrmann, *The Communion of the Christian with God* (Engl. transl.

by J. S. Sandys Stanyon, revised in accordance with the 4th German edition of 1903 by R. W. Stewart), London, 1930, p. 78.

27. R. Bultmann, "Welchen Sinn hat es, von Gott zu reden?" *Glauben und Verstehen*, Vol. I, 2nd ed., Tübingen, 1954, p. 33; also *Jesus Christ and Mythology*, New York, 1958. "The question of God and the question of myself are identical," p. 53.

28. For an excellent recent appraisal of Gunkel's work, *v.* James Muilenburg, "The Gains of Form Criticism in Old Testament Studies," *ET*, LXXXI (May 1960), 229 ff.

29. Bultmann acknowledges his particular indebtedness to Gunkel in Berlin: "Autobiographical Reflections," *Existence and Faith: Shorter Writings of R. Bultmann* (Engl. transl. by Schubert M. Ogden), New York, 1960, p. 284.

30. J. Wellhausen's work on the Synoptics moved in the same direction. "Without the later influence of Jesus on the community we cannot discern anything of the religious personality of Jesus. It always appears only as reflected, interrupted by the medium of the Christian faith"—*Einleitung in die drei ersten Evangelien*, Berlin, 1905, p. 114.

31. M. Albertz, *Die synoptischen Streitgespräche: ein Beitrag zur Formengeschichte des Urchristentums*, Berlin, 1921.

32. J. Jeremias, *The Parables of Jesus* (Engl. transl. by S. H. Hooke), London, 1954. C. H. Dodd has also applied the Form-criticism method of analysis to the Easter stories of the Gospels with considerable success in "The Appearances of the Risen Christ: An Essay in Form-Criticism of the Gospels," *Studies in the Gospels: Essays in Memory of R. H. Lightfoot*, Oxford, 1955.

33. There was, however, a positive side. *V.* Vincent Taylor's estimate in his *The Formation of the Gospel Tradition*, London, 1933, pp. 20–21. "Form-Criticism has certainly succeeded in pointing out definite narrative forms which meet us in popular tradition, and has made important suggestions regarding the life-story of these and the causes which gave them shape. But its most valuable service is that it helps us to penetrate the hinterland of the decades from 30 to 50 A.D. and place ourselves in imagination among the young Palestinian communities."

34. R. H. Lightfoot, *History and Interpretation in the Gospels*, London, 1934, p. 225.

35. R. Bultmann, *Der Begriff der Offenbarung im Neuen Testament*, Tübingen, 1929, p. 25.

36. Bruno Bauer, *Kritik der Evangelien und Geschichte ihres Ursprungs*, 2 vols., Berlin, 1850–51.

37. Paul-Louis Couchoud, *The Creation of Christ: An Outline of the Beginnings of Christianity* (Engl. transl. by C. Bradlaugh Bonner of *Jésus, Dieu fait homme*), London, 1939.

38. M. Goguel, *Jesus the Nazarene—Myth or History?* (Engl. transl. by F. Stephens), New York, 1926. Goguel argued (1) that if Paul's Christ had been a purely spiritual and celestial Being, he would never have contradicted himself by connecting his Messiah with a human lineage; (2) that there was an organic connection between the preaching of Jesus and the Church's doctrine of salvation; (3) that the development of Christology grew directly out of the impression Jesus himself had made on his disciples; (4) that no early pagan or Jewish polemic had denied that Jesus actually lived. In attacking Couchoud, Goguel addressed himself at the same time to the parallel views of P. Alfaric, "Christianisme et Gnosticisme," *Revue d'Histoire*, CXLV (1924), and Salomon Reinach, *Orpheus*, 1909 (Engl. transl. by Florence Simmonds, New York, 1930).

39. S. Kierkegaard, *Philosophical Fragments* (Engl. transl. by David Swenson), Princeton, 1936, p. 87.

40. R. Bultmann, "Das Verhältnis der urchristlichen Christusbotschaft zum historischen Jesus," *Sitzungsberichte der Heidelberger Akademie der Wissenschaften*, Heidelberg, 1960.

41. R. Bultmann, "New Testament and Mythology," *Kerygma and Myth*, Vol. I (Engl. transl. by R. H. Fuller), ed. H. W. Bartsch, London, 1953, pp. 17–33; also *Jesus Christ and Mythology*, New York, 1958.

42. K. Barth, *Rudolf Bultmann: Ein Versuch ihn zu verstehen*, Zürich, 1953, p. 17. Available in translation by R. H. Fuller, *Kerygma and Myth*, Vol. II, ed. H. W. Bartsch, London, 1962, pp. 83 ff.

43. O. Eissfeldt, "Religionsgeschichtliche Schule," *Die Religion in Geschichte und Gegenwart: Handwörterbuch für Theologie und Religionswissenschaft*, ed. by H. Gunkel and L. Zscharnak, 2nd ed., Tübingen, 1927–32, Vol. IV, col. 1900.

44. Cf. W. Heitmüller, "Zum Problem Paulus und Jesus," *ZNW* (1912), p. 330; also W. Bousset, *Kyrios Christos*, 3rd ed., Göttingen, 1926, pp. 75 ff.

45. A. Schweitzer, *Die Mystik des Apostels Paulus*, Tübingen, 1930, p. 31. Engl. transl., *The Mysticism of Paul the Apostle*, London, 1931.

46. W. Heitmüller, "Zum Problem Paulus und Jesus," p. 331; H. J. Schoeps, *Paul: The Theology of the Apostle in the Light of Jewish Religious History* (Engl. transl. by H. Knight), Philadelphia, 1961, p. 62.

47. C. H. Dodd, *History and the Gospel*, New York, 1938, pp. 53–4.

48. A. Deissmann, *Light from the Ancient East* (Engl. transl. by L. R. M. Strachan), London, 1927, pp. 349–62.

49. W. Bousset, op. cit. p. 99.

50. Kurt Rudolph's recent two-volume work on the Mandeans postulates and defends a pre-Christian date for the Mandean myth: *Die Mandäer*, Göttingen, 1960–61. The difficulty of controlling the available evidence so as to arrive at a firm conclusion in this respect is, I think, still apparent in Rudolph's study. Forty and more years ago, R. Reitzenstein held that Mandeism was Christian and acted as a channel for the transmission of Iranian ideas into Christianity—*Das mandäische Buch des Herrn der Grosse und die Evangelien-überlieferung*, 1919. The publication of Mandean texts by M. Lidzbarski (*Das Johannesbuch der Mandäer*, 1905 and 1915; *Mandäische Liturgien*, 1920; *Ginza: Der Schatz oder das grosse Buch der Mandäer*, 1925) was followed by what M. Goguel called "une fièvre mandéenne." The influence of the "Mandean hypothesis" regarding Christian origins was clearly discernible in Walter Bauer's *Das Johannesevangelium* (Handbuch zum Neuen Testament, 6), 2. Aufl., 1925, as it is in Bultmann's commentary on the Fourth Gospel. For opposition to the theory of Mandean influence on primitive Christianity, v. A. Loisy, *Le Mandéisme et les origines chrétiennes*, 1934; M.-J. Lagrange, "La Gnose mandéenne et la tradition évangélique," *Revue Biblique*, 1928, p. 36. *V.* also C. H. Dodd, *The Interpretation of the Fourth Gospel*, Cambridge, 1953.

51. C. H. Dodd, op. cit. p. 97; R. McL. Wilson, *The Gnostic Problem*, London, 1958, pp. 65–9; Johannes Munck, "The New Testament and Gnosticism," *Current Issues in New Testament Interpretation*, ed. William Klassen and Graydon Snyder, New York, 1962, p. 234.

52. R. M. Grant, *Gnosticism and Early Christianity*, New York, 1959.

53. R. Reitzenstein, *Die hellenistischen Mysterienreligionen*, Leipzig, 1927, p. 56.

54. W. D. Davies, *Paul and Rabbinic Judaism*, London, 1955, pp. 260–68.

55. Bultmann has of course readily conceded that there are clear points of

difference between Gnosticism and early Christianity. Especially significant for him is the contrast between Gnosticism's call to repentance and the call present in Christian preaching. Gnosticism's summons to become aware of one's alienation from the world can only be given a positive turn by the furnishing of mystagogical or cosmological instruction, and so lacks the urgency of Christian preaching's call to decision—*Primitive Christianity in Its Contemporary Setting* (Engl. transl. by R. H. Fuller), London and New York, 1956, p. 201. Yet the main weight of Bultmann's emphasis is on the Gnostic character of the Pauline kerygma (which has been somewhat naïvely interwoven with Jewish apocalyptic elements), and in this Bultmann resembles Reitzenstein and is rather less reserved than Bousset.

56. Cf. R. McL. Wilson, *The Gnostic Problem*, p. 76.

57. On the Gnostic side of the hotly disputed question, *v.* H. Schlier, *Christus und die Kirche im Epheserbrief*, Tübingen, 1930; E. Käsemann, *Leib und Leib Christi*, Tübingen, 1932; R. Bultmann, *Theology of the New Testament*, Vol. I, London, 1955, pp. 192 ff. For other views, *v.* J. A. T. Robinson, *The Body*, London, 1952, pp. 55 ff.; E. Schweizer, "The Church as the Missionary Body of Christ," *NTS*, VIII (Oct. 1961), 5–6. Schweizer does not admit the Gnostic thesis as a possibility.

58. J. M. Robinson, "Basic Shifts in German Theology," *Interpretation*, XVI (Jan. 1962), 79.

59. R. Bultmann, *Primitive Christianity in Its Contemporary Setting*, p. 197.

60. Ibid. p. 201.

61. Cf. A. E. J. Rawlinson, *The New Testament Doctrine of the Christ*, New York, 1926, p. 90, n. 5: "For St. Paul there is only one Christ—Jesus of Nazareth. What he is repudiating is not a fleshly kind of Christ but a fleshly kind of knowledge." *V.* also W. D. Davies's refutation of Reitzenstein's view that Paul no longer needs to know Jesus after the flesh since he is already subject to "spirit" and is undergoing a metamorphosis from glory to glory—*Paul and Rabbinic Judaism*, pp. 194 ff.

62. G. Koch, *Die Auferstehung Jesu Christi*, Tübingen, 1959, p. 147.

63. Donald Baillie, *God Was in Christ*, New York, 1948, p. 49.

64. R. Bultmann, "Die Bedeutung der neuerschlossenen mandäischen und manichäischen Quellen für das Verständnis des Johannesevangeliums," *ZNW*, XXIV (1925), 100–146.

65. For example, John 5:28 f.; 6:51–8 and similar minor additions. R. Bultmann, *Primitive Christianity in Its Contemporary Setting*, p. 231, n. 23. *V.* also *Das Evangelium des Johannes* (Meyer: Kritisch-exegetischer Kommentar), 11th ed., Göttingen, 1950.

66. G. H. C. Macgregor, *The Gospel of John* (Moffatt N.T. Commentaries), London, 1940, p. xxxvii. E. Käsemann has recently sought to show the affinity between the positive concern of the primitive Christian apocalyptic outlook with history and the Fourth Gospel: "Die Anfänge christlicher Theologie," *ZTK*, LVII (1960), 176.

67. N. A. Dahl, "The Johannine Church and History," *Current Issues in New Testament Interpretation*, ed. William Klassen and Graydon Snyder, New York, 1962, pp. 131–32. Dahl seems to me to be correct in stating that in the context of chapter 12, where John is alluding to the teaching and work of the earthly Jesus, the reference in 12:41, "Isaiah said this because he saw his glory and spoke of him," can only be to the incarnate and crucified life of Jesus of Nazareth.

68. Although it would be widely agreed that there are traces of a "Gnostic" tendency in the sect of the Dead Sea Scrolls, it would be safe to say, at the present stage of development of Qumran studies, that the sect is not to be considered

Gnostic. There is much to commend the view that the Scrolls' stress on *knowledge*, as knowledge of God's glories in creation, of the fulfillment of prophecy, and of the laws revealed by God to man, can be explained from a Hebrew background, and that therefore we have to be extremely careful in positing a direct relationship between the Scrolls and any fully developed Gnosticism. K. G. Kuhn, *ZTK*, XLIX (1952), 200 ff., 296 ff.; W. D. Davies, *Harvard Theological Review*, XLVI (1953),113 ff.

69. C. K. Barrett, *The New Testament Background: Selected Documents*, New York, 1961, p. 91. Cf. H. J. Schoeps, *Paul*, p. 20: "We know too little about the character of these mysteries to be in a position to make a material comparison between them and the Christian ones."

70. W. Bauer, *Rechtgläubigkeit und Ketzerei im ältesten Christentum*, Tübingen, 1934.

71. Cf. Helmut Köster, "Häretiker im Urchristentum," *Die Religion in Geschichte und Gegenwart*, 3rd ed., 1959, 17–21. In direct contrast with Schmithals, Köster points up the distinction between the various heretical tendencies Paul encountered in his different congregations, e.g. in Galatia, Judaizers of the Diaspora, whose brand of syncretism had been subjected to Oriental influences; in I Corinthians, a group who were more definitely of a true gnosticizing type.

72. H. Jonas, *Gnosis and spätantiker Geist*, Vol. I, Göttingen, 1934. Vol. II, Part I, appeared in 1954.

73. H. Jonas, *The Gnostic Religion*, Boston, 1958, p. 33.

74. Ibid. p. 17.

75. *Evangelium Veritatis*, ed. by M. Malinine, H.-C. Puech, G. Quispel, Zürich, 1956. *V.* R. M. Grant, *Gnosticism and Early Christianity*, New York, 1959, pp. 6–13.

76. J. Munck, "The New Testament and Gnosticism," *Current Issues in New Testament Interpretation*, ed. William Klassen and Graydon Snyder, New York, 1962, p. 234. To Munck's essay I owe a good deal more than these few words.

77. Günter Wagner, *Das religionsgeschichtliche Problem von Römer 6:1–11*, Zürich, 1962. *V.* also W. D. Davies, *Paul and Rabbinic Judaism*, pp. 88 ff.

78. C. Colpe, "Gnosis I. Religionsgeschichtlich," *Die Religion in Geschichte und Gegenwart*, 3rd ed., Vol. II, 1648–52.

79. E. Bevan, "The Gnostic Redeemer," *Hellenism and Christianity*, London, 1932, Essay V, pp. 89 ff.

80. F. C. Burkitt, *Church and Gnosis*, Cambridge, 1932.

81. R. Bultmann, "New Testament and Mythology," *Kerygma and Myth*, Vol. I, ed. H. W. Bartsch, p. 15.

82. R. Bultmann, *Theology of the New Testament*, Vol. II (Engl. transl. by K. Grobel), London, 1955, pp. 33 ff., and especially p. 49.

83. Donald Baillie, *God Was in Christ*, New York, 1948, p. 53.

84. Karl Barth, *Church Dogmatics*, Vol. IV, Part 2 (Engl. transl. by G. W. Bromiley), Edinburgh, pp. 154 ff.

Chapter II

1. E. Stauffer, *Jesus and His Story* (Engl. transl. by Richard and Clara Winston), New York, 1960.

2. Ibid. pp. vii-xiv.

3. Ibid. pp. 152–3.

4. Ibid. pp. 143–5.

5. E. Stauffer, "Entmythologisierung oder Realtheologie," *Kerygma und Mythos*, Vol. II, ed. H. W. Bartsch, Hamburg-Volksdorf, 1952, pp. 16–17.

6. Amos Wilder, "Biblical Hermeneutic and American Scholarship," *Neutestamentliche Studien für Rudolf Bultmann*, ed. W. Eltester, Berlin, 1954, p. 27.

7. R. Niebuhr, "How My Mind Has Changed," *Christian Century*, May 11, 1960, p. 568.

8. Schubert M. Ogden, *Christ Without Myth*, New York, 1961, p. 131, n. 4.

9. S. J. Case, *The Social Origins of Christianity*, Chicago, 1923, p. 1.

10. A. Wikgren, "History and Scripture," *Early Christian Origins*, ed. A. Wikgren, Chicago, 1961, p. 143.

11. S. J. Case, *The Evolution of Early Christianity*, Chicago, 1914. p. 25.

12. C. T. Craig, "The Apostolic Kerygma in the Christian Message," *Journal of Bible and Religion*, XX (July 1952), 185.

13. Amos Wilder, "Biblical Hermeneutic and American Scholarship," op cit. p. 30.

14. F. C. Grant, *Ancient Judaism and the New Testament*, New York, 1959. In an age of "Iron Curtains" and intolerance on a grand scale, one has the greatest respect for Dr. Grant's appeal for a Christianity that is truly catholic in outlook and truly concerned for men of every race and creed, and also, at the critical level, for his continuing advocacy of the Jewish emphasis in Christianity.

15. Otto J. Baab, *The Theology of the Old Testament*, New York, 1949.

16. R. H. Pfeiffer, *Religion in the Old Testament: the History of a Spiritual Triumph* (ed. C. C. Forman), New York, 1961.

17. Early Christian Origins, ed. A. Wikgren, Chicago, 1961.

18. A. Barnett, "Jesus as Theologian," ibid. p. 18: "His knowledge and power come to focus in his administration of creation in the interest of the welfare of persons."

19. Ibid. pp. 22–3.

20. Ibid. p. 16.

21. A. Kalthoff, *Das Christusproblem grundlinien zu einer Sozialtheologie*, Leipzig, 1902.

22. E. Troeltsch, *The Social Teaching of the Christian Churches*, Vol. I (Engl. transl. by Olive Wyon), New York, 1931, pp. 43 ff.

23. Ibid. pp. 57 ff.

24. F. C. Grant, "The Economic Background of the New Testament," *The Background of the New Testament and Its Eschatology*, ed. W. D. Davies and D. Daube, Cambridge, 1956, p. 101.

25. A. N. Wilder, "Early Christian Eschatology," *Early Christian Origins*, ed. A. Wikgren, Chicago, 1961, p. 75.

26. John Macquarrie, *The Scope of Demythologizing*, p. 244.

27. J. Lowe, "The Recovery of the Theological Interpretation of the Bible," *The Interpretation of the Bible*, ed. C. W. Dugmore, London, 1944, pp. 118–19.

28. C. H. Dodd, *The Apostolic Preaching and Its Developments*, London, 1936, p. 78.

29. C. H. Dodd, *Thirty Years of New Testament Study* (Inaugural Lecture), Cambridge, 1936.

30. C. H. Dodd, *The Apostolic Preaching and Its Developments*, p. 55.

31. Ibid. pp. 47 and 52.

32. Ibid. p. 46. *V.* also C. H. Dodd, "The Framework of the Gospel Narrative," *ET*, XLIII (June 1932), 396 ff.

33. J. M. Robinson, *A New Quest of the Historical Jesus*, London, 1959, p. 58.

34. C. H. Dodd, *The Apostolic Preaching and Its Developments*, p. 20. *V.* also

J. de Zwaan, *The Beginnings of Christianity*, ed. F. Jackson and K. Lake, Part I, Vol. II, London, 1922, pp. 30–65.

35. The essay appeared first in Εὐχαριστήριον *für Hermann Gunkel*, II, pp. 27–49, and was reprinted in *Aufsätze zur Apostelgeschichte*, ed. H. Greeven, 2nd ed., Berlin, 1953, pp. 9–28 (Engl. transl. by Mary Ling, *Studies in the Acts of the Apostles*, New York, 1956).

36. Cf. H. J. Cadbury, "The Speeches of Acts," *The Beginnings of Christianity*, Vol. V, ed. K. Lake and H. J. Cadbury, 1933, pp. 402–27. The same position is reflected here.

37. Ph. Vielhauer, "Zum 'Paulinismus' der Apostelgeschichte," *Evangelische Theologie*, 10, n.f. No. 5 (1950–51), pp. 1–15.

38. H. Conzelmann, *The Theology of St. Luke* (Engl. transl. by G. Buswell), London, 1960. *V.* also "Zur Lukasanalyse," *ZTK*, XLIX (1952), 16–33, and "Die Rede des Paulus auf dem Areopag," *Gymnasium Helveticum*, XII (1958), 18–32.

39. For further details on the shift of perspective in Lucan studies, *v.* Ernst Haenchen, *Die Apostelgeschichte*, 12th ed., Göttingen, 1959, pp. 37 ff. Haenchen speaks of himself as having, in the tenth edition of his work, joined the chorus of these voices, albeit with moderation. *V.* also J. M. Robinson, *A New Quest of the Historical Jesus*, pp. 58–9, n. 1. C. F. Evans also comes down on the side of Dibelius's view of the speeches in Acts, "The Kerygma," *JTS*, new series, VII (April 1956), 25–41. On the conservative side, however, the case against the "Thucydidean assumptions" concerning Lucan historiography has been continued: *v.* N. B. Stonehouse, *Paul before the Areopagus and other New Testament Studies*, London, 1957, where an attempt is made to refute Dibelius's position, pp. 1–40 and 151–85; C. S. C. Williams, *The Acts of the Apostles* (Black's N.T. Commentaries), 1957; in the commentary on Acts in the *Interpreter's Bible*, G. H. C. Macgregor says a *cautious* "Yes" to Lucan authorship of the speeches. Most recently H. N. Ridderbos has seen the lack of developed theology in the speeches as a mark of reliable historiography and not inventive genius, *The Speeches of Peter in the Acts of the Apostles* (Tyndale Lecture), London, 1962, p. 9. A. M. Hunter, *Paul and His Predecessors*, 2nd ed., Philadelphia, 1961, follows Dodd in thinking of the speeches in Acts as preserving an outline of the kerygma recognizably in line with a received N.T. substructure. S. S. Smalley holds that, although we cannot confirm the reliability of Luke's use of sources in his second volume, there is no *prima facie* reason for assuming that it differs widely from its character in the first; we have to distinguish, in the methodology of Luke's historiography, between summary edition and *ab initio* invention— S. S. Smalley, "The Christology of Acts," *ET*, LXXIII (1962), No. 12, pp. 358 ff. The debate continues, with the main weight still on the trend initiated by Dibelius.

40. C. H. Dodd, *The Bible To-day*, New York, 1947, p. 96.

41. C. H. Dodd, *History and the Gospel*, New York, 1938, p. 105. *V.* R. R. Niebuhr, *Resurrection and Historical Reason*, New York, 1957, pp. 24–5.

42. V. Taylor, *The Person of Christ in New Testament Teaching*, London–New York, 1958, p. 305.

43. Ibid. p. 271.

44. Ibid. pp. 186 and 301.

45. Ibid. p. 306.

46. A. M. Farrer, *St. Matthew and St. Mark*, London, 1954; P. Carrington, *The Primitive Christian Calendar*, Cambridge, 1952. *V.* V. Taylor, *The Life and Ministry of Jesus*, Nashville, 1955, pp. 37–44.

47. M. Goguel, *Jesus and the Origins of Christianity*, Vol. II: *The Life of Jesus* (Engl. transl. by Olive Wyon), New York (Harper Torchbooks), 1960, p. v.

48. V. Taylor, *The Life and Ministry of Jesus*, pp. 35 and 186.

49. Ibid. pp. 152 ff.
50. T. W. Manson, "The Foundation of Christianity," *Church Quarterly Review*, XI (1933), 12.
51. T. W. Manson, "Is It Possible To Write a Life of Christ?" *ET*, LIII (1941–42), 251.
52. T. W. Manson, "The Life of Jesus: Some Tendencies in Present-Day Research," *The Background of the New Testament and Its Eschatology*, ed. W. D. Davies and D. Daube, Cambridge, 1956, p. 216.
53. In his excellent account of Biblical theology in *Jesus Christ the Risen Lord*, New York, 1956, F. V. Filson has allowed the Resurrection to be the organizing center of all aspects of unity in the Biblical message.
54. W. Marxsen, *Der Evangelist Markus*, Göttingen, 1956.
55. T. W. Manson, "The Gospel Miracles," *Religion in Education*, XIX (1952), 50–51.
56. T. W. Manson, *The Servant Messiah*, Cambridge, 1953, p. 96.
57. Recent British Biblical scholarship has, of course, no more than American been simply a one-way traffic. We have merely sought to delineate briefly the major movement.
58. Although he may seem to have overstated the case, there is probably some substance in the protest of Prof. James D. Smart: "The rather dangerous impression has grown in some circles of British and American Biblical scholarship that whereas the Europeans have always fluctuated wildly between extremes in an unbalanced fashion, 'we' have ever followed a more balanced, sane, middle-way tradition. Our history does not support such pretensions. Our middle way has only too often been an eclecticism in which we have tried to have the best out of contradictory theologies without ever facing clear-sightedly the issues that divide them"—*The Interpretation of Scripture*, Philadelphia, 1961, p. 283.
59. E. Hoskyns and F. N. Davey, *The Riddle of the New Testament*, pp. 10 f.
60. H. Riesenfeld, *The Gospel Tradition and Its Beginnings: A Study in the Limits of "Formgeschichte,"* London, 1957. *V*. the concluding section of the present book for a brief discussion of how Riesenfeld's proposals have lately been developed in detail by one of his followers, Birger Gerhardsson.
61. C. H. Dodd, *History and the Gospel*, New York, 1947, pp. 90–101. The passages are these: Mark 2:14, 15–17; Luke 7:36–48; John 7:53–8:11; Luke 15:4–7 = Matt. 18:12–13; Luke 18:10–14; Matt. 11:16–19 = Luke 7:31–5; Matt. 21:32.
62. J. M. Robinson, "The Formal Structure of Jesus' Message," *Current Issues in New Testament Interpretation*, ed. William Klassen and Graydon Snyder, New York, 1962, pp. 96–7.
63. G. Ebeling, *The Nature of Faith* (Engl. transl. by R. G. Smith), Philadelphia, 1961, p. 56: "What Jesus says cannot be separated from his Person, and his Person is one with his way. The way which he goes raises the question of what his words mean. And his words explain the meaning of his way."
64. Most recently, Matthew Black, *The Scrolls and Christian Origins*, New York, 1961.

Chapter III

1. For the view that Jesus intended the Church, *v*. R. Newton Flew, *Jesus and His Church*, New York, 1938. For the view that the Church was called into being by the Resurrection, *v*. George Johnston, *The Doctrine of the Church in the New*

Testament, Cambridge, 1943. Cf. Théo Preiss, *Life in Christ* (Engl. transl. by Harold Knight), London, 1954.

2. A. Fridrichsen, *This Is the Church,* ed. Anders Nygren (Engl. transl. by C. C. Rasmussen), Philadelphia, 1952, p. 22.

3. John Knox, *Criticism and Faith,* New York, 1952, pp. 47 ff.

4. E. Brunner, *The Mediator* (Engl. transl. by Olive Wyon), New York, 1934, p. 159 n.

5. R. R. Niebuhr, *Resurrection and Historical Reason,* p. 62.

6. John Knox, *Criticism and Faith,* pp. 85, 107, 113.

7. James Denney, *The Death of Christ,* London, 1902, p. 94.

8. John Knox, *Christ the Lord,* Chicago, 1945, p. 60.

9. Jean Daniélou, *Christ and Us* (Engl. transl. by Walter Roberts), New York, 1961. Cf. J. L. Leuba, *L'Institution et l'évènement,* 1950, where it is maintained that the concepts of "institution" and "prophetic event" are parallel in the New Testament.

10. John Knox, *Criticism and Faith,* p. 82. Cf. *Chapters in a Life of Paul,* New York, 1950, pp. 125 f.

11. John Knox, *Criticism and Faith,* p. 82.

12. Ibid. pp. 51–2.

13. R. R. Niebuhr, *Resurrection and Historical Reason,* pp. 70–71.

14. Cf. Rom. 4:4. Paul thinks of the "reward of grace" in distinction from any price to be paid for works accomplished, and in this he seems to parallel Jesus' own teaching.

15. The tendency for "meaning" or "interpretation" to become a substitute for the historical reality of the event itself, as the place in which God acts, has been noticed by James Muilenburg in connection with the Exodus. "The Exodus was no deduction on the part of a clever and gifted people from what had happened; it was not Israel's interpretation of the meaning or significance of what had occurred at the Sea of Reeds. . . . The deed was revelation and the meaning of the deed was revelation"—*The Way of Israel: Biblical Faith and Ethics,* New York, 1961, pp. 48 f.

16. J. Jeremias, "The Present Position in the Controversy Concerning the Problem of the Historical Jesus," *ET,* LXIX (1957–58), 333–9.

17. Ibid. p. 338.

18. Ibid. p. 336.

19. Ibid. p. 339.

20. R. H. Fuller, *The Mission and Achievement of Jesus,* London, 1954.

21. O. Cullmann, *The Christology of the New Testament* (Engl. transl. by S. C. Guthrie and C. A. M. Hall), Philadelphia, 1959, pp. 3–4. *V.* also "The Reply of Professor Cullmann to Roman Catholic Critics," *SJT,* XV (March 1962), 36 ff. Professor Cullmann here re-emphasizes his view of the *functional* character of N.T. Christology, and of both Testaments of the Bible as telling about *the action of God in the world.* Yet he does at the same time concede that the question of the *natures* of Christ, as raised by the Church in the doctrinal controversies of the early centuries, was necessitated by the different heresies that were impinging upon the Christological problem as a result of the influence of Greek concepts alien to the Bible—the Church may have displaced the N.T. center of gravity from a Christological point of view, but did not follow a path *contrary* to the N.T., and the formulation of Chalcedon "corresponds to what the N.T. presupposes." Cf. E. Käsemann, "Kritische Analyse von Phil. 2:5–11," *ZTK,* XLVII (1950), 313–60. Käsemann points out that in the hymn of the self-

emptying of Christ, the emphasis is not on what or who Christ was, but on his work.

22. R. H. Fuller, op. cit. pp. 103–8.
23. Ibid. p. 117.
24. W. C. van Unnik, "Jesus the Christ," *NTS*, VIII (Jan. 1962), 101 ff.
25. Among recent studies, *v*. Vincent Taylor, *The Names of Jesus*, New York, 1953, pp. 25 ff.; O. Cullmann, *The Christology of the New Testament*, p. 134.
26. E. G. Selwyn, "Image, Fact and Faith," *NTS*, I (May 1955), 246.
27. H. Lietzmann, *Der Menschensohn*, Freiburg and Leipzig, 1896.
28. R. Bultmann, *Theology of the New Testament*, Vol. I, pp. 26 ff.
29. J. Y. Campbell, *JTS*, XLVIII (1947), 145 ff.; G. S. Duncan, *Jesus, Son of Man*, New York, 1949.
30. E. Stauffer, *New Testament Theology* (Engl. transl. by John Marsh), London, 1955, pp. 26 ff.
31. O. Cullmann, op. cit. p. 162.
32. R. H. Fuller, op. cit. pp. 98–105.
33. G. Bornkamm, *Jesus of Nazareth* (Engl. transl. by Irene and Fraser McLuskey with J. M. Robinson), New York, 1960, p. 230.
34. G. Bornkamm, op. cit. pp. 103 ff., also pp. 176–7.
35. The separateness of statements about the Son of Man and the coming kingdom of God is recognized by E. Schweizer, *Lordship and Discipleship*, London, 1961, pp. 22 and 40 (notes). Cf. Ph. Vielhauer in *Festschrift für Günter Dehn*, Neukirchen, 1960, pp. 177–8.
36. J. M. Robinson, *A New Quest of the Historical Jesus*, pp. 100 ff.
37. J. Y. Campbell, *ET*, XLVIII (Nov. 1936), 91 f.; K. W. Clark, *JBL*, LIX (1940), 367 ff.
38. W. G. Kümmel, *Promise and Fulfilment* (Engl. transl. by Dorothea M. Barton), London, 1957, p. 144.
39. R. Bultmann, *Jesus and the Word* (first published in Germany in 1926 under the title *Jesus*), New York, 1958, p. 52.
40. W. G. Kümmel, op. cit. p. 146.
41. C. H. Dodd, *The Apostolic Preaching and Its Developments;* also *The Parables of the Kingdom*, London, 1941 (first publ. 1935). It has quite frequently been noted that Dodd's interpretation is Platonic rather than Hebraic in character.
42. H. Schlier in *Evangelische Theologie*, VIII (1948–49), 462–73.
43. W. G. Kümmel, op. cit. p. 148. Cf. Théo Preiss, "The Vision of History in the New Testament," *Life in Christ*, p. 66: Preiss contends that we must not demythologize the conception of time in the New Testament, especially with regard to the end of history. *V*. also O. Cullmann, *Christ and Time* (Engl. transl. by F. V. Filson), London, 1951, p. 53.
44. M. Werner, *Die Entstehung des christlichen Dogmas problemgeschichtlich dargestellt*, 2nd ed., Bern, 1953.
45. P. Wernle, *Jesus*, Tübingen, 1917.
46. For example, J. Weiss, *Die Predigt Jesu vom Reiche Gottes*, pp. 100 ff.
47. The interjected comment in Mark 13:14, "Let the reader understand," would seem to indicate the literary nature of the composition of Mark 13.
48. W. G. Kümmel, op. cit. pp. 88 ff.
49. G. Bornkamm, *Jesus of Nazareth*, p. 93.
50. R. H. Fuller, op. cit. p. 50.
51. W. Michaelis, *Reich Gottes und Geist Gottes nach dem Neuen Testament*, 1947, p. 15. C. K. Barrett, *The Holy Spirit and the Gospel Tradition*, London, 1947, p. 63.

52. W. G. Kümmel, op. cit. p. 109: "It is the meaning of the mission of Jesus, when announcing the *approach* of the kingdom of God, to make this future at the same time already now a present reality." We can justly speak about a consensus in recent scholarship regarding the intricate interweaving of present and future in Jesus' eschatological message (*v.* the interpretations of the parables also by J. Jeremias and E. Fuchs). It is well known that C. H. Dodd has latterly wished to modify his "realized eschatology" concept to "self-realizing eschatology" (*sich realisierende Eschatologie*)—*The Interpretation of the Fourth Gospel*, p. 447, n. 1. The stress, however, in the works of T. W. Manson and Vincent Taylor is very much on "realized eschatology."

53. R. H. Fuller, op. cit. p. 120.

54. R. Bultmann, "Jesus and Paul," *Existence and Faith* (shorter writings of Bultmann selected and translated by Schubert M. Ogden), New York, 1960, p. 196.

55. For the discussion about the Baptist and especially the question of the authenticity of Jesus' confession to the Baptist in Matt. 11:11–14, as well as for the relevant literature, *v.* J. M. Robinson, *A New Quest of the Historical Jesus*, pp. 114–19.

56. William Manson, *Jesus, the Messiah*, Philadelphia, 1946, p. 50.

57. J. Chr. K. von Hofmann, *Biblische Theologie des Neuen Testaments* (posthumously edited by W. Volck), 1886. Also von Hofmann's earlier work *Weissagung und Erfüllung* (1840–44) in which the basic thesis is that all Biblical history is prophecy and all prophecy history: every event carries within itself the seed of what follows. All history is in the last analysis a prophecy of the definitive religious encounter between God and men, and the terminal phase is opened by Christ who is the end of all history and prophecy. How influential this has been for Cullmann can be gathered from his "pilot" work, *Christ and Time; v.* especially pp. 90 ff.: "The history of salvation as a whole is prophecy" (p. 97).

58. E. Stauffer, *New Testament Theology*.

59. O. Cullmann, "Les récentes études sur la formation de la tradition évangélique," *Revue d'histoire et de philosophie religieuse*, V (1925), 459–77 and 564–79. For an excellent description of the early development of Cullmann's thought, *v.* Jean Frisque, *Oscar Cullmann: Une théologie de l'histoire du salut*, Tournai, 1960, pp. 16 ff.

60. O. Cullmann, *Christ and Time*, pp. 20, 21, 23, 49, 82 f., 94.

61. Ibid. pp. 136, 139, 140, 152, 157.

62. O. Cullmann, *The Christology of the New Testament* (Engl. transl. by S. C. Guthrie and C. A. M. Hall), Philadelphia, 1959.

63. Ibid. p. 9.

64. O. Cullmann, *Christ and Time*, p. 109; *The Christology of the New Testament*, p. 9.

65. John Macquarrie, *The Scope of Demythologizing*, pp. 62 ff.

66. O. Cullmann, *The Christology of the New Testament*, p. 255.

67. Ibid. p. 8: "The early Church believed in Christ's messiahship only because it believed that Jesus believed himself to be the Messiah. In this respect Bultmann's faith is fundamentally different from that of the early Church."

68. R. Bultmann, "History of Salvation and History," *Existence and Faith*, pp. 232 and 233.

69. W. Eichrodt, *Theology of the Old Testament*, Vol. I, concluding excursus on von Rad's method. Cf. Johannes Hempel, "Alttestamentliche Theologie in protestantischer Sicht heute," *Bibliotheca Orientalis*, XV (1958), 206–14.

70. J. Macquarrie, op. cit. p. 79.

71. O. Cullmann, *Christ and Time*, p. 98. Revealed prophecy, says Cullmann, "raises historically verifiable facts to the status of an object of faith."

72. G. Ebeling, *The Nature of Faith*, pp. 84 ff. and 102 ff. *V.* also J. M. Robinson, "Basic Shifts in German Theology," *Interpretation*, XVI (Jan. 1962), 93. Robinson seeks to show that *Heilsgeschichte* should be construed as the all-embracing event of the revelation, "the whole movement of the subject matter, from historical occurrences through their historic commemoration in language," by relating it to the philosophy of the later Heidegger and the category of *Lichtungsgeschichte* ("clearing-history"), through which language is understood as the speech evoked by the subject matter (in this case the God who acts) clearing its way into thought.

73. R. Bultmann, in *Existence and Faith*, pp. 234 f.

74. O. Cullmann, *Christ and Time*, p. 40.

75. Ibid. p. 43.

76. James Barr, *The Semantics of Biblical Language*, London, 1961; "Hypostatization of Linguistic Phenomena in Modern Theological Interpretation," *Journal of Semitic Studies*, VII (Spring 1962); *Biblical Words for Time*, London, 1962. The other side of Cullmann's "time-line" thesis is his understanding of αἰών as the *whole of time* or *endless time*. Barr points out that, in the light of the classical Hebrew usage of 'ôlâm, which provides the background for N.T. usage, αἰών in such phrases as ἐκ τοὺ αἰῶνος and εἰς τὸν αἰῶνα does not mean a "precisely limited period of time," and the most natural translation is simply "from all eternity" or "forever."

77. E. Käsemann, *ZTK*, LVII (1960), 174–6.

78. R. Bultmann, in *Existence and Faith*, p. 237.

79. E. Käsemann, *ZTK*, LVII (1960), 183.

80. E. Schweizer, "The Church as the Missionary Body of Christ," *NTS*, VIII (Oct. 1961), 1–4. Schweizer remarks concerning his brief exposition of Romans: "I learned most from A. Schlatter, *Gottes Gerechtigkeit* (1935) and from occasional discussion with E. Käsemann whose commentary on the letter to the Romans is eagerly awaited."

81. J. Munck, *Paul and the Salvation of Mankind* (Engl. transl. by Frank Clarke), Richmond, 1959.

82. W. D. Davies's review of Munck's work in *Christian Origins and Judaism*, Philadelphia, 1962, p. 198.

83. For example, C. H. Dodd, *The Bulletin of the John Rylands Library*, Vol. XVII (1933) and Vol. XVIII (1934).

84. O. Cullmann, *The Christology of the New Testament*, pp. 316–17.

85. Ibid. p. 319.

Chapter IV

1. R. Bultmann, *Jesus and the Word* (Engl. transl. by L. P. Smith and E. H. Lantero of the German work entitled *Jesus*), New York, 1958, p. 11.

2. T. W. Manson, *The Teaching of Jesus*, Cambridge, 1945, pp. 81, 291 ff.

3. Ibid. pp. 17 ff. J. Jeremias has made full use of this criterion in his attempt to trace the parables back to their *Sitz im Leben Jesu, The Parables of Jesus*, London, 1954.

4. T. W. Manson, op. cit. pp. 291 f.

5. G. Bornkamm, *Jesus of Nazareth*, p. 58.

6. Ibid. pp. 60 ff. Cf. T. W. Manson, op. cit. pp. 45–81.

7. T. W. Manson, op. cit. p. 81.
8. G. Bornkamm, op. cit. pp. 69 ff.
9. T. W. Manson, op. cit. p. 12.
10. T. W. Manson, "The Life of Jesus: Some Tendencies in Present-Day Research," *The Background of the New Testament and Its Eschatology*, ed. W. D. Davies and D. Daube, Cambridge, 1956, p. 216.
11. G. Bornkamm, op. cit. pp. 53–5.
12. Ibid. pp. 62 f.
13. Ibid. p. 212, n. 3.
14. Ibid. p. 63.
15. Ibid. pp. 124 ff.; cf. T. W. Manson, op. cit. pp. 89 ff.
16. T. W. Manson, op. cit. p. 102.
17. Ibid. pp. 104, 112 f.
18. For basic discussions of this passage, v. E. Norden, *Agnostos Theos*, 1913, pp. 277 ff.; J. Bieneck, *Sohn Gottes als Christusbezeichnung der Synoptiker*, 1951, pp. 75 ff. *V.* also the recent excellent summary by A. M. Hunter, "Crux Criticorum—Matt. XI 25–30—A Re-appraisal," *NTS*, VIII (April 1962), 241.
19. The description originated with K. von Hase, *Geschichte Jesu*, 1876, p. 422.
20. J. Weiss, *The History of Primitive Christianity*, New York, 1937, p. 121; R. Bultmann, *Die Geschichte der synoptischen Tradition*, Göttingen, 1958, pp. 171–2; A. E. J. Rawlinson, *The New Testament Doctrine of the Christ*, New York, 1926, p. 263; T. W. Manson, *The Sayings of Jesus*, London, 1949, p. 80.
21. V. Taylor, *The Names of Jesus*, London, 1953, pp. 59–65.
22. W. G. Kümmel, *Promise and Fulfilment*, London, 1957, p. 41.
23. W. D. Davies, "Knowledge in the Dead Sea Scrolls and Matthew 11:25–30," *Christian Origins and Judaism*, Philadelphia, 1962, pp. 119 ff.
24. E. Schweizer's comment is apt: "What Jesus himself felt at his baptism we simply cannot know"—*Lordship and Discipleship*, London, 1960, p. 44, n. 3.
25. I refer here only to one or two recent discussions. The view, on the grounds mentioned, that Mark 13:32 is not wholly a community saying, is shared by O. Cullmann, *The Christology of the New Testament*, pp. 288–9; W. G. Kümmel, op. cit. p. 42; and V. Taylor, *The Gospel According to St. Mark*, London, 1952, p. 439. *V.* also E. Schweizer, op. cit. p. 43.
26. O. Cullmann, op. cit. p. 288: "Precisely when one accepts as genuine Matt. 11:27, which points to Jesus' omniscience, does the saying in Mark 13:32 with its limitation of that omniscience become understandable as a saying of Jesus."
27. A. M. Hunter, op. cit. p. 245. The admirable recent scholarly work of B. M. F. van Iersel must be noted, *'Der Sohn' in den synoptischen Jesusworten: Christusbezeichnung der Gemeinde oder Selbstbezeichnung Jesu?* Leiden, 1961. After a clear account of the history of the debate concerning the title "Son" or "Son of God" in the N.T., van Iersel makes a good case for the independence of the "Son" logia of Jesus over against the confessional statements of the primitive Church. In the early Christian preaching (particular reference is made to Acts 1–13) and confessions (e.g. Rom. 1:4), Jesus is explicitly referred to as "the Son of God," the term being connected with such O.T. testimonies as Psalm 2:7 and II Samuel 7:14 (discussion of the connection between "the Son of God" title and that of the Servant of the Lord leads to the conclusion that the Servant passages exerted a greater influence on the catechetical phase of the tradition than on the earliest kerygma). By contrast with the kerygmatic passages and hymns and confessions alluding to "the Son of God" (which, although secondary, are by no means late, bound up as they are with the Resurrection of Jesus, Rom.

1:4, Acts 13:33), the "Son" sayings of Jesus in the Synoptic tradition (on which van Iersel is prepared to concede the impact of the theology of the community) are vague and even bald and make no reference to O.T. testimonies or the Resurrection. So van Iersel holds that the "Son" logia of Jesus may be taken to be independent of and prior to the kerygmatic statements and confessions, and that, although Jesus makes no express claim to be the Son of God, his sayings are a *reflection* of his consciousness of Sonship. Sonship is therefore "the hidden ground of his perceptible form" (p. 181). I think it is not unfair to say that, amid the detail of linguistic and theological arguments in this study, the *Sitz im Leben Jesu* of the "Son" sayings remains somewhat unclear, and the suggestion that Matt. 11:27 is a reply to the discussion about the authority of Jesus (Matt. 13:54–6) hardly carries conviction (pp. 151–7). What could the self-designation "Son" have meant to the contemporaries of Jesus? There is still considerable obscurity at this point. If the "Son" sayings only *reflect* Jesus' own consciousness of being the Son of God, and if only later, after the Resurrection, the disciples recognized him to be the true Son of God both in his earthly ministry and his preexistence (p. 184), are we to suppose that their new recognition was founded in some way upon an unadulterated transmission of such a saying as Matthew 11:27 or not? Since this question is scarcely answered, it seems not unjust to say that the obstacles in the way of taking Matthew 11:27 in its present form to represent the *ipsissima verba* of Jesus have not quite been overcome.

28. J. M. Robinson, *A New Quest of the Historical Jesus,* pp. 100 ff.

29. G. Bornkamm, op. cit. p. 128.

30. T. W. Manson, op. cit. pp. 265 ff.

31. For example, W. H. Brownlee, "Messianic Motifs of Qumran and the New Testament," *NTS,* III (Nov. 1956), 12 ff., and III (1957), 195 ff.

32. M. Dibelius, *Jesus,* Philadelphia, 1949; R. H. Fuller, *The Mission and Achievement of Jesus,* London, 1954.

33. R. Bultmann, *Theology of the New Testament,* Vol. I, pp. 26 ff.

34. G. Bornkamm, *Jesus of Nazareth,* p. 178.

35. Ibid. p. 169.

36. Bultmann is satisfied to think of Jesus' death as a political capital punishment that was carried through as a result of political misunderstanding. "Das Verhältnis der urchristlichen Christusbotschaft zum historischen Jesus," *Sitzungsberichte der Heidelberger Akademie der Wissenschaften,* Heidelberg, 1960, p. 12. But when we press the question of how the misunderstanding could have arisen, we are led to think that the Jews must have pointed to Jesus as an insurgent (*v.* I Thess. 2:15).

37. E. Schweizer, *Lordship and Discipleship,* London, 1960.

38. F. Gogarten, *Der Mensch zwischen Gott und Welt,* Stuttgart, 1956, pp. 263 ff.

39. W. C. van Unnik, "Jesus the Christ," *NTS,* VIII (Jan. 1962), 102 ff.

40. Heinz E. Toedt, *Der Menschensohn in der synoptischen Überlieferung,* Gütersloh, 1959.

41. Cf. E. Schweizer, op. cit. p. 40, n. 2. Schweizer argues that the Parousia sayings of the Son of Man are not original. Rather the sayings that describe him walking the earth in humility can most certainly be traced back to Jesus. To be sure, one must allow that the term "Son of Man" includes humility (the possibility of a background in Ezekiel is, incidentally, neglected by E. Schweizer) as well as an eschatological pre-existence. See O. Cullmann, *The Christology of the New Testament,* pp. 137–52. But cf. G. S. Duncan, *Jesus, Son of Man;* also E. M. Sidebottom, "The Son of Man in the Fourth Gospel," *ET,* LXVIII (Feb. 1937), 231 ff., (Mar. 1937), 280 ff.) as well as an eschatological

role. The weight of scholarly opinion, however, still favors a background for the title in Daniel, Enoch, and IV Ezra, and so an emphasis on the eschatological role. At all events, the view that Jesus purposely used "Son of Man" as an ambiguous title, hinting now at his humiliation, now at his coming eschatological, heavenly glory, seems unlikely. One might add that it seems less probable that the high apocalyptic interest of the 40's and 50's A.D. could have led the Church to invent the Parousia sayings of the Son of Man, than that remembered words of Jesus about the imminent coming of the heavenly Son of Man could have heightened the fervent eschatological expectation (I Thess. 4:15).

42. T. W. Manson, *The Teaching of Jesus*, pp. 140 f.

43. W. G. Kümmel, *Promise and Fulfilment*, pp. 151–5.

44. W. Manson, *Jesus the Messiah*, p. 50.

45. G. Bornkamm, *Jesus of Nazareth*, p. 93.

46. Ibid. p. 21.

47. H. Conzelmann, *The Theology of St. Luke*, New York, 1961. Other *Redaktionsgeschichte* works, e.g. W. Marxsen on Mark, and G. Bornkamm, H. J. Held, and Gerhard Barth on Matthew, are referred to elsewhere in this book.

48. For a good summary of recent discussion about the Baptist (particularly in opposition to Bultmann's rejection of *all* the logia about the Baptist, both positive and negative, *Die Geschichte der synoptischen Tradition*, 3rd ed., 1957, pp. 177 ff.) v. J. M. Robinson, *A New Quest of the Historical Jesus*, pp. 116 ff.

49. G. Bornkamm, *Jesus of Nazareth*, p. 62.

50. K. Barth, *Church Dogmatics*, Vol. I, Part 2: *The Doctrine of the Word of God*, pp. 126, 463.

51. D. Baillie, *God Was in Christ*, p. 67.

52. Schubert M. Ogden, *Christ Without Myth*, New York, 1961.

53. Ibid. p. 143.

54. Ibid. p. 145.

55. Ibid. p. 161.

56. Ibid. pp. 162–3.

57. While Ogden admits that "*in some sense* Christ is in very truth 'the Son of God'" (p. 158), he baffles us by refusing to allow this to carry through fully to the idea of the concrete historicity of the revelation in the earthly ministry of Jesus.

58. Otto Piper, "A Unitary God with Jesus as His First Theologian" (Review of Bornkamm's *Jesus*), *Interpretation*, XV (Oct. 1961), 473 ff.

59. S. M. Ogden, op. cit. p. 143.

60. While Ogden appears to characterize Jesus mainly as "mankind's preacher," he is not altogether silent about the "objective" reality of revelation in the deed as well as the word of Jesus, for he confesses that in his conduct the offer of forgiveness to the "lost" was effected (cf. p. 69 with p. 81).

61. J. M. Robinson, op. cit. pp. 95 ff.

62. G. Bornkamm, op. cit. p. 21.

63. Ibid. p. 158.

64. J. M. Robinson, "The Formal Structure of Jesus' Message," *Current Issues in New Testament Interpretation*, ed. William Klassen and Graydon Snyder, New York, 1962, pp. 91 ff.; v. p. 104.

65. Ibid. pp. 104–5.

66. E. Fuchs, "Die Frage nach dem historischen Jesus," *ZTK*, LIII (1956), 210–29.

67. Cf. Paul Tillich, *Systematic Theology*, Vol. II, Chicago, 1957, pp. 121 ff.

68. G. Bornkamm, *Jesus of Nazareth*, p. 178.

69. Johannes Munck, "The New Testament and Gnosticism," *Current Issues in New Testament Interpretation*, p. 232.

Chapter V

1. A. M. Ramsey, *The Resurrection of Christ*, London, 1956.

2. K. Barth, *Kirchliche Dogmatik*, Vol. III, Part 2, p. 531.

3. F. V. Filson, *Jesus Christ the Risen Lord*, Nashville, 1956, pp. 25–9.

4. Barnabas Lindars, *New Testament Apologetic*, Philadelphia, 1961, p. 286.

5. James S. Stewart, *A Faith To Proclaim*, New York, 1953, p. 109.

6. Hans Fr. von Campenhausen, "Der Ablauf der Osterereignisse und das leere Grab," *Sitzungsberichte der Heidelberger Akademie der Wissenschaften*, 1958. G. D. Yarnold, *Risen Indeed: Studies in the Lord's Resurrection*, New York, 1959.

7. M. Goguel, *La Foi à la Résurrection de Jésus dans le christianisme primitif*, Paris, 1933, pp. 213 ff. E. Bickermann, "Das leere Grab," *ZNW*, XXIII (1924), 281–92. Strack-Billerbeck, *Kommentar zum N.T. aus Talmud und Midrasch*, I, pp. 753 ff.

8. M. Goguel, *The Birth of Christianity* (Engl. transl. by H. C. Snape), London, 1953, pp. 66 ff. E. G. Selwyn, *The First Epistle of St. Peter*, London, 1947, pp. 256–7. R. Bultmann, *Theology of the New Testament*, Vol. I, pp. 45, 82.

9. E. Schweizer, *Lordship and Discipleship*, London, 1960.

10. R. H. Fuller, "The Resurrection of Jesus Christ," *Biblical Research* (Papers of the Chicago Society of Biblical Research), IV, 1960.

11. Rodney Branton, "Resurrection in the Early Church," *Early Christian Origins*, ed. A. Wikgren, Chicago, 1961, p. 44.

12. C. F. D. Moule, "The Resurrection Appearances in the Light of Festival Pilgrimages," *NTS*, IV (Oct. 1957), 58 ff.

13. K. Lake, *The Historical Evidence of the Resurrection of Jesus Christ*, New York, 1907. J. P. Gardner-Smith, *The Narratives of the Resurrection*, London, 1926. V. also J. M. Creed, *The Gospel According to St. Luke*, London, 1930, p. 317: "Is it conceivable that Mark would have allowed an angel to say, 'There [in Galilee] ye [the Apostles] shall see him, as he said to you,' if he did not accept a tradition that in fact they did so?" On the other hand, A. M. Ramsey notes that least of all should the inscrutable angelic message be taken as a clue to the course of events and the reconstruction of the *history* (op. cit. p. 71).

14. L. E. Elliott Binns, *Galilean Christianity*, London, 1956, p. 41.

15. J. Weiss, *Die Schriften des Neuen Testaments*, 1, p. 208, contends that προάξω ὑμᾶς (Mark 14:28) means "I will lead you," and points to Jerusalem as the scene of the Resurrection appearances and to Galilee as the first center of the Christian community. V. also A. M. Ramsey, op. cit. p. 70. For the view that προάξω ὑμᾶς means "I will forestall you in Galilee," v. V. Taylor, *The Gospel According to St. Mark*, p. 549.

16. H. J. Cadbury, *The Making of Luke—Acts*, New York, 1927. B. S. Easton, *Early Christianity: The Purpose of Acts and Other Papers*, ed. Frederick C. Grant, Greenwich, Conn., 1954.

17. Ernst Lohmeyer, *Galiläa und Jerusalem*, Göttingen, 1956 (first published 1936).

18. Professor Matthew Black has recently given enthusiastic endorsement to Lohmeyer's thesis of a double origin of Christianity, *The Scrolls and Christian*

Origins, New York, 1961, pp. 81 ff. Picking up the evidence cited by Lohmeyer, Dr. Black suggests (tentatively) that the oldest root of the Christian movement in Galilee is to be sought in a group of dedicated Nazirites, and that if Epiphanius' "Nasareans" were a sectarian survival of this ancient order, we may have in such a North Palestinian sect the actual historical link between the primitive Church and Qumran Judaism. But the hypothesis of a fairly clearly defined "Galilean" Nazirite group or community is questionable (Prof. W. D. Davies's protest against distinguishing rigidly between the Judaism of Galilee and the orthodox Judaism of Jerusalem has its own bearing on the case: "Apocalyptic and Pharisaism," *Christian Origins and Judaism,* Philadelphia, 1962, p. 21). Questionable also would be the suggestion of a close affinity between the Nazirites and Essene asceticism. For while the condition of the individual Nazir, sacrificed in his person to the Lord, parallels the state of the serving priest and holy warrior of Qumran, we have to notice the incompatibility between the Essene use of *tîrôs,* "new wine," and the absolute Nazirite ban on any fruit of the vine, as also between the Essene practice of keeping their dead so close to their living quarters and the rites of purification required for the Nazirite if he incurred defilement through accidentally touching a dead body. I am indebted to my colleague Prof. John Strugnell for discussing Dr. Black's book with me.

In general, we have no information concerning a Church in Galilee, *v.* W. Marxsen, *Der Evangelist Markus,* Göttingen, 1956, p. 60; J. M. Robinson, *A New Quest of the Historical Jesus,* pp. 102–3, n. 2. The only definite mention of Christianity in Galilee in Acts is 9:31, "the Church throughout Judea, Galilee and Samaria had rest," and that is so broad as to disclose nothing about a rigidly differentiated branch of Galilean Christianity. L. E. Elliott Binns, for his account of Galilean Christianity, has to rely most heavily, and precariously, on the Epistle of James. For a most useful earlier discussion of Lohmeyer's thesis, *v.* F. C. Grant, *The Earliest Gospel,* New York–Nashville, 1943, pp. 147 ff.

19. K. Lake, op. cit. p. 253. A. M. Ramsey, op. cit. pp. 51–2.

20. Paul Tillich, *Systematic Theology,* Vol. II, Chicago, 1957, pp. 155–6.

21. E. G. Selwyn, "The Resurrection," *Essays Catholic and Critical,* ed. E. G. Selwyn, London, 1938 (first published 1926).

22. Ibid. p. 319.

23. M. C. Perry, *The Easter Enigma,* London, 1959.

24. M. Goguel, *The Birth of Christianity* (Engl. transl. by H. C. Snape), London, 1953, pp. 66 ff.

25. John Macquarrie, *The Scope of Demythologizing,* p. 86.

26. G. Bornkamm, op. cit. p. 185.

27. G. Ebeling, *The Nature of Faith* (Engl. transl. by R. G. Smith), Philadelphia, 1961, p. 69.

28. In the Preface to the Second Edition of his work on *The Resurrection of Christ,* London, 1956, Archbishop Ramsey observes that the historical problems of the Resurrection "have too often been discussed in separation from the Gospel with which the history is bound up and from the Theology which made the story of Easter worth the telling."

29. R. Bultmann, *Die Geschichte der synoptischen Tradition,* 4th ed., Göttingen, 1958, pp. 160–61, 308–16.

30. R. Bultmann, "New Testament and Mythology," *Kerygma and Myth,* Vol. I.

31. R. Bultmann, *Theology of the New Testament,* Vol. I, p. 45; also "Das Verhältnis der urchristlichen Christusbotschaft zum historischen Jesus," Heidelberg, p. 27.

32. James Denney, *The Death of Christ*, London, 1902, pp. 309–10.
33. Ibid., pp. 310–11.
34. J. S. Stewart, *A Faith To Proclaim*, New York, 1953, p. 111.
35. R. Bultmann, *Theology of the New Testament*, Vol. I, pp. 43–4.
36. The interpretation of Rom. 1:3–5 has of course been much debated. The explanation we have favored is supported by W. Sanday and A. C. Headlam, *The Epistle to the Romans* (I.C.C.), New York, 1926, pp. 7–8: they hold that Paul did not think that the Son of God *became* Son only by the Resurrection, but that the Resurrection simply designated and manifested his prior "concealed" Sonship to men.

The formulary style and confessional ring of the passage, together with the persuasion that it does indeed reflect a primitive "adoptionist" Christology, has led to the quite widespread conclusion that we are dealing here with a Pre-Pauline creedal statement, for Paul's own Christological doctrine is not "adoptionist" but "incarnationist" (e.g. Rom. 8:3; I Cor. 10:4; II Cor. 8:9; Gal. 4:4). Why then does the apostle include a statement that is out of accord with his own more fully developed Christological position? The answer given by C. H. Dodd is that he makes a concession to his Roman readers by employing a formula (almost certainly Palestinian) that was already familiar to them and could provide a starting-point for further discussion—*The Epistle of Paul to the Romans*, New York, 1932, pp. 4–5. From this basis, such scholars as C. K. Barrett and A. M. Hunter follow the "adoptionist" interpretation. "Christ belongs to two orders of existence, denoted respectively by flesh and Spirit," writes Barrett; "in these He can be described as Son of David and Son of God. He was born as Son of David, *appointed* Son of God. We have no grounds for taking any other than the most natural view, that the birth preceded the appointment. Exactly when the appointment took place is not stated. Perhaps at Baptism, or perhaps the further words 'after His resurrection from the dead' belonged to the original formula"—*Commentary on the Epistle to the Romans*, New York, 1957, pp. 19–20. Hunter proposes that we follow the triadic division presupposed by the Peshitta: (1) who was born of the seed of David according to the flesh; (2) who was appointed Son of God with power according to the Holy Spirit; (3) as a result of the resurrection of the dead Jesus Christ our Lord. In that case we have still the clear suggestion of adoptionism; the Baptism is the birthday of the Son of God—*Paul and His Predecessors*, Philadelphia, 1961, pp. 25–6 (on this showing the view would be upheld that it was not the Resurrection that effected any radical transformation in Jesus' status as Son).

We are faced, however, with the acute problem of how much of our passage belongs to the original pre-Pauline formula; Barrett particularly has sensed this difficulty. If the phrase "concerning his son" (Rom. 1:3) belonged to the original formula, any adoptionist understanding is ruled out. Similarly with the phrase "with power": is it to be taken adjectivally as qualifying "Son of God" rather than adverbially as modifying "appointed," and so as denoting Paul's *own* intention to soften the adoptionism of the words quoted?—Barrett, in op. cit. p. 20. In this regard, A. M. Hunter's cautionary words concerning the establishment of pre-Pauline formulas are wise: "Absolutely conclusive proof is not to be expected: the reader must decide in each particular instance whether on a balance of probabilities the case is made out," in op. cit. p. 24.

There is lastly the problem of the meaning of ὁρισθέντος "appointed," "designated," "declared" (*v.* W. Bauer's *Lexicon*). Linguistic evidence seems to favor the meaning "appointed." But even so, this one word does not necessarily connote an "adoptionist" standpoint in the sense that Jesus was *made* by the Resurrection something he had not been before. Long ago H. C. G. Moule observed that never for an hour had Jesus ceased to be in fact Son of God, but there was an hour when he became openly and officially what he always is naturally, somewhat as a born king is "made" king by coronation; historical act (Resurrection) then affirmed independent fact—*The Epistle of St. Paul to the Romans*, 1899, p. 17. Cf. Walther Lüthi, *The Letter to the Romans*, Edinburgh, 1961, p. 6. It is perhaps significant that C. K. Barrett points out that, although the formula seems to imply the adoption of Jesus Christ as Son of God by the Resurrection, *it does not prove that Jesus was actually not Son of God before the Resurrection*, in op. cit. p. 20.

37. R. Bultmann, *Theology of the New Testament*, Vol. I, p. 45.

38. R. Bultmann, "Revelation in the New Testament," *Existence and Faith* (transl. by S. M. Ogden), New York, 1960, p. 72.

39. R. Bultmann, "The Historicity of Man and Faith," op. cit. p. 110.

40. Dr. Paul Tillich speaks much the same language about Easter as Bultmann, at least in the first instance: the one who was supposed to bring in the new eon was destroyed by the powers of the old eon and "this meant that the disciples either had to accept the breakdown of their hope or radically transform its content"—*Systematic Theology*, Vol. II, Chicago, 1957, p. 118. But Tillich goes on to show a greater concern for the event-character of the Resurrection in his "restitution theory" of the Easter event. The symbol of the Resurrection necessarily implies a factual element which historical research is justified in seeking to elaborate (p. 155). Death could not confine Jesus to the past. Wherever the New Being is present, he is present. His presence has the character of spiritual presence. "In this way the concrete individual life of the man Jesus of Nazareth is raised above transitoriness into the eternal presence of God as Spirit (p. 157). Tillich's "restitution theory" accords quite well with the presentation we have been making.

41. R. Bultmann, "New Testament and Mythology," *Kerygma and Myth*, Vol. I, p. 39.

42. H. Diem, *Dogmatics*, Edinburgh, 1959, p. 124.

43. M. Goguel, *The Birth of Christianity*, p. 42; E. Bammel, *Theologische Zeitschrift*, XI (1955), 401–19.

44. *Gen. Rab.* LVI:1 (Engl. transl. of the *Midrash Rabbah*, publ. by the Soncino Press, London, 1951, p. 491); *Deut. Rab.* 7:6 (Soncino ed., p. 137); *Esther Rab.* 9:2 (Soncino ed., p. 112).

45. Barnabas Lindars, *New Testament Apologetic*, Philadelphia, 1961, pp. 59 ff.

46. Vincent Taylor, *The Gospel According to St. Mark*, ad loc.

47. B. M. Metzger, "I Cor. XV 4b," *JTS*, VIII, New Series (1957), 118 ff. Metzger holds that "according to the scriptures" relates only to the verb, i.e. "was raised according to the scriptures." "On the third day" is not foreshadowed in the O.T., and denotes that his Resurrection took place "on the third day," i.e. "he was raised according to the scriptures *and* it took place 'on the third day.'" He finds support in I Maccabees 7:16: "Alcimus seized sixty of them [the Hasidim] and killed them in one day, in accordance with the word which was written, 'the flesh of thy saints and their blood they poured out round about Jerusalem, and there was none to bury them.'" The O.T. passage contains no reference to "in one day," so only the slaughter itself was prefigured by the Psalmist *and* it took place *in one day*.

48. *Theologisches Wörterbuch zum Neuen Testament*, ed. G. Kittel, Stuttgart, 1932 ff., I, p. 753; *v*. also B. M. Metzger, in loc. cit. The N.T. does not appe ir to

have had any equivalent for our conception of a text in the sense of a specific separate passage, and simply uses such technical introductory formulae as καθὼς γεγράπται, γεγράπται γάρ. V. A. M. Ramsey, *The Resurrection of Christ*, p. 26; E. Schweizer, "Two New Testament Creeds Compared," *Current Issues in New Testament Interpretation*, ed. William Klassen and Graydon Snyder, New York, 1962, p. 163.

49. W. Zimmerli, *Das Alte Testament als Anrede*, München, 1956.

50. H. J. Schoeps, *Paul: The Theology of the Apostle in the Light of Jewish Religious History* (Engl. transl. by H. Knight), Philadelphia, 1961, pp. 72 ff. Schoeps participates in the tendency to correct the exaggerated emphases of the Tübingen school on the difference between Paul and the prime apostles(Gal. 2:2), and expounds the view that Paul's bitterest strife was with the Jerusalem extremists, of whom "some from James" (Gal. 2:12) and "the false brethren brought in secretly" (Gal. 2:4) were the messengers, pp. 67 ff. *V.* also R. Bultmann, *Theology of the New Testament*, Vol. I, p. 185; W. G. Kümmel, "Jesus und Paulus," *Theologische Blätter*, 1942, p. 213.

51. Bo Reicke, *Diakonie, Festfreude und Zelos in Verbindung mit der altchristlichen Agapefeier*, Uppsala, 1951, pp. 279 ff.

52. W. Schmithals, *Die Gnosis in Korinth*, Göttingen, 1956, pp. 82–134. *V.* also R. McL. Wilson, "Some Recent Studies in Gnosticism," *NTS*, VI (Oct. 1959), 32 ff.

53. W. Marxsen, *Der Evangelist Markus*, Göttingen, 1956.

54. R. H. Lightfoot, *The Gospel Message of St. Mark*, Oxford, 1950.

55. E. Lohmeyer, *Das Evangelium des Markus*, Göttingen, 1937, pp. 355 f. Cf. V. Taylor, *The Gospel According to St. Mark*, p. 608.

56. M. Goguel, *La Foi à la résurrection de Jésus*, pp. 317 ff. R. Bultmann, *Die Geschichte der synoptischen Tradition*, Göttingen, 1958, pp. 278–81.

57. G. H. Boobyer, *St. Mark and the Transfiguration Story*, pp. 11–16; A. M. Ramsey, *The Glory of God and the Transfiguration of Christ*, London–New York, 1949, pp. 118 f.

58. That it is Mark who has here fixed the Resurrection as a terminus is acknowledged even by more conservative critics; for example, Vincent Taylor admits that this was probably expressed less explicitly by Jesus—*The Gospel According to St. Mark*, p. 393.

59. A. M. Ramsey, *The Resurrection of Christ*, p. 77.

60. R. H. Lightfoot, *History and Interpretation in the Gospels*, London, 1935, p. 92.

61. A. G. Hebert, "The Resurrection-Narrative in St. Mark's Gospel," *SJT*, XV (March 1962), 66 ff.

62. The mss. are D, Θ, 565; also some Syriac and Latin versions.

63. William Manson, *Jesus the Messiah*, pp. 39–40.

64. Nice as is Father Hebert's typological interpretation, it may hardly stand on linguistic grounds. Whether the phrase λίαν πρωΐ *must mean* "before daybreak" is very much open to question. Πρωΐ meaning "early" appears to be quite indefinite, *v.* W. Bauer's *Lexicon*. J. Jeremias has pointed out how Mark 16:2 is an example of the apparent rule of his Gospel that where two dates are given and the second seems to be merely pleonastic, it is in fact intended to interpret the first (1:35; 14:2; 15:42 as well as 16:2). So here "when the sun had risen" shows that "very early" still indicates a time after sunrise (πρωΐ itself meaning either "before" or "after" sunrise). *V.* J. Jeremias, *The Eucharistic Words of Jesus* (Engl. transl. by A. Ehrhardt), New York, 1955, p. 3.

65. B. W. Bacon, *Studies in Matthew*, New York, 1930, pp. 265 ff. G. D.

Kilpatrick's view of Matthew as a "revised Gospel lectionary" has Bacon's
notion of the Gospel as the *nova lex*, and of chapters 3–25 as a deliberate imitation of the Pentateuch, at its foundation; *v. The Origins of the Gospel According to St. Matthew*, Oxford, 1946, pp. 107 f. G. Bornkamm finds Bacon's thesis
unconvincing on the ground that the historical function of Jesus as Messiah for
Matthew is not the giving of a *nova lex* but the interpretation of the Law of
Moses; *v.* G. Bornkamm, G. Barth, and H. J. Held, *Überlieferung und Auslegung
im Matthäusevangelium*, Neukirchen, 1960, p. 32, n. 2. Bornkamm agrees about
the presence of a Moses typology in Matthew, but argues that Jesus does not
represent an antithesis to Moses, as in the Fourth Gospel, 1:17; 6:32 ff. The
"but I say unto you" of Matthew is not a Revelation word like the "I am" of the
Fourth Gospel. Jesus is above all the Teacher, interpreting the Law (p. 32; cf.
H. J. Held, p. 143). Krister Stendahl counsels caution about finding a Moses
typology in Matthew—*The School of St. Matthew*, Uppsala, 1954. F. V. Filson
has also recently noted that there are fewer references to Moses in Matthew than
in the other Gospels, plays down Matthew's affinities with Qumran, and points
up his universalism. Matthew's purpose, according to Filson, was "to provide the
Church's teachers with a basic tool for their work"—*The Gospel According to
St. Matthew* (Black's N.T. Commentaries), London, 1960. However, although
little overt expression is given to the "second Moses" theme in Matthew, it is
not infrequently implied. In Matthew 2:15 Jesus is proclaimed as the one coming
out of Egypt according to scriptural prophecy. In the Sermon on the Mount he is
not the abrogator of the Mosaic Torah, but the one who brings it to its full
fruition. The ten miracles wrought by God in Moses' time (*v. Pirke Aboth* 5:4)
seem to be paralleled by the ten mighty works of Jesus in Matthew 8 and 9.
Jewish Messianic expectation had of course a place for a figure similar to Moses;
v. the Intertestamental literature, e.g. the Psalms of Solomon, also the citation of
Deuteronomy 18:18 in the Messianic testimonies of Qumran, and the figure of
the Righteous Teacher in the history or theology of the Qumran sect. The Rabbinic literature frequently compares the work of the Messiah with that of Moses;
v. G. Kittel, *Theologisches Wörterbuch des Neuen Testament*, IV, 846 f., and
W. D. Davies, *Torah in the Messianic Age and/or the Age To Come* (Society of
Biblical Lit. and Exegesis, 1952), pp. 29 ff. *V.* also G. Barth, *Überlieferung und
Auslegung im Matthäusevangelium*, pp. 143 ff.

66. E. Lohmeyer, "Mir ist gegeben alle Gewalt," *In Memoriam Ernst Lohmeyer*, ed. W. Schmauch, Stuttgart, 1951, pp. 22 ff.

67. O. Michel, "Der Abschluss des Matthäusevangeliums," *Evangelische Theologie*, X (1950–51), 16–26. J. Jeremias, *Jesus' Promise to the Nations*, London,
1958, pp. 38–9. In I Timothy 3:16, Philippians 2:9–11; Hebrews 1:5–14 we also
have coronation texts after the fashion of the ancient Egyptian coronation ritual.
The connection of Matthew 28:18b with the enthronement of the Son of Man in
Daniel 7:14 has also frequently been noticed.

68. O. Michel, op. cit. pp. 17 ff. G. Barth, op. cit. n. 65, p. 124.

69. C. H. Dodd, *New Testament Studies*, Manchester, 1953, p. 56. J. Jeremias, op. cit. p. 39. G. Barth, op. cit. p. 125. A. M. Ramsey writes: "Mark views
the Resurrection as itself the coming of the end: the Son of Man has returned, the
age-to-come is breaking in. Matthew rather looks ahead to the Parousia that still
lies in the future when he writes"—*The Resurrection of Christ*, p. 79. But the
tension, "the day is come: the day is still to come" exists not only *between* Mark
and Matthew, but within Mark and even more clearly within Matthew itself.

70. If the Church's message consists of *all* that God did in and through Jesus
Christ, there can be no gospel without this Jesus.

71. Eusebius' text reads only "Go ye therefore and teach all nations in my name." It is hard to decide whether Eusebius was abbreviating the text of the Gospel or citing the text in its original form, in which case "baptizing in the triadic name" would probably be a second-century liturgical addition. However, all the Greek mss. and the versions do contain the longer clause. *V. F. C.* Conybeare, "The Eusebian Form of the Text Mt. 28:19," *ZNW* (1901), pp. 275 ff.; W. C. Allen, *St. Matthew* (I.C.C.), 1907, pp. 307–8; G. Barth, *Überlieferung und Auslegung im Matthäusevangelium,* p. 126.

72. Matthew makes it plain that the Church's missionary obedience arises not from a decision in regard to any theological abstraction or soteriological proposition, but a decision in regard to *Jesus* the Christ, with all that the name Jesus implied. *V. J. J.* Vincent, "Discipleship and Synoptic Studies," *Theologische Zeitschrift,* XVI, Heft 6 (Nov.-Dec. 1960), 456 ff.; also H. W. Bartsch, "The Still Unsettled Debate on Demythologizing," *Religion in Life,* XXX (Spring 1961), 167 ff.

73. G. Barth, *Überlieferung und Auslegung im Matthäusevangelium,* p. 128.

74. O. Michel, op. cit. pp. 16–26, n. 86.

75. Théo Preiss, "The Mystery of the Son of Man," *Life in Christ,* 1954. *V.* also Roger Mehl, *La Rencontre d'autrui: Remarques sur le problème de la communication,* Paris-Neuchâtel, 1955, pp. 53 ff. "Si j'annonce que Christ est présent actuellement, je dois du même coup croire que mon partenaire, qu'il le sache ou non, est assumé par Christ comme je le suis moi-même et qu'ainsi en Christ une communication plénière est possible entre lui et moi" (p. 55).

76. A. R. C. Leaney, "The Resurrection Narratives in Luke (XXIV: 12–53)," *NTS,* II (Nov. 1955), 110 ff.

77. Edward Lohse, *Die Auferstehung Jesus Christ: Im Zeugnis des Lukasevangeliums* (Biblische Studien 31), Neukirchen, 1961, pp. 32–3. Quite aside from attempts to find a background for Luke's Emmaus story, it is not a particularly fruitful exercise to try to reconstruct his source or sources. We cannot achieve much beyond inferring from the other less-developed types of appearance-story that Luke may have begun with a kernel consisting of verses 13, 15b, 16, and 28–31. *V.* A. R. C. Leaney, in op. cit. p. 111.

78. We follow the longer text of B, C, and other mss. "While he blessed them he parted from them and was carried up into heaven. And they worshiped him and returned to Jerusalem with great joy, and were continually in the temple blessing God." It is sometimes argued that the word ἀναφέρειν, which is used in Hebrews of offering a sacrifice, cannot have that connotation here, and so in its plain sense of "carry up" would be too colorless a word for Luke to use for something so important to his theology as the Ascension. The authenticity of the words "was carried up into heaven" may be defended on the following grounds: (a) the longer text of B and C is likely to be correct. The shorter Western text, in its harmonizing tendency, may well have wished to resolve the difficulty of variant reports of the Ascension by omitting these words; (b) the words "was carried up into heaven" are necessary to complete the order of sentences in Luke 24:50–53; (c) the concrete meaning of ἀναφέρειν suits the realistic theology of Luke in this chapter. P. A. van Stempvoort, "The Interpretation of the Ascension in Luke and Acts," *NTS,* V (Oct. 1958), 36. E. Haenchen observes "that *even if* the shorter reading, omitting these words, is original, the ἀνελήμφθη of Acts 1:2 indicates that διέστη ἀπ' αὐτῶν in Luke 24:52 means the Ascension"—*Die Apostelgeschichte,* p. 109, n. 3.

79. A. M. Ramsey, op. cit. p. 81.

80. In regard to the later stage of the Fourth Gospel also, Siegfried Schulz has

made a good case for the dependence of the Johannine tradition on the worship of the Johannine congregation—*Untersuchungen zur Menschensohn-Christologie im Johannesevangelium*, Göttingen, 1957, p. 176.

81. P. A. van Stempvoort, op. cit. pp. 30 ff.

82. The question of the integrity of Luke 24:50–53 (briefly touched on in note 78 above) and Acts 1:1–12 has been hotly debated. Among reasons suggested for rejecting both passages in whole or in part are the following: (a) the apparent conflict between the dating of the Ascension in Luke 24:51 and Acts 1:3; (b) the μέν *solitarium* of Acts 1:1 with no answering δέ (but is not this a fairly common usage?); (c) the disturbed state of the text with several variants in Luke 24:51–2 and Acts 1:2 (but full weight should be given to the possibility that even good old texts did not wish to retain two accounts of the Ascension!); (d) the weight of Harnack's judgment that Acts 1:1–12 really tells us nothing of the contents of the book (but must it do so in view of the special transition Luke has to make between his Gospel and his history of the Church?). The Lucan origin of Acts 1:1–12 has been rejected by a formidable list of scholars—to those cited by W. G. Kümmel in *Theologische Rundschau*, 1948, p. 9, n. 1, namely, E. Meyer, M. Goguel, H. W. Beyer, and a conservative critic like O. Bauernfeind, should be added also E. Preuschen, A. Loisy, J. Weiss, and E. Norden; *v.* E. Haenchen, *Die Apostelgeschichte*, p. 116. H. Sahlin suggested that Luke 24:50–53 and Acts 1:1–5 were added in the second century when Luke's work was divided into two sections—*Der Messias und das Gottesvolk: Studien zur protolukanischen Theologie*, Uppsala, 1945, pp. 11–18. The same position was taken by K. Lake, *The Beginnings of Christianity*, Vol. V, pp. 1–4. P. H. Menoud accepts this hypothesis and holds that Luke 24:50–53 is very loosely connected with the rest of the chapter and is scarcely Lucan (Acts 1:6 seems also to follow naturally on Luke 24:49), and also that Luke 24:50–52 seems like a résumé of the scene described in Acts 1:9–12, and Luke 24:53 like an abbreviation of Acts 2:46–7—"Remarques sur les textes de l'ascension dans Luke-Acts," *Neutestamentliche Studien für Rudolf Bultmann*, p. 152. A. R. C. Leaney has recently adopted this view in a modified form: he omits with D the words "and was carried up into heaven" in Luke 24:51, and excludes only from the prologue of Acts chapter 1:3–5—*The Gospel According to St. Luke* (Harper's N. T. Commentaries), New York, 1958, p. 295. Over against this, I find van Stempvoort's defense of the originality of Luke 24:50–53 (and of Acts 1:1–11) on textual, stylistic, and semasiological grounds convincing—the word "bless" occurs fourteen times in the Gospel and twice in Acts; the "temple" figures prominently throughout Luke's work; and the noun "joy" is found eight times in the Gospel and twice in Acts (van Stempvoort, op. cit. pp. 34 ff.). In regard to this last point, I cannot follow Menoud's argument that the "great joy" of the disciples in Luke 24:52 has no motive since the Ascension as such would much rather be a cause for grief (P. H. Menoud, op. cit. p. 152), inasmuch as Luke would certainly share the view that, by the Ascension, Jesus entered into his heavenly Lordship, and would see in it every reason for rejoicing and praising God.

H. Conzelmann, who rejects Luke 24:50–53 because of "the non-Lucan setting in Bethany and the lack of any clear delimitation of the period of the appearances" (*The Theology of St. Luke*, p. 203), seems to find in these verses a stumbling block to his presentation of Luke's "theology of saving history," for which Acts 1:3 and 1:9–11 are pivotal. But Jerusalem, the center of Luke's "theological geography," is very much in the picture in Luke 24:50–53, and Luke writes that Jesus led his disciples *from* Jerusalem ἕως πρὸς βηθανίαν.

If we are not persuaded by the arguments against the integrity of Luke 24:50–

53 and Acts 1:1-11, is there then any necessary incongruity between Luke's two accounts of the Ascension? It is at this point that we must take fully into consideration the different intentions or purposes by which Luke may have been motivated in closing his Gospel on the one hand, and in composing the prelude to his history of the primitive Church on the other. In the conclusion of the Gospel he appears to be focusing on the gladness of faith in the heavenly enthronement of Christ in fulfillment of the prophecy of Psalm 110:1. In the preface to Acts the stress is on the Ascension as a "declaration of acted finality" (C. F. D. Moule, "The Ascension," *ET,* LXVIII (1957), 208), marking the termination of the epoch of Jesus' history and the inauguration of the new time of the Church under the Spirit and of its mission to the world. Accordingly E. Haenchen suggests, we think reasonably, that most readers would have found no incompatibility between Luke 24:50-53 and Acts 1:3. The unadorned and undetailed nature of the tradition of the "forty days" made it easy for Luke to introduce it, as part of his "realistic interpretation" of the Ascension in Acts 1, into the same material with which he described the last encounter of the disciples with Jesus at the end of the Gospel.

83. Paul Schubert, "The Structure and Significance of Luke 24," *Neutestamentliche Studien für Rudolf Bultmann,* 1954, p. 185: "It is this theology [Luke's theology of "sacred history"] which determines his chronological interest. The latter does not determine his theology." How little the Church was interested in the "forty days" as a mere chronological fact can be inferred from the neglect of the tradition in the Patristic writings—not until Tertullian is it expressly mentioned. The Church besides knew of other traditions: Irenaeus testifies that Ptolemy and the Ophites assigned a period of eighteen months; Coptic Gnostic texts like the *Pistis Sophia* speak of eleven or twelve years—*v.* M. Goguel, *La Foi à la Résurrection de Jésus dans le christianisme primitif,* Paris, 1933, pp. 354 f.

84. Barnabas Lindars, "The Composition of John XX," *NTS,* VII (1961), 142-7.

85. The most obvious difficulty in the way of this interpretation is the seeming contradiction between Jesus' injunction to Mary *not* to touch him and his later invitation to Thomas to touch him. C. F. D. Moule has recently proposed that the words to Mary mean that she need not cling to the Rabbi for he is still "with her" and has not yet withdrawn from sight. By contrast, Thomas needs to be met on his own ground, and, since he has demanded tactual evidence, to be offered it, if only to convince him, in the very act, that it can be dispensed with. "On this showing, the contrast lies entirely in the needs and circumstances of the two disciples, and not in any difference in the state of the Lord as between the two encounters"—"The Individualism of the Fourth Gospel," *Novum Testamentum,* V (July 1962), 175. Professor Moule's suggestion, interesting though it is, seems unlikely. Mary's recognition of her risen Master has already taken place (John 20:16). Jesus' "touch me not" to Mary (John 20:17) would seem to imply something more or other than merely a confirmation that it is he, Jesus of Nazareth, who is "with her." The same is true of Matthew 28:9-10 (in which Moule finds a parallel to John 20:17): "Jesus met them, saying: 'All hail.' And they came and held him by the feet and worshiped him. Then said Jesus to them: 'Be not afraid: go tell my brethren . . .'" The "be not afraid" means here also, according to Moule, that they are to have no misgivings, for it is really the Lord whom they see; he has not yet ascended; he is no phantom. But here once again, the risen Jesus has already been recognized and indeed worshiped (Matt. 28:9), and it seems more likely that this "be not afraid" means that they should not

allow their reverential awe in his presence to keep them from spreading the news (Matt. 28:10).

It is, I think, preferable to follow the view of C. H. Dodd and others that the apparent contradiction between the "touch me not" to Mary and "reach hither thy finger" to Thomas is simply that between the two the Ascension has, as John understands it, been consummated. It may be that, as is not infrequently suggested, John has High Priestly notions in view: the High Priest became "touchable" only after he had completed the sacrifice and then finished his intercession for the people in the Holy of Holies. At all events, the two stories appear to be in accord in their main *theological* point—faith lives out of the whole consummated way of Jesus through Death, Resurrection, and Exaltation to the Father, and not by grasping any particular "moment" of it such as Jesus' earthly or physical appearance alone (v. the climax of the Thomas story in John 20:29).

86. R. Bultmann, "History and Eschatology in the New Testament," *NTS,* I (Sept. 1954), 15.

87. Sir Edwyn Hoskyns contended strongly that we are dealing here not with an identification of the resurrected Christ and the Spirit, but with a distinct Resurrection appearance—E. Hoskyns and F. N. Davey, *The Fourth Gospel,* London, 1947, p. 459. Cf. C. K. Barrett, *The Gospel According to St. John,* New York, 1957, p. 387. Even if, however, we hesitate to speak of the total identification of the risen Christ and the Spirit, John does plainly place the gift of the Spirit on Easter Day, and so seems to indicate that in the *experience* of the Church, at least, the two are most closely connected.

It is another and an open question also whether John has lost sight altogether of any *future* eschatological consummation. Did John intend to substitute the Paraclete for the Parousia? John 14:16 is quoted in support of such a view. But, as C. F. D. Moule has noted, εἰς τὸν αἰῶνα here need only mean "for good and all" in a relative sense and in contrast to the earthly ministry of Jesus about to be terminated. There is hardly sufficient evidence to show that the Spirit is conceived differently in John from Paul, for whom it denotes the abiding presence of God with His Church on earth and the firstfruits or pledge of a consummation yet to come. Cf. Romans 8:23, where the Spirit is a pledge of something still to come; cf. also I John 3:24, which recognizes the presence of the Spirit, but at the same time adds in 3:2 εαν φανερώθη. The "now is" sayings of John 4:23 and 5:25 only represent the combination of realized with future which is a recognized phenomenon also in the Synoptists. *V.* C. F. D. Moule, "The Individualism of the Fourth Gospel," *Novum Testamentum,* V (July 1962), 178 ff.

88. R. Bultmann, *Theology of the New Testament,* Vol. II, pp. 56 ff.; also *Das Evangelium des Johannes,* p. 539.

89. H. Grass, *Ostergeschehen und Osterberichte,* Göttingen, 1956, p. 72.

90. E. Schweizer, "The Concept of the Church in the Gospel and Epistle of St. John," *New Testament Essays: Studies in Memory of T. W. Manson,* Manchester, 1959, pp. 230–45.

91. The Fourth Gospel in this respect is quite different from later narratives of the appearance to Thomas, like the *Epistola Apostolorum,* and from Ignatius' Letter to the Smyrnans, where "faith" or "believing" plays hardly any role. *V.* Helmut Wenz, "Sehen und Glauben bei Johannes," *Theologische Zeitschrift,* XVII, Heft 1 (Jan.-Feb. 1961), 17 ff.

92. O. Cullmann, "Εἶδεν καὶ ἐπίστευσεν, La vie de Jésus, objet de la 'vue' et de la 'foi,' d'après le quatrième Évangile," *Aux Sources de la tradition chrétienne,* Paris, 1950, pp. 52 ff. Cullmann holds that the verb θεᾶσθαι ("we beheld his glory," John 1:14) might well refer to "seeing with the eyes," facing the words

and deeds of Jesus, *and* to spiritual apprehension thereof. He points to the interplay between the verbs ὁρᾶν and πιστεύειν and γινώσκειν in 14:7, 9, 17, and to the combination of "seeing" and "believing" in the story of the beloved disciple's entry into the tomb (John 20:8), and holds that this connection between "seeing" and "believing" matches the stress in the Fourth Gospel on the full humanity of Jesus on the one hand and his full divinity on the other. By contrast, Bultmann (*Theology of the New Testament,* Vol. II, p. 72), while observing that inner sight may paradoxically coincide with a sensory perceiving of Jesus (1:14; 6:40; 12:45; 14:9), maintains that the specifically Johannine usage indicates inward comprehension of matters that are not perceptible to the senses.

93. Paul Tillich, *Systematic Theology,* Vol. II, Chicago, 1957, pp. 156–8.

94. Gerhard Koch, *Die Auferstehung Jesu Christi* (Beiträge zur Historischen Theologie, 27), Tübingen, 1959, pp. 157 ff.

95. N. A. Dahl, "The Johannine Church and History," in William Klassen and Graydon Snyder, *Current Issues in New Testament Interpretation,* pp. 135–6.

96. E. Hoskyns and F. N. Davey, *The Fourth Gospel,* pp. 270, 320.

97. G. Bornkamm, *Jesus of Nazareth,* pp. 185–6.

Chapter VI

1. M. Kähler, *Der sogenannte historische Jesus und der geschichtliche, biblische Christus,* Leipzig, 1892. New ed., München, 1956, pp. 23, 49.

2. W. Wrede, *Das Messiasgeheimnis in den Evangelien,* Göttingen, 1901. J. Wellhausen, *Einleitung in die drei ersten Evangelien,* Berlin, 1905.

3. A. Drews, *Das Markusevangelium als Zeugnis gegen die Geschichtlichkeit Jesu,* Jena, 1921. For an excellent concise account of the main trends in Marcan research, *v.* J. M. Robinson, *The Problem of History in Mark,* London, 1957, pp. 7 ff.

4. M. Dibelius, *Formgeschichte des Evangeliums,* Tübingen, 1919 (recently revised by G. Bornkamm, Tübingen, 1959). Engl. transl. by B. L. Woolf, *From Tradition to Gospel,* New York, 1935.

5. R. Bultmann, *Die Geschichte der synoptischen Tradition,* p. 374; also *Theology of the New Testament,* Vol. II, pp. 124–6.

6. J. Schreiber, "Die Christologie des Markusevangeliums," *ZTK,* LVIII, Heft 2 (1961), 154 ff.

7. W. Marxsen, *Der Evangelist Markus.* Cf. J. M. Robinson, op. cit. Robinson also brings out the overlapping in Mark between the history of the believer and the history of Jesus. In the history he records, Mark speaks in the cosmic language of a struggle between the Spirit and Satan. The history is seen in its unity by Mark as the eschatological action of God, who defeats the force of evil and establishes the reign of God in history by the Resurrection of Jesus Christ. Robinson goes on to draw attention to the continuation of the same cosmic struggle which Jesus began, in the "Marcan history after A.D. 30," and, in a final investigation of "communal history" in Mark, he shows that Mark understood his own time and experience in the same way as he understood the history of Jesus.

8. I am indebted in this section to two essays by T. A. Burkill, "St. Mark's Philosophy of History," *NTS,* III (Jan. 1957), 142–8, and "Strain on the Secret: An Examination of Mark 11:1–13:37," *ZNW,* LI (1960), 31 ff.

9. This address is found on the lips of two blind men (9:27), a woman of Canaan (15:22), two blind men in Jericho (20:30–31), the crowds (21:9), and children (21:15).

10. Matthew's reproduction of the Q saying gives a greater breadth to the perception of the disciples than does the Lucan form: "Blessed are the eyes which see *what you see*" (Luke 10:23–4).

11. G. Bornkamm, *Überlieferung und Auslegung im Matthäusevangelium*, p. 43—"Abweisung des Petrus-Bekentnisses." Matthew has transferred Jesus' rebuke of Peter to a different context (16:21–3). Here it follows upon Jesus' speaking about his rejection and death preceding the Resurrection. When Peter objects, he is upbraided. The way of the Cross, for both Master and disciple, is inescapable (Matt. 16:24–7).

12. From the voluminous literature on this text, I mention, in support of the view presented, only G. Johnston, *The Church in the New Testament*, Cambridge, 1943, p. 48; G. Bornkamm, *Überlieferung und Auslegung im Matthäusevangelium*, pp. 41 ff.; and *Jesus of Nazareth*, pp. 186 ff. For another recent point of view, *v*. O. Cullmann, *Peter, Disciple, Apostle, Martyr* (Engl. transl. by F. V. Filson), 2nd revised ed., Philadelphia, 1962.

13. G. Bornkamm, "Die Sturmstillung im Matthäusevangelium," *Überlieferung und Auslegung im Matthäusevangelium*, pp. 48 ff. Cf. Paul J. Achtemeier, "Person and Deed, Jesus and the Storm-tossed Sea," *Interpretation*, XVI (April 1962), 169 ff. After adducing evidence from the Babylonian and Hebraic traditions for the concept of the sea as symbolizing the threat of chaos, Achtemeier detects three main motifs in the Gospel accounts of Jesus' stilling the sea: (1) he does what God alone can do (Psalm 107:28 f.); (2) the stilling of the sea is the final redemptive act by which the creation is secured against its arch-enemy, chaos (Psalm 74); (3) in the very earthly presence of Jesus the demonic is vanquished, so that "with him the victory of God over evil and its prince, begun with the creation, is about to be consummated." With this background in view, we may better appreciate the depth of meaning involved for the Church in the "storm-stilling."

14. Gerhard Barth plausibly finds here an analogy to the Shekhinah (cf. *Aboth* 3, 2). The *name* of Jesus takes the place of the Torah, and Jesus himself is present in place of the Shekhinah—*Überlieferung und Auslegung im Matthäusevangelium*, p. 127.

15. The "individuality" of the authorship of the Gospel is debated in recent scholarship. Krister Stendahl admits that "there is no *a priori* reason why the Matthean revision of Mark was not the ingenious work of one man, 'the author,' whether his name was Matthew or not." Nevertheless, his thesis is that behind Matthew's Gospel lies the activity of a scribal school in the Church where he lived and served—*The School of St. Matthew*, Uppsala, 1954, pp. 30 ff. G. Bornkamm accepts this thesis, but thinks (rightly, we believe, in view of the extremely careful formulation and planning of the work of Matthew) that Stendahl has underestimated the *individuality* of the theological reflection and interpretation of the Tradition in the Gospel. Matthew 13:52 may indeed be the best characterization of the author: "Every scribe instructed unto the kingdom of heaven is like a man who is a householder, who brings forth out of his treasure things new and old," *Überlieferung und Auslegung im Matthäusevangelium*, p. 46 and p. 47, n. 2.

16. The designation "formula quotation" is used because these citations include a special introductory formula. Οὐκ ἐρίσει (Matt. 12:19: "he shall not strive") has no parallel either in the M.T. or LXX of Isaiah 42:2. It looks like Matthew's interpretation of Jesus' refusal to engage in open conflict with the Pharisees (Matt. 12:14–15). *V*. K. Stendahl, op. cit. p. 112; also Gerhard Barth, op. cit. pp. 118–19. Again in Matthew 12:20, "A bruised reed shall he not break,

and smoking flax shall he not quench, till he send forth judgment unto victory."
There is no parallel to Matthew's εἰς νῖκος ("unto victory") in the M.T. or LXX,
or in the Targum or Peschitta. Stendahl believes that this εἰς νῖκος reflects the
influence of Habakkuk 1:4: yēçē' laneçaḥ mishpaṭ and that εἰς νῖκος is an
Aramaism since the Aramaic neçaḥ means "victory"—op. cit. p. 113. G. Barth
insists that we must ask the further question why Matthew has made this change.
And he finds in the conjunction of 12:20a, "A bruised reed shall he not break,
and smoking flax shall he not quench," and 12:20b, "till he send forth judgment
unto victory," Matthew's own Christological conception. In 12.20a is recalled
not only Jesus' work of healing (12:15) but also his preaching (11:5). All the
Lord's saving work, indeed his final victory, already resides in his humiliation
as the Servant of God—op. cit. pp. 119–20.

17. E. Lohmeyer, *Gottesknecht und Davidssohn*, Göttingen, 1953.

18. W. C. van Unnik, "Jesus the Christ," *NTS*, VIII (Jan. 1962), 101 ff.

19. G. W. H. Lampe, "The Lucan Portrait of Christ," *NTS*, II (Feb. 1956), 170.

20. Philo, *De Spec. Leg.* I, 65. *V.* O. Cullmann, *The Christology of the New Testament*, pp. 16 ff., also G. W. H. Lampe, in op. cit. p. 168.

21. C. F. Evans has compared the great central section of Luke's Gospel, the so-called "travel-narrative," to a new Deuteronomy, in which the teaching of Moses is followed through step by step. If it is meant to be so, the Mosaic character of the role of Jesus in Luke would of course be strongly corroborated. C. F. Evans, "The Central Section of St. Luke's Gospel," *Studies in the Gospels*, ed. D. E. Nineham, Oxford, 1955, pp. 37–53. The description of what was to be accomplished at Jerusalem as an "exodus" may confirm the "second Moses" idea as applied to Jesus by Luke. G. W. H. Lampe, in op. cit. p. 69.

22. O. Cullmann, *The Christology of the New Testament*, p. 44.

23. W. C. van Unnik, in op. cit. pp. 113–14.

24. G. W. H. Lampe, "The Holy Spirit in the Writings of St. Luke," *Studies in the Gospels*, ed. D. E. Nineham, pp. 159 ff.

25. E. Hoskyns and F. N. Davey, *The Riddle of the New Testament*, p. 160.

26. G. Ebeling, *Theologie und Verkündigung*, Tübingen, 1962, pp. 55 f. Ebeling holds that the existential method has to be viewed as one form of the historical-critical method: inquiry into the facts is inquiry into what is exposed in the facts.

27. E. Hoskyns and F. N. Davey, op. cit. p. 260.

28. Bo Reicke, "Incarnation and Exaltation," *Interpretation*, XVI (April 1962), 162.

29. H. Strathmann, in Kittel's *Wörterbuch*, Vol. IV, p. 505.

30. N. A. Dahl, "The Johannine Church and History," *Current Issues in New Testament Interpretation*, ed. William Klassen and Graydon Snyder, pp. 124 ff.

31. E. Schweizer, "Discipleship and Belief in Jesus as Lord from Jesus to the Hellenistic Church," *NTS*, V (Nov. 1955), 87 ff.

32. James Denney, *The Death of Christ*, London, 1902, p. 280.

33. G. Bornkamm, *Jesus of Nazareth*, p. 23.

34. R. Bultmann, *Theology of the New Testament*, Vol. I, p. 185. But for a defense of the positive importance of the *Verba Christi* in the Epistles as a mark of the authority of Christ, *v.* E. G. Selwyn, "The Authority of Christ in the New Testament," *NTS*, III (Jan. 1957), 83 ff.

35. T. W. Manson, "The Argument from Prophecy," *JTS*, XLVI (Jan.-April 1945), 129–36.

36. W. D. Davies, *Paul and Rabbinic Judaism*, pp. 250 ff.

37. E. Käsemann, "Kritische Analyse von Phil. 2:5–11," *ZTK*, XLVII (1950), 313 ff.
38. H. J. Schoeps, *Paul*, pp. 153–7.
39. For example, A. M. Hunter, *Paul and His Predecessors*, p. 46; A. E. J. Rawlinson, *The New Testament Doctrine of the Christ*, p. 134; W. D. Davies, *Paul and Rabbinic Judaism*, pp. 41–2, 274.
40. E. Schweizer, *Lordship and Discipleship*, pp. 61–3.
41. J. M. Robinson, "The Quest of the Historical Jesus Today," *Theology Today*, XV (July 1958), 193.
42. E. Schweizer, op. cit. p. 62.
43. W. L. Knox, *St. Paul and the Church of the Gentiles*, Cambridge, 1939, pp. 87 f. *V*. W. D. Davies, op. cit. p. 107.
44. M. Noth, "Die Vergegenwärtigung des Alten Testaments in der Verkündigung," *Evangelische Theologie*, XII (1952), 6–17.
45. For the most recent support of this view, *v*. Günter Wagner, *Das Religionsgeschichtliche Problem von Römer* 6:1–11, Zürich, 1962, pp. 299–305.
46. M. Dibelius, *Paulus und die Mystik*, Munich, 1941.
47. W. D. Davies, op. cit. p. 88.
48. G. Ebeling, *Theologie und Verkündigung*, Tübingen, 1962; cf. R. Bultmann, *Jesus and the Word*, p. 8.
49. J. M. Robinson, "The Quest of the Historical Jesus Today," *Theology Today*, XV (July 1958), 183–97.
50. Van A. Harvey and Schubert M. Ogden, "Wie neu ist die 'Neue Frage nach dem historischen Jesus'?" *ZTK*, LIX, Heft 1 (1962), 46–87.
51. James Denney, *The Death of Christ*, p. 100.
52. John Macquarrie, *The Scope of Demythologizing*, pp. 84–5.
53. E. Schweizer, *Lordship and Discipleship*, p. 67.
54. H. Wheeler Robinson, *Redemption and Revelation*, London, 1942, pp. 232–3.
55. E. G. Selwyn, *The First Epistle of St. Peter*, London, 1949, p. 129.
56. O. Cullmann, *The Christology of the New Testament*, pp. 91–2.
57. A. D. Galloway, *The Cosmic Christ*, London, 1951, pp. 212–3.
58. H. P. Owen, *Revelation and Existence*, Cardiff, 1957, p. 116.
59. O. Cullmann, op. cit. p. 93.
60. Ibid.; E. Schweizer, op. cit. p. 71.
61. C. Spicq, *L'Epître aux Hebreux*, Vol. II, p. 39, relates τελειοῦν in Hebrews to Jesus' saying from the Cross in John 19:30, τετέλεσται. *V*. O. Cullmann, op. cit. p. 92.
62. O. Cullmann, op. cit. p. 95.
63. E. Käsemann, *Das wandernde Gottesvolk*, 1939, p. 58.
64. W. Manson, *The Epistle to the Hebrews*, 1951, pp. 57 f.; E. Schweizer, op. cit. pp. 74–5.
65. The writer appears to see the present work of Christ not as an offering either of himself or his work in the Holy of Holies, but rather as a resumption of his ordinary work as Israel's representative before God now that the once-for-all and unrepeatable act of expiation had been consummated—"where there is remission of these there is no more offering for sin" (Heb. 10:18). Further the writer seems also to point up the contrast between the priests who are *standing* in their day to day serving (as indeed they were required to stand), and the Christ who has perfected for ever those who are being sanctified and so can *sit down*. Thus Christ is depicted as having finished for good and all his sacrificial work and as having entered upon his ongoing royal work (cf. II Samuel

7:18, 24, 26, 27, 29) of intercession while now *seated* before God. Wilfrid Stott, "The Conception of 'Offering' in the Epistle to the Hebrews," *NTS*, IX (Oct. 1962), 62 ff.

66. E. Underhill, *Worship*, 2nd ed., London, 1937, p. 33. I am indebted here to an unpublished paper by Prof. F. Herzog at Duke University on "The Norm and Freedom of Christian Worship."

67. O. Cullmann, op. cit. p. 98.

68. H. P. Owen, *Revelation and Existence*, p. 115.

69. James Denney, *The Death of Christ*, p. 238.

70. Supra, n. 65.

71. O. Cullmann, op. cit. p. 101.

72. E. Schweizer, op. cit. p. 90.

73. Cf. I Timothy 6:12–16. *V.* O. Cullmann, *The Earliest Christian Confessions* (Engl. transl. by J. K. S. Reid), London, 1949, pp. 23–5.

74. C. K. Barrett, "The Lamb of God," *NTS*, I (Feb. 1955), 216.

75. The view that the Seer has combined the idea of the glorified Christ with that of the slain Lamb, without any sense of antinomy between them, is shared by R. H. Charles, *The Revelation of St. John*, Vol. I, Edinburgh, 1920, pp. cxiii-cxiv; I. T. Beckwith, *The Apocalypse of John*, New York, 1922, p. 316; and V. Taylor, *The Names of Jesus*, London, 1954, pp. 116–17. The interpretation of the Baptist's words in John 1:29, "Behold the Lamb of God, who takes away the sin of the world," is a special, and controversial, question. C. H. Dodd finds here no cultic and sacrificial reference, but rather the apocalyptic Lamb of God of Revelation, the bellwether of God's flock, the victorious Messiah—*The Interpretation of the Fourth Gospel*, pp. 230–38. C. K. Barrett, however, holds that, whereas the Baptist thought of the Messiah as the Apocalyptic Lamb, Christian theology reflected on the meaning of Jesus' death and Christian liturgy developed the notion of the Christian Passover. The Fourth Evangelist therefore brought the resultant wealth of material together, apocalyptic, theological, liturgical, and poured it in, so to speak, to the designation "Lamb of God."—C. K. Barrett, op. cit. pp. 210–18. Geza Vermes has recently connected the Lamb with the Akedah, the Binding of Isaac (Gen. 22:8): "The Fourth Gospel consciously emphasizes the two traditional expressions—Passover Lamb and Suffering Servant—of the one fundamental reality, namely, the sacrifice of the new Isaac, the 'son of God' "—*Scripture and Tradition in Judaism*, Leiden, 1961, pp. 223–5. Cf. A. Richardson, *An Introduction to the Theology of the New Testament*, New York, 1958, p. 228.

76. A. Schweitzer, op. cit. pp. 78–9.

77. Théo Preiss, "Was the Last Supper a Paschal Meal?" *Life in Christ* (Engl. transl. by Harold Knight), London, 1954.

78. J. Jeremias, *The Eucharistic Words of Jesus*, Oxford, 1955, pp. 106 ff. W. D. Davies, *Paul and Rabbinic Judaism*, p. 246.

79. This is the view of Vincent Taylor, *Jesus and His Sacrifice*, London, 1937, p. 205.

80. A. Schweitzer, *Die Mystik des Apostels Paulus*, Tübingen, 1930, p. 156. Engl. transl. by W. Montgomery, *The Mysticism of Paul the Apostle*, London, 1931.

81. W. D. Davies, op. cit. p. 248.

82. H. Lietzmann, *An die Korinther* (Handbuch zum Neuen Testament), 3rd ed., Tübingen, 1931, p. 57. Cf. recently Johannes Munck, *Paul and the Salvation of Mankind* (Engl. transl. by Frank Clarke), Richmond, 1959, p. 18. Munck argues that we must not take too literally Paul's assertion, on the ground of his

Damascus experience, that his call and his gospel were directly from the Lord. "It can scarcely be doubted that he was baptized in Damascus. A human mediation of this kind, bringing to him baptism and the tradition of the Christian Church, does not prejudice his assertion that both his call and his way of presenting the Gospel were from God and not from man." It is largely a matter of emphasis, for recognition of the human factors involved in the mediation of Paul's call and gospel should not be allowed to obscure the importance for him of the notion of the controlling influence of the living Christ on the tradition. *V.* the words of I Corinthians 7:12: "To the rest say I, not the Lord." O. Cullmann has shown how in such a case "the Lord" is equivalent to the tradition of the Apostolic Church understood as *the voice of the living Christ*—"Κύριος as Designation for the Oral Tradition Concerning Jesus," *SJT,* III (June 1950), 180–97.

83. W. D. Davies, op. cit. pp. 249–51.

84. Ibid. p. 252.

85. H. J. Schoeps, *Paul,* pp. 116–17.

86. G. Bornkamm, "Geschichte und Glaube im Neuen Testament," *Evangelische Theologie,* XXII (1962), 1–15.

87. J. Jeremias, *Die Abendmahlsworte Jesu,* 3rd ed., Göttingen, 1960, pp. 234–46. Although he accepts Jeremias' premises in regard to εἰς τὴν ἐμὴν ἀνάμνησιν, G. Vermes has recently maintained (rightly, we think) that Jeremias has not sufficiently stressed the sacrificial aspect of a rite "uniting, in a liturgical drama, both *past* and future within a continuous present." Linking the Eucharistic meal with the theology of the Akedah, the Binding of Isaac, in its Targumic representation, Vermes finds that, just as in the Akedah theology the remission of sin as well as present and future salvation were the result of the unique sacrifice of Isaac, so in the Christian sacrament there is "the perpetual remembrance of the one perfect Sacrifice until the Kingdom comes." G. Vermes, *Scripture and Tradition in Judaism,* Leiden, 1961, pp. 225–7. The Epistle of Barnabas furnishes the earliest evidence in Christian literature of the notion of Isaac on Moriah as the O.T. "type" of the Passion of Christ (Barnabas 7:3): the theme was also well known to the Church Fathers and figured prominently in Christian art from the fourth century A.D. on, notably in the frescoes of Dura-Europos. It is not unnatural to assume that Paul was familiar with the *Akedath Isaac* tradition, especially as in 4 Maccabees 7:14; 13:12, etc., Isaac is presented as a prototype of the martyrs. Nor is it unnatural to assume that, particularly in connection with the Lord's Supper, Paul may have had in mind the Isaac:Moriah–Christ:Golgotha typology—he would have been familiar with the Isaac tradition from the liturgy of the *Rosh ha-shana,* as well as with the tradition that the sacrifice of Isaac, typifying the paschal lamb, took place on a Passover day (the *Akedath Isaac* being dated in ancient sources on 15th Nisan, when the Passover lamb was slaughtered) and could quite easily have substituted God for Abraham and Jesus for Isaac. However, it is very much open to question whether we should go so far as H. J. Schoeps in finding in the *Akedath Isaac* "the very model for the elaboration of Pauline soteriology." H. J. Schoeps, *Paul,* pp. 141 ff. It is doubtful, for example, whether Romans 8:32 ("God did not spare his own Son but gave him up for us all") reflects the Septuagint text of Genesis 22:16 and so alludes to the Binding of Isaac. Doubtful also is the supposed connection of the προέθετο of Romans 3:25 with the yir'eh of Genesis 22:8. Abraham said: "God will provide himself the lamb for the burnt offering"; with which is associated: "God has provided him (Christ) as an expiatory sacrifice"—Schoeps, op. cit. p. 146. A glance at W. D. Davies's detailed discussion of the meaning of the verb προτίθεσθαι and the noun ἱλαστήριον (*Paul and Rabbinic Judaism,* pp. 237 ff.)

in the context of Romans 3:25 will show how difficult it is to go beyond the conclusion, established by C. H. Dodd (*The Bible and the Greeks,* London, 1935, pp. 82 ff.), that ἱλάσκεσθαι and its cognates denote not the placating or propitiation of the deity but expiatory sacrifice, in order to discover what *particular* ideas or picture of expiation Paul had in mind in regard to the death of Christ.

88. G. Bornkamm, *Jesus of Nazareth,* pp. 160–61.

89. This was the view of A. Deissmann, *Paul: A Study in Social and Religious History* (Engl. transl. by W. E. Wilson), London, 1926, pp. 198 ff. *V.* also E. Käsemann, "Auliegen und Eigenart der paulinischen Abendmahlslehre," *Evangelische Theologie,* VII (1947–48), 266.

90. J. A. T. Robinson, *The Body,* London, 1952, pp. 55–6.

91. Ibid. p. 58. *V.* also Barnabas Lindars, *New Testament Apologetic,* Philadelphia, 1961, p. 73. The idea of the Body, denoting a special relationship between Christians and the risen Lord, "is derived primarily from reflection on the meaning of the Resurrection of the person of Jesus."

92. J. A. T. Robinson, op. cit. pp. 60 ff. For the view that Paul's language is not to be taken literally but metaphorically, *v.* E. Best, *One Body in Christ,* London, 1955, pp. 98–101.

93. M. Barth, "A Chapter on the Church—The Body of Christ," *Interpretation,* XII (1958), 141, 148.

94. W. D. Davies, "A Normative Pattern of Church Life in the New Testament?" *Christian Origins and Judaism,* Philadelphia, 1962, p. 225.

95. D. O. Via, "Darkness, Christ and the Church," *SJT,* XIV (June 1961), 186–7.

96. E. Schweizer, "The Church as the Missionary Body of Christ," *NTS,* VIII (Oct. 1961), 6 ff. Schweizer finds also in Ephesians 2:11–22 and 3:1–3 as well as in I Timothy 3:16 the same development of ideas as in the Colossians hymn.

97. Arnold Toynbee, *An Historian's Approach to Religion,* New York, 1956, p. 298.

98. John Macquarrie, *The Scope of Demythologizing,* p. 181.

99. D. Baillie, *God Was in Christ,* p. 209.

100. Bo Reicke, "Incarnation and Exaltation," *Interpretation,* XVI (April 1962), 161.

101. L. Hodgson, *The Doctrine of the Trinity,* London, 1943, p. 35.

102. T. W. Manson, *Ministry and Priesthood: Christ's and Ours,* Richmond, 1959, p. 21.

103. H. P. Owen, *Revelation and Existence,* Cardiff, 1957, p. 120.

104. E. Schweizer, *Lordship and Discipleship,* p. 116.

Conclusion

1. Paul Winter, *On the Trial of Jesus,* Berlin, 1961.

2. B. Gerhardsson, *Memory and Manuscript: Oral Tradition and Written Transmission in Rabbinic Judaism and Early Christianity* (Engl. transl. by E. J. Sharpe), Lund-Copenhagen, 1961.

3. Günter Wagner, *Das religionsgeschichtliche Problem von Römer 6:1–11,* Zürich, 1962.

4. Carsten Colpe, *Die religionsgeschichtliche Schule: Darstellung und Kritik ihres Bildes vom gnostischen Erlosermythus,* Göttingen, 1961.

5. Most recently, Gerhard Ebeling, *Theologie und Verkündigung,* Tübingen, 1962, pp. 55 f.

6. D. Baillie, *God Was in Christ*, p. 47.
7. A. E. J. Rawlinson in *The Christian Faith: Essays in Explanation and Defence*, ed. W. R. Matthews, 2nd ed., London, 1944, p. 92.
8. C. H. Dodd, *History and the Gospel*, New York, 1938, p. 28.
9. J. Schniewind, *Kerygma and Myth*, Vol. I, ed. H. W. Bartsch, London, 1953, p. 83.
10. W. Herrmann, *The Communion of the Christian with God* (Engl. transl. by J. S. S. Stanyon), revised ed., London, 1930, pp. 140–42.
11. H. R. Mackintosh, *The Christian Experience of Forgiveness*, London, 1941 (first publ. 1927), pp. 48–9.
12. N. A. Dahl, "Der historische Jesus als geschichtswissenschaftliches und theologisches Problem," *Kerygma und Dogma*, Göttingen, 1955, pp. 119 ff.
13. James Muilenburg, *The Way of Israel: Biblical Faith and Ethics*, New York, 1961, p. 46.
14. A. Schweitzer, *The Quest of the Historical Jesus* (Engl. transl. by W. A. Montgomery), 2nd Engl. ed., London, 1922, pp. 400–401.

Selected Bibliography*

Althaus, P. *The So-called Kerygma and the Historical Jesus,* transl. by D. Cairns. Edinburgh and London, 1959.

Bacon, B. W. *Studies in Matthew.* New York, 1930.

Baillie, D. *God Was in Christ.* New York, 1948.

Barr, J. *The Semantics of Biblical Language.* London, 1961.

———. *Biblical Words for Time.* London, 1962.

Barrett, C. K. *The Holy Spirit and the Gospel Tradition.* London, 1947.

———. *The Gospel According to St. John.* New York, 1957.

———. *The New Testament Background: Selected Documents.* New York, 1961.

Barth, G. *See* Bornkamm, G., G. Barth, and H. J. Held.

Barth, K. *The Epistle to the Romans,* 2nd ed. London, 1921.

———. *R. Bultmann, Ein Versuch ihn zu verstehen.* Zürich, 1953.

———. *Church Dogmatics,* Vol. IV, Part 2, transl. by G. W. Bromiley. Edinburgh, 1958.

———. *The Humanity of God,* transl. by J. N. Thomas and T. Weiser. Richmond, 1960.

Bartsch, H. W., ed. *Kerygma and Myth,* Vol. I, transl. by R. H. Fuller. London, 1953.

———. *Kerygma und Mythos,* Vol. II. Hamburg-Volksdorf, 1952.

Bauer, W. *Rechtgläubigkeit und Ketzerei im ältesten Christentum.* Tübingen, 1934.

Best, E. *One Body in Christ.* London, 1955.

Bevan, E., ed. *Hellenism and Christianity.* London, 1932.

Binns, L. E. Elliott. *Galilean Christianity.* London, 1956.

* From the voluminous periodical literature there are listed here only a few articles which represent landmarks in the recent "Jesus of history"–"Christ of faith" debate. Standard commentaries and reference works, alluded to in the Notes, are also, for the most part, omitted from this list.

355

Black, M. *The Scrolls and Christian Origins*. New York, 1961.

Bornkamm, G. *Jesus of Nazareth*, transl. by Irene and Fraser McLuskey with J. M. Robinson. New York, 1960.

Bornkamm, G., G. Barth, and H. J. Held. *Überlieferung und Auslegung in Matthäusevangelium*. Neukirchen, 1960. *Tradition and Interpretation in Matthew*, transl. by Percy Scott. London, 1963.

Bousset, W. *Kyrios Christos*, 3rd ed. Göttingen, 1926.

Bultmann, R. *Der Begriff der Offenbarung im Neuen Testament*. Tübingen, 1929.

——. *Das Evangelium des Johannes* (Meyer: Kritischexegetischer Kommentar), 11th ed. Göttingen, 1950.

——. *Theology of the New Testament*, Vol. I, transl. by K. Grobel. London, 1952. Vol. II, London, 1955.

——. *Primitive Christianity in Its Contemporary Setting*, transl. by R. H. Fuller. London and New York, 1956.

——. *Jesus Christ and Mythology*. New York, 1958.

——. *Existence and Faith: Shorter Writings of R. Bultmann*, transl. by S. M. Ogden. New York, 1960.

——. *Jesus and the Word*, transl. by L. P. Smith and E. H. Lantero from the German work entitled *Jesus*, 1926. New York, 1960.

——. "Das Verhältnis der urchristlichen Christusbotschaft zum historischen Jesus," in *Sitzungsberichte der Heidelberger Akademie der Wissenschaften*. Heidelberg, 1960.

——. *Die Geschichte der synoptischen Tradition*. Göttingen, 1957. *The History of the Synoptic Tradition*, transl. by John Marsh. Oxford, 1963.

Burkitt, F. C. *Church and Gnosis*. Cambridge, 1932.

Cadbury, H. J. *The Making of Luke-Acts*. New York, 1927.

Carrington, P. *The Primitive Christian Calendar*. Cambridge, 1952.

Case, S. J. *The Evolution of Early Christianity*. Chicago, 1914.

——. *The Social Origins of Christianity*. Chicago, 1923.

Collingwood, R. G. *The Idea of History*. London, 1946.

Conzelmann, H. *The Theology of St. Luke*, transl. by G. Buswell. London, 1960.

Couchoud, P.-L. *The Creation of Christ: An Outline of the Beginnings of Christianity*, transl. by C. B. Bonner. London, 1939.

Cullmann, O. *The Earliest Christian Confessions*, transl. by J. K. S. Reid. London, 1949.

——. *Christ and Time*, transl. by F. V. Filson. London, 1951.

——. *The Christology of the New Testament*, transl. by S. C. Guthrie and C. A. M. Hall. Philadelphia, 1959.

——. *Peter, Disciple, Apostle, Martyr*, transl. by F. V. Filson, 2nd revised ed. Philadelphia, 1962.

Daniélou, Jean. *Christ and Us*, transl. by W. Roberts. New York, 1961.

Daube, D. *See* Davies, W. D., and D. Daube.

Davey, F. N. *See* Hoskyns, E., and F. N. Davey.

Davies, W. D. *Torah in the Messianic Age and/or the Age To Come* (Society of Biblical Literature and Exegesis). Lancaster, Pa., 1952.

——. *Paul and Rabbinic Judaism*. London, 1955.

——. *Christian Origins and Judaism*. Philadelphia, 1962.

——., and D. Daube, eds. *The Background of the New Testament and Its Eschatology*. Cambridge, 1956.

Deissmann, A. *Paul: A Study in Social and Religious History*, transl. by W. E. Wilson. London, 1926.

Denney, J. *The Death of Christ*. London, 1902.
Dibelius, M. *From Tradition to Gospel*, transl. by B. L. Woolf. New York, 1935.
———. *Jesus*. Philadelphia, 1949.
———. *Studies in the Acts of the Apostles*, transl. by Mary Ling. New York, 1956.
Diem, H. *Dogmatics*, transl. by H. Knight. Edinburgh, 1959.
Dodd, C. H. *The Epistle of Paul to the Romans*. New York, 1932.
———. *The Bible and the Greeks*. London, 1935.
———. *The Apostolic Preaching and Its Developments*. London, 1936.
———. *Thirty Years of New Testament Study*. Cambridge, 1936.
———. *History and the Gospel*. New York, 1938.
———. *The Parables of the Kingdom*. London, 1941.
———. *The Bible Today*. New York, 1947.
———. *The Interpretation of the Fourth Gospel*. Cambridge, 1953.
Dugmore, C. W., ed. *The Interpretation of the Bible*. London, 1944.
Duncan, G. S. *Jesus, Son of Man*. New York, 1949.
Easton, B. S. *Early Christianity: The Purpose of Acts and Other Papers*, ed. by F. C. Grant. Greenwich, Conn., 1954.
Ebeling, G. *The Nature of Faith*, transl. by R. Gregor Smith. Philadelphia, 1961.
———. *Theologie und Verkündigung*. Tübingen, 1962.
Eichrodt, W. *Theology of the Old Testament*, Vol. I, transl. by J. A. Baker. Philadelphia, 1961.
Eltester, W., ed. *Neutestamentliche Studien für Rudolf Bultmann*. Berlin, 1954.
Farrer, A. M. *St. Matthew and St. Mark*. London, 1954.
Filson, F. V. *Jesus Christ the Risen Lord*. New York, 1956.
———. *The Gospel According to St. Matthew* (Black's N. T. Commentaries). London, 1960.
Flew, R. Newton. *Jesus and His Church*. New York, 1938.
Frisque, Jean. *Oscar Cullmann: Une Théologie de l'histoire du salut*. Tournai, 1960.
Fuchs, E. *Zur Frage nach dem historischen Jesus*. Tübingen, 1960.
Fuller, R. H. *The Mission and Achievement of Jesus*. London, 1954.
Galloway, A. D. *The Cosmic Christ*. London, 1951.
Gardner-Smith, J. P. *The Narratives of the Resurrection*. London, 1926.
Gerhardsson, Birger. *Memory and Manuscript: Oral Tradition and Written Transmission in Rabbinic Judaism and Early Christianity*, transl. by E. J. Sharpe. Lund and Copenhagen, 1961.
Goguel, M. *Jesus the Nazarene—Myth or History?*, transl. by F. Stephens. New York, 1926.
———. *La Foi à la Résurrection de Jesus dans le christianisme primitif*. Paris, 1933.
———. *The Birth of Christianity*, transl. by H. C. Snape. London, 1953.
———. *Jesus and the Origins of Christianity*, Vol. II: *The Life of Jesus*, transl. by Olive Wyon. Paperback. New York, 1960.
Grant, F. C. *The Earliest Gospel*. New York and Nashville, 1943.
———. *Ancient Judaism and the New Testament*. New York, 1959.
Grant, R. M. *Gnosticism and Early Christianity*. New York, 1959.
Grass, H. *Ostergeschehen und Osterberichte*. Göttingen, 1956.
Haenchen, E. *Die Apostelgeschichte*, 12th ed. Göttingen, 1959.
Harnack, A. von. *History of Dogma*, Vol. I, transl. by N. Buchanan. New York, 1958.
Headlam, A. C. *See* Sanday, W., and A. C. Headlam.

Held, H. J. *See* Bornkamm, G., G. Barth, and H. J. Held.

Herrmann, W. *The Communion of the Christian with God*, transl. by J. S. Sandys Stanyon, revised in accordance with the 4th German edition of 1903 by R. W. Stewart. London, 1930.

Hodgson, L. *The Doctrine of the Trinity*. London, 1943.

Hoskyns, E., and F. N. Davey. *The Riddle of the New Testament*. New York, 1931.

Hunter, A. M. *Paul and His Predecessors*, 2nd ed. Philadelphia, 1961.

Iersel, B. M. F. van. *"Der Sohn" in den synoptischen Jesusworten: Christusbezeichnung der Gemeinde oder Selbstbezeichnung Jesu?* Leiden, 1961.

Jackson, F., and K. Lake. *The Beginnings of Christianity*, Vols. I-II, London, 1922. Vol. V, eds. K. Lake and H. J. Cadbury, London, 1933.

Jeremias, J. *The Parables of Jesus, transl. by S. H. Hooke*. London, 1954.

———. *The Eucharistic Words of Jesus*, transl. by A. Ehrhardt. New York, 1955.

———. "The Present Position in the Controversy Concerning the Problem of the Historical Jesus," in *Expository Times*, LXIX (1957–58), 333–9.

———. *Jesus' Promise to the Nations*. London, 1958.

Johnston, G. *The Doctrine of the Church in the New Testament*. Cambridge, 1943.

Jonas, H. *The Gnostic Religion*. Boston, 1958.

Kähler, M. *Der sogenannte historische Jesus und der geschichtliche, biblische Christus*. Leipzig, 1892. New ed., München, 1956.

Käsemann, E. "Das problem des historischen Jesus," in *Zeitschrift für Theologie und Kirche*, LI (1954), 125–53.

Kalthoff, A. *Das Christusproblem grundlinien zu einer Sozialtheologie*. Leipzig, 1902.

Kilpatrick, G. D. *The Origins of the Gospel According to St. Matthew*. Oxford, 1946.

Klassen, W., and G. Snyder, eds. *Current Issues in New Testament Interpretation*. New York, 1962.

Knox, John. *Christ the Lord*. Chicago, 1945.

———. *Chapters in a Life of Paul*. New York, 1950.

———. *Criticism and Faith*. New York, 1952.

Knox, W. L. *St. Paul and the Church of the Gentiles*. Cambridge, 1939.

Koch, G. *Die Auferstehung Jesu Christi*. Tübingen, 1959.

Kümmel, W. G. *Promise and Fulfilment*, transl. by Dorothea M. Barton. London, 1957.

Lake, K. *The Historical Evidence of the Resurrection of Jesus Christ*. New York, 1907.

———. *See* Jackson, F., and K. Lake.

Lietzmann, H. *An die Korinther* (Handbuch zum Neuen Testament), 3rd ed. Tübingen, 1931.

Lightfoot, R. H. *History and Interpretation in the Gospels*. London, 1935.

———. *The Gospel Message of St. Mark*. Oxford, 1950.

Lindars, Barnabas. *New Testament Apologetic*. Philadelphia, 1961.

Lohmeyer, E. *Galiläa und Jerusalem*. Göttingen, 1956 (first published 1936).

———. *Das Evangelium des Markus*. Göttingen, 1937.

———. *Gottesknecht und Davidssohn*. Göttingen, 1953.

Lohse, E. *Die Auferstehung Jesus Christi: Im Zeugnis des Lukasevangeliums* (Biblische Studien 31). Neukirchen, 1961.

Macgregor, G. H. C. *The Gospel of John* (Moffatt N. T. Commentaries). London, 1940.

Mackintosh, H. R. *The Christian Experience of Forgiveness.* London, 1941 (first published 1927).

Macquarrie, J. *The Scope of Demythologizing.* New York, 1960.

Manson, T. W. *The Teaching of Jesus.* Cambridge, 1945.

———. *The Sayings of Jesus.* London, 1949.

———. *The Servant Messiah.* Cambridge, 1953.

———. *Ministry and Priesthood: Christ's and Ours.* Richmond, 1959.

Manson, William. *Jesus, the Messiah.* Philadelphia, 1946.

Marxsen, W. *Der Evangelist Markus.* Göttingen, 1956.

Matthiae, K. *See* Ristow, H., and K. Matthiae.

Muilenburg, J. *The Way of Israel: Biblical Faith and Ethics.* New York, 1961.

Munck, J. *Paul and the Salvation of Mankind,* transl. by Frank Clarke. Richmond, 1959.

Niebuhr, R. R. *Resurrection and Historical Reason.* New York, 1957.

Nineham, D. E., ed. *Studies in the Gospels: Essays in Memory of R. H. Lightfoot.* Oxford, 1955.

Ogden, Schubert M. *Christ Without Myth.* New York, 1961.

Owen, H. P. *Revelation and Existence.* Cardiff, 1957.

Perry, M. C. *The Easter Enigma.* London, 1959.

Preiss, Théo. *Life in Christ,* transl. by H. Knight. London, 1954.

Rad, G. von. *Theology of the Old Testament,* transl. by D. G. Stalker. Edinburgh and London, 1962.

Ramsey, A. M. *The Glory of God and the Transfiguration of Christ.* London and New York, 1949.

———. *The Resurrection of Christ.* London, 1956.

Rawlinson, A. E. J. *The New Testament Doctrine of the Christ.* New York, 1926.

Reicke, Bo. *Diakonie, Festfreude und Zelos in Verbindung mit der altchristlichen Agapefeier.* Uppsala, 1951.

Reitzenstein, R. *Die hellenistischen Mysterienreligionen.* Leipzig, 1927.

Richardson, A. *An Introduction to the Theology of the New Testament.* New York, 1958.

Riesenfeld, H. *The Gospel Tradition and Its Beginnings: A Study in the Limits of "Formgeschichte."* London, 1957.

Ristow, H., and K. Matthiae, eds. *Der historische Jesus und der kerygmatische Christus.* Berlin, 1960.

Robinson, H. Wheeler. *Redemption and Revelation.* London, 1942.

Robinson, J. A. T. *The Body.* London, 1952.

Robinson, J. M. *The Problem of History in Mark.* London, 1957.

———. *A New Quest of the Historical Jesus.* London, 1959.

Rudolph, Kurt. *Die Mandäer,* 2 vols. Göttingen, 1960–61.

Sanday, W., and A. C. Headlam. *The Epistle to the Romans* (I.C.C.). New York, 1936.

Schmithals, W. *Die Gnosis in Korinth.* Göttingen, 1956.

Schoeps, H. J. *Paul: The Theology of the Apostle in the Light of Jewish Religious History,* transl. by H. Knight. Philadelphia, 1961.

Schweitzer, A. *Geschichte der paulinischen Forschung.* Tübingen, 1911.

———. *The Quest of the Historical Jesus,* transl. by W. A. Montgomery, 2nd Engl. ed. London, 1922.

————. *The Mysticism of Paul the Apostle*, transl. by W. A. Montgomery. London, 1931.

Schweizer, E. *Lordship and Discipleship*. London, 1961.

Selwyn, E. G. *The First Epistle of St. Peter*. London, 1947.

————, ed. *Essays Catholic and Critical*. London, 1938. See especially Selwyn's essay "The Resurrection."

Smart, J. D. *The Interpretation of Scripture*. Philadelphia, 1961.

Snyder, G. *See* Klassen, W., and G. Snyder.

Stauffer, E. *New Testament Theology*, transl. by John Marsh. London, 1955.

————. *Jesus and His Story*, transl. by Richard and Clara Winston. New York, 1960.

Stendahl, K. *The School of St. Matthew*. Uppsala, 1954.

Stewart, J. S. *A Faith To Proclaim*. New York, 1953.

Taylor, V. *The Formation of the Gospel Tradition*. London, 1933.

————. *Jesus and His Sacrifice*. London, 1937.

————. *The Gospel According to St. Mark*. London, 1952.

————. *The Names of Jesus*. New York, 1953.

————. *The Life and Ministry of Jesus*. Nashville, 1955.

————. *The Person of Christ in New Testament Teaching*. London and New York, 1958.

Tillich, Paul. *Systematic Theology*, Vol. II. Chicago, 1957.

Toedt, Heinz E. *Der Menschensohn in der synoptischen Überlieferung. Gütersloh, 1959.

Toynbee, Arnold. *An Historian's Approach to Religion*. New York, 1956.

Troeltsch, E. *The Social Teaching of the Christian Churches*, Vol. I, transl. by Olive Wyon. New York, 1931.

Vermes, Geza. *Scripture and Tradition in Judaism*. Leiden, 1961.

Wagner, Günter. *Das religionsgeschichtliche Problem von Römer 6:1–11*. Zürich, 1962.

Weiss, J. *Die Predigt Jesu vom Reiche Gottes*, 2. Aufl. Göttingen, 1900.

————. *The History of Primitive Christianity*, 2 vols., transl. by F. C. Grant and others. New York, 1937.

Wellhausen, J. *Einleitung in die drei ersten Evangelien*. Berlin, 1905.

Werner, M. *Die Entstehung des christlichen Dogmas problemgeschichtlich dargestellt*, 2nd ed. Bern, 1953.

Wernle, P. *Jesus*. Tübingen, 1917.

Wikgren, A., ed. *Early Christian Origins*. Chicago, 1961.

Williams, C. S. C. *The Acts of the Apostles* (Black's N. T. Commentaries). London, 1957.

Wilson, R. McL. *The Gnostic Problem*. London, 1958.

Winter, Paul. *On the Trial of Jesus*. Berlin, 1961.

Wrede, W. *Das Messiasgeheimnis in der Evangelien*. Göttingen, 1901.

Yarnold, G. D. *Risen Indeed: Studies in the Lord's Resurrection*. New York, 1959.

Index of Scripture References

Old Testament

GENESIS
2:7 234
3 219
18 228
22:8 350 n.75,
351 n.87

EXODUS
8:19 130
9:3 130
15:6 130
19:3f. 271
24:8 295

DEUTERONOMY
6:23 276
18:15 256
18:18 341 n.65

I SAMUEL
2:7f. 193
10:1ff., 9ff. 257
16:13 257

II SAMUEL
7:14 333 n.27

II KINGS
20:5 212

JOB
22:29 193

PSALMS
2:7 284, 333 n.27
16:10 214
22:17 35
40:7f. 282
107:28f. 347 n.13
110:1 255

PROVERBS
8:30f. 272
29:23 193

ISAIAH
7:14 226, 247
42:1–4 251, 252

50:7 254
53:4 252
53:12 254

DANIEL
7:14 341 n.67

HOSEA
6:1f. 212f.

JONAH
1:17 212

HABAKKUK
1:4 348 n.16

ZECHARIAII
9:9 252
14:4 221

MALACHI
4:2 221

New Testament

MATTHEW
1:22f. 226, 247, 248
2:2 248

2:5, 15, 17, 23 248
2:15 341 n.65
3:13–15 248

4:14 248
4:17 165
5:1 224

361

5:12 *112*
5:21–2, 27–8, 31–2,
  33–4, 38–9, 43–4
  247
5:44ff. *159*
6:8 *159*
6:10 *128, 166*
6:32 *159*
7:28 *222*
8:4 *247*
8:17 *252*
8:20 *123*
8:22–7 *251*
9:30 *247*
10:10 *267*
10:29f. *159*
10:32f. *123*
10:38f. *253*
11:1 *222*
11:4–6 *128*
11:5 *164, 166*
11:11–14 *331 n.55*
11:12f. *170*
11:19 *123, 179*
11:20 *128*
11:20–24 *249*
11:25–30 *156*
11:27 *157ff., 333 n.26*
12:14–21 *251*
12:16 *247*
12:19f. *347 n.16*
12:22–37 *249*
12:28 *126, 165*
12:29 *131*
12:38–42 *249*
13:11, 13–15, 16–17,
  51 *249*
13:52 *347 n.15*
13:53 *222*
13:54–6 *334 n.27*
14:33 *249*
15:10–20 *249*
15:29 *224*
16:13 *123*
16:13–23 *249*
16:17 *104*
16:17–19 *106, 249,
  250*
16:21–3, 24–7
  347 n.11

17:1 *224*
17:20 *221*
18:3 *177*
18:17 *250*
18:20 *251*
19:1 *222*
19:28–30 *129*
20:15 *58*
20:16 *112*
21:5 *248, 252*
23:12 *178*
23:16–28, 34–7 *249*
24:3 *224, 248*
24:27 *122*
24:37 *122, 143*
24:39, 44 *122*
25:14ff. *112*
25:21, 23 *128*
25:31–46, 34, 40 *248*
25:40 *226*
26:1 *222*
26:24 *248*
26:28 *225*
26:54, 56 *248*
26:64 *121*
27:11, 29, 37, 42 *248*
27:51–3 *192, 193, 223*
27:62–6 *223*
28:2–4 *223*
28:11–15 *199, 223*
28:12ff., 15 *58, 227*
28:16–20 *233ff., 251,
  252*
28:19 *342 n.71*
28:20 *239, 258*

MARK
1:1–13 *218*
1:9–11 *248*
1:11 *156, 158, 218*
1:13 *219*
1:15 *126, 165*
1:23–5 *31, 245*
1:34, 44 *245*
2:10 *122*
2:15f. *166*
2:28 *112, 123*
3:11f. *31, 245*
3:20–27 *180*
3:21 *164*

3:27 *131*
4:10–13 *31*
4:13 *249*
4:35–41 *251*
5:43 *245*
6:50–52 *31, 245, 249*
7:17–23 *31, 245*
7:36 *31, 245*
8:17, 26 *245*
8:27 *123*
8:27–33 *249*
8:30 *31, 245*
8:31 *123, 124, 245*
8:34ff. *245, 278*
8:38 *122, 123, 124,
  129, 164*
9:2ff. *87, 219f., 245*
9:9–13 *219, 245*
9:31 *123*
9:43, 45, 47 *128*
10:7–12 *267*
10:17 *128*
10:30 *141*
10:33f. *123*
10:35–45 *246*
11:23 *221*
11:27–33 *170*
12:6–8 *158*
13 *174*
13:1–27 *129*
13:3ff. *246, 248*
13:14 *330 n.47*
13:14–23 *246*
13:32 *158, 333 n.26*
13:33–7 *129, 167*
14:3ff. *245*
14:24 *291*
14:25 *128, 166, 296*
14:28 *197, 336 n.15*
14:53ff. *289*
14:58 *213*
14:62 *119, 122, 245*
15:2, 9, 26 *119*
16:1–8 *191, 221*
16:2 *221*
16:4 *220*
16:6 *194, 218*
16:6f. *195, 219*
16:7 *196, 197, 199*
16:8 *196, 222, 227*

LUKE
1:1 *82, 217, 226*
1:1–3 *253*
1:5 *227*
1:13 *230*
1:25 *227*
1:35 *256*
2:25–38 *227*
2:49 *158*
3:22 *121, 256*
4:1, 14 *121, 256*
4:21, 22, 24 *256*
4:31–6 *255*
4:43 *256*
6:12, 17 *168*
6:20f., 25 *178*
8:22–5 *251*
8:22–39 *168*
9:28–36 *168*
9:51 *227*
10:7f. *267*
10:16 *258*
10:18 *166*
10:21f. *156*
10:22 *157*
10:23f. *253*
11:20 *130, 164, 165, 166*
12:8 *122*
12:8f. *123, 124*
12:28 *130*
12:32 *129*
13:32f. *255*
15:11ff. *159, 160*
15:32 *128*
16:8 *128*
17:6 *221*
17:33 *178*
18:9–14 *112*
19:38 *255*
22:14–30 *259*
22:16 *177*
22:19 *293*
22:37 *254*
22:69 *255*
23:43 *193*
24 *344 n.83*
24:1–7 *227*
24:5 *186*
24:6 *197*
24:13ff. *203, 228*

24:36–43 *229*
24:37 *200*
24:41 *224*
24:44 *258*
24:44–7 *229*
24:48 *230, 263*
24:50–53 *230, 231, 342 n.78, 343 n.82*

JOHN
1:1 *237, 273*
1:1–18 *218*
1:14 *163, 236, 263, 346 n.92*
1:17 *341 n.65*
1:18 *299*
1:29 *221, 350 n.75*
1:32–4 *263*
2:4 *264*
2:23 *236*
3:11 *263*
3:13 *299*
3:14 *193, 262*
3:19 *7*
3:35 *157*
4:23 *345 n.87*
4:39 *263*
4:47ff. *236*
5:24f. *7*
5:25 *345 n.87*
5:39, 46 *263*
6:32ff. *341 n.65*
6:42 *265*
6:46 *299*
6:48 *262*
6:51–8 *324 n.65*
6:63 *265*
7:5 *236*
7:7 *239, 299*
7:8 *264*
7:39 *234, 262*
8:12 *262, 264*
8:13–18 *263*
8:20 *264*
8:28 *262*
8:29 *174*
8:38 *122*
8:58 *262*
10:7, 9, 11, 14 *262*
10:11–16 *299*
10:14–15 *299*

10:15 *157*
10:17f. *174, 264*
11:25 *262*
11:25f. *7, 235*
11:39 *214*
12:16 *262*
12:24–8 *264*
12:31 *7, 235*
12:32 *193, 262, 264*
12:32f. *299*
12:34 *193, 262*
12:41 *47, 238, 324 n.67*
12:45 *346 n.92*
12:46 *264*
12:47f. *263*
13:7, 20 *264*
13:26 *122*
13:31 *262*
13:36, 37, 38 *264, 299*
14:2 *264*
14:6 *235, 262, 264*
14:7 *264*
14:7, 9, 17 *346 n.92*
14:8f. *236*
14:10f. *264*
14:15–17 *236*
14:16 *345 n.87*
14:17 *53*
14:18 *236*
14:21–4 *265*
14:26 *239, 264*
14:29 *264*
14:62 *121, 122*
15:12f., 15 *299*
15:18–21 *239, 299*
15:26 *236*
15:27 *217*
16:2–3, 4 *239, 299*
16:11 *235*
16:13ff. *53*
16:22 *236*
16:24 *264*
16:26 *234*
16:28 *264*
17:1–5 *262*
17:8, 14 *299*
17:17–19 *288*
17:18 *299*
17:20, 21, 22 *239*
17:20, 22 *299*

18:36–7 289
19:30 264
19:35 265
20:1–10 227
20:1–29 233ff.
20:8 346 n.92
20:16f. 344 n.85
20:17 299
20:18 219
20:21 299
20:22 264
20:25 219
20:29 219, 236,
  345 n.85
20:31 262
21 196
24:24 263

ACTS
1:1—5:16 81
1:1–12 230ff.,
  343 n.82
1:2 342 n.87
1:4 196
1:7 142
1:10f. 227
1:11 239
1:21f. 217, 263
2:22–4 120, 208, 255
2:24 209
2:25–32 120, 255
2:25–8, 31 209
2:32f. 231
2:33 193
2:36 120, 121, 208,
  255
3:15 187
3:22 257
4:26 121
5:32 217
6–8 40
6:7 310
7:37 257
7:56 122
9:31 337 n.18
9:31—11:18 81
10 80, 257
10:38 121, 257
11 40
12:24 310
13 80

13:33 334 n.27
15:1–36 44
19:20 310

ROMANS
1:3f. 208, 209, 269,
  270, 333 n.27,
  338 n.36
1:5, 16 144
1:18—3:20 144
3:21—8:39 144
3:25 43, 270, 351 n.87
4:4 329 n.14
5 273
5–8 145
5:6 271
5:8f. 43
5:10 271
5:18f. 270, 277
6:1–11 51, 274, 275f.
6:4 269
6:5 299
6:10 288
6:11–12 275
8:3 338 n.36
8:17 275, 298
8:22 279
8:23 130, 345 n.87
8:29 193
8:32 351 n.87
9–11 145
10:8–10 217
10:9 268
12 300
12–15 145
12:5 298

I CORINTHIANS
1:12 217
2:2 208
2:8 243
2:8, 10, 14f. 42
5:7 271
7:1ff. 310
7:10f. 267
7:12 351 n.82
7:23 271
8:6 273
9:1 219
9:1ff. 310

9:14 267
10:4 273, 338 n.36
10:16f. 293, 297
11:1 274
11:2ff. 310
11:3 298
11:23 269, 292
11:23–6 43, 271,
  291ff., 310
11:26 296
12:3 268
12:12–31 297
13 43
15 42, 51, 200, 240
15:3–5 195, 218, 268,
  269
15:3–8 189, 191, 194,
  197, 203, 204, 211ff.,
  270, 310
15:8 190, 208
15:14 187
15:20–23 193, 205,
  217, 240, 271

II CORINTHIANS
1:22 257
4:5 268
4:6 42
4:10f. 205
5:14f. 205
5:16 216, 269
5:16, 17 44
6:8–10 279
8:9 338 n.36
10–13 49
11:5 216
12:11 216

GALATIANS
1:11f. 267
2:4 340 n.50
2:9 216
2:12 340 n.50
2:20 276, 298
3:1 269
3:28 298
4:3 42
4:4 269, 338 n.36
4:9 42
5:13f. 43

EPHESIANS
1:7–8, 23 298
2:14–18 44
4:8–10 44
4:13–16 302
4:15 299

PHILIPPIANS
2:6–11 163, 243, 268f.,
271ff., 278, 329 n.21
2:8 269
2:9 193
2:9–11 341 n.67
2:11 268
2:12 276
3:1 276
3:10 274

COLOSSIANS
1:5f. 301
1:15–20 300, 301
1:18 193, 301
1:22f. 301
1:24 300
1:24–9 301
2:6 268

I TIMOTHY
2:6 142
3:16 163, 341 n.67

HEBREWS
1:1–4 286

1:3–13 193
1:3 282, 283
1:4f 284
1:5–14 341 n.67
1:10 282
2:9 284, 286
2:10 286
2:10, 11 288
2:14–18 286
2:15 287
3:2, 5 282
3:8–10 282
4:12 281
4:14 163, 284
4:15 283
5:7 282
8:1 193
9:9 141
9:11–28 284
10:5–10 283
10:10, 12 284
10:22, 37 286
11:1 286
12:2 282, 287
12:22f. 281
13:12f. 287
13:13, 14 282

I PETER
1:3 240, 280
1:3–9 280
1:5 240
1:7–9 280

1:10–12 280
1:21 280
2:22–4 280
3:15–17 279
3:18–22 280
3:21 280
4:1 280

II PETER
1:16–18 219

I JOHN
1:1 265
3:2 345 n.87
3:5f., 16–18 265
3:24 345 n.87
4:2f. 265
4:9–11 265
5:8 265

REVELATION
1:4–6 289
1:5 289, 290
1:13ff. 122
2:8, 10, 13, 26–8 289
4–6 290
7:14, 17 290
12:5, 11 289
14:4 290
17:13ff. 290
19:11ff. 290
21–22 290

Index of Authors

Adam, K. 22
Albertz, M. 32, 33
Althaus, P. 6, 181
Aron, R. 26

Baab, O. J. 69
Bacon, B. W. 222
Baillie, D. 54, 172, 312
Barnett, A. 70ff.
Barr, J. 141f.
Barrett, C. K. 290, 338 n.36, 350 n.75
Barth, K. 5, 6, 8, 11, 22, 23, 24, 29, 54, 107, 176, 187, 211, 315
Barth, M. 298
Bauer, B. 35
Bennett, J. 63
Bevan, E. 52
Black, M. 336f. n.18
Bornkamm, G. 10, 22, 149ff., 166ff., 169ff., 173, 174ff., 181f., 202, 251, 293f., 314
Bousset, W. 6, 40
Brown, W. A. 62f.
Brownlee, W. H. 334 n.31
Brunner, E. 107, 312
Bultmann, R. 3, 4, 6, 8, 9, 11, 12, 14, 15, 21, 24ff., 28ff., 32–41, 44–8, 50, 51, 53–5, 69, 75, 92, 94, 105, 107, 119, 122, 126, 127, 131, 138, 141, 143, 149f., 155, 159, 162, 174, 176, 179, 181, 183, 187, 202, 205ff., 235f.,

243, 260, 276f., 304, 312, 315
Buri, F. 8, 21
Burkitt, F. C. 33, 52, 196

Cadoux, C. J. 160
Campbell, J. Y. 125
Campenhausen, H. F. von 190
Carrington, P. 85
Case, S. J. 64ff.
Clark, K. W. 125
Collingwood, R. G. 9, 26, 181
Colpe, C. 52, 311
Conzelmann, H. 10, 81, 134ff., 168, 343 n.82
Couchoud, P.-L. 35
Craig, C. T. 66
Creed, J. M. 336 n.13
Cullmann, O. 123, 134ff., 147, 257, 281, 282, 285, 287, 345 n.92

Dahl, N. A. 263
Daniélou, J. 110
Davey, F. N. 17, 260
Davies, W. D. 43, 145, 271, 276, 292, 293, 337 n.18
Deissmann, A. 40
Denney, J. 108, 206, 265, 277, 286
Dibelius, M. 30, 32, 81, 243, 276
Dilthey, W. 5, 7, 9, 26, 174, 181
Dodd, C. H. 79ff., 94, 100, 119, 125ff., 153, 165f., 225, 313, 345 n.85

366

Drews, A. *243*
Driver, S. R. *77f.*

Easton, B. S. *33*
Ebeling, G. *10, 11, 12, 204, 314*
Eichrodt, W. *4*
Eissfeldt, O. *38*
Evans, C. F. *327 n.39*

Farrer, A. M. *85*
Filson, F. V. *187*
Fridrichsen, A. *329 n.2*
Frisque, J. *331 n.59*
Fuchs, E. *10, 11, 179f., 314*
Fuller, R. H. *117ff., 147, 166, 194f.*

Gardner-Smith, J. P. *196*
Gerhardsson, B. *309f.*
Gogarten, F. *6, 174*
Goguel, M. *16, 17, 35, 91, 192ff., 199, 202*
Gore, C. *78*
Grant, F. C. *68, 73*
Grant, R. M. *42*
Greeven, H. *81*
Gressmann, H. *30*
Gunkel, H. *30, 38*

Haenchen, E. *231*
Harnack, A. von *16, 17, 18, 20, 68, 118*
Hebert, A. G. *220f., 340 n.64*
Heidegger, M. *6, 7, 174, 181*
Heitmüller, W. *7, 40*
Herrmann, W. *11, 28, 29, 313, 314*
Hodgson, L. *304*
Horton, W. *63*
Hoskyns, E. *17, 186, 260*
Hunter, A. M. *157f., 338 n.36*

Iersel, B. M. F. van *333 n.27*

Jaspers, K. *8, 302*
Jeremias, J. *33, 90, 114ff., 170, 224, 295, 313, 340 n.64, 351 n.87*
Jonas, H. *49, 50*

Kähler, M. *5, 12, 26, 27, 28, 29, 80, 84, 133, 176, 183, 242, 313*
Käsemann, E. *8, 9, 10, 17, 18, 100, 143, 144ff., 182*
Kalthoff, A. *72*

Keim, T. *201*
Kierkegaard, S. *36*
Knox, J. *107ff., 147*
Knox, W. L. *275*
Koch, G. *46*
Köster, H. *325 n.71*
Kümmel, W. G. *126f.*

Lagrange, M.-J. *323 n.50*
Lake, K. *196, 198, 199*
Leaney, A. R. C. *342 n.77*
Lietzmann, H. *292*
Lightfoot, R. H. *33, 218f., 220*
Lindars, B. *212f., 336 n.4*
Lohmeyer, E. *197f., 219, 252*
Lohse, E. *228*
Loisy, A. *323 n.50*
Lowe, J. *78*

McGiffert, A. C. *63*
Mackintosh, H. R. *314*
McNeile, A. H. *33*
Macquarrie, J. *8, 137, 139, 202, 277f., 302*
Manson, T. W. *67, 79, 88ff., 150ff., 166, 271, 305, 313*
Marxsen, W. *92, 218, 244*
Matthiae, K. *320 n.17*
Menoud, P. H. *343 n.82*
Metzger, B. *214, 339 n.47*
Meyer, E. *89*
Michaelis, W. *330 n.51*
Michel, O. *224, 226*
Minear, P. S. *69*
Morrison, C. C. *107*
Moule, C. F. D. *196, 232, 344 n.82, 344 n.85, 345 n.87*
Munck, J. *50, 182, 350 n.82*

Niebuhr, H. R. *107*
Niebuhr, Reinhold, *63*
Norden, E. *333 n.18*
Noth, M. *275*

Ogden, S. M. *13, 172f.*
Ott, H. *12*

Perry, M. C. *202*
Pfeiffer, R. H. *69*
Piper, O. *173*
Preiss, T. *106*

Rad, G. von   *4, 139*
Ramsey, A. M.   *196, 197, 220, 230*
Ranke, L. von   *59, 61*
Raven, C. E.   *278*
Rawlinson, A. E. J.   *312, 333 n.20*
Reicke, B.   *217, 304*
Reitzenstein, R.   *39, 41, 42, 46, 50, 51, 52, 311*
Renan, E.   *100, 185, 201*
Ridderbos, H. N.   *327 n.39*
Riesenfeld, H.   *99*
Ristow, H.   *320 n.17*
Ritschl, A.   *115, 165*
Robinson, H. W.   *279*
Robinson, J. A. T.   *297f.*
Robinson, J. M.   *9, 69, 80, 100, 149, 175, 176ff., 276, 314, 346 n.7*
Rudolph, K.   *323 n.50*

Sahlin, H.   *343 n.82*
Sanday, W.   *78*
Schlatter, A.   *144*
Schlier, H.   *127*
Schmidt, K. L.   *31, 155*
Schmithals, W.   *48, 49, 217*
Schniewind, J.   *313*
Schoeps, H. J.   *40, 273, 293, 351 n.87*
Schreiber, J.   *243f.*
Schubert, P.   *344 n.83*
Schweitzer, A.   *5, 17, 18, 19–22, 39, 115, 126, 128, 166, 292*
Schweizer, E.   *144f., 163, 193, 273, 274, 287f., 300, 301, 305*
Selwyn, E. G.   *122, 201f.*
Smith, G. A.   *77f.*
Spitta, F.   *199*
Stauffer, E.   *57ff., 94, 134*
Stempvoort, P. A. van   *230ff.*

Stendahl, K.   *347 n.15 and 16*
Stewart, J. S.   *189, 208*
Stonehouse, N. B.   *327 n.39*
Strathmann, H.   *263*
Strauss, D. F.   *34*

Taylor, V.   *79, 83ff., 89, 91, 94, 308*
Thielicke, H.   *8*
Tillich, P.   *64, 200, 237, 339 n.40*
Toedt, H. E.   *334 n.40*
Toynbee, A.   *302*
Troeltsch, E.   *67, 72, 73, 174*

Underhill, E.   *284*
Unnik, W. C. van   *12, 13, 120ff., 164, 209, 257*

Vermes, G.   *350 n.75, 351 n.87*
Vielhauer, P.   *81*

Wagner, G.   *51, 311*
Weber, M.   *26*
Weiss, J.   *5, 115, 165, 197*
Wellhausen, J.   *30, 243*
Werner, M.   *21, 128*
Wernle, P.   *330 n.45*
Wilder, A. N.   *62, 69, 73f.*
Williams, C. S. C.   *327 n.39*
Winter, P.   *309*
Wrede, W.   *5, 19, 20, 31, 131, 152, 243*
Wright, G. E.   *69*

Yarnold, G. D.   *190, 191*
Yorck, G. P.   *7*

Zimmerli, W.   *215*
Zwaan, J. de   *81*